World Yearbook of Education 2008

Geographies of Knowledge, Geometries of Power: Framing the Future of Higher Education

Edited by
Debbie Epstein, Rebecca Boden,
Rosemary Deem, Fazal Rizvi and
Susan Wright

Routledge
Taylor & Francis Group

NEW YORK AND LONDON

D0209812

First published 2007
by Routledge
270 Madison Ave, New York, NY 10016

Simultaneously published in the UK
by Routledge
2 Park Square, Milton Park, Abingdon, Oxon OX14 4RN

Routledge is an imprint of the Taylor & Francis Group, an informa business

© 2007 Taylor & Francis

Typeset in Galliard by
HWA Text and Data Management, Tunbridge Wells
Printed and bound in the United States of America on acid-free paper by
Sheridan Books Inc.

Library of Congress Cataloging-in-Publication Data
A catalog record has been requested for this book

ISBN10: 0–415–96378–8 (hbk)
ISBN10: 0–203–93234–X (ebk)

ISBN13: 978–0–415–96378–7 (hbk)
ISBN13: 978–0–203–93234–6 (ebk)

World Yearbook of Education Series
Series editors: Terri Seddon, Jenny Ozga and Evie Zambeta

World Yearbook of Education 1989
HEALTH EDUCATION
Edited by Chris James, John Balding and Duncan Harris

World Yearbook of Education 1990
ASSESSMENT AND EVALUATION
Edited by Chris Bell and Duncan Harris

World Yearbook of Education 1991
INTERNATIONAL SCHOOLS AND
INTERNATIONAL EDUCATION
*Edited by Patricia L. Jonietz and
Duncan Harris*

World Yearbook of Education 1992
URBAN EDUCATION
*Edited by David Coulby, Crispin Jones
and Duncan Harris*

World Yearbook of Education 1993
SPECIAL NEEDS EDUCATION
*Edited by Peter Mittler, Ron Brouilette
and Duncan Harris*

World Yearbook of Education 1994
THE GENDER GAP IN HIGHER
EDUCATION
*Edited by Suzanne Stiver Lie,
Lynda Malik and Duncan Harris*

World Yearbook of Education 1995
YOUTH, EDUCATION AND WORK
Edited by Leslie Bash and Andy Green

World Yearbook of Education 1996
THE EVALUATION OF HIGHER
EDUCATION SYSTEMS
Edited by Robert Cowen

World Yearbook of Education 1997
INTERCULTURAL EDUCATION
*Edited by David Coulby,
Jagdish Gundara and Crispin Jones*

World Yearbook of Education 1998
FUTURES EDUCATION
*Edited by David Hicks and
Richard Slaughter*

World Yearbook of Education 1999
INCLUSIVE EDUCATION
*Edited by Harry Daniels and
Philip Garner*

World Yearbook of Education 2000
EDUCATION IN TIMES OF
TRANSITION
*Edited by David Coulby, Robert Cowen
and Crispin Jones*

World Yearbook of Education 2001
VALUES, CULTURE AND
EDUCATION
*Edited by Roy Gardner, Jo Cairns and
Denis Lawton*

World Yearbook of Education 2002
TEACHER EDUCATION: DILEMMAS
AND PROSPECTS
Edited by Elwyn Thomas

World Yearbook of Education 2003
LANGUAGE EDUCATION
Edited by Jill Bourne and Euan Reid

World Yearbook of Education 2004
DIGITAL TECHNOLOGY,
COMMUNITIES AND EDUCATION
Edited by Andrew Brown and Niki Davis

World Yearbook of Education 2005
GLOBALIZATION AND
NATIONALISM IN EDUCATION
*Edited by David Coulby and
Evie Zambeta*

World Yearbook of Education 2006
EDUCATION RESEARCH
AND POLICY: STEERING THE
KNOWLEDGE-BASED ECONOMY
*Edited by Jenny Ozga, Terri Seddon and
Tom Popkewitz*

World Yearbook of Education 2007
EDUCATING THE GLOBAL
WORKFORCE: KNOWLEDGE,
KNOWLEDGE WORK AND
KNOWLEDGE WORKERS
Edited by Lesley Farrell and Tara Fenwick

World Yearbook of Education 2008

Contents

Figures

Tables

Contributors

David Ashton is Honorary Professor at Cardiff University School of Social Sciences and Emeritus Professor at Leicester University. He founded the Centre for Labour Market Studies at Leicester University and has published widely on labour markets and skills issues. His current interests are in the field of work organisations skills and performance and in the impact of globalisation on national systems of education and training. He is involved in a major study, financed by the UK Economic and Social Research Council, into the skill strategies of multinational corporations in seven countries. He has served in an advisory capacity to government agencies in the UK and abroad as well as the European Union and International Labour Organisation.

Rebecca Boden is a professor of critical management and director of the Institute for Social Innovation at the University of Wales Institute Cardiff, UK. She has also held posts at the Universities of Manchester, Sheffield and the West of England. Her major area of research interest is the effects of management and accounting regimes of control on publicly funded sites of knowledge creation. Rebecca has published widely across a number of disciplines and has held a variety of ESRC awards, including a current project with colleagues at the University of Manchester that is exploring the role of universities in regional innovation networks. She was a co-organiser on the ESRC funded seminar series that led to the production of this *World Yearbook* and, along with Debbie Epstein and Jane Kenway, she authored the *Academic's Support Kit* – a six-volume survival guide for early career academics in contemporary, globalised, universities.

Rodrigo Britez is a doctoral student at the University of Illinois at Urbana-Champaign. He was born in Argentina, grew up in Paraguay and came to the United States as a Fulbright scholar. His major research interests include: globalisation and education policy, higher education policy in South America, and networks of governance in higher education policy. He is currently working on issues relating to social networks and the role of trans-national agencies in policy processes in higher education. He is also the editor of a blog in global studies in education.

Rachel Brooks is a senior lecturer in social policy at the University of Surrey, UK and co-convenor of the British Sociological Association's Youth Study Group. She was awarded a PhD from the University of Southampton for her work on young people's higher education choices (subsequently published as *Friendship and Educational Choice: Peer Influence and Planning for the Future*, Palgrave, 2005). Since completing her doctoral research, she has explored the interface between higher education and lifelong learning through an ESRC-funded project on 'Young Graduates and Lifelong Learning' and is currently working on a British Academy-funded project on international higher education (with Johanna Waters at Liverpool University).

Phillip Brown is a Research Professor in the School of Social Sciences, Cardiff University. His academic career took him to Cambridge University and the University of Kent before joining Cardiff University in 1997. His current research interests include globalisation and the knowledge economy; the future of education, work and the labour market; and theorising positional competition. He has written, co-authored and co-edited fourteen books, the most recent is *Education, Globalization and Social Change*, edited with H. Lauder, J.A. Dillabough and A.H. Halsey (Oxford University Press, 2006). He is currently involved in a major seven-country study of the corporate strategies of multinational companies and the future of skills (funded by the Economic and Social Research Council of Great Britain).

Penny Ciancanelli is Senior Lecturer in the Faculty of Business at the University of Strathclyde. She is a trained economist whose work adopts an interdisciplinary perspective on the architecture of international finance and its consequences for income distribution and social justice. Of late, her research has focused on the links between financial deregulation and privatisation of public benefit services (including, *inter alia*, bank regulation, public health, and higher education). She is a member of an international research team studying financial deregulation and bank lending in Mexico and an enthusiastic supporter of efforts to promote Open Access to the knowledge commons.

Bill Cope is a Research Professor at the University of Illinois at Urbana-Champaign, as well as an adjunct professor at RMIT University in Australia. He is also the founding director of Common Ground, an organisation that organises a large number of conferences, including the Learning conference, which has now been held annually for almost twenty years, and specialises in flexible modes of knowledge production and publishing. Bill is a historian, who has had a distinguished career as a researcher and senior civil servant, including a period as the Director of the Office of Multicultural Affairs in Australia. He has written extensively on issues of cultural diversity, new approaches to learning and developments in digital media and their implications for learning designs.

Roger Dale is Professor of Education at the University of Bristol. Until 2002, he was Professor of Education at the University of Auckland. Before moving to Auckland, he was involved in producing courses in sociology of education and education policy at the Open University for almost 20 years. Whilst at Auckland he led (with Susan Robertson) a major research study into the responses to globalisation of four education systems in Alberta (Canada), New Zealand, Scotland and Singapore. One strand of investigation was the role of regional organisations in national responses to globalisation. This led to a major interest in the EU and education policy, which is now the main focus of his work, complementing and extending qualitatively his earlier work on the state and education policy. It led to him becoming Academic Coordinator of the EU Erasmus Thematic Network, GENIE (Globalisation and Europeanisation in Education) which was based in Bristol. Together with Susan Robertson, he co-founded the journal *Globalisation, Societies and Education*, the first volume of which was published in 2003.

Rosemary Deem is Professor of Education and Research Director for the Faculty of Social Sciences and Law at the University of Bristol, an Academician of the Academy of Social Sciences and Vice-Chair of the Society for Research into Higher Education. She has also worked at Lancaster University (where she was Dean of Social Sciences 1994–7 and founding Director of the University Graduate School 1998–2000), the Open University (1980–91) and the former North Staffordshire Polytechnic (1975–9). Her research interests include higher education policy and management, organisational cultures, equity and education, the relationship between research and teaching in universities and the connections between urban lifestyles and environmental interventions. She is currently co-directing, with colleagues at Cardiff Business School, an Economic and Social Research Council funded project on change agency and leadership development in UK public services, including hospital and primary health care trusts, secondary schools and higher education.

Debbie Epstein is Professor of Education in the School of Social Sciences at Cardiff University. She became an academic after nearly 20 years of teaching in schools and working as a Teacher Advisor for Birmingham (UK) Local Education Authority. Prior to working at Cardiff, she worked at the University of Central England (1991–4), the Institute of Education, London (1994–2001) and Goldsmiths College, London, where she was Head of the Education Department (2001–3). Her research concerns a range of inequalities (particularly sexuality and gender) and their intersections and she is particularly interested in understanding how the dominant is kept in place. Together with Rebecca Boden and Jane Kenway, she has written the *Academic's Support Kit*, consisting of six volumes each offering mentoring advice to early career academics. She was the principal investigator for the ESRC funded seminar series that led to the production of this *World Yearbook*. She is co-editor, with Emma Renold and Mary Jane Kehily, of *Gender and Education*.

Johannah Fahey is a research fellow in the Faculty of Education at Monash University, Australia. She has a PhD in cultural studies from Macquarie University, Sydney. She is interested in post-structuralist theories of language and textuality; post-colonial models of subjectivity, corporeality and ethnicity; mobility and globalisation; and contemporary Australian visual arts. Her latest co-authored book is *Haunting the Knowledge Economy* (Routledge). Her earlier book is *David Noonan: Before and Now* (Thames & Hudson). She is currently working on a new book called *Globalising the Research Imagination* (Routledge).

Steve Fuller is Professor of Sociology at the University of Warwick, UK. Originally trained in the history and philosophy of science, he is most closely associated with the research programme of 'social epistemology', which is the name of the journal he founded in 1987, as well as the first of fifteen books. His most recent books include *The Intellectual* (Icon, 2005), *The New Sociological Imagination* (Sage, 2006), and *The Knowledge Book: Key Concepts in Philosophy, Science and Culture* (Acumen, 2007). His works have been translated into fifteen languages. He is currently writing a book on the sociology of academic and intellectual life, to be published by Sage. In 2007, he was awarded a 'higher doctorate' (D.Litt.) by Warwick.

Mary Kalantzis has, since August 2006, been the Dean of the College of Education at the University of Illinois at Urbana-Champaign. Before that she was an Innovation Professor and Dean of the Faculty of Education at RMIT University Australia, as well as the President of the Australian Deans of Education. She completed her PhD in History from Macquarie University in Australia, and has held academic appointments at University of Wollongong, James Cook University and University of Technology Sydney. She has published extensively on educational policy, issues of language and literacy, cultural diversity and social justice and more recently on the new science of education, which is the subject of her new book, jointly authored with Bill Cope, *New Learning* (Cambridge University Press).

Jane Kenway holds a Chair in Global Education Studies in the Faculty of Education, Monash University, Australia. Her research focuses on the links between educational change and socio-economic and cultural change. Her books include her co-authored *Haunting the Knowledge Economy* (Routledge), *Masculinity Beyond the Metropolis* (Palgrave/Macmillan) and *Consuming Children: Entertainment, Advertising and Education* (Open University Press). Her co-edited books include *Innovation & Tradition: The Arts, Humanities and the Knowledge Economy* and *Globalizing Education: Policies, Pedagogies, & Politics* (both Peter Lang). She is currently working on a new book called *Globalising the Research Imagination* (Routledge).

Terri Kim is a Lecturer at Brunel University, and an Associate of the Centre for Higher Education Research and Innovation (CHERI), Open University in the UK. Previously, she worked as a research consultant for OECD/CERI; a Visiting Research Scholar in International Relations at LSE in London; a Brain Korea 21 Contract Professor at Seoul National University in Korea; and a Visiting Scholar at the IEC, Collège de France in Paris. The areas of her academic research include state–university relations, international politics and neoliberal economic globalisation, higher education policy, international academic recruitment policy and practice, and transnational academic mobility and identities. She is International Convener of the Higher Education Thematic Group for the World Council of Comparative Education Societies, and has recently participated in the OECD 'University Futures Project'. She received the CESE 'Women's Network Prize for Excellence in presenting a comparative research paper' at the XXII CESE (Comparative Education Society in Europe) Conference held in Granada, 2006.

Marek Kwiek is the founder (in 2002) and director of the Center for Public Policy (www.cpp.amu.edu.pl) and professor in the Department of Philosophy of Poznan University, Poland. He is a former Fulbright scholar, Kosciuszko Foundation scholar, Reagan–Fascell Democracy Fellow, OSI International Policy Fellow; and currently, a Fulbright 'New Century Scholar' (2007–8). His research interests include globalisation and education, European educational policies, international organisations, welfare state reforms, the modern institution of the university, transformations of the academic profession, private higher education, as well as philosophy of education and intellectual history. He has published 80 papers and eight books, most recently *The University and the State: A Study into Global Transformation*, a monograph about the impact of global reformulations of the role of the state on the future of public universities. He serves as an editorial board member in a number of international journals, including *Higher Education Quarterly, European Educational Research Journal,* and *Globalisation, Education, and Societies.*

Hugh Lauder is Professor of Education and Political Economy at the University of Bath. His recent books include with Phil Brown, Jo-Anne Dillabough and A.H. Halsey (eds) *Education, Globalization and Social Change* (Oxford University Press, 2006); with Phil Brown and Andy Green *High Skills: Globalisation, Competitiveness and Skill Formation* (Oxford University Press, 2001) and with Phil Brown *Capitalism and Social Progress: The Future of Society in a Global Economy* (Basingstoke, Palgrave Press, 2001; reprinted in Chinese, 2007). He is currently working with Phil Brown and David Ashton on an ESRC funded project: 'The Global Skill Strategies of Multinational Companies' and is Principal Investigator for the Progress at Primary Schools Study (also ESRC funded).

Simon Marginson is a Professor of Higher Education in the Centre for the Study of Higher Education at the University of Melbourne in Melbourne, Australia, and holds a government-funded Australian Professorial Fellowship on the nomination of the Australian Research Council. His work draws on political philosophy and political economy, global sociology and cultural theory and focuses on higher education and education policy in the context of globalisation. Simon worked on recent studies for the OECD on the internationalisation of higher education in the Asia-Pacific region, globalisation and higher education, and tertiary education in the Netherlands. He publishes in such journals as *Higher Education, Journal of Studies in International Education, Comparative Education Review*, and *Thesis Eleven*. The author of *Markets in Education* (1997) and the award winning *The Enterprise University* (2000, with Mark Considine), his most recent book is the edited collection *Prospects of Higher Education: Globalization, Market Competition, Public Goods and the Future of the University* (Sense, Rotterdam, 2007).

Gigliola Mathisen has a Master in Public Administration from the Department of Administration and Organization Theory, University of Bergen. Her current position is as Researcher on the project 'The steering of universities' – SUN/PRIME (6th EU framework programme). With participation from seven European countries, this project is studying policy evolution and implementation in the steering of universities in Western Europe. Gigliola, together with Professor Ivar Bleiklie, is carrying out the Norwegian element: 'Changes in conditions for research at Norwegian universities'. Her wider research interests are in globalisation and higher education and in multilateral organisations' policies on higher education, as reflected in her publication, 'Chasing quality. WTO and UNESCO; multilaterals at work', in T. Halvorsen, G. Mathisen and T. Skauge (eds) *Identity Formation or Knowledge Shopping. Education and Research in the New Globality* (SIU, Bergen, 2005).

Gunnar Guddal Michelsen gained a Doctorate in Political Science from Bergen University. His thesis, 'Institutional legacies at work in African Telecommunications', compared important developmental traits of Ghana and The Ivory Coast. He was appointed as a post-doctoral researcher (professor stipend) at the Rokkan Centre for Social Science Studies, University of Bergen. Under the Norwegian Research Council's programme 'Identity formation or knowledge shopping', he focused on changes in Africa. His particular interest was Senegal. There he did most of his fieldwork on higher education, on which the current chapter is based. He has published widely on the role of telecommunication and use of ICT. His broad interest in higher education was presented in the article 'Identity formation or knowledge shopping. Globalisation and the future of university education and research in Africa' (together with Tor Halvorsen) in *Qelle Université pour L'Afrique?* edited by Noble Akam and Rland Ducasse (Maison des Sciences de L'Homme D'Aquitaine, 2002).

At Christmas 2005 Gunnar was taken ill in Senegal and due to unfortunate circumstances he died. He was a young scholar with outstanding potential who was dearly loved by his colleagues in Senegal and at Bergen, who still mourn and miss him.

Rajani Naidoo directs the Doctorate of Business Administration in Higher Education Management at the University of Bath. She took her PhD at the University of Cambridge. Before this, she contributed to setting up an institution which aimed to transform higher education in apartheid South Africa by disseminating innovative academic programmes and progressive teaching strategies. She is Honorary Secretary of the Society for Research in Higher Education and is on the editorial boards of the *British Journal of Sociology of Education* and *Studies in Higher Education*. Her research interests include the global commodification of higher education, higher education and social justice, the changing nature of academic work and higher education and international development. Her publications include 'Fields and Institutional Strategy: Bourdieu on the relationship between higher education, inequality and society'. *British Journal of Sociology of Education*, 25(4), pp. 457–71 (2004).

Maria Nedeva is Senior Lecturer at PREST and Associate Dean for Postgraduate Research of the Faculty of Humanities, University of Manchester. Her background is in the sociology of science and technology and her main contributions are in the broad area of social, organisational and cognitive dynamics. Her research expertise is in studying science systems and science and technology policy issues such as the relationships between higher education institutions and industry, and research infrastructure and its impact on quality of research. More recently Maria has been contributing to the debates on the organisational dynamics of knowledge producing institutions and the dynamics of the European Research Area and its policy instruments.

Michael A. Peters is Professor of Education at the Universities of Illinois (Urbana-Champaign) and Glasgow where he teaches policy and global studies. He is the editor of three international journals: *Educational Philosophy & Theory*, *Policy Futures in Education* and *E-Learning*. His research interests are in educational philosophy and policy studies with a focus on the significance of both contemporary philosophers (Nietzsche, Wittgenstein, Heidegger) and movements of post-structuralism, critical theory and analytic philosophy on the framing of educational theory and practice. His major current projects include work on knowledge futures, educational policy futures, critical theory anthologies, and the rise of global science. Recent publications include *Knowledge Economy, Development and the Future of the University* (2007), *Building Knowledge Cultures: Education and Development in the Age of Knowledge Capitalism*, with A.C. Besley (2006), and *Deconstructing Derrida: Task for the New Humanities* (2005).

Fazal Rizvi is a professor in educational policy studies at the University of Illinois at Urbana-Champaign, where he directs the Global Studies in Education programme (gse.ed.uiuc.edu). During the 1990s, he held a number of senior academic and administrative positions in Australia, including Pro Vice Chancellor (International) at RMIT University. He has published widely on globalisation and educational policy, the cultural politics of education and internationalisation of higher education. His recent books include a co-edited volume, with Nadine Dolby, *Youth Moves: Identities and Education in a Global Context*, and a forthcoming book, jointly authored with Bob Lingard, *Globalizing Education Policy*. He has also served on a number of government committees as a member of the Australia Council for the Arts, the Australia Foundation for Culture and the Humanities and currently as an international panel member on the UK's Research Assessment Exercise RAE2008.

Wei Shen is a PhD Candidate in Geography, Loughborough University. Originally from Shanghai, China, Wei Shen is currently a doctoral researcher at Loughborough University in association with Sciences Po de Paris (CERI/CNRS) where he is a UACES Scholar funded by the European Commission. Wei's research interests are international migration and student/labour mobility, globalisation of business education, inter-city networks, international migration and Asia–Europe relations. Wei studied business for his undergraduate degree in Rotterdam and later obtained master's qualifications in urban management and law and economics from Erasmus Universiteit Rotterdam and Stockholms Universitet respectively. He has also studied in Milano (Bocconi), Hamburg, Linköping, Warwick and Brussels (ULB) and has been a worker/intern for a number of international organisations including IFAD, UNESCO, IOM and the Asia–Europe Foundation.

Jani Ursin is a senior researcher at the University of Jyväskylä, Finland. In his PhD study (Characteristics of Finnish medical and engineering research group work, 2004) he examined research group work characteristics from the perspective of the work design approach. After completing his doctoral studies his research has focused primarily on quality assurance in higher education, but he has also done comparative research on the implementation of the Bologna Process in Finland and in Italy (with the Higher Education Studies research group at the Institute for Educational Research) as well as a study on university teachers' competencies in Finnish universities (together with Dr. Susanna Paloniemi at the University of Jyväskylä). He is also a co-convenor of the European Educational Research Association's (EERA) Network 22: Research in Higher Education.

Antoni Verger was awarded a PhD from the Universitat Autònoma de Barcelona (UAB) for his work on WTO/GATS and Higher Education. Since 2003 he has been a member of the research group 'Analysis of Social Policies Seminar', part of the Department of Sociology of the UAB (www.

uab.es/gr-saps). Currently, he is a postdoctoral researcher of the AMIDSt (Amsterdam Institute for Metropolitan and International Development Studies) of the Universiteit van Amsterdam (www.fmg.uva.nl/amidst). His principal research topics are globalisation and education politics, as well as education quality, knowledge and international development.

Matt Waring is a Senior Lecturer in the Cardiff School of Management at the University of Wales Institute Cardiff (UWIC), specialising in Human Resource Management (HRM) and Employee Relations. He has wide experience in programme management and has previously chaired the HRM/Law discipline group in the School. Matt's main research interest is HRM within the higher education sector and he is currently undertaking doctoral research to explore this further. He is also a member of the British Universities Industrial Relations Association (Buira) and the South West Higher Education Network.

Anthony R. Welch works in the Faculty of Education and Social Work, University of Sydney, where he was until recently, Head, School of Policy and Practice. Widely published on Australian and international education, he has been Visiting Professor in Japan, USA, Germany and the UK, and has significant Asia experience, as both researcher and consultant. He was recently awarded the prestigious Fulbright New Century Scholar Fellowship. His two most recent books are *The Professoriate: Profile of a Profession* (Springer, 2005) and the jointly authored *Education, Change and Society* (Oxford, 2007).

Susan Wright (D.Phil. in Anthropology, Oxford University) is Professor of Educational Anthropology at the Danish School of Education, Århus University. With a team of researchers, she is currently studying Danish university reform. This builds on previous studies of changes to universities in the UK, audit culture, and the anthropology of policy (Shore and Wright (eds) *Anthropology of Policy. Critical Perspectives on Governance and Power*, London, Routledge, 1997). A main interest is to study changing practices of learning and teaching within the context of changing institutional management and national and international policies. This is the focus of the journal she co-edits, *Learning and Teaching: International Journal of Higher Education in the Social Sciences,* and of her previous work as founding director of C-SAP, the UK Higher Education Academy's subject centre for the social sciences.

Zhang Zhen works in the English Department of Tianjin University, Tianjin, China, and recently completed her MA in Education at the University of Sydney. She has previously published on communication networks among the Chinese knowledge diaspora in the Chinese journal *Comparative Education Review* (Beijing), in 2005.

Series editors' introduction

This 2008 volume of the *World Yearbook of Education* explores the state of higher education in globalised conditions of knowledge production, use and exchange. Its title – *Geographies of Knowledge, Geometries of Power: Framing the Future of Higher Education* – illuminates the perspective on knowledge and power that shapes the volume, and that provides energy and critical direction to the discussion of the global university contained in its pages. It also signals the attentiveness of the contributors to emergent trends in higher education, and their identification of key technologies and relations that map its production into the future.

Put briefly, this volume is focused on the uneven and unequal consequences of changing knowledge production, especially where different countries and regions find themselves positioned in different ways in relation to knowledge production, control, use and exchange. The fragmented and uneven distribution of intellectual resources – within nations and regions as well as across them – has significant consequences for the crucial, informed assessment and study of processes of change, which in turn generate unequal conditions of knowledge production, with consequences for the protection of democratic practices and relations in research. In adopting this perspective, the volume editors – Debbie Epstein, Rebecca Boden, Rosemary Deem, Fazal Rizvi and Susan Wright – have created a focused and securely grounded counter-narrative to the rather dominant themes that direct the university towards service of the 'knowledge economy'. The outlines of that economy – its shifting locations and its consequences for producers and users in higher education – are made more visible through the contributions in this volume, and pertinent questions are raised about the impact of 'mobility' on regional and national capacities; the steering of knowledge production by transnational agencies and agreements, and the emergence of powerful trading 'blocs' for the production and use of knowledge. As well as addressing questions that focus on the production and circulation of knowledge, and the marketing and consumption of knowledges to different audiences, the volume interrogates the assumptions that drive this circulation, and records their impacts on academic workers and on the increasingly mobile students who consume knowledge in different contexts. In addition, there is a necessary focus on the relationship between various funding regimes and the kinds of knowledge that are preferred by publishers and that attract investment from business and industry.

As series editors of the *World Yearbook of Education*, we are fortunate to have worked with such insightful and committed editors. Debbie Epstein, Rebecca Boden, Rosemary Deem, Susan Wright and Fazal Rizvi have combined to bring a formidable range of expertise together and have exploited a rich vein of continuing work on higher education and its management, politics and directions that has ensured that the volume is serious, substantial and combines theoretical resources with empirical evidence. The reach of the collection is impressive, as networks have been drawn upon to provide contributions drawn from or directly addressing contrasting contexts, including central and eastern Europe, China, India, England, North America and Australia.

The volume continues the project for the *World Yearbook of Education* that we are committed to as series editors; that is to go beyond the documenting of worldwide developments in education in order to map significant emergent issues as a contribution towards framing research agendas at the cutting edge of the field. This volume achieves that ambition, and does so in new ways that foregrounds the old and essential questions about 'who benefits' and 'who loses' in the university in globalised conditions.

As the editors point out, the *World Yearbook of Education 2008* challenges those who work in universities, engaged in research and technological development, to consider the implications of their work for the transformation of geographies and geometries of power/knowledge.

Jenny Ozga, Terri Seddon and Evie Zambeta
Edinburgh, Melbourne and Athens, 2007

1 Introduction

Geographies of knowledge, geometries of power: framing the future of higher education

Debbie Epstein

Does it matter what happens in and to higher education (HE) either locally – in specific nation-states – or globally – in terms of developments that can be seen across countries and continents and in the role of inter-, trans- and supra-national organisations in determining and influencing what happens in and to universities? It is the contention of the editors and authors of this *World Yearbook* that it does for a number of reasons. First, participation in the global 'knowledge economy' has become an increasingly important policy imperative in developed and developing countries, as discussed in the *World Yearbook of Education 2005* (Coulby and Zambeta 2005). Second, one of the key functions of universities is to act as both producers of knowledge through research and transmitters of knowledge through their teaching role. Third, the massification of higher education in very many countries, with ever more young people (mainly) becoming undergraduates, is both a result of these policy imperatives and a reason for being concerned about what is happening in and to universities, what the experiences of students and academics are, and what technologies of control and regimes of truth are in place (and in contention) within them. These, then, are the primary reasons for the choice of higher education, its globalisation, commercialisation and the impacts thereof as the key themes of this particular *World Yearbook of Education*.[1]

Higher education practices, processes and institutions are widely acknowledged to be both globalised and marketised (Marginson 2004a), exhibiting a compression of time and space, flows of people and ideas across national boundaries and a significant degree of homogenisation (Scott 1998). In other words, higher education is an increasingly global business, with international markets for both students and knowledge. This increasing commodification and marketisation has led to a rapid rate of change, which, together with the ability for (some) people to move to and from their own countries to others and the push towards international collaboration (though simultaneously towards international competition) all contribute to what Jane Kenway so memorably called the ' "now" university', operating in the context of 'fast capitalism' (Kenway with Langmead 2000: 155).

Two market contexts appear important in HE: that for knowledge and the capacity to produce it (the so-called 'knowledge economy') and that for students (Naidoo 2003; Ram 2003; Sauve 2002). The knowledge market is marked by a high degree of knowledge commodification (Baskaran and Boden 2004), competition, increasing homogeneity through managerial practices, and mobility of highly skilled research labour. The whole is embedded in discourses of 'governance' and 'accountability' – managerialist regimes that may serve to capture and control what happens in universities (Deem 2001; Strathern 2000; Vidovich 2004). Simultaneously, the global supply of and demand for student places is marked by commercial, competitive pressures (Walker 2001). As in all markets, there are imbalances of power within the markets for knowledge and of higher education: between institutions in single countries; between countries; and between the richer countries of the 'West'/global North and poor to middle income countries of the global South, struggling to enter, develop and maintain their place within the global knowledge economy.

There is a symbiotic relationship between knowledge production activities and the international movement of students. It is widely believed that a prestigious research reputation, measured by formal (but contested) performance indicators (Codd 2004; Strathern 1997), fuels student demand (Currie *et al.* 2007). Recruiting overseas fee-paying students offers both the prospect of enhanced funding and the possibility of students carrying different social, cultural and intellectual capitals back to their own countries. Moreover, graduate students bring with them ideas and knowledges that have the potential to make inroads into the hegemony of 'Western' knowledges at their host institutions (Marginson 2004b). This global market for education may in turn create global labour markets for highly skilled workers that exhibit inequities between different countries and their peoples (Brown and Hesketh 2004).

Universities participate in global developments in knowledge recognition, production, control and usage, acting as incubators and conduits for knowledge production and flows. They achieve this by research 'outputs' and the movement of real bodies. These processes have repercussions for local educational practices, likely to be most severely felt in places subject to 'epistemic colonisation'. Appadurai (1999, 2001) argues for producing and sharing knowledge about globalisation in ways that create new forms of critical dialogue between academics from different societies in the 'globalisation of knowledge and the knowledge of globalisation' (Appadurai 2001: 4).

The globalisation of HE is, thus, best analysed in terms of relations of power that are spatial, historic and economic. There are distinct *geometries of power* as the knowledge production capability of HE is increasingly globalised. As argued above, the changes in HE organisation and practice and the demands on universities have tended to travel from the 'West to the rest', making for interesting developments in the *geographies of knowledge:* its recognition, production, control and usage in different regions of the world. As Appadurai (2001: 4) argues:

> Globalisation as an uneven economic process creates a fragmented and uneven distribution of just those resources of learning, teaching, and

cultural criticism that are most vital for the formation of democratic research communities that could produce a global view of globalisation. That is, globalisation resists the possibility of just those forms of collaboration that might make it easier to understand or criticize.

In producing this book, we have resisted the temptation to try to achieve maximum coverage of the countries of the world. Rather, this *Yearbook* explores the consequences of the developing global market and the reinscription of universities within new globalised socio-cultural meanings and economic roles in four key areas that provide the interlinked themes for the volume, each with its own part editor:

• Producing and reproducing the university, edited by Rosemary Deem
• Supplying knowledge, edited by Rebecca Boden
• Demanding knowledge – marketing and consumption, edited by Susan Wright
• Transnational academic flows, edited by Fazal Rizvi

These themes, introduced more fully by the respective part editors than can be done in this brief introduction to the *World Yearbook*, are explored by authors from a variety of different disciplinary backgrounds: education; sociology; critical management studies, science and technology studies; anthropology; public policy studies; accounting and finance; and human geography. Drawing on a range of empirical and policy studies, they use their own disciplinary approaches to theorise and illuminate questions, problems and issues that arise in most universities in most countries, albeit nuanced by local visions, discourses and materialities that create diversity in the mission and focus of particular higher education systems and institutions.

Part I: Producing and reproducing the university

This part is concerned with the ways in which the higher education sector has been re-formed and has reformed itself in the face of globalising pressures. The chapters in this part are concerned with complex questions not only of how such reforms (reformation) have worked themselves out in different local contexts and with regard to the politics of different places and nations but also with the deep questions of what universities are and how they can be understood in current times. In considering these issues, the part throws light on both the ways in which we think about universities, what they can do, what their purposes are, and what the consequences of globalisation and the accompanying commercialisation of knowledge are for students, academics, the nature of knowledge itself and socio-economic development.

As Rosemary Deem points out in her introduction to the part, debates about the nature and purposes of universities have existed virtually for as long as universities themselves, but have intensified over the past two or three decades. The part consists of five chapters beginning with the broad sweep of

Roger Dale's critique of existing work on universities, illustrated by reference to policies and strategies in the European Union. It continues with Marek Kwiek's fine-grained account of the reform of universities particularly in the former communist countries and how this relates to the transformation of both welfare and nation states, in part through the intervention of supra- or trans-national bodies such as the World Bank. Steve Fuller's provocative examination of 'Academic Caesarism', that is the current state of leadership/ management of higher education, and the development of universities as 'part Vatican and part Vegas' draws on developments in the USA and the UK to develop possible strategies for their futures.

The final two chapters of the part, by Penny Ciancanelli and Maria Nedeva, provide nuanced theoretical accounts of how pressures of funding and the ways in which this takes place are changing the nature of knowledge and what counts as knowledge produced within universities. Ciancanelli offers detailed exploration of the impact of neo-liberal policies and globalisation on the sharing of knowledge and the free exchange of ideas through an economic analysis of academic publishing. Nedeva suggests that the emphasis on 'third mission' functions with their overt link to business and economic development, is significantly changing both the nature of knowledge and of universities themselves.

Part II: Supplying knowledge

Moving on from questions about the production and re-production of the university, this part, edited by Rebecca Boden, picks up some of the questions raised by Ciancanelli and Nedeva and interrogates the re-forming of universities as free market suppliers of knowledge. The four chapters in this part explore the structural and cultural changes required for universities to make the transition to being able to fulfil, at least in part, the role thus assigned to them. The part begins with Antoni Verger's critical appraisal of the regulatory framework developed by the General Agreement on Trade in Services (GATS) as part of the World Trade Organisation's (WTO) wider brief to bring about free markets in goods and services – a framework which purports to open the field to competition but which actually weights the scales heavily on the side of the already rich universities (and the nation states within which they are primarily based).

Of course, regulation takes place not only at the level of international agreements but also within countries (and, indeed, individual universities). Jani Ursin's chapter picks up the question of how 'quality' can be 'assured' for the purposes of marketing universities and the knowledge they produce. Using Finnish universities as a case study, he gives a detailed account of the impact of the globalised discourse of 'quality assurance' (QA) and the regulatory regimes that accompany it, on the disposition of universities in local contexts. Drawing on empirical data from universities in Wales and England, the next chapter, by Matt Waring, considers how 'human resources management' (HRM) tools are used to control and pacify workers in universities through the individualisation of employee responsibility and accountability and the imperative for them, individually, to respond and adapt to risks to the organisation within which they work.

The final chapter in the part, by Jane Kenway and Johannah Fahey, is concerned with the ways in which the 'mobility' of academics is a key element of the globalised knowledge economy. They use a range of metaphors to describe the different ways in which researchers are (and are made to be) mobile – as 'tourists', 'exiles', 'explorers', 'strangers' and 'hobos'. This chapter looks forward to the final part of the book in its consideration of the mobility of academics, knowledge and power and the relationship between such movement and the cultural and economic geographies of the world of higher education and beyond.

Part III: Demanding knowledge – marketing and consumption

This part, edited by Susan Wright, moves the focus from the supply of knowledge to its marketing and the demands for it. The part as a whole questions the assumption that western countries will automatically dominate in the global market for knowledge. It consists of six chapters, beginning with Phillip Brown, Hugh Lauder and David Ashton's challenge to the notion of a global division of knowledge labour. Based on extensive empirical work, involving interviews in several countries with senior managers from 20 leading transnational companies and policy makers, they show that the emergent economies (particularly of China and India) are in the process of generating their own knowledge-workers, transporting the previously well-established Taylorisation of manufacturing to financial and service industries. They argue that this is a process which is beginning and will continue to happen in the university sector, with consequent 'unbundling' and outsourcing of different aspects of academic work to places where knowledge work comes cheaper than in the global North. Wei Shen's study of Chinese students' roles and motivations on their international migrations follows. He shows that these people tend not to migrate permanently but to return to family and other social responsibilities at home once they have acquired the education and skills they came for. Thus, while they may act as a 'cash cow' for universities which charge fees, as in the UK, they do not join the local labour force in the countries in which they are attending university. Shen's study of migratory Chinese students is followed by Rachel Brooks' chapter in which she explores how graduates in England view their education as a kind of credentialising process in which they gain the basic ticket for employment and which does nothing to disturb existing social differentiation.

The fourth chapter in this part, by Rajani Naidoo, offers a closely argued and critical examination of the actions of the World Bank, which first compelled developing countries to disinvest in universities as part of structural adjustment programmes and is now pressurising these same countries to create the market conditions for private and foreign universities to trade. This can be seen as a process of knowledge colonisation that clearly demonstrates both the geographies of knowledge and geometries of power that we are concerned about in this volume.

Gigliola Mathisen's chapter continues the theme of de/regulation of markets in higher education. The role of two further international agencies, the Organisation for Economic Cooperation and Development (OECD) and the United Nations Education, Science and Culture Organisation (UNESCO), are examined here. Whereas Ursin, in the previous part, investigated quality assurance measures in Finland, Mathisen records how the OECD and UNESCO, worried about the impact of free trade in higher education allowing all and sundry to offer something called 'university education', drew up guidelines to try to provide quality control and good information about providers in the global market in higher education. In this context the question arises as to whether poor countries have either the infrastructure or the resources necessary to be able to follow these guidelines and whether, even if they did, this would have any impact on the potentially damaging effects of free trade as required by GATS (see also Verger, this volume). The final chapter in this part by Gunnar Guddal Michelsen provides a case study of Senegal which is very much to the point. He vividly outlines the Senegalese government's inability to follow the UNESCO guidelines, or to provide any quality control, leaving the field open to 'academic entrepreneurs', who hoped that Senegal could become a hub in the global knowledge economy from which they could profit.

Part IV: Transnational academic flows

The final part of the *Yearbook* explores both the flows of people, knowledge and capital that characterise contemporary, globalised capitalism, and the disjunctures that this creates. In his introduction, Fazal Rizvi points out that student flows, as discussed in the previous part, have not been the only type of movement. University teachers and researchers, too, have become part of global knowledge networks and, as Kenway and Fahey (this volume) showed in their chapter, have joined the flows of people to and from universities around the world. Rizvi notes that flows are never smooth but are always disjunctive. Neither do flows look the same from every angle.

The part begins with Simon Marginson's chapter about the cross-border flows of academics. Marginson shows that, notwithstanding Brown *et al.*'s caution in Part III, the global academic labour market is shaped by and infused with the dominant Anglo-American linguistic and cultural traditions in higher education. Nevertheless, as Marginson notes, local/national career structures, systems and traditions continue to operate, albeit at a level residualised on the global scale, leading to the problem of 'brain drain' from poorer to richer countries in ways that entail the effective subsidy of the knowledge production in the global North by the global South. However, as Terri Kim points out in the next chapter, the picture is more complicated than simply a brain drain to the US. While academic mobility is not new, it has intensified and speeded up in the twenty-first century, while simultaneously being constrained by exclusive national policies in a number of countries and by the 'war on terror' insofar as access to the US is concerned.

The third chapter in this part follows on with Anthony Welch and Zhang Zhen's study of Chinese-born academics around the world conceptualised as an intellectual diaspora. Unlike Shen's students, these academics do not necessarily intend to return to China, but retain emotional and familial connections with home, and make a significant contribution to the development of China's scientific stature. They argue that China is able to draw on its diasporic intellectuals as a resource in the building of its knowledge economy through the use of extensive communication and collaboration that deploys contemporary electronic methods.

Rodrigo Britez and Michael Peters also consider the social networks produced through cross-border mobility. Just as Welch and Zhen's Chinese diasporic intellectuals use contemporary information technologies to stay in and make contact, Britez and Peters point to the importance of digital communication in the creation of the term 'cosmopolitical university', which might form part of a democratic, ethical project which is international in scope and origin.

In the final chapter of this part and, indeed of the *Yearbook*, Bill Cope and Mary Kalantzis also point to the importance of digital technologies not only in flows of knowledge but also in the emergence of new 'social webs', which have the potential to blur boundaries of institution, space and time. The *World Yearbook 2008* thus ends with a challenge for those engaged in research, technological development and higher education to develop relationships of learning that are 'more apt to today's social conditions, more dynamic, and which engage learners more effectively'. In meeting this challenge, it may be that both geographies and geometries of power/knowledge can be transformed.

Note

1 This volume emerges from a seminar series funded by the Economic and Social Research Council (RES-451-25-4144). Many of the chapters were first given as papers at the seminars. We would like to thank the ESRC for this support.

References

Appadurai, A. (1999) 'Globalization and the research imagination', *International Social Science Journal*, 160 (June): 229–38.

Appadurai, A. (2001) *Globalization*, Durham and London: Duke University Press.

Baskaran, A. and Boden, R. (2004) 'Science: a controversial commodity', *Science, Technology and Society*, 9(1): 1–27.

Brown, P. and Hesketh, A. (2004) *The Mismanagement of Talent: Employability and Jobs in the Knowledge Economy*, Oxford: Oxford University Press.

Codd, J.A. (2004) 'Measuring research performance: the origins and outcomes of New Zealand's Performance-Based Research Fund'. Paper presented to the Annual

Conference of the Australian Association of Research in Education, University of Melbourne: 28 November–2 December.

Coulby, D. and Zambeta, E. (2005) *World Yearbook of Education 2005: Globalization and Nationalism in Education*, New York: Routledge.

Currie, J. Vidovich, L. and Yang, R. (2007) 'Changing accountabilities in higher education as China "opens up" to globalization', *Globalization, Societies and Education*, 5(1): 89–107.

Deem, R. (2001) 'Globalisation, new managerialism, academic capitalism and entre-preneurialism in universities: is the local dimension still important?', *Comparative Education*, 37(1): 7–20.

Kenway, J. with Langmead, D. (2000) 'Fast capitalism, fast feminism and some fast food for thought', in Ali, S., Coate, K. and wa Goro, W. (eds) *Global Feminist Politics: Identities in a Changing World*, London: Routledge.

Marginson, S. (2004a) 'National and global competition in higher education', *Australian Educational Researcher*, 31: 1–28.

Marginson, S. (2004b) 'Global public space and global marketplace: rethinking the public/private divide in higher education'. Plenary address to the Society for Research in Higher Education Annual Conference, University of Bristol, 14–16 December.

Naidoo, R. (2003) 'Repositioning higher education as a global commodity: opportunities and challenges for future sociology of education work', *British Journal of Sociology of Education*, 24(2): 249–59.

Ram, R. (2003) 'The global market for higher education: sustainable competitive strategies for the new millennium', *Economics of Education Review*, 22(6): 650.

Scott, P. (ed.) (1998) *The Globalisation of Higher Education*, Buckingham: Open University Press.

Strathern, M. (1997) '"Improving ratings": audit in the British university system', *European Review*, 5: 305–21.

Strathern, M. (ed.) (2000) *Audit Cultures: Anthropological Studies in Accountability, Ethics and the Academy*, London and New York: Routledge.

Suave, P. (2002) 'Trade, education and the GATS: what's in, what's out, what's all the fuss about?', *Higher Education Management and Policy*, 14(3): 47–78.

Vidovich, L. (2004) 'Global-national-local dynamics in policy processes: a case of "quality" policy in higher education', *British Journal of Sociology of Education*, 25: 342–54.

Walker, P. (2001) 'Market or circus? Reflections on the commodification of British higher education from the international student experience', *Education and Social Justice*, 3(2): 33–9.

Part I

Producing and reproducing the university

Rosemary Deem

The globalisation of national economies and of higher education itself are now central elements in explaining what is happening to contemporary universities, although local factors also remain extremely relevant to understanding the characteristics of particular national systems of higher education (Deem 2001; Marginson and Sawir 2005). The geographies of knowledge and geometries of power relevant to the concept of 'producing' and 'reproducing' the university are highly complex. Three key questions tackled in this part are: Who and what have been involved in the production and reproduction of the university in recent decades and in what spaces have they worked? What do we now understand a university to be in the context of a more globalised and interconnected world and how are its purposes changing? What are the consequences of the production and reproduction of the university at the present time for students, academics, knowledge and socio-economic development?

Despite or perhaps because of the historically close linkages between universities and nation states, there has never been a single conception of what a university is and what it is for. There are some long-standing controversies over what the purposes of the university actually are (Von Humboldt 1970; Newman 1976), particularly in respect of the centrality or marginality of both research and teaching. From the nineteenth century onwards, as the foundations were laid for the modern and post-modern university, different notions of what constitutes the university have vied for organisational and systemic hegemony and, particularly in the twenty-first century, competed for global status and recognition (Marginson 2006). How universities should be led, governed and managed and the process of re/identifying their core functions (teaching and research, plus the so-called 'third mission' via links to industry and commerce and public engagement with academic research) have also become preoccupations of both university leaders and policy-makers, as declining public funds for public services encourage questioning of the extent to which higher education is a public benefit or private good. At the same time, international and supra-national bodies like the European Commission and World Bank are replacing national governments as key education and economic policy-makers. Moreover the power of multinational companies (such as the publishing conglomerates) and new definitions of post-school education (such as life-long learning), which embrace but go well beyond higher education, also question the place, power and significance of the university as an institution. The five chapters in this part explore how a range of these developments and reforms are affecting the re/production of the university.

Dale's chapter criticises existing work on how universities have changed in the last few decades for often having an institutional rather than systemic focus, over-emphasising national factors and nation states and not being sufficiently detached from the academic context. He notes how post World War II universities across the globe have been affected by the separation of the twin trajectories of capitalism and modernity and the extent to which their reconstitution has been marked, on the one hand by a managerialist hollowed-out organisational core concerned with performativity, quality and excellence, and on the other by an increasing emphasis on their contribution to global innovation and the knowledge economy. Dale contends that individual institutions of higher education and higher education systems are increasingly operating as parallel universes. He suggests that universities' historic attachment to the concept of emancipation has been tempered by a more recent emphasis on regulation (by the market, states and transnational bodies). Dale illustrates his arguments by reference to the work of the European Commission in putting university reform at the heart of its economic strategy and the new Knowledge sector, a process that is already reaching well beyond the geography and power geometries of Europe itself.

Kwiek's chapter takes up some of the themes of Dale's chapter, in discussing the consequences of the extent to which publicly-provided higher education in Europe (particularly in those central and eastern European countries which have recently joined the European Union) and elsewhere, is increasingly in competition with other public services such as pensions and healthcare for scarce state expenditure. This, he contends, both threatens the traditional uniqueness of universities and also leads to questions about the purposes of higher education and whether it is still deserving of public funding. This in turn is leading to debates about whether all higher education should be funded through student fees and other private means, thus moving from being a public to a private good. The author considers the links between the renegotiation of the foundations of the European welfare and communist/post-communist states and globalisation. He suggests that the reform and re/production of higher education need to be linked to wider issues of the transformation of both welfare and nation states, as well as to the involvement in these processes of transnational bodies such as the World Bank. Kwiek's argument is illustrated by reference to the World Bank's interventions in Poland in the late 1990s. The chapter also examines different theory and practice in reforming public services at the global level, and in both the established European Union countries of Western Europe and the new-EU (accession) countries of central Europe. In relation to the latter, Kwiek notes that the post-communist model of mass higher education has been for (underfunded) public and private institutions of higher education to exist side by side, with the public sector providing but also charging for part-time education provided at weekends, so that in one way or the other most non-traditional students end up paying for their higher education. Higher education, Kwiek contends, has also become focused on goals of international competitiveness that are new to both institutions and academics, with students being more consumerist in their attitudes and higher education itself increasingly viewed as a private good.

Fuller's chapter is concerned with examining the current state of academic leadership (particularly a variant he terms Academic Caesarism) and how that is affecting the re/production of the university. He considers the ways in which the university has both paralleled the development of the nation state in its historical acquisition of organisational autonomy and also owes its contemporary existence to actions taken by states to consolidate national identity and train their future leaders. He argues that both the university and the state have been attacked in recent times, particularly by post-modernists, for their failure of representation, the state in respect of people and the university in respect of knowledge. Fuller contends that universities have responded to post-modernity by acquiring some of the functions of the state, absorbing responsibility not only for education but for the provision of healthcare and sometimes even domestic security (which he calls Academic Imperialism) and also by developing dictatorial forms of leadership (Academic Caesarism) which both seek to protect and limit their complex and potentially divisive constituencies, including students and alumni, academics, politicians and business. The chapter sets out the characteristics of Academic Caesarism and how it relates to the reproduction of the university in a form described by Fuller as part church, part casino. Fuller also explores how university leaders may still be able to uphold the view that higher education is a public good whilst balancing the often contradictory interests of the various constituencies. The arguments made are illustrated by reference to examples from both the USA and the UK. Fuller then outlines a radical strategy for the future development of universities, which sheds new light on the question of the desirable relationship between research and teaching in higher education institutions and suggests removing public funding from higher education in favour of greater investment in education at school level.

Ciancanelli's chapter examines recent changes in the financial situation of universities, institutions that she argues were once tailored to fit national circumstances but are now subject to the effects and impact of neo-liberalism, globalisation and 'financialisation'. The author explores how 'financialisation' has affected the widely used, long-standing system of scholarly communication in universities based on the free exchange of ideas. This exchange has benefited considerably from recent developments in internet and other communication technologies. At the same time, greater commercial involvement in publishing for profit, the outputs of research which are then sold back to the academic community, has tended to thwart the realisation of the emancipatory potential of technologies that could (and arguably should) provide open and free access to the knowledge that universities produce. The contrast between journals produced by learned societies or public universities and those produced by the five global publishing conglomerates that now dominate academic publishing are quite strikingly different. The chapter provides a case study of the University of California, demonstrating the extent to which commercially produced citation indexes of academic work published in journal articles not only increasingly drive where academics publish, their promotion prospects and the national and global status of their universities but also which journals university libraries purchase. Soon even universities in high-income countries will be unable to afford the cost of some commercial academic journals, which increasingly come in digitised forms (such that back copies of paper journals no longer form a knowledge commons which universities can keep in perpetuity if they wish). Open access journals are available but have been slow to gain academic credibility and legitimacy in many fields. Ciancanelli argues that the production and reproduction of much new university knowledge is now well outside the control of any nation state or individual higher education institution and hence brings into question the extent to which higher education anywhere is still a service for public benefit.

Nedeva's chapter focuses on the extent to which global pressures on universities and funding crises as well as attempts to redefine the role of higher education have increasingly led to the explicit diversification and framing of university missions beyond teaching and 'blue skies' research, into what is sometimes termed the 'third mission' or 'third stream', including public engagement in the processes and outcomes of academic research, entrepreneurial activities of many kinds, undertaking applied research for industry and other fund-raising pursuits and an overt link between universities, society and the economy. Nedeva suggests that greater emphasis on a set of 'third mission' functions is not merely adding to or being absorbed into the existing functions of higher education institutions but is significantly changing and deflecting the more traditional core activities of universities and how those functions are carried out. 'Third mission' activities are, she contends, leading towards a different relationship between universities, societies and their economies, in an increasingly global context. Thus the development of teaching programmes largely concerned with imparting employability and skills rather than knowledge to students, the selling of knowledge 'products' and the shaping of research problems by what funding is available rather than by academic curiosity, are all examples of how a closer relationship between higher education and the economy is transforming and reproducing the university. Comparing two hypothetical cases of universities pursuing different versions of the 'third mission', one a for-profit university and the other a publicly-funded university, Nedeva illustrates how the 'third mission' may lead to some teaching-oriented universities losing public respect, a deflection of the activities of more research-oriented institutions, a re-assessment of how universities' teaching and research activities are organised and funded and whom they benefit, and ultimately the disappearance or diminution of the idea of higher education's provision of research and teaching as a public good.

References

Deem, R. (2001) 'Globalisation, new managerialism, academic capitalism and entrepreneurialism in universities; is the local dimension still important?', *Comparative Education*, 37(1): 7–20.

Marginson, S. (2006) 'Dynamics of national and global competition in higher education', *Higher Education*, 52(1): 1–39.

Marginson, S. and E. Sawir (2005) 'Interrogating global flows in higher education', *Globalisation, Societies and Education*, 3(3): 281–310.

Newman, J. H. (1976) *The Idea of the University*, Oxford, Clarendon Press.

Von Humboldt, W. (1970) 'University reform in Germany: reports and documents', *Minerva*, 8: 242–50.

2 Repairing the deficits of modernity

The emergence of parallel discourses in higher education in Europe

Roger Dale

The main argument of this chapter turns around the surely uncontentious claim that over the past half century, universities in particular, and higher and tertiary education in general (the labels are significant) have undergone enormous changes. However, while the claim may be uncontentious, the analysis of its substance and consequences have tended to be confined and constricted by what have been called the theoretical and methodological 'isms' of the study of education policy – methodological nationalism, methodological statism and methodological educationism (see Dale and Robertson, forthcoming). In each case, the 'ism' is used to suggest an approach to the objects that takes key elements of them as unproblematic and assumes a constant and shared meaning; they become 'fixed, abstract and absolute' (Fine 2003: 465), and the source of the danger lies in the nominal continuity provided by the ostensibly similar concepts. As Smith warns, 'a whole series of key concepts for the understanding of society derive their power from appearing to be just what they always were and derive their instrumentality from taking on quite different forms' (Smith 2006: 628). What is meant by the first two isms, methodological nationalism and statism, may be seen as relatively straightforward, though their exact nature and consequences can be matters for dispute. In a nutshell, the first relates to the tendency in social science as a whole to take the 'nation-state' as the container of society, and the national as the appropriate level of analysis, while the second relates to the tendency to take 'the state' as the universal, and ubiquitous, model for governing societies. These assumptions also characterise a great deal of work on higher education. Universities are widely and unproblematically regarded as 'national' institutions, which involve some element of regulation by the relevant state. Of course, those assumptions remain largely accurate. However, the assumption that universities necessarily and always take the same fundamental form is not justified.

In the context of this chapter, educationism relates to two tendencies: (a) to take a relatively abstract and fixed model of 'the University' as the fundamental if shifting object and basis of study (interesting analysis of the forms this might take is to be found in Trow 2005); and (b) to assume the existence of a static University or higher education *sector* in which those institutions are embedded, and which is taken for granted as embracing a collection of activities that naturally, even necessarily, go together. One very specific element of educationism in the area of higher education is the fact that the very great majority of the literature on the topic is produced by people working in universities, often with a scant empirical base, writing about what they experience as well as what they observe, with the writers having clear 'interests' in the future of the institution. This not only makes 'detachment' difficult, but it also makes it more challenging to 'stop seeing the things that are conventionally "there" to be seen' (Becker 1971). More than this, it could be argued that this insider view has tended to affect the focus of studies of higher education, with particular emphasis on the governance of the University as an organisation, and to a lesser extent, governance of higher education as a sector, and the factors influencing these, at the expense of a broader analysis that would examine not just the governance of the organisation and the sector, but the wider meaning of the University and the higher education sector. As the quotation from Gavin Smith suggests, names (and, we might add, activities) may stay the same, but as their place in the changing social structures and social formations of which they are part changes, so does the meaning of those activities, disguised though it may be by the nominal continuity.

The intention of this chapter, then, is to try to open up questions of the nature of the broader changes within which the University is changing, in order to understand the nature and possible consequences of those changes more broadly, especially at the level of the higher education sector, in a way that goes beyond methodological nationalism, statism and educationism. I will examine the consequences for what were once solely national institutions, in an era when economies were national, as the economic fulcrum is increasingly moving to supranational level.

I will focus on higher education in the European Union to provide a basis for examining some of the questions generated by the broader theoretical analysis of the changes in the wider world that form the structuring context for the changes in meaning of the University and the higher education sector. I shall argue in particular that (a) rather than the main consequence being forms of *diversification* of the *organisations* of higher education, which is where most of the literature is concentrated, the main consequence is a tendential *differentiation* of higher education as a *sector*; and (b) that the logic of going beyond the isms undermines the still pervasive logic of regarding relationships between scales as necessarily based on producing an outcome that includes both existing scales, whether that outcome be zero sum, hybrid or convergence. Rather than seeking to establish how the two scales are reconciled, for instance through identifying the 'effect' of one on the other, it may be useful to approach the issue abductively, and to consider not just 'either/or' relationships between scales, but 'both/and' and I shall attempt to elaborate this by pointing to a tendential emergence of *parallel discourses* of higher education at national and European levels.

Theoretically, the argument is set at a very broad level. It suggests that the current state of the Universities, like other institutions of modernity, is fundamentally a reflection of and a response to the changing nature of the relationship between capitalism and modernity. In developing the fundamental argument, I follow Boaventura de Sousa Santos (2002) in suggesting that it is crucial to the understanding of the current global predicaments to distinguish between the trajectories of capitalism (as found currently in the form of neoliberal globalisation) and modernity and to examine the relationships between them. As Santos puts it,

> Western modernity and capitalism are two different and autonomous historical processes ... (that) have converged and interpenetrated each other. ... It is my contention that we are living in a time of paradigmatic transition, and, consequently, that the sociocultural paradigm of modernity ... will eventually disappear before capitalism ceases to be dominant ... partly from a process of supersession and partly from a process of obsolescence. It entails supersession to the extent that modernity has fulfilled some of its promises, in some cases even in excess. It results from obsolescence to the extent that modernity is no longer capable of fulfilling some of its other promises.
>
> (Santos 2002: 1–2)

He goes on, 'Modernity is grounded on a dynamic tension between the pillar of regulation ((which) guarantees order in a society as it exists in a given moment and place) and emancipation ... the aspiration for a good order in a good society in the future' (ibid.: 2). Modern regulation is 'the set of norms, institutions and practices that guarantee the stability of expectations' (ibid.); the pillar of regulation is constituted by the principles of the state, the market and community (typically taken as the three key agents of governance (see Dale 1997). Modern emancipation is the 'set of oppositional aspirations and tendencies that aim to increase the discrepancy between experiences and expectations' (ibid.: 2). It is constituted by 'three logics of rationality ...: the aesthetic-expressive rationality of the arts and literature, the cognitive-instrumental rationality of science and technology, and the moral-practical rationality of ethics and the rule of law' (ibid.: 3). However, 'what most strongly characterises the sociocultural condition at the beginning of the century is the collapse of the pillar of emancipation into the pillar of regulation, as a result of the reconstructive management of the excesses and deficits of modernity which ... were viewed as temporary shortcomings and as problems to be solved through a better and broader use of the ever-expanding material, intellectual and institutional resources of modernity ... (and which) have been entrusted to modern science and, as a second best, to modern law' (ibid.: 7 and 4–5). Further, these two pillars have now ceased to be in tension but have become almost fused, as a result of the 'reduction of modern emancipation to the cognitive-instrumental rationality of science and the reduction of modern regulation to the principle of the market' (ibid.: 9). We may put these arguments in summary form by suggesting that what they mean is that modernity is no longer the best possible shell for capitalism in its global neoliberal form (see Dale, forthcoming).

The central argument of the chapter will be that universities do provide a very good illustration of Santos' (2002) argument. It does not seem too far-fetched to see in the recent history of the University just the kind of fusing of emancipation and regulation to which Santos refers. Historically, it will be argued, the modern university could be seen as very much more attached to the pillar of emancipation than to the pillar of regulation, while more recent experience points to first, the increasing involvement of the University with the pillar of regulation, and second, the increasing absorption of that pillar by the rules and practices of the market. In particular, the changes to the University might also be seen as forms of 'reconstitutive management' of the deficits of modernity. Thus, the consequences of these changes are not seen as transcending modernity, but as an intensified use of the tools of modernity, producing what might be seen as a form of ultra-modernity, especially through the shifting of the scales of problem identification and solution. It will be suggested that while neither the extent nor the outcome of those processes are yet decided, (a) it is clear that the nature of those outcomes are contingent rather than determined; (b) that they are not to be found only at a national level; and (c) that they are likely to be characterised not by fusion or hybridity or convergence, but by a functional and scalar division of labour between parallel discourses (see Dale 2002, and Dale, forthcoming).

The chapter is organised as follows. The next section will cover the development of the University away from its association with the pillar of emancipation towards the pillar of regulation, initiated by the rise of the instrumentalisation of the University and of the planning and management of its activities after World War II. Following this, I will look a little more closely at the main forms taken by the reconstitutive management of the deficits of modernity, as reflected in changes in the University and the higher education sector, with a particular focus on the UK. And finally, I will consider recent changes in the University and the higher education sector associated with the increasing involvement of Europe in the sector.

The university – from emancipation to regulation?

Very briefly, we might follow Bill Readings in suggesting that 'the modern University has had three ideas: the Kantian concept of reason, the Humboldtian idea of culture, and now the techno-bureaucratic notion of excellence' (Readings 1996: 14), a suggestion that seems to parallel Santos' (2002) distinction between emancipation and regulation, and the collapse of the first into the second. In this section, I will start from the very broad assumption that the Humboldtian idea of the University remained dominant up to the World War II, but that since then it has been subjected to increasing, and increasingly differentiated, forms of critique and pressure.

The end of World War II brought about significant changes to the contexts within which Universities operated. Chief among these are the Cold War, and decolonisation.

The Cold War took the form it did in part because of the explosion of the Atomic Bomb over Hiroshima and Nagasaki, which had a number of very profound consequences for the relationship between Universities and modernity. One of these was that those explosions represented the ultimate demonstration that science could be used for destructive as well as beneficent ends. In a sense, this parallels Bauman's (2000) argument about the Holocaust representing the apogee, or inevitable outcome, of modernity; humanity had proved capable of destroying itself, and the power to determine whether that would happen was to become, and has remained, in more complex ways, the single most significant issue facing the people of the planet. A second was that warfare was no longer about the size of armies and guns, but about scientific knowledge. From the race between the two camps of a newly bipolar world to capture the leading German brains in 1944–5, to the jolt given to the West a little more than ten years later by Russia launching the Sputnik, having the best scientists, and being better educated, was becoming strategically more important than being able to field the largest and best equipped army.

Decolonisation also had a great impact on the conception and nature of the University. We might see this as taking two forms. First, although Universities had been set up in the colonies of Western European countries before decolonisation, these tended to be very much 'extensions' of the 'home' institution, rather than autonomous institutions. With decolonisation being interpreted as creating 'modern' nation-states in the ex-colonies, on the basis of possessing the characteristics and trappings of existing, 'proper' nation-states, having a national university became almost a sine qua non of membership of the international system of states that emerged as part of the construction of the United Nations. If the first form can be seen as essentially political, part of the process of nation-building, the second is more involved with economic development. Under the dominant aegis of 'Modernisation Theory' (see Rostow 1960) 'underdeveloped' countries were to 'develop' by following as closely as possible the stages followed by the already developed world in the course of their development, including the adoption of the institutions that had enabled their progress – which included, of course, Universities.

The key point of these two different kinds of changes for the present purpose is that they *both* involved a new level of *instrumentalisation* of knowledge and a new relationship with the state, now to be seen as Principal, with the University to be seen as its Agent. And they both involved, independently, some *routinisation* of the idea of the University as an institution, and the installation and implementation of that idea through the ideas of *planning and management*, which were, of course, key elements of the expanding 'scientisation' of the world (see Schofer and Meyer 2005) that was a logical outcome of modernity, and especially of modern social science.

This latter is exemplified through the creation at the end of WWII of two key international organisations, the United Nations Educational, Scientific and Cultural Organisation (UNESCO) and the Organisation for European Economic Cooperation (OEEC), later to become the Organisation for Economic Cooperation and Development (OECD). 'Planning made its first official appearance' as applied to education in the UNESCO/IBE International Conference on Public Education held in 1951 (UNESCO, 1996: 183), where the participants also called for assistance by UNESCO in setting up national planning services. This developed to take the form of the International Institute for Educational Planning which was set up in 1963 to carry out research and higher education activities.

In the countries of North West Europe, the idea of planning was a central element of states that were to organise and improve their societies, and once again, the idea that this would be useful in the case of Universities also was evident, for instance in the case of the early 1960s UK Robbins report (Committee on Higher Education 1963) which laid down principles about access to University that are still appealed to today.

Perhaps even more significant for the current issue is the entry on to the scene of the idea that Universities required 'management', and of a specific kind. This is signalled most clearly in the creation of the IMHE – the Institute for Management in Higher Education – by the OECD in 1966 (see Henry *et al.* 2001); Levasseur 1996). A key stage in this process was the events of 1968 in Paris, whose outcome was, perhaps paradoxically, a qualitative shift in the idea of the modern University as a 'managed' institution. As Readings (1996: 137) put it, 'the students ... resisted both the existing feudal structure and the state's attempt to modernize it. This fed into a general critique of the nation-state ... So, the question was not how to make the University into a proper state institution but how to think about the University outside the terms laid down by the nation-state, while also recognizing that the old feudal structure was dysfunctional'.

Instrumentalisation and managerialism continued to develop in the sector, but were by the mid-1970s beginning to be absorbed into – and possibly to shape the response to – changes brought about as the transnationalisation of the economy and the earlier stages of globalisation gathered pace, and began to expose the fading role of 'national' economies, with both the capacity and the appropriateness of the state retaining a National University system with the same values and same funding, provision and governance as previously under scrutiny.

We might see these changes as having come about through: (a) the decline of the national state as the basis of the economy (without a national economy it is more difficult to build a national welfare state, for instance), with the reversal of the relationship between the economic and the social, from one where the former served the latter to its opposite; and consequently (b) the declining influence of borders, especially as constraints on the movement of capital, as well as the growth of international organisations that carry out many of what were formerly regarded as 'national' prerogatives and responsibilities; (c) the recognition (particularly in the form of the New Public Management, see, e.g., Kettl 1997; Pollitt and Bouckaert 2004) that many of what had come to be seen as 'obviously' state activities, could, and should, be funded and provided by other, often private, bodies, with benefits to both state expenditure and quality of service; (d) the dominant role of the state becoming the promotion of national economic prosperity, on the assumption that the wealth so created would trickle down so that all would eventually benefit from it; (e) the associated shift of state activity towards economic activity; and (f) a shift from state to individual responsibility for security and risk, especially in the area of employment.

The contemporary university, and the reconstitutive management of the deficits of modernity

The University and higher education sector, were not, of course, immune from the effects of these attempts at what might be seen as another phase of the reconstitutive management of the deficits of modernity as providing the institutional base for neoliberal capitalism. We might see a dual characterisation of the deficits of modernity as registered in discussions of the University. On the one hand, we find deficits arising from inadequate governance of Universities, their shortcomings as part of neoliberal polities. The problem is that they are perceived as ineffective and inefficient, and hence not fit for the purposes they were intended to serve. On the other hand, their mandate and capacity is inadequate to meet the new demands placed on them by neoliberal globalisation, especially in the form of the Knowledge Economy.

In terms of the first of these, we may see three aspects of the changes to governance in the critique of the University: (a) Universities' funding was cut, and they were required to find a much higher proportion of their income from non-state sources, which brought new stakeholders (a concept new to university governance) and partners into University governance as well as significantly altering the relationship between existing stakeholders; (b) much more direct governmental control over the allocation of funding to Universities, symbolised in England by the replacement in 1988 of the University Grants Committee, which had acted as a traditional buffer institution between government and Universities, by the Universities Funding Council (Taggart 2003); and (c) their integration into the broader process of reform of the public sector initiated in the 1990s, usually known as the New Public Management (NPM).

It will be useful to elaborate a little on the NPM, since it appears to have provided a kind of template for reforms to University governance. A great deal has been written about the NPM, but for present purposes it may be sufficient to point to its critique of the poor performance of the public sector, its lack of responsiveness to clients, its lack of accountability, and its tendency to provider capture, which were taken to characterise the public sectors of what had been social democratic countries.[1] Four aspects of the NPM are important here (though it is also important to note that it has been to a degree succeeded in some places by what is referred to as the 'new managerialism' (see Deem and Brehony 2005; Deem *et al.* 2007). First, it was a central feature of the NPM that it was equally applicable to all sectors; it was a set of principles for public management that held irrespective of whether the sector was police or health, or education. Such sectors were 'mainstreamed' (see Dale and Jesson 1992), meaning that they were to be treated alike, with no possible recourse to any kind of special (sectoral) pleading, with a very narrow definition of mutatis mutandis. Second, the NPM involved prescription *and* diagnosis as well as both solution and framing of the problem. It embodied and was the mechanism through which key elements of neoliberalism were installed in public sectors around the world.[2] Third, it involved the replacement of a relationship of trust between the University and what would now (and in consequence of this shift) be called its stakeholders, by a relationship of contract. And fourth, it was concerned with the formal relationship between process and outcomes (or, more narrowly, outputs[3]), not with outcomes themselves. In some versions of the NPM there was a sense that the guiding slogan was 'get the process right and the outcomes will be bound to follow' (see Dale 2001). However, the concentration on outputs did have some perverse effects on what Universities did, such as measuring outputs against quite inflexible formulae, and the reduction of responsibility for outcomes to accountability for outputs (see Schick 2001). This is particularly important in the context of this chapter because it indicates how 'content-free' the remedies for the perceived deficits were. 'One size fits all' may be valid in terms of process, but it tells us nothing about the substance of what is to be achieved.

One major consequence of this was to prioritise issues of process over issues of substance, which were to a degree to be met through proxies of performance, rather than established through explicit policy. A considerable amount of critical work has been done on this form of substitution, the best known of which is probably Lyotard's (1984 [1979]) famous notion of *performativity*. I have suggested elsewhere (Dale 1992) that the notion of 'quality' fills a similar role, due to its 'tofu-like' character, which sees it having no taste of its own but absorbing the taste of whatever environment it is placed in, or whatever set of indicators are used to indicate its presence. Of particular value in this context is Bill Readings' version of this argument. He suggests that

> The nation state and culture arose together, and ... are ... ceasing to be essential to an increasingly transnational global economy. This shift has major implications for the University, which has historically been the primary institution of national culture in the modern nation-state ... the (most notable) implication (is) the emergence of a discourse of *'excellence'* in place of prior appeals to the idea of culture as the language

in which the University seeks to explain itself to itself and to the world at large.

(Readings 1996: 12, emphasis added)

Very briefly, then, we may suggest that by the end of the last century, issues of University governance dominated the work and approaches of the higher education sector, at least in the UK and Western Europe (and far beyond, through the patronage of the World Bank; see Dale 2001 and Kwiek in this volume), with a concomitantly reduced emphasis on the mandate and capacity of the system, beyond the point where they were, not entirely incidentally, shaped by the changes in governance. National culture as the cement/glue holding higher education sectors together and forming a mandate for Universities was eroding into performativity, quality and excellence at national level, aimed at making the sector more efficient and also more aligned to economic rather than social goals. In the following section, we will consider the increasing influence of the European level on these issues, through the development of an agenda for the modernisation of the University for the Europe of Knowledge.

Modernising the university for the Europe of knowledge

In this final section of the chapter, I will attempt to trace the development of European efforts at modernising the University, chiefly for the purpose of enhancing its contribution to economic competitiveness. I will suggest that this has involved the construction of a new agenda, new institutions and effectively a new 'Knowledge' sector of which higher education – or at least a part of it – is a key component. I shall not be paying significant attention to the 'effects' of these changes on individual organisations, which seems to be the main focus of most existing research in the area, or how far the Bologna process reforms[4] of achieving common degree programmes/ credits and quality assurance arrangements have been implemented. Rather, my focus will be on the differentiation of the sector at and between national and European levels.

The first official recognition and naming of the problem came in the European Commission's Communication, *The role of the universities in the Europe of Knowledge*, which also demonstrated the increasingly powerful role adopted by the EC in driving (and funding) the Bologna Process, making it a key element of the response to the Lisbon agenda, rather than 'merely' a means of increasing mobility and the creation of a common degree architecture. The Communication sought to 'start a debate on the role of the Universities within the knowledge society and economy in Europe' and stated that 'The creation of a Europe of Knowledge has been a prime objective for the European Union since the Lisbon European Council of March 2000' (CEC 2003: 2, 3). The conclusions of that Council were that Europe should 'become the most dynamic, competitive knowledge-driven economy in the world, with sustained growth, more and better jobs and greater social cohesion', and universities are seen in the Communication as having a major role to play in this process. The Europe of Knowledge was based on two planks, the European Research Area, and the Commission's work in education. At that stage, the nature of the education contribution was rather general and unspecific, and there was little liaison between the two components. The 2003 Communication identified five new challenges facing European universities: the increased demand for higher education; the internationalisation of education and research; developing cooperation between universities and industry; proliferation of knowledge production spaces; and the reorganisation of knowledge. Most notably, it also pointed to the increasing divergence between 'the organisation of universities at member state level and the emergence of challenges which go beyond national frontiers', which required 'a joint and coordinated endeavour ..., backed up and supported by the EU, in order to move towards a genuine Europe of Knowledge' (ibid.: 9, 10). At this stage, however, it was not possible to point to significant actions that might assist in this cause. Three main priorities were identified: ensuring sufficient resources and their efficient use; consolidating excellence in research and teaching; and opening up universities to the outside and increasing their international effectiveness. Though the tenor and urgency of later documents changed, this Communication effectively laid down the dual basis of the agenda for modernisation of the University – effectively, organising existing activities more productively, which was referred to in later documents as 'unleashing the potential' of Europe's universities – and developing new, knowledge-related capacities.

The next significant contribution, *Mobilising the brainpower of Europe: enabling universities to make their full contribution to the Lisbon Strategy* (CEC 2005a) continued but intensified and added more detail to this agenda. It significantly extended the scope of universities' potential contribution to the achievement of the Lisbon goals, identifying them, in a new and rather narrower expression of the mandate for higher education, as 'essential' in all three 'poles of Europe's knowledge triangle: education, research and innovation', but 'not in a position to deliver their full potential contribution' (p. 2). This was associated with three main challenges – achieving world-class quality and increasing attractiveness, improving governance, and increasing and diversifying funding, and attractiveness, governance and funding came to form the basis of the 'Core Modernisation Agenda', which was named and effectively formalised in this document. Also of significance in this document is that obstacles to achieving these goals are identified on the basis of comparative studies with other HE systems worldwide, specifying the nature and size of the gaps to be filled by European universities (see also Marginson 2006). In particular, explicit comparisons were made, in tables comparing levels of performance, with the United States and Japan. We can begin to see some differentiation of the sector and responsibilities here. In the area of governance, which had as its priority 'unleashing universities' potential within the national context' (p. 9), Europe's role appears to be one of coordinating national efforts. In the other two areas, however, it is rather more interventionist. Enhancing attractiveness, for instance, requires diversification and specialisation of roles between universities, and 'diversity demands organization at European level' (p. 6). For funding, a wider range of sources is called for but here, a much more radical claim is made: 'Higher education is not just the sum of its education, training and research activities ... (but) also a fundamental economic and social sector in its own right in need of resources for redeployment. The EU has supported the conversion process of sectors like the steel industry, or agriculture; it now faces the imperative to modernize its "knowledge industry" and in particular its universities' (p. 10). Here we see, then, not just a new agenda but the suggestion that it can only be enabled through the reconstruction of the sector, by 'Europe'.

These arguments were further developed in a series of speeches by the present EU Commissioner for Education, Jan Figel. The common basis of these speeches is that Europe is lagging behind the rest of the world, especially the United States (and, more recently, India and China), and that it is essential to recognise why, and what may be done in response. One major perceived problem is the fragmentation of Europe's universities, which is 'inherent in a Europe made up largely of small countries (who) all want their own universities ... research funding systems, ... controls, ... and cultures' (Figel 2006a: 9). Thus,

> if we compare the number of universities which consider themselves to be 'research-intensive', we have in Europe 14 times more than in the US. Alas, they aren't (sic). The American sector is much more sharply segmented between those which see themselves as providers of tuition and those who aspire to engage in globally significant research ... In Europe, research funding is sprinkled between some 2000 institutions ... Europe's universities should be allowed to diversify and specialize; some may be able to play in the major league, but others should concentrate on regional and local needs and perhaps more on teaching.
>
> (Figel 2006b: 3; 2006c: 7)

The importance of moving beyond the national level is another key theme:

> The challenges (that the Modernisation agenda is designed to address) used to be regarded as mainly national ones. But things are changing in that respect. Top higher-education institutions operate in a truly global market, so the only viable solutions for our universities are European in scope and global in ambition ... (the challenges) have become common European ones and require *a concerted approach in the EU context.*
>
> (Figel 2006d: 3; 2006c: 3, emphasis in original)

Two main institutional means of addressing these issues are identified in the speeches. One is the Bologna Process, which is seen as a framework for success: the essential condition for success is the root and branch reform of the way our universities are managed, structured, funded and regulated, ... (though) ... important as they are the curricular and other reforms under the heading of 'Bologna', cover only one aspect of how we urgently need to modernize our higher education systems.

(Figel 2006c: 5)

The other is the European Institute of Technology (EIT), a project initiated by President Barroso as part of the mid-term review of the Lisbon strategy. The EIT

will become a symbol of the integrated European Innovation, Research and Education Area, generating innovations in areas of key economic or societal interest. The ambition is that the EIT becomes a reference for managing innovation, by promoting new forms of collaboration among the type of partner organisations involved in the Knowledge triangle as well as for the modernisation of higher education and research institutions in the EU, both directly, through its activities and outputs, and indirectly through its governance ... (it) will encourage and promote innovation through trans- and inter-disciplinary strategic research and education in areas of key economic or societal interest and by exploiting its knowledge outcomes to the benefit of the EU. It will build a 'critical mass' of human and physical resources in these fields of knowledge, attracting and retaining private sector investment in innovation, education, and R&D, as well as students at master level, doctoral candidates and researchers at all levels of their careers from both the scientific and business sectors.

(CEC 2006b: 7, 3)

What is most remarkable about the EIT is that the work on it was done by the Directorate General responsible for education and training. It places education, and universities in particular, right at the centre of the EU's innovation and knowledge economy strategies.

The most recent document in the series is *Delivering on the Modernisation Agenda for universities: education, research and innovation* (CEC 2006a). It is interesting that the subheading qualifying and specifying 'the Modernisation Agenda' is in fact comprised of what were described in *Mobilising the brainpower*, as 'the poles of the knowledge triangle' (Education, Research and Innovation (CEC 2005a; see above)), while the Core Modernisation Agenda of Governance, Funding and Attractiveness announced there is not mentioned in the 2006 document. The Communication suggests that 'Discussions at European level show an increasing willingness to modernize systems and the agenda mapped out below is not, in essence, contested' (p. 4). However, the agenda, made up of nine 'changes that will be key to success' (p. 5) is somewhat broader, particularly in its promotion of a new European Research Institute mandate, than the CMA of *Mobilising brainpower*. It contains three items that seem to be more related to the ERI knowledge triangle than to the CMA. These are: 'Provide the right mix of skills and competences for the labour market ... to equip Europe with the skills and competences necessary to succeed in a globalised, knowledge-based economy' (p. 6), while it is also significant that this change is explicitly linked to the lifelong learning agenda, the basis for all the EU's activities in education; 'Enhance interdisciplinarity and transdisciplinarity' which requires a focus '*less on scientific disciplines and more on research* domains' (p. 8, emphasis in original); and (the slightly ambiguous) 'Reward excellence at the highest level', which emphasises the importance of competition, and of the EIT and the ERC. Here, then, we find further evidence of the emergence and extension, through the added prominence given to the ERI over the CMA, of a dual agenda, and further evidence of the view that the ERI can only be achieved at the European level.

Overall, what this set of papers indicates is a wish for a new role, or rather new and differentiated roles, for an institution that now more clearly and distinctly than ever has to meet two distinct sets of demands, the global knowledge-economic/innovative, and (the mainly national) social cohesion.

Conclusion

I have argued in this chapter that the roots of new problems for the University are very deep seated, and to be found in the separation of the trajectories of modernity and capitalism in its latest, neoliberal, phase. This has serious and entirely novel consequences for universities as classic institutions of modernity. It is argued that there are two main consequences of this for analysts; there is a need to rethink the nature of the sources, the nature and scope of the problems perceived by the contemporary university; and there is a need to look beyond the theoretical and methodological tools that have been deployed to analyse the problems of modernity.

Specifically, following Santos, the argument has been that the separation of modernity and capitalism, and the waning of the capacity of the institutions of the former to provide an effective 'shell' for the latter, has created a need for the reconstitution of the institutions of modernity and the repair of their deficits, and it has been through this perspective that the current state of higher education has been analysed here. This involved looking at how the remedying of these deficits was tackled in an era when the national level had been to a degree superseded, when governance was both pluriform and multiscalar rather than national and 'statist', and when the consequences of the initial attempt to interpret and repair the deficits, by means of NPM-style interventions, were such as to hollow out the core of the University, leaving it to operate within a husk comprised of 'performativity', 'excellence' and 'quality'.

As the final section of the chapter shows, there is quite compelling evidence that this is the case, with an incipient division of labour between matters associated with the competitiveness agenda moving towards the EU level, and those to do with governance of universities remaining at national level, albeit with some element of attempted coordination at the European level. There is also evidence[5] to suggest that the former is to be achieved effectively through the construction of a new sector, the Knowledge sector, of which higher education, or at least some parts of it, are to be part, leaving the remaining parts to contribute to a 'social policy' sector, into which the national level activities of higher education systems will be folded (see Dale, forthcoming; Dale and Robertson, 2005). An analysis that closely matches that advanced here, though without suggesting a division of labour, is Brine's (2006) very well-documented account of the almost complete bifurcation of lifelong learning policy into strands for HKS (high knowledge and skills) students, who are destined for membership of the Knowledge *Economy*, and LSK (low knowledge and skills) students, who will end up in the Knowledge *Society* (ibid.). The final point of the argument is that the relationship between these scales need not be the kind of hybrid model, or convergence, that is assumed by and a paradoxical product of, the zero sum approaches that seem to characterise much discussion in this area, but parallel discourses, based in effectively different sectors, that exist in relationship to each other but are not reducible to each other.

Finally, if we consider the three major questions that frame this section of the Yearbook, we might say that universities are now all, directly and/or indirectly (and here it is important to recall Saskia Sassen's point that globalisation can take place *within* the national), involved in processes of globalisation. They might be seen as transnational (as well as national) organisations, operating in transnational (as well as national) spaces, and all related to the discourse or the imaginary of the global knowledge economy. The examples discussed here have been drawn from the most fully developed and clearest example of these shifts, the EU, and the European Higher Education Area, but it would be short-sighted to assume that the global influence is confined to these areas. Second, universities have now to be understood as not homogeneous or single-purpose institutions (if they ever were) with an essential and unchanging 'core business'. The European version of this sketched out here points to a reconstituted *sector, differentiated* into knowledge policy and social policy related activities, rather than an increasingly *diversified institution*. And finally, it might be expected that these changing realities will be reflected in multiple and contingent ways in the experiences, values and achievements of all those associated with them.

Notes

1 While the NPM was originally an Anglo-American phenomenon, and most rigidly enacted in New Zealand, it is clear, as we shall see below, that it has very clearly penetrated the vocabulary and practice of HE systems across Europe.
2 This is not to suggest that NPM was installed everywhere in the same way, or that it was somehow parachuted in with no human agency. It was 'made', or 'done', through mundane practices, which were performed in accordance with its central tools of audit, benchmarking, etc.

3 The difference between outputs and outcomes is itself a key distinction within the NPM. Essentially 'outputs' are the services, activities and products that organisations deliver, and 'outcomes' are the intended consequences of the delivery of the specified outputs. The distinction is basic to the idea of purchaser–provider splits; for instance, the purchaser sets outcomes and the outputs through which these are to be achieved and the provider is accountable for the delivery of those outputs.

4 Formally, the Bologna Process is the most important and wide-ranging reform of higher education in Europe since the founding of the EU, though membership of the process is not confined to EU members, and the European Higher Education Area, which the Process has brought into being, now extends from the most westerly point to Vladivostok on the Pacific. It developed from the Sorbonne Declaration, signed by the French, German, Italian and British Ministers of Education, which set out to create an 'open European area for higher education', through removing barriers to student and teaching staff mobility and cooperation; increasing the external and internal readability of higher education; and thus enhancing Europe's international appeal and competitiveness.

This laid the ground for the signing of the Bologna Declaration on 19 June 1999, by 29 European Ministers of Education. The aim of the Process was to 'establish a European Higher Education Area by 2010 in which staff and students can move with ease and have fair recognition of their qualifications, and which advances European higher education as a single and coherent system in order to increase Europe's competitiveness and its share in the global higher education market'. This overall goal was reflected in the six main goals defined in the Bologna Declaration:

• adoption of a system of easily readable and comparable degrees;
• adoption of a system essentially based on two main cycles, undergraduate and graduate;
• establishment of a system of credits – such as in the ECTS system – as a proper means to promoting the most widespread student mobility;
• promotion of mobility by overcoming obstacles to the effective exercise of free movement;
• promotion of European co-operation in quality assurance with a view to developing comparable criteria and methodologies; and
• promotion of the necessary European dimensions in higher education.

These goals were augmented by three further actions proposed at the Prague meeting of the Bologna Process in 2001:

• a commitment to lifelong learning;
• involvement of higher education institutions and students; and
• promoting the attractiveness of European higher education.

The 2003 Berlin meeting added a further goal of 'developing the EHEA and the European Research Area as two pillars of the knowledge-based society'. However, the mere addition of the extra goal, significant though it was in itself, does not exhaust the importance of the shift in the process between Prague and Berlin. This point will be elaborated in the second half of this chapter.

5 'Reforms are facilitated by a favourable economic and social context, and where there are high levels of public and private investment in knowledge, skills and competences, but also where modes of governance of the systems are coherent and coordinated ... (such as) Effective inter-ministerial synergy between "knowledge policies" (education, training, employment/social affairs, research, etc.) ...' (CEC 2005b: 11).

References

Barroso, José Manuel Durão (2007) 'Helping Europe to lead the knowledge revolution' Speech at the Opening of Netherlands House for Education and Research, Brussels, 21 February.

Bauman, Z. and D. Bauman (2000) *Modernity and the Holocaust*, Ithaca, NY: Cornell University Press.

Becker, Howard S. (1971) 'Note' in Wax, M. and Wax, R., 'Great tradition, little tradition and formal education', in Wax, M., Diamond, S. and Gearing, E. (eds) *Anthropological Perspectives on Education*, New York: Basic Books, p. 10.

Brine, Jacky (2006) 'Lifelong learning and the knowledge economy: those that know and those that do not – the discourse of the European Union', *British Educational Research Journal*, 32(5): 649–65.

Commission of the European Communities (2003) 'Communication from the Commission: the role of the universities in the Europe of knowledge', COM (2003) 58, Brussels, 5 February.

Commission of the European Communities (2005a) 'Mobilising the brainpower of Europe: enabling universities to make their full contribution to the Lisbon Strategy', COM (2005) 152, Brussels, 4 April.

Commission of the European Communities (2005b) 'Communication from the Commission: Modernising education and training: a vital contribution to prosperity and social cohesion in Europe'. Draft 2006 Joint Progress Report of the Council and the Commission on the Implementation of the 'Education & Training 2010 Work Programme' {SEC(2005) 1415} COM (2005) 549 final/2, Brussels, 30 November.

Commission of the European Communities (2006a) 'Communication from the Commission to the Council and the European Parliament: Delivering on the modernisation agenda for universities: education, research, innovation', COM (2006) 208, Brussels, 10 May.

Commission of the European Communities (2006b) 'Proposal for a Regulation of the European Parliament and the Council establishing the European Institute of Technology', COM (2006) 604 final/2 2006/0197 (COD) Brussels, 13 November.

Committee on Higher Education (1963) *Higher Education: Report of the committee under the chairmanship of Lord Lionel Robbins*, London: HMSO.

Dale, R. (1997) 'The state and the governance of education: an analysis of the restructuring of the state-education relationship', in A. Halsey, H. Lauder, P. Brown and A. Stuart Wells (eds) *Education, Culture, Economy and Society*, Oxford: Oxford University Press.

Dale, R (2001) 'Constructing a Long Spoon for Comparative Education: charting the career of the "New Zealand model"', *Comparative Education*, 37(4): 493–500.

Dale, R. (2002) 'The construction of a European education space and education policy'. Paper presented to European Social Fund Exploratory Workshop on Globalisation, Educational Restructuring and Social Cohesion in Europe. Barcelona, 3–5 October.

Dale, R. (2005) 'Globalisation, knowledge and comparative education', *Comparative Education*, 41(2): 117–50.

Dale, R. (forthcoming) 'Neoliberal capitalism, the modern state and the governance of education', *Tertium Comparationis*, 13(2).

Dale, R. and J. Jesson (1992) 'Mainstreaming education; the role of the State Services Commission', *New Zealand Annual Review of Education*, 2: 7–34.

Dale, R. and S. L. Robertson (forthcoming) 'Beyond methodological "isms"', in A. Kazamias and R. Cowen (eds) *Comparative Education in an Era of Globalisation*.

Deem, R. and K. J. Brehony (2005) 'Management as ideology: the case of "new managerialism" in Higher Education', *Oxford Review of Education*, 31 (2): 213–31.

Deem, R., S. Hillyard and M. Reed (2007) *Knowledge, Higher Education and the New Managerialism: The Changing Management of UK Universities*, Oxford: Oxford University Press.

Figel, Jan (2006a) 'International competitiveness in higher education – a European perspective'. Speech to AHUA Conference, Oxford, 3 April.

Figel, Jan (2006b) 'Higher education needs bold reforms'. Presentation at Centre for European Reform, Brussels, 18 July.

Figel, Jan (2006c) 'The modernization agenda for European universities'. Speech at Ceremony of the 22nd Anniversary of the Open University of the Netherlands. Heerlen, 22 September.

Figel, Jan (2006d) 'Modernising Europe's higher education: making initiatives work'. Dinner speech at the presentation of the Global Engineering Excellence study titled 'In Search of Global Engineering Excellence, educating the next generation of engineers for the global workplace', Frankfurt/Main, 9 November.

Fine, R. (2003) 'Taking the "ism" out of cosmopolitanism', *European Journal of Social Theory*, 6(4): 451–70.

Henry, M., B. Lingard, F. Rizvi and S. Taylor (2001) *The OECD, Globalisation and Education Policy*, Amsterdam: Pergamon.

Kettl, Donald (1997) 'Global revolution in public management: driving themes, missing links', *Journal of Policy Analysis and Management*, 16(3): 446–62.

LeVasseur, Paul (1996) '1970–1995: an IMHE perspective on higher education in transition', *Higher Education Management*, 8(3): 7–14.

Lyotard, Jean François (1984 [1979]) *The Postmodern Condition*, Minneapolis: University of Minnesota Press.

Marginson, S. (2006) 'Dynamics of national and global competition in higher education', *Higher Education*, 52(1): 1–39.

Pollitt, Christopher and Bouckaert, Geert (2004) *Public Management Reform: A Comparative Analysis*, 2nd edition, Oxford: Oxford University Press.

Readings, Bill (1996) *The University in Ruins*, Cambridge, MA: Harvard University Press.

Rostow, W. W. (1960) *The Stages of Economic Growth: A Non-Communist Manifesto*, Cambridge: Cambridge University Press.

Santos, Boaventura de Sousa (2002) *Toward a New Legal Common Sense*, London: Butterworths.

Sassen, Saskia (2006) *Territory, Authority, Rights: From Mediaeval to Global Assemblages*, Princeton, NJ: Princeton University Press.

Schick, Allen (2001) 'Reflections on the New Zealand Model', Wellington: New Zealand Treasury.

Schofer, Evan and Meyer, John (2005) 'The worldwide expansion of higher education in the twentieth century', *American Sociological Review*, 70: 898–920.

Smith, Gavin (2006) 'When "the logic of capital is the real which lurks in the background": programme and practice in European regional economies', *Current Anthropology*, 47(4): 621–39.

Taggart, G. J. (2003) 'A critical review of the role of the English Funding Body for Higher Education in the relationship between the state and higher education in the period 1945–2003'. Unpublished EdD thesis, Graduate School of Education, University of Bristol, Bristol.

Trow, Martin A. (2005) 'An American perspective on British higher education: the decline of diversity, autonomy and trust in post-war British higher education', Institute of Governmental Studies. Paper WP2005-3. Accessed May 2007 from http://repositories.cdlib.org/igs/WP2005–3.

UNESCO (1996) *50 Years for Education*, Paris: UNESCO.

3 The university and the welfare state in transition

Changing public services in a wider context

Marek Kwiek

Introduction

This chapter relates current transformations in higher education in European economies to current transformations of the public sector in general, and changes in higher education to changes in other public services provided within traditional European welfare states. In particular, it links ongoing discussions about the future of the welfare state under the pressures of globalisation and changing demographics to discussions about the future of public investment in higher education and to the wider question of the production and reproduction of the university. It discusses the position that the World Bank is taking with respect to the state, public sector reforms and higher education reforms, both in general and for transition economies, and highlights the contrast between its publications on the future of the welfare state and the future of public higher education. The World Bank has been particularly involved in both the conceptualisation and implementation of reforms of major public services, especially but not only in developing and transition countries: the reforms of education, healthcare, and pensions. Further, the chapter discusses the state's changing fiscal conditions and major competitors to higher education among welfare (and other) services, especially in the European transition countries. It links the question of the reformulation of the pact between the nation-state and the modern university to the issue of the renegotiation of the post-war welfare contract in general. The chapter finds it useful to view higher education in the context of changing welfare state policies as higher education is a significant part of the public sector and welfare state services, in general, have been under severe pressures, both on the theoretical and practical levels. Finally, tentative conclusions are given.

The welfare state, globalisation, and public investment in higher education

Social scientists have divergent views about the causes of the current pressures on the traditional Keynesian post-war European models of the welfare state (both the Continental, Anglo-Saxon, Scandinavian, and Southern European, although to different degrees and with different intensity). They seem to agree on a single point though: we are facing the radical reformulation of the welfare state as we know it in most industrialised nations in Europe.[1] There does not seem to be a major disagreement, broadly speaking, about the future of the welfare state in its current European post-war forms: its foundations, for a variety of internal and external reasons and due to a variety of international and domestic pressures, need to be renegotiated today (see Kwiek 2007b). The idea of the welfare state will probably continue, albeit in modified, adapted forms. Major differences between social scientists researching the area of welfare state are based on different explanations about what has been happening to the European welfare state regimes since the mid-1970s until now, about different variations and paths of restructuring in different European countries, and different degrees of emphasis concerning the scope of welfare state downsizing in particular European countries in the future. The impact of globalisation on the welfare state is an issue that sharply divides researchers on welfare issues (see Genschel 2004: 632, or Kwiek on globalists, skeptics, and moderates, 2006a: 169–214). The question debated today is not whether recasting the European welfare state has come to be seen as necessary by the national governments of most affluent Western democracies, international organisations (such as the OECD), global organisations and development agencies (such as the World Bank) and the European Commission; it is rather why it is seen as necessary, and here the answers include economic integration and/or demographic changes, changes in societal norms etc. As Maurizio Ferrera explained the fundamental logic that is guiding policy solutions to the reform processes of the welfare state today: 'system-wide searches for novel, economically viable, socially acceptable and politically feasible policy solutions are underway' (Ferrera 2003: 596).[2]

Under these new circumstances, the prospects for the future in those countries with largely publicly funded higher education seem to be that higher education will be increasingly seen as just one part of public services (as it already is seen in many countries), with its traditional uniqueness removed, with many consequences. The public sector, especially in transition countries, is often viewed as ineffective and unaccountable, in need of being restructured. One way to break away from this perspective is to view higher education as a social investment, rather than a social burden, crucial for the development of 'knowledge-based' societies and economies, or to view higher education through the lens of social capital formation. Martin Carnoy sounds moderately optimistic when he concludes in his book about globalisation and educational reforms that:

> Because knowledge is the most highly valued commodity in the global economy, nations have little choice but to increase their investment in education.

> (Carnoy 1999: 82)

The question is which level of education Carnoy means above; it is interesting to note Gøsta Esping-Andersen's arguments against *increasing* public investments in higher education for knowledge-based societies (as opposed to massive public investments in early schooling and families with children).[3] In his view, a knowledge-intensive economy will lead to a new social polarisation. The long-term scenario might very well be 'a smattering of "knowledge islands" in a great sea of marginalized outsiders'. To avoid this bleak development, cognitive capacities and the resource base of citizens must be strengthened. On numerous occasions, he recommends increased public investment in families with children, rather than in higher education (e.g. Esping-Andersen 2002: 3; 2001: 134–5). This argument, if taken seriously by national governments, could be used against free ('tax-based') higher education in major parts of Europe – especially together with the argument that higher education is increasingly a private and individual (rather than public and collective) good. Interestingly, the European Commission, perhaps for the first time, has emphasised recently that free access to higher education 'does not necessarily guarantee social equity. Member States should therefore critically examine their current mix of student fees and support schemes in the light of their actual efficiency and equity' (EC 2006: 7; see also Kwiek 2004a, 2004b).

The claim shared by many economists, sociologists and welfare analysts is that the limits of public expenditure and taxation have probably already been reached in the EU member countries. Investment for the knowledge society is already subject to strong external constraints. Esping-Andersen rightly mentions 'new winners and losers' and a deepening gulf between those with and without skills.[4] He suggests two ground rules for policy making: one, 'we cannot pursue too one-dimensionally a "learning society", a human capital-based strategy in the belief that a tide of education will lift all boats. Such a strategy inevitably leaves the less-endowed behind'; and two, 'new social policy challenges cannot be met by any additional taxation or spending as a per cent of GDP. We must accordingly concentrate on how to improve the status quo' (Esping-Andersen 2001: 146–7). So the same (or sometimes smaller in transition economies) pie may have to be divided up differently. Between 1995 and 2002, the growth in public expenditure per student in most EU countries was still the same or higher than the growth in the number of students, Sweden being the only exception; the opposite trend was observed in new EU entrants in most of which growth in numbers was not accompanied by growth in per student funding; see OECD (2006: 175).

It looks like the whole traditional post-war slice-cutting of the pie of state funding may have to be renegotiated. Former winners may be future losers (and vice versa) under changing priorities, growing inequalities and possibly new ideas regarding what counts most in our societies and what counts less. Even though the outcome of these changing priorities is uncertain, so far public higher education has not competed successfully with two major welfare areas, pensions and healthcare (there are indications of a new theoretical context, though, in which there is a possibility of a 're-calibration of social insurance from "old-age protection" to "societal integration" and "human capital upgrading"', Ferrera 2003: 592, which might lead to new ideas favouring higher education more than today). The effects of changing priorities may be different in different countries; in the EU transition economies, though, this may mean the introduction of cost-sharing elements in public higher education, following the UK example. One can expect these to include a mixture of student fees, loans, and grants.

Thus although it is possible to claim substantial increases in the share in the GDP of the public funds for national public higher education systems using the 'knowledge-based society' and 'human capital upgrading' argumentation, in practice it has not worked in any of the major OECD countries or European transition countries so far (as opposed to public per student expenditure, public expenditure on educational institutions as a percentage of GDP in 2002 was smaller than the total public and private expenditure in 1995 in the vast majority of OECD countries, including the UK, Norway, Australia, France, Portugal, the USA, Finland, Austria, Germany and the Netherlands; the few exceptions include Denmark, Poland, Greece and Turkey; see OECD 2006: 180). The situation of financing higher education better recalls that of raising taxes for the sake of raising the standards of welfare provisions: even though transition countries would like to have better public universities, their citizens do not seem willing to pay higher taxes for this reason (compare the generally supportive attitude towards welfare opposed to the unwillingness to be taxed accordingly, and the number of transition countries in which flat tax was introduced; additionally, OECD countries are experiencing a shrinking tax base: as Pierre Pestieau put it recently, 'the share of regular, steady salaried labor is declining in a large number of countries, and thus the share of payroll tax base in the GDP is shrinking', Pestieau 2006: 35).

The option of more public funding for higher education (or research and development) in Europe in the future is explicitly excluded even by the European Commission which suggests substantially more private funding, both for teaching (through fees) and research (from private companies).[5] In general terms, ongoing (and envisaged for the future) reformulations of the welfare state in European economies, no matter whether related only to globalisation and economic integration, or only to domestic national factors connected, for example, to demographic changes, or finally related to both, at the moment do not provide promising ground for policies treating higher education as public investment. This may have fundamental effects on both students and academics: fee-paying students can increasingly view themselves as customers of services provided by academics and as clients of university services (as is the case in the booming private sector of higher education in several transition countries, Poland included), there may be more managerialism and stronger business orientation of academic units less reliant on core state public subsidies, more market ideology and sets of practices drawn from the world of business, more reliance on market forces and non-core non-state 'earned' income, and the intensification of work of the increasingly contracted academic staff etc. Higher education is increasingly viewed as a public cost/burden and a private good. But – as commentators stress – welfare transfers still, under strong globalisation-related pressures, remain a political choice (Gizelis 2005: 159) and the role of electorates in democratic systems is fundamental in determining the depth and character of welfare state restructuring (Swank 2001: 198).

Globalisation and the public sector: the World Bank story revisited

Thus the debate on the future of (public) higher education today comes as part and parcel of a much wider, and often ideological, debate on the future of the public sector in general (and state intervention in, or provision of, different, traditionally public, services; on pension reforms globally, see Schwarz *et al.* 1999, on pension reforms in Europe, see Holzmann 2004, Holzmann *et al.* 2003, and Holzmann and Palacios 2001; on healthcare reforms in Central and Eastern Europe (CEE), see Adeyi *et al.* 1997, Kornai *et al.* 2001, and on CEE and globalisation, see Orenstein *et al.* 2002). Certainly in the period of the traditional Keynesian post-war welfare state regimes in Europe it was the state – rather than the market – that was deeply involved in the economy and in the protection of nation-state citizens against the potential social evils of post-war capitalism. As the World Bank's flagship publication on the role of the state (*The State in a Changing World*) argued, for much of the twentieth century people looked to government or the state to do more; but since the 1980s, the pendulum has been swinging again, and the existing conceptions of the state's place in the world have been challenged by such developments as, for example, the collapse of command-and-control economies or the fiscal crisis of the welfare state. Consequently, today, politicians are asking again what government's role ought to be and how its roles should be played (World Bank 1997: 17).

It was in CEE, exposed to the influences of global agencies in redefining their national welfare policies following the collapse of communism in 1989, that the direct link between the new 'effective' state on the one hand (with a downsizing of the public sector and a redefined minimal welfare state) and higher education policies on the other, was very much visible. With almost no exceptions, higher education in the 1990s was the lowest priority in transition countries, with chronic underfunding as a permanent feature. Still another paradox, largely overlooked, was that the policies for the ten accession countries which joined the EU in 2004, generally promoted and praised in subsequent accession countries' reports by the European Commission, were not exactly 'European' policies rooted in European models of the welfare state with its generally accepted 'European social model'. On the contrary, as Zsuzsa Ferge convincingly demonstrates (and as many of us Central Europeans know very well from policies actually being implemented in the healthcare, pensions, higher education and other public sectors), these policies are largely neoliberal.[6] That is another reason to take the link between the reformulations of the welfare state and emergent higher education policies seriously in Central and Eastern Europe; it is here that educational policies, and consequently the future of public universities, may be going hand in hand with changing welfare policies, as in the traditional World Bank formulation of the 'third wave of privatisation' where changes in (higher) education follow changes in the two major claimants on welfare state resources: healthcare services and public pensions systems (see Rama 2000; Torres and Mathur 1996; Kritzer 2002, 2005).

To refer to an image used by numerous commentators – that of a state/market pendulum (see Evans 1997: 83): the pendulum had swung from the statist development model to the 'minimalist state' model of the 1980s. The countries involved in implementing 'reinventing government' policies had squeezed programmes in education and health but the result of this 'overzealous rejection of government' was, the World Bank admits, the 'neglect of the state's vital functions, threatening social welfare and eroding the foundations for market development' (World Bank 1997: 24). So, after a few years, probably for the first time in the World Development Report of 1997 referred to here, the World Bank, heavily involved in implementing structural adjustment policies in developing countries, had to admit that the idea of the 'minimal state' did not work. It is here that a crucial passage which shows a considerable change in the Bank's attitude to the state appears: 'Development – economic, social, and sustainable – without an effective state is impossible. It is increasingly recognized that an effective state – not a minimal one – is central to economic and social development' (World Bank 1997: 25).

The state is thus viewed by the World Bank not as a direct provider of growth but a 'partner, catalyst, and facilitator', not as a sole provider but a 'facilitator and regulator', not as a 'director' but a 'partner and facilitator' (World Bank 1997: 1, 2, 18). The state should certainly be assisting households to cope with certain risks to their economic security but 'the idea that the state alone must carry this burden is changing'.[7] Coming back to the picture of the state/market pendulum, citizens (especially from the developing world) should not look for solutions provided by the state – but should focus instead on solutions provided by the market. The consequences for the public sector, including higher education, are far-reaching: 'although the state still has a central role in ensuring the provision of basic services – education, health, infrastructure – it is not obvious that the state must be the only provider, or a provider at all' (World Bank 1997: 27). An 'effective state' can leave some areas to the market and the areas where markets and private spending can meet most needs are 'urban hospitals, clinics, universities, and transport' (World Bank 1997: 53).

New publications on the tertiary education sector in the World Bank carry different overtones, though. *Constructing Knowledge Societies: New Challenges for Tertiary Education* (2002) was very careful in describing a state's obligations with respect to higher education: obligations include working within a coherent policy framework, providing an enabling regulatory environment, and working towards financial incentives; the state's role is guidance rather than steering, and in the elaboration of a clear vision for the long-term development of the education system on a national level (World Bank 2002: xxii–xxiv). Despite diminished fiscal resources and competing claims from other sectors, governments in the World Bank's account still have at least three strong reasons for supporting the higher educational sector: investments in higher education generate external benefits essential for economic and social development; capital market imperfections make loans largely unavailable to students on a large scale, in a wide range of programmes; and finally, higher education plays a key role in supporting basic and secondary education (World Bank 2002: 76). The report does not leave much doubt about the need to adequately finance higher education from the public purse when it presents a long list of the social and economic costs of under-investment in higher education:

> [T]he cost of insufficient investment in tertiary education can be very high. These costs can include reduced ability of a country to compete effectively in global and regional economies; a widening of economic and social disparities; declines in the quality of life, in health status, and in life expectancy; an increase in unavoidable public expenditures on social welfare programs; and a deterioration of social cohesion.
>
> (World Bank 2002: xxiii)

Higher education plays a crucial role in the construction of knowledge societies and the rationale for the state support of higher education (within clearly defined limits) is surprisingly strong here. But the difference between the Bank's major publications, including those on the role of the state, privatisation of public services, reforms in healthcare and pensions, and the future of the welfare state on the one hand, and its (somehow niche) publications on the education sector on the other, has to be borne in mind. There is a tremendous difference between the Bank's writings on the state and related issues and its writings on higher education. The difference has been evident from the Bank's first book on the education sector published in 1994 (*Higher Education. The Lessons of Experience*) to *Constructing Knowledge Societies* (2002). There is an interesting incompatibility between the way the Bank in general views the role of the state vis-à-vis higher education, and the way the relationship is viewed by its education sector. Consequently, such flagship publications as subsequent World Development Reports are not compatible in their views on the state/market relationships with most of the books published by its education sector. From a wider perspective, higher education seems to be still viewed by the World Bank as a unique part of the public sector which still needs substantial public investments. Also its package of reform policies is developed in greatest detail with reference to pensions (away from 'pay-as-you-go' systems towards 'multipillar' ones), less to healthcare provision, and still less to higher education and its funding.[8]

The state's fiscal condition and competitors to higher education

How could public funding of education and education spending (as part of social expenditure within the welfare state undergoing restructuring) be seen as an investment rather than a cost, and why should it be? Paradoxically, the unwillingness or inability of the state to increase the level of public funding for higher education (or in more general terms, to use Philip G. Cerny's expression, the recently decreased state's potential for 'collective action', Cerny 1995: 618) is accompanied by a clear realisation that – in the new global era – higher education is more important for social and economic development than ever before. The United Nations' report on 'globalisation and the state' argues that countries that want to benefit from globalisation must invest in education, to upgrade their citizens' skills and knowledge (United Nations 2001: 84). Higher education in most transition countries is still highly selective and access to it is not equitable. Martin Carnoy concludes that what is needed is a coherent and systemic effort by the public sector – which 'usually means more, as well as more effective, public spending' (Carnoy 1999: 86). There is thus an interesting tension between what most education sector specialists and academics dealing with *higher education issues* say about the future of higher education and what political economists, political scientists or sociologists say about the future of the *state*, as well as the welfare state and its services in particular, including higher education.

State funding for higher education, as for any other part of the public sector, depends on the overall outlook for state finances. The difference between higher education funding in the EU-15 and in post-communist new EU countries is substantial: while in major European higher education systems (France, Italy, Germany and the UK) total private and public expenditure per tertiary student in PPP in thousand euros is between 8 and 10 (and for Norway reaching 12, Denmark 13.6, Sweden 14 and Switzerland 19) – for most CEE countries it is about 3 (Poland 3.9, Latvia 3.0, Lithuania 3.1, Bulgaria 3.2, Romania 3.4), and reaches higher levels only for Slovakia 4.9, the Czech Republic 5.2 and Hungary 7.0. In short, total expenditure per student in most CEE countries is three times lower than in the biggest EU-15 economies, except for the Czech Republic, Slovakia and Hungary where it is two times lower (see data for 2001 in EC 2005: 35). The projections for the future suggest that the tight fiscal environment will continue, if not intensify, in the coming years. Basically, the situation faced by governments, under current fiscal conditions, is that of a zero-sum game: gains in share by one programme (e.g. higher education) basically would have to come at the expense of other programmes such as for example social protection. But at the same time social expenditures increase almost everywhere in the EU. The total expenditure for social protection – which does not include education – between 1990 and 2001 has increased in all EU-15 countries except Ireland, Luxembourg, and the Netherlands. In the vast majority of them, the single most expensive social service is old-age pensions; in others, it is health services (Pestieau 2006: 22–4).

This lose-lose situation is very clear in most post-communist transition countries: there are priorities in the transformation processes, the pie to be distributed is small indeed and it is largely current politics – rather than explicitly formulated long-term government policies – that determines how the pie is cut. In most affluent EU democracies, the selection of top priorities is still not so urgent, although unavoidable in the near future. As Andrei Marga sadly remarked in a paper about 'reforming the postcommunist university': 'politics and law, macroeconomics and finance, civil rights and liberties, the church and the family, have all been objects of consideration. But universities – despite the vital roles they play in providing research and expertise and in selecting and forming the leaders of tomorrow – have not' (Marga 1997: 159). It was no different for welfare policies in general in European transition countries: Bob Deacon notes that 'what became immediately evident ... was that debates of any kind about social policy became relegated to almost last place in the priority of many of the new governments' (Deacon *et al.* 1997: 92).

Higher education in CEE countries (much more than in the old EU countries) has to compete with other forms of state spending, and the costs of other forms of social needs are growing steadily, although not as rapidly as between the Second World War and 1980 (on the 'long rise of social spending' from a longer historical perspective, see Lindert 2004). Higher education has not been competing successfully with other programmes for state funding over the last decade in most CEE countries. It is enough to see the data on the generally declining public funding for higher education and research and development in almost all of them in the 1990s. Allocating priority to different programmes is a highly political issue in every country and it does not seem to be any different in Europe, or in CEE countries, for that matter. The prospects in the future for increasing public funding for public higher education, including public universities, are low unless some unexpected new shifts in global thinking about it occur; as mentioned, the European Commission does not propose such actions either for higher education or for research and development, suggesting instead, as in the case of the '3 per cent' goal of national GDPs devoted to R&D activities in EU Member countries by 2010, that private funds contribute to reaching this goal. One of the solutions for public universities to thrive in the new setting could be to follow Burton Clark and Michael Shattock's models of the 'entrepreneurial university' in which universities increasingly rely on non-core non-state income (for CEE countries, see Kwiek 2006d, 2006b).

Renegotiating two social contracts, open economies, and the politics of austerity

In wider terms, the current situation of higher education and the welfare state can be described in Europe as follows: we are facing the simultaneous renegotiation of the post-war social contract concerning the welfare state in Europe and the accompanying renegotiation of a smaller-scale, by comparison, modern social pact between the university and the nation-state.[9] The renegotiation of the latter is not clear outside of the context of the former, as state-funded higher education formed one of the bedrocks of the European welfare system. Current transformations to the state under the pressures of globalisation (and/or demographics, or both) will not eventually leave the university unaffected, and consequently it is useful to discuss the university in the context of the current global transformations of the state. The institution of the university in most advanced OECD economies seems already to have found it legitimate and necessary to evolve together with radical transformations of its social setting. Universities are often becoming powerful economic organisations, increasingly willing to play regional if not global roles, opening off-shore campuses and charging fees from overseas students, getting engaged in entrepreneurial activities and restructuring their less financially successful units. They reformulate their missions, become more accountable to their stakeholders and often behave more like businesses. They do not seem to be longing for the old humanistic Humboldtian and Napoleonic models, closely tied into the nation-states. For in the new global order, against the odds, universities are striving to maintain their traditionally pivotal role in society. The role of universities as engines of economic growth, contributors to economic competitiveness and suppliers of well-trained workers for the new knowledge-driven economy is being widely acknowledged, especially outside of the academy. But it is undoubtedly a radical reformulation of the traditional social roles of the modern university which meant training citizen subjects of the nation-state, watching over the spiritual life of the people, producing and inculcating national self-knowledge or providing the social glue necessary to keep the citizens of the nation-states together (on the Humboldtian model, see Kwiek 2006c). The main reasons for these transformations of the university include the globalisation pressures on the nation-state and its public services, the end of the 'golden age' of the Keynesian welfare state as we have known it, and the emergence of knowledge-based societies and knowledge-driven economies (in more financial terms, what seems crucial is what D. Bruce Johnstone called 'diverging trajectories' of costs of higher education and revenues available to it, which according to him are a function of three forces: increasing per-student costs, increasing participation rates, and dependence on an increasingly inadequate governmental revenue (Johnstone and Marcucci 2007: 1)).

More generally, the processes affecting the university today are not any different from those affecting the outside world; under both external pressures (like globalisation) and internal pressures (like changing demographics, the ageing of societies, maturation of welfare states, emergent post-patriarchal family patterns etc.), the processes in question are the individualisation (and recommodification) of our societies and the denationalisation (and desocialisation) of our economies. On top of that, we are beginning to feel at universities the full effects of the universalisation (or massification – in most transition countries) of higher education and the increasing commodification of research.

Off-loading the state through increasing private income for public universities and keeping the competition between public and private providers in education is a regional variation in CEE countries of the global theme of privatisation in higher education. We have been witnessing the pressures of global forces on both national policies with respect to the welfare state and on national budgets accompanied by the ideas (and ideals) of the 'minimalist' – or, more recently, 'effective', 'intelligent' etc. – state with smaller social duties than Western Europe under post-war welfare systems was familiar with. These pressures are even more direct in CEE where the need for welfare services reforms may be (economically) more urgent than in Western Europe. In the case of higher education, the emergence of private providers fits neatly into the picture (see Kwiek 2007a). Other examples include multi-pillar pension schemes being introduced in many countries of the region (on Poland, see Chlon *et al.* 1999; Gomulka 2000) and the (sometimes partial) privatisation of healthcare services (see Adeyi *et al.* 1997; for Poland, see Berman 1998; Girouard and Imai 2000; Golinowska 2002). We are witnessing more general attempts at a reformulation of the post-war social contract which gave rise to the welfare state in its various European forms. In CEE, the social contract, including the question of which social benefits are universally available for citizens (or more often, for working citizens) and which are not, on what terms and conditions, needs to be substantially re-written as the social setting provided by communism does not exist any more.

The economic space of the nation-state and national territorial borders no longer coincide (see Scharpf 2000; Ruggie 1997). Consequently, the post-war 'embedded liberalism compromise' – the social contract between the state, market, and labour – does not work any more as it was designed to work within closed national economies. At the time, however, when major European welfare state regimes were being constructed, it was not fully realised how much the success of market-correcting policies depended on the capacity of the territorial nation-states to control their economic boundaries. Under the forces of globalisation, though, this controlling capacity was lost. 'The "golden years" of the capitalist welfare state came to an end' (Scharpf 2000: 255). The social contract which had allowed the nation-states in advanced capitalist countries to be accompanied by a welfare state originated right after the Second World War. With the advent of globalisation, it is eroding, though, to different extents in different countries.

The privatisation of the educational sector in selected CEE countries – especially in its more evident variant of booming new private institutions (see Kwiek 2007c) and its less evident variant, as in Poland, of privatisation of the public sector through offering fee-paying education – fits nicely into the new picture of smaller social responsibilities of the state, and more responsibility of the individual for his or her future. The individual comes first; but also the individual, increasingly, pays first. Economic policies are becoming increasingly denationalised and the state is increasingly unable, or unwilling, to keep its promises from the golden age of the welfare state. And the welfare state has traditionally been one of the main pillars in the appeal of nation-state construction.

The power of the nation-state, and the power of the loyalty of its citizens, has rested on a firm belief in (historically unprecedented) welfare rights. When the Keynesian welfare state was formed, the role of the state was to find a fair balance between the state and the market – which had fundamentally transformed post-war social relations in all the countries involved in this social experiment (and now we are experiencing what Ulrich Beck called in *World Risk Society* a 'domino effect': 'Things which used to supplement and reinforce one another in good times – full employment, pension savings, high tax revenue, leeway for government action – now tend *mutatis mutandis* to endanger one another' Beck 1999: 11). The impact of globalisation on the nation-state is through undermining the founding ideas behind the post-war welfare state: through liberalisation and the opening up of economies, nation-states begin to lose their legitimacy provided, in vast measure, by a social contract valid in closed, national economies.

In the post-war Keynesian welfare state in Europe, higher education was very important – as testified by the constant growth of student enrolments, an increasing number of higher education institutions, and the relatively lavish public research funding available to universities. This massification of higher education was in full swing in Europe, with universalisation as its aim. The stagnation which began in the second half of the 1970s in Europe was perhaps the first symptom that the welfare system in the form designed for one period (the post-war reconstruction of Europe) might not be working in a different period. The social agenda of the 1980s and 1990s changed radically: after the policies of the golden age of expansion, European welfare states have been shaped by what Paul Pierson, a Berkeley-based political scientist, termed the *politics of austerity* (Pierson 2001).

And the social agenda in post-1989 CEE changed even more radically: suddenly, the region was exposed to new economic pressures, but also to new market-oriented opportunities which in many cases required better skills and higher competencies from its citizens, provided by new, vocationally-focused private institutions. While in Western Europe the emergence of the private sector in education is both marginal and often revolutionary (see the example of Buckingham University in the UK, with a strong Thatcherite ideological underpinning), in most CEE countries it might be even considered as one of the more realistic options available – in the situation of the chronic underfunding of public institutions and, in many instances, their structural inability to face new challenges, with the huge social need to raise the enrolment levels at the forefront. To give a Polish example: the number of students increased from 400,000 in 1990 to almost 2,000,000 in 2006, about 32 per cent of which are enrolled in 315 private institutions. The capacities of the public sector have not changed dramatically in the period: both the number of faculty and educational premises available have been at roughly the same level. New students used the avenues available to them through the process of privatisation: they either entered fee-paying part-time studies in the public sector or fee-paying studies in the emergent private sector. Relatively liberal legislation regarding the private sector, accompanied by genuine interest of the public sector faculty in both running fee-paying weekend studies and creating out of scratch the private sector made possible this impressive transformation of Polish higher education; see Kwiek (2007a).

Seeing higher education policies in isolation from larger welfare state policies would be assuming a short-sighted perspective: higher education is a significant (and often significantly fund-consuming) part of the public sector and a part of the traditional welfare state that is right now under severe pressures, even though they may not be as strong as pressures on the two main parts of the welfare state, healthcare and pensions. In still more theoretical than practical terms, these phenomena had their powerful impact on thinking about public services, including public higher education, in CEE. The theoretical impact was already translated into changed national legislation in the case of the pensions reform and health care reforms at the end of the 1990s.

Conclusions

What we increasingly see today as universities' missions seem highly influenced by the two decades of reformulations (both in theory and in practice) of the role of public sector services; in wider terms, the university, as other public sector institutions, is increasingly viewed in the context of economic competitiveness of nations, global pressures on national economies, and global pressures on national welfare states. For public universities, these are absolutely new contexts; they are new to academics as well. The consequences of this shift are far reaching: for just a little more than a decade, international and supra-national organisations and bodies have been involved in the production of new university missions (both the World Bank, the European Commission and the OECD became seriously interested in the university in the second half of the 1990s, except for a few reports published earlier). Their influence on policy thinking and policy making has been tremendous all over Europe: they seem to be providing major concepts in which university futures are currently being discussed, and the economic spaces increasingly seem to converge with the academic spaces in ongoing discussions (the subsumption of the goals of the Bologna Process, of the ideas of the 'Europe of Knowledge' and of knowledge-based societies under the overall EU 'Lisbon Strategy' of 'more growth/more jobs' being a good example). A substantially more 'economic' space in which public universities are currently discussed (at the expense of the traditional 'academic' space of the discourse on its roles, missions, and futures) affects institutions, academics, and students alike. As in the case of other major public services, healthcare and pensions, the economic dimension of functioning of universities comes to the fore, especially in the transition countries. Students in massified systems increasingly view themselves as consumers and view academics as providers of educational services; institutions increasingly want to view individual academics as part-time knowledge workers rather than tenured professors making use of academic freedom in their quest for truth, as in traditional university models, and academic collegiality is losing out to managerialism and business approaches; societies increasingly view higher education as a private good and are more inclined to pay from their pockets for this good (especially in those transition countries where the private sector is large and the public sector is still restrictive and elitist); finally, governments view universities as bedrocks of knowledge-based economies. The links between rethinking universities and rethinking the welfare state are powerful and need to be taken into account in thinking about the production and reproduction of the university in the last two decades.

The welfare state in its traditional post-war European forms, and its services, including public higher education, seems to be undergoing substantial transformations in most parts of Europe, and especially in the European transition countries. Lines of these changes and argumentation in support of them (whether by the European Commission, the OECD or national governments) point in a similar direction, which is more financial self-reliance of public universities, rethinking the introduction of student fees in the context of equitable access to higher education, academic entrepreneurialism leading to more non-core non-state income etc. (even though the concepts used may be different in different systems). Many discussions in Western Europe about welfare state futures seem academic in the transition economies: what they shyly predict for affluent democracies is in fact already happening there. There is certainly a lot of social experimentation with respect to welfare going on in the transition countries. Nowadays, as the reformulation of the welfare state in general progresses smoothly (and mostly in an unnoticeable manner, for example through new legislation) in most parts of the world, social contracts with regard to most areas of state benefits and state-funded services may have to be renegotiated. In many respects, higher education and pensions (in transition countries and elsewhere) seem to be an experimental area and a testing ground on how to reform public sector institutions in general. The end-products of these experimentations are still largely hard to predict. What perhaps counts most in this context is a historical phenomenon that universities are highly adaptable institutions which tend to thrive under ever-changing circumstances. There is a plethora of nationally-specific and culture-related choices to be made by both policymakers and academic institutions, and the effects of these choices are still largely hard to predict.

Notes

1 This chapter is a revised version of a lecture I gave at the seminar 'Geographies of Knowledge, Geometries of Power: Higher Education in the 21st Century', Gregynog, University of Wales, 18 January 2006. I would like to express my gratitude for the invitation and logistical support I received from Rosemary Deem and Debbie Epstein, as well as for lively comments from, and interesting

discussions with, the seminar participants. I would also like to thank Rosemary Deem for her comments on an earlier draft of this chapter.

2 The Finnish generous model of the welfare state provides a special case in which information society is able to create a financial basis for the (renewed) welfare state. Castells and Himanen argue that 'so far, the evidence supports the conclusion that, in spite of the pressures of the global information economy, Finland continues to be a different form of an information society, which combines with it a generous welfare state' (Castells and Himanen 2002: 85).

3 Esping-Andersen argues that vocational training and increased participation in higher education are unlikely, by themselves, to solve the problems caused by a fall in the demand for low-skill labour: 'If fighting social exclusion through employment remains the principal policy goal of the European social model in the early 21st century, the learning offensive will have to be complemented with strategies of raising employment opportunities for *low skill* workers through other means' (Esping-Andersen *et al.* 2001: 230).

4 An interesting distinction between the 'knowledge rich' and the 'knowledge poor' was drawn in a European Commission communication on *Investing Efficiently in Education and Training* (EC 2003: 8).

5 What is needed in the EC's view is therefore a 'combination of targeted public investments and higher private contributions' (EC 2003: 15).

6 Ferge finds the neoliberal tendency dominant in CEE countries. It is 'practically ubiquitous' and 'seems to be dictated by concerns allegedly related to globalization pressures' (Ferge 2001: 129–30).

7 The picture and recommendations are clear: 'Innovative solutions that involve businesses, labor, households, and community groups are needed to achieve greater security at lower cost. This is especially important for those developing countries not yet locked into costly solutions' (World Bank 1997: 5).

8 In transition countries, there was a strong influence of the Washington Consensus institutions – through political pressure and aid and loan conditionalities. Compared with Western Europe, some CEE countries in the 1990s have gone much further down the road of neoliberal reforms of, for example, pension systems. World Bank ideas were subsequently implemented in such diverse countries as Poland, Bulgaria, Croatia, Estonia, Hungary, Latvia, Slovakia, Macedonia, Romania, Ukraine and Uzbekistan, in different variants. To date, 31 countries have implemented some type of personal accounts as part of their mandatory retirement income systems (see Kritzer 2005). For most CEE countries, the social security reform was not the priority in the first wave of reforms; it was only in the second half of the 1990s that pension reforms became unavoidable as the pay-as-you-go traditional systems were consuming an enormous percentage of GDP (Poland establishing perhaps a record in 1996 among the OECD countries by spending 16 per cent of its GDP on pensions, see Holzmann 2004: 3).

9 Some arguments in this section have been adapted from Kwiek (2005b).

References

Adeyi, Olusoji, Gnanaraj Chellaraj, Ellen Goldstein, Alexander Parker and Dena Ringold (1997) 'Health status during the transition in Central and Eastern Europe: development in reverse?', *Health Policy and Planning*, 12(2).

Beck, Ulrich (1999) *World Risk Society*, Cambridge: Polity Press.

Berman, Peter (1998) 'National health insurance in Poland: a coach without horses?', Boston: Harvard School of Public Health.

Carnoy, Martin (1999) *Globalization and Educational Reform: What Planners Need to Know*, Paris: UNESCO, International Institute for Educational Planning.

Castells, Manuel and Pekka Himanen (2002) *The Information Society and the Welfare State: The Finnish Model,* Oxford: Oxford University Press.

Cerny, Philip G. (1995) 'Globalization and the changing logic of collective action', *International Organization,* 49(4), Autumn: 595–625.

Chlon, Agnieszka, Marek Gora and Michal Rutkowski (1999) 'Shaping pension reform in Poland: security through diversity'. Social Protection Discussion Paper Series No. 9923.

Deacon, Bob, with Michelle Hulse and Paul Stubbs (1997) *Global Social Policy. International Organizations and the Future of Welfare,* London: Sage.

Esping-Anderson, Gøsta (2002) *Why We Need a New Welfare State,* New York: Oxford University Press.

Esping-Andersen, Gøsta (2001) 'A welfare state for the 21st century', in Anthony Giddens (ed.) *The Global Third Way Debate,* Cambridge: Polity Press.

Esping-Andersen, Gøsta, Duncan Gallie, Anton Hemerijck and John Myles (2001) 'A new welfare architecture for Europe?' Report submitted to the Belgian Presidency of the European Union. Available at www.ccsd.ca/pubs/2002/europe.pdf.

European Commission (2003) *Investing Efficiently in Education and Training: An Imperative for Europe,* Brussels, COM (2002) 779.

European Commission (2005) 'European Higher Education in a Worldwide Perspective', Commission Staff Working Paper, Brussels, SEC(2005) 518.

European Commission (2006) 'Delivering on the modernisation agenda for universities: education, research and innovation', Brussels, COM (2006) 208 final.

Evans, Peter (1997) 'The eclipse of the state? Reflections on stateness in an era of globalization', *World Politics,* 50(1): 62–87.

Ferge, Zsuzsa (2001) 'Welfare and ill-fare systems in Central-Eastern Europe', in Robert Sykes, Bruno Palier and Pauline M. Prior (2001) *Globalization and European Welfare States: Challenges and Change,* New York: Palgrave.

Ferrera, Maurizio (2003) 'Reforming the European social model: dilemmas and perspectives', *The European Legacy,* 8(5): 587–98.

Ferrera, Maurizio, Anton Hemerijck and Martin Rhodes (2001) 'The future of social Europe: recasting work and welfare in the new economy', in Anthony Giddens (ed.) *The Global Third Way Debate,* Cambridge: Polity Press.

Genschel, Philipp (2004) 'Globalization and the welfare state: a retrospective', *Journal of European Public Policy,* 11(4): 613–36.

Girouard, Nathalie and Yutaka Imai (2000) *The Health Care System in Poland,* Paris: OECD.

Gizelis, Theodora-Ismene (2005) 'Globalization, integration, and the European welfare state', *International Interactions,* 31(2): 139–62.

Golinowska, Stanislawa (2002) 'Health care reform in Poland after 3 years: challenges for new authorities', Warsaw: CASE Foundation.

Gomulka, Stanislaw (2000) 'Pension problems and reforms in the Czech Republic, Hungary, Poland and Romania', London: LSE (Globalisation Programme).

Holzmann, Robert (2004) 'Toward a reformed and coordinated pension system in Europe: rationale and potential structure', Social Protection Discussion Paper Series, No. 0407, Washington, DC: World Bank.

Holzmann, Robert and Robert Palacios (2001) 'Individual accounts as social insurance: a World Bank perspective', Social Protection Discussion Paper Series No. 0114, Washington, DC: World Bank.

Holzmann, Robert, Mitchell Orenstein and Michal Rutkowski (2003) *Pension Reform in Europe: Process and Progress*, Washington, DC: World Bank.

Johnstone, D. Bruce and Pamela Marcucci (2007) *Worldwide Trends in Higher Education Finance: Cost-Sharing, Student Loans and the Support of Academic Research*. The paper commissioned by the UNESCO Forum on Higher Education, Research, and Development, available from www.gse.buffalo.edu.org/IntHigherEdFinance.

Kornai, János (1997) 'The reform of the welfare state and public opinion', *The Transition from Socialism*, 87(2): 339–43.

Kornai, János, Stephan Haggard and Robert R. Kaufman (2001) *Reforming the State. Fiscal and Welfare Reform in Post-Socialist Countries*, Cambridge: Cambridge University Press.

Kritzer, Barbara E. (2002) 'Social security reform in Central and Eastern Europe: variations on a Latin American theme', *Social Security Bulletin*, 64(4).

Kritzer, Barbara E. (2005) 'Individual accounts in other countries', *Social Security Bulletin*, 66(1).

Kwiek, Marek (2004a) *Intellectuals, Power, and Knowledge: Studies in the Philosophy of Culture and Education*, Frankfurt am Main and New York: Peter Lang.

Kwiek, Marek (2004b) 'The emergent European educational policies under scrutiny. The Bologna process from a Central European perspective', *European Educational Research Journal*, 3(4), December: 759–76.

Kwiek, Marek (2005a) 'Renegotiating the traditional social contract? The university and the state in a global age', *European Educational Research Journal*, 4(4), December.

Kwiek, Marek (2005b) 'The university and the state in a global age: renegotiating the traditional social contract?', *European Educational Research Journal*, 4(4): 324–41.

Kwiek, Marek (2006a) *The University and the State. A Study into Global Transformations*, Frankfurt am Main and New York: Peter Lang.

Kwiek, Marek (2006b), 'Academic entrepreneurship vs. changing governance and institutional management structures at European universities', available from www.euerek.info.

Kwiek, Marek (2006c) 'The classical German idea of the university revisited, or on the nationalization of the modern institution', Poznan: CPP Research Papers Series. 1 (2006), available from www.cpp.amu.edu.pl.

Kwiek, Marek (2006d), 'Academic entrepreneurship and private higher education (in a comparative perspective)', available from www.euerek.info.

Kwiek, Marek (2007a) 'On accessibility and equity, market forces, and entrepreneurship: developments in higher education in Central and Eastern Europe', *Higher Education Management and Policy*, 19(3) (forthcoming).

Kwiek, Marek (2007b) 'The future of the welfare state and democracy: the effects of globalization from a European perspective', in Ewa Czerwinska-Schupp (ed.) *Globalisation and Norms in the Age of Globalization*, Frankfurt and New York: Peter Lang.

Kwiek, Marek (2007c) 'The European integration of higher education and the role of private higher education', in Daniel C. Levy and Snejana Slantcheva (eds) *In Search of Legitimacy: Private Higher Education in Central and Eastern Europe*, Dordrecht: Springer.

Lindert, Peter H. (2004) *Growing Public. Social Spending and Economic Growth Since the Eighteenth Century*, Cambridge: Cambridge University Press.

Marga, Andrei (1997) 'Reforming the postcommunist university', *Journal of Democracy*, 8: 2.

OECD (2006) *Education at a Glance: OECD Indicators 2005*, Paris: OECD.

Orenstein, Mitchell A. and Martine R. Haas (2002) 'Globalization and the development of welfare states in post-Communist Europe'. International Security Program. Belfer Center for Science and International Affairs.

Pestieau, Pierre (2006) *The Welfare State in the European Union. Economic and Social Perspectives*, Oxford: Oxford University Press.

Pierson, Paul (2001) 'Coping with permanent austerity: welfare state restructuring in affluent democracies', in P. Pierson (ed.) *The New Politics of the Welfare State*, Oxford: Oxford University Press.

Rama, Martin (2000) 'Public sector downsizing: an introduction', *The World Bank Economic Review*, 13(1): 1–22.

Ruggie, John Gerard (1997) 'Globalization and the embedded liberalism compromise: the end of an era?'. Max Planck Institute for the Studies of Societies, Working Paper No. 1.

Scharpf, Fritz (2000) 'Negative integration: states and the loss of boundary control', in Christopher Pierson and Francis G. Castles (eds) *The Welfare State Reader*, Cambridge: Polity Press.

Schwarz, Anita M. and Asli Demirguc-Kunt (1999) 'Taking stock of pension reforms around the world', Social Protection Discussion Paper Series No. 9917.

Swank, Duane (2001) 'Political institutions and welfare state restructuring: the impact of institutions on social policy change in developed democracies', in Paul Pierson (ed.) *The New Politics of the Welfare State*, Oxford: Oxford University Press.

Sykes, Robert, Bruno Palier and Pauline M. Prior (2001) *Globalization and European Welfare States. Challenges and Change*, New York: Palgrave.

Torres, Gerver and Sarita Mathur (1996) 'The third wave of privatization: privatization of social sectors in developing countries', Washington, DC: World Bank.

United Nations (2001) *World Public Sector Report: Globalization and the State 2001*, New York: UN.

World Bank (1994) *Higher Education: The Lessons of Experience*, Washington, DC: World Bank.

World Bank (1997) *The State in a Changing World*, World Development Report 1997, Washington, DC: World Bank.

World Bank (2002) *Constructing Knowledge Societies: New Challenges for Tertiary Education*, Washington, DC: World Bank.

4 University leadership in the twenty-first century

The case for Academic Caesarism

Steve Fuller

All roads lead to Rome. At least so I shall argue with regard to the search for ideals for the future of higher education. Much has been written about how the university is being forced to redefine its place in society in light of developments largely originating outside its precincts and over which it has relatively little control. These developments fall under the category neatly labelled, 'neo-liberal political economy of knowledge production'. In narratives where this phrase would provide an adequate title, if not plot summary, the university straddles two fates. At best the university is portrayed as a supple organism adaptive to a fluid environment. At worst it appears as a living fossil artificially maintained by a declining national support system. However, there is an alternative way to think about the university's current predicament, one that draws more deeply from the university's common legal ancestry with the state and the church. It involves the embodiment of the institution's corporate personality in a style of academic leadership I call *Academic Caesarism*, a phrase designed to draw attention to both the promise and the peril of universities' acquiring leaders who so strongly identify with their institution that they may feel they must protect its identity even from its own academic constituency.

Seeing the university as a state: the Roman precedent

The university is related to the state in an historically twofold fashion: on the one hand, both the university and the state (more exactly, the city-state) acquired their organisational autonomy under medieval Roman law in much the same way – that is, as instances of *universitas*, normally translated as 'corporation'. Indeed, the ordinary use of 'corporation' to refer to universities and states (and guilds and churches) predates its use for business firms by at least five centuries. On the other hand, most actual universities in the modern era (outside the US) were founded as institutions of the state, designed to consolidate national identity by providing a crucible for forging the next generation of society's leaders. In either case, the legal status of *universitas* implied that these corporate entities were 'artificial persons', whose autonomy consists in pursuing their own ends, as distinct from those of the particular individuals who constitute this artificial person at any given point. Aside from a sense of self-direction, the university's corporate autonomy is also defined in terms of the self-selection of its members and the self-organisation of its activities, including the provision of material support.

Not surprisingly, given this history, the legitimacy of both the state and the university have come under attack in these postmodern, neo-liberal times. The attacks are most directly felt in terms of the provision of material support, where both have been subject to a shrinkage in discretionary public sector funding. At a more conceptual level, the attacks on the legitimacy of the university and the state have also pursued a parallel course: postmodern attacks on the university's ability to represent and integrate knowledge resemble neo-liberal attacks on the state's ability to represent and integrate people. At the same time, many universities have adjusted to postmodernism and neo-liberalism by acquiring functions previously reserved to the state. A precedent for this tendency can be found in US universities, many of which – including most of the Ivy League – had been established as autonomous institutions prior to American national independence. While it is easy to dismiss the US experience as exceptional, in fact it serves as a reminder of the medieval origins of universities and states as legal siblings. In this respect, the US may provide clues on how universities may reassert their autonomy as state-like institutions.

The practical implications of universities acquiring state-like functions are epitomised in two phrases: *Academic Imperialism* and *Academic Caesarism*. The former refers to the tendency for universities to absorb the state's welfare functions, e.g. the provision and regulation of healthcare, education and perhaps even domestic security. The latter refers to a leadership style among university chief executives that resembles a dictator who extends his or her institutional authority while both protecting and limiting the power exerted by a group of potentially divisive constituencies. In what follows, I shall develop the concept of Academic Imperialism through that of Academic Caesarism, following the historic pattern of ancient Rome.

Like Athens in its classical period, republican Rome treated citizenship as the measure of equality in society. In particular, all citizens were equally invested in the republic's well-being, by virtue of having owned and managed property there for several generations. This created a presumption of roughly equal willingness and ability to take dictatorial powers, whenever there was a need for the republic to take action against a common enemy. Such states of emergency were assumed to be temporary, after which the dictator would resume his ordinary life as a citizen. However, as Rome expanded its borders, eventually to overseas colonies, the dictator's role metamorphosed from an office that, at least in principle, any citizen could hold to an office worthy only of people possessing special qualities required for the role's expanded scope. Thus, as the republic became an empire, the dictator became a Caesar.

A similar trajectory can be charted in the history of the university, whose republican phase corresponds to institutional governance on a collegial basis. Here the leader would be expected to have come up the academic ranks in the same or a comparable institution. Indeed, Oxbridge and the US Ivy League often seem to operate with a default policy of hiring their own graduates. It is easy nowadays to dismiss this practice as simply so much academic snobbery, if not outright nepotism. However, the practice harks back to the university's legal status as an artificial person, where intellectual lineage acquires the role of biological lineage in natural persons. Thus, each new university matriculant is portrayed as born anew – hence, the university's personification as *alma mater*, 'nurturing mother'. In this respect, the university's entrance examinations and degree certifications are comparable to baptism and holy orders, respectively, as initiation rites in the church, another of the university's institutional siblings. Both sets of rites require that individuals undergo a trial of faith, the successful outcome of which is the acquisition of a new identity as part of the larger corporate structure.

And just as Rome's self-understanding underwent a gradual transformation from republic to empire – bracketed by the careers of Julius and Augustus Caesar – so too has the university's. The university's imperial phase began when the institution diversified its functions to such an extent that satisfying the interests of its official 'citizenry' (that is, academics on the payroll and perhaps enrolled students) constituted only part of the task of maintaining the institution's autonomy. I allude here to the university's proto-state activities, ranging from economic pump-priming through the provision of welfare, both typically at the local regional level, to more client-centred delivery of skills, products and services. In this context, the university's stakeholders expand to approximate the range that would normally have an interest in the decisions taken by a state assembly. Some universities – including the US land-grant colleges and the universities created under European imperial rule – were specifically chartered in anticipation of their expanded capacity. They are not unreasonably seen as governing in lieu of the state, in terms that both universities and states have found more or less mutually satisfying. Where the states saw the universities as organising regions and recruiting leaders, the universities saw the states as licensing the extension of their research activities. Not surprisingly, with the decline of both state power in the first world and imperial power in the third world, universities created in this imperial mode have acquired still more state-like functions, sometimes even serving as *de facto* alternative governments.

Some universities, including Oxbridge and the US Ivy League, have drawn out the transition from republic to empire in their self-understanding – though not their actual functions – as long as possible. They have perpetuated the image that the university's chief executive is really a *primus inter pares*, even though his or her decisions extend way beyond what those who normally roam the campus might see as being in their own interests. Not surprisingly, serious cracks increasingly appear in the image.

A case in point is the ongoing controversy surrounding John Hood, Oxford's first vice-chancellor to have been chosen from outside its own academic faculties in the university's 900-year history. He was appointed to reorganise the university's corporate structure, specifically by separating and streamlining the academic and financial functions – in both cases, shifting power from the colleges to the departments and central administration, as per most modern universities. The speed with which he has tried to transform Oxford's time-honoured traditions easily gives the impression of self-aggrandisement. And while Hood's initiatives have suffered some notable setbacks, nevertheless they enjoy the support of roughly 40 per cent of the academic staff and most of those outside the staff, including students and alumni, who constitute the greater Oxford community.

Perhaps an even clearer case of the difficulties facing universities as they shift from republican to imperial mode is captured in the saga of Larry Summers, whose tenure as Harvard President came to an ignominious end in 2006. Unlike Hood, a New Zealander who was parachuted into Oxford thirty years after he last appeared on campus as a first-class cricketer for the university team, Summers had been one of the youngest tenured professors at Harvard, a recipient of the main professional award for economists under the age of 40. A lifelong Democrat, Summers was appointed chief economist at the World Bank and then Secretary of the Treasury in rapid succession when Bill Clinton was US President. However, once the Republican George W. Bush became president, Summers returned to Harvard, this time as its president. By all accounts, his management style was to dictate without consultation, presuming that as himself a 'Harvard man' there was no need to solicit opinion more widely. On his own, then, Summers continued Harvard's international outreach and development programmes, while stressing the university's traditional emphasis on a broad undergraduate liberal education to which its distinguished faculty were expected to contribute regularly and responsibly.

These policies made Summers very popular with students and alumni, who increased their financial support to this richest of universities. But they also earned him the enmity of tenured academics, who were less appreciative of Harvard's global meddling and, in any case, had become accustomed to offloading their teaching to untenured staff members and graduate students. However, the tipping point against Summers came when he openly asserted that evolutionary psychologists might be correct about the genetic basis for women's inferior scientific performance. This provided a rhetorical pretext for the faculty to declare that they could not work under someone with such odious views based on such an unproven area of science. As it turns out, Summers' permanent successor, Drew Gilpin Faust, is not only the first woman but also, and more remarkably, the first non-Harvard-trained person to become its president. (Harvard, America's oldest university, was founded in 1636.) However, she comes to the job having run the university's institute for advanced studies.

These vignettes of less-than-best practice, combined with the more general historical and theoretical considerations about Caesarism as a mode of governance, suggest the follow defining features of a successful Academic Caesar (AC):

1   The AC, while perhaps not currently a practising academic, should be sufficiently connected to academic culture to be able to easily articulate the university's goals in ways that practising academics can recognise as reflective of their own values and aspirations.

2   When the AC's actions elicit opposition from the university's constituencies, s/he can deftly distinguish the values and ideals upheld by his/her institution from the various interests of those constituencies, including current academic staff. The AC has a very clear sense of the difference between institutional autonomy and individual (or group) selfishness – and can turn that difference to his/her advantage. Thus, the AC may be inclined to take a strong stand against the establishment of academic fiefdoms while strongly defending the academic freedom of an unpopular colleague.

3   Since even universally endorsed academic values can be – and have been – taken in multiple contradictory or incommensurable directions, the AC can gain and maintain power simply by upholding this plurality, thereby preventing any particular interpretation of those values from becoming dominant. Thus, the AC's hand is naturally strengthened vis-à-vis particular constituencies by expanding their number, not least through 'affirmative action'.

4   However, the AC must also maintain a clear distinction between the university's 'internal' and 'external' constituencies – say, on the one hand, academic staff, students and alumni, and on the other, representatives of politics, business, etc. This is how a university in the imperial mode retains its republican core, and the AC can legitimise his/her exercise of power in terms of the protection of institutional autonomy.

5   The AC must prevent external constituencies from unduly influencing the governance of the internal constituencies, say, by allowing a large client-oriented grant to an academic department to set a standard to which other departments are then held accountable. Rather, the AC should see such grants as, in the first instance, upsetting the institution's equilibrium, which of course need not be negative. However, the AC must then use grant overheads creatively to engage in compensation or redistribution across the institution.

In the rest of the chapter, I explore this last feature of Academic Caesarism by elaborating its underlying political economy, which envisages the university as part church and part casino, possessing what I call in the next section 'a Vatican face and a Vegas heart'. In short, the successful Academic Caesar upholds his/her institution's autonomy by securing and expanding the material base that can sustain the most intellectual adventure possible within its borders. On the one hand, this feat requires an imaginative forward-looking macro-economic strategy, which is detailed in the next section. On the other hand, it also calls on the Academic Caesar to make the university less directly sensitive to market pressures by reasserting the distinctiveness of its knowledge as a second-order, or public, good, in terms of which other forms of private and first-order knowledge may be evaluated and regulated. This topic, which I regard as the Academic Caesar's 'ultimate weapon' is discussed in the final section.

A Vatican face with a Vegas heart: the Academic Caesar's political economy

The US sociologist Craig Calhoun has recently challenged higher education thinkers, practitioners and researchers to come up with a business plan for today's university that demonstrates that only by adhering to classical academic norms can it effectively serve the social and economic ends increasingly demanded of the institution. My proposal to meet this challenge is meant to be fit for an Academic Caesar. It starts from the counter-intuitive assumption that whatever model of political economy is used to rationalise the university, it should *not* be based on modern industry's fixation on 'productivity', that is, the efficient translation of labour and capital into goods and services. Although the rhetoric surrounding the 'entrepreneurial university', not to mention the pervasive and casual use of the phrase 'knowledge production', appears indebted to this model, the resemblance is superficial – a conflation of (undoubted) *increased production* and (doubtful) *increased productivity*. But while our speech may be confused, our actions are loud and clear: the main academic performance indicators are based not on productivity but on sheer production – of students (enrolled, graduated, or employed), research (funded, published, patented, or cited), income (received or generated), etc. By these standards, the United States is the world's sole academic superpower and its undisputed capital is Harvard.

But is the US the most *productive* academic nation-state? This is a sensitive matter in the United Kingdom, where higher education has been repeatedly congratulated for doing more with fewer resources. For the last quarter-century, the UK has been arguably the most productive academic nation on Earth. For example, the combined endowment and annual income of Harvard is seven times that of Oxford and Cambridge combined. Is Harvard *seven* times better than Oxbridge? Maybe two or three times, but surely not seven! Perhaps unsurprisingly, as an American who has now lived in the UK for a dozen years, my knee-jerk response upon returning to a US campus is to observe the plush resources that go wasted or underutilised by tenured academics who quaintly fuss over the content of their courses as preludes to research they might conduct someday. The US is the world's largest academic producer by virtue of being its most conspicuous consumer.

I call my response 'knee-jerk' so as not to belittle the American norm, which, despite many local challenges, remains reasonably robust. On the contrary, the success of US-style conspicuous consumption in academia reveals an important, albeit complex, truth: that universities are institutions that produce with impunity. Classical ways of thinking about this phenomenon usually include the image of following the trail of truth wherever it may lead. This image is taken from the bygone era of what Derek de Solla Price called 'little science', where the main resources were one's own time, energy, and money – not great amounts of equipment, manpower, and other people's money. The image is continuous with the political economy implicit in Aristotle's injunction to turn to 'philosophy' (a proxy for any systematic intellectual inquiry) only once the household chores were done. To recall a point Marxists used to relish, Aristotle treated philosophy as quite literally a kind of mental gymnastics that was not expected, any more than competitive sports, to feed back into the relief of humanity's secular burdens. Rather, it was the consummate leisured activity, one devoted to contemplating how and why the world is as it is.

This attitude has persisted in the West well into the modern era, even as it came into conflict with Muslim, Christian, and ultimately Enlightenment ideologies of knowledge as a collective legacy and universal entitlement for the betterment of humanity, indeed, perhaps to create 'a Heaven on Earth'. In *The Decline and Fall of the Roman Empire*, Edward Gibbon may have demonised Caliph Omar as philistine for casting all of ancient wisdom to the flames when he torched the Library of Alexandria in 640 AD, yet similar feelings of contempt were expressed by his own contemporaries – including such Enlightenment icons as Hume and Smith, Voltaire and Diderot – towards the 'useless' knowledge then amassed in European universities. The existence of tomes produced in the name of 'curiosity', written in languages few could understand and to which even fewer would have access, manifested the intellectual equivalent of greed, a mortal sin for the faithful and idle capital for everyone else.

Embarrassingly good economic sense informs this philistine contempt. The most efficient means for a state to improve its citizenry's stock of human capital for purposes of increasing overall national wealth is to invest in primary and secondary education, even at the expense of higher education and original research. And if the state must invest in university teaching and research at all, the national interest is best served by an investment strategy that encourages free access between academics and those capable of turning their ideas into marketable products.

There are lessons here for both third and first world countries, which business schools now dispense in the name of 'knowledge management': no number of showcase research institutes can compensate for mass deficiencies in basic literacy and numeracy, and no number of registered patents can replace direct involvement in industrial research and development. It is clear, then, that a budget-conscious state keen on making its mark in the world's increasingly knowledge-based economy would adopt a two-pronged strategy toward higher education.

First, the state would redistribute education funding from the tertiary to the primary and secondary levels, so that people can acquire the requisite competitive skills as early as possible, thereby assuring quick and decisive entry into a globalised labour market. This strategy would help to counteract 'credentials creep', the need for each new generation of students to spend more time in formal schooling to acquire comparable qualifications. While it follows that fewer people would initially require university training (or if so, for a shorter period), the innovation-induced volatility of the global knowledge economy ensures that whatever financial losses universities incur in the short term will be recovered later through recidivism – a.k.a. 'lifelong learning' – whereby late-breaking skills are acquired by those not lucky enough to have been originally exposed to them. In this respect, ambient incentives to generate innovation are like temptations to commit crime or susceptibilities to suffer illness: that is, persuasive justifications for the public funding of what Erving Goffman called 'total institutions'. Universities can thus position themselves in the market next to prisons and hospitals as 'social equilibrium providers'.

The second prong of the state's strategy would be to maintain the porosity of the boundary dividing academia from industry and the private sector more generally. This would probably lead to a widening of the variance in academic salaries, perhaps decoupling them from academic rank altogether. Universities could adopt the British practice of justifying further public expenditure by pointing out the diminishing burden they place on taxpayers to fund their activities, as academics accumulate grants, patents, consultancies, and so forth. In the long term, universities might even renounce their non-profit legal status, assuming they could persuade their trustees and perhaps alumni to think of themselves as corporate shareholders – and academics to think of themselves as employees.

However, I reject the premise that universities should be seen primarily as suppliers of capital – both human (in education) and non-human (in research) – for the global knowledge economy. This is not because they should stand above – or outside – economic considerations. Rather, universities should lead rather than follow. Combining the insights of Wilhelm von Humboldt, the architect of the Enlightenment model of the university as a state function, and Joseph Schumpeter, the theorist of entrepreneurship, I have elsewhere defined the unique corporate function of the university as the 'creative destruction of social capital'. By this phrase I mean to update the dynamic unity that Humboldt held to exist between education and research, but now seen as alternating phases of an endless cycle. Humboldt's innovation was to turn the university into an engine of social progress – specifically, progress of the 'nation', the spirit of which state policy tries to embody, however imperfectly. Schumpeter, writing over a century later, recognised that the universities have been the most reliable, and sometimes effective, source of anti-establishment thought.

Research initially generates social capital by forging new alliances between ideas, people, processes, and things. However, a university dedicated purely, or even primarily, to research would simply polarise the populace between, so to speak, the 'knows' and the 'know-nots', a kind of epistemological feudalism. But luckily, here the teaching function enters to level this emergent difference by spreading the fruits of research as widely as possible. Significantly, students are often far from the original networks responsible for the research in which they are being instructed, but their appreciation is vital for its continued social support and, more importantly, for taking the research in unexpected directions. This, in turn, will forge new alliances and redistribute competitive advantage across society.

It follows that the soul of the university as the creative destroyer of social capital resides in curriculum committees empowered with deciding which aspects of new research are worth incorporating into, say, a discipline-based major or a general liberal arts requirement. In this respect, the 'canon wars' now simmering on US campuses for the last quarter-century merely bring a level of self-consciousness and media attention to a process that has been endemic to the modern history of the university. The only difference now is that possibly the amount and rate of replacement of course content is greater than in the past. If true, this might be a reflection of the enlarged and diversified student body of recent years, the composition of which can more easily conjure up the idea that society's future should be significantly different from its past.

There is a model for this ever expanding and forward-looking vision of the university. It is the oldest legally incorporated private sector entity, the self-supporting church, out of which the original universities evolved in the twelfth century. The economic side of proselytism is that church finances typically flow 'forward' not 'backward'. Rather than requiring potential converts to pay upfront to join a church before they have received any benefits (however defined), those whose lives have been already transformed by their membership in a community of faith donate some percentage of their subsequent income to allow others to share in the same fellowship. This attitude toward universities is uniquely anchored in the United States because of the nation's origins in British religious dissenters. Consequently, by any world standard, even officially state-funded universities enjoy enviable alumni contributions that enable them to retain a large measure of their institutional autonomy, even in the face of external economic and political pressures.

Two features of this autonomy are worth highlighting: the university's discretion to select a considerable number of students who cannot pay anything near full tuition costs and to permit a considerable number of faculty members to survive on relatively low research productivity. Ideally, such students will turn out to be generous alumni, and such faculty inspiring teachers. Of course, the ideal is not always realised. Nevertheless, generous alumni tend to invoke inspiring teachers – not the acquisition of job-related skills – as motivating their endowments. Moreover, such alumni will not necessarily have been promising students, nor the teachers especially productive researchers. This suggests to me that at least some, if not most, American universities have designed a successful long-term financial strategy based on 'spirit' rather than 'matter'. They are valued for what their long-term employees, the faculty, value.

The relative ease with which Americans have been able to apply the financial model of the church to the university is what I mean by the 'Vatican face' of the university in the title of this section. The charge of Humboldt and other state officials has been to try to recreate that sentiment in the public sector, where it is more natural to think of education, like health, as a 'service' whose value rests on how well it enables people to cope with life-chances for which the state is ultimately held responsible. Expressed in most general terms, the practical problem is how to justify a financial regime for universities that does not cause the people funding them to expect most of the benefits to accrue close to the point of service delivery. My solution is what I call the 'Vegas heart' of the university, to which the rest of this section is devoted. Its financial plan is modelled on that of a casino – that is, dedicated to the encouragement of risk-taking.

Evidence for the university's Vegas heart appears initially as budgetary cross-subsidisation. This is the time-honoured practice of taking from the rich and giving to the poor academic departments. In the extreme case, the profits generated by the medical school may underwrite philosophy classes with three students. That universities successfully impose overhead costs on external funders partly reflects the legitimacy generally accorded to such cross-subsidisation. A university is not simply a marketplace where the various disciplines set up their stalls, but a corporate entity expressly dedicated to the maintenance of all forms of systematic inquiry. Lest we be sentimental, this show of intellectual integrity amounts to a strategy for pooling risk. The underlying economic rationale is that, lacking any long-term correlation between funding research and producing significant knowledge, it is wisest for those lucky enough to have struck rich to underwrite those unlucky enough to have struck poor. After all, fortunes are likely to be, if not reversed, at least levelled, in the future – say, once other medical schools acquire the knowledge that accorded the innovator an initial advantage.

But the Vegas heart of academia is, perhaps unwittingly, shared by society at large. Because universities today are expected to provide skills directly relevant to the increasing number of people who are destined for, in twentieth-century parlance, 'white collar' jobs, it is often forgotten that the state has traditionally regarded universities as public-spirited casinos in which citizens are forced to gamble some proportion of their wealth via tax payments. Until a half- to a quarter-century ago, the vast majority of people whose taxes funded universities had to tell a rather complicated story to justify the investment. Perhaps a relative or friend used academic achievement as a vehicle for personal advancement and upward class mobility. But more likely a complete stranger advanced knowledge in a way that benefited everyone, say, by curing a common disease or expanding our understanding of reality. When such singular 'Einstein' moments occur, people appear willing to excuse all their previous tax expenditure that subsidised the education of people who, for whatever reason, had squandered their opportunity.

This attitude is quite rational under certain economic conditions. The most obvious one is that the investors can benefit as freely as possible from the intellectual windfall. While it took Albert Einstein to come up with the theory of relativity, any of a number of people could have arrived at the theory under the right circumstances, and there was no prior reason to believe that Albert would be that person. To be sure, it might have happened somewhat earlier or later than it did. But if we truly believe that Einstein made a lasting contribution to knowledge (perhaps because he hit upon something deep about the nature of reality), not that he was riding the wave of the latest intellectual fad, then this is how those who subsidised his education should respond. Einstein received his reward upfront as an incentive for him to do something to merit the investment in him, as one of a number of academically trained people. Had Einstein failed to produce the goods, he would not have been penalised, but equally his success does not warrant his receiving *additional* financial benefit. The financial gamble on Einstein was taken not by Einstein himself but the society forced to bet on him (and others) through their taxes because he passed some state-sanctioned academic examinations. Einstein's success is simply grounds for society to continue trusting the state's investment of its taxes, at least in higher education.

Intellectual property law generally accepts that Einstein does not deserve additional remuneration – but for the wrong reasons. Thus, Einstein is not entitled to a patent for the theory of relativity, but lawyers say this is because his intellectual work consisted in discovering laws of nature that did not require human effort for their existence and over which no human could thereby exercise ownership. The legal justification harks back to a theologised version of the labour theory of value, whereby human discoveries are essentially acts of copying God's inventions. However, the Vegas heart of the university implies a critique that recalls the most probing examination of the labour theory of value as defended by Karl Marx, perhaps its last champion in economics.

The author was Eugen von Böhm-Bawerk, the late nineteenth-century Austrian finance minister and Joseph Schumpeter's economics teacher at the University of Vienna. He argued that workers did not deserve a share in the profits gained from their labours because they had been already paid in wages for work whose market value had yet to be determined. Part of the risk that an entrepreneur undertakes is the employment of labour to produce things that perhaps no one will buy. Workers rightly demand fair wages regardless of consumer fickleness. In this respect, Böhm-Bawerk took the labour theory of value more literally than Marx, who, like his Christian predecessors (but unlike Böhm-Bawerk), did not believe that the labour market was a natural guarantor of fair wages. But by the same token, workers are not entitled to additional payment if the products happen to sell. That would turn the entrepreneur's calculated risk into a sure loss, thereby creating a disincentive to industry.

The lesson for universities is clear: the state ministry, board of trustees, or senior academic administrators should behave like corporate entrepreneurs who adopt a liberal attitude toward investment but a conservative attitude toward returns. This entails protecting students and staff even when their returns as investments are poor without extravagantly rewarding them when they are good. Thus, student fees and stipends across disciplines should not be excessively influenced by graduates' anticipated incomes, and similarly faculty salaries should not mimic the spread in the demand for different types of knowledge. In short, university finances should not be tightly bound to fluctuating market indicators. After all, the market advantage currently enjoyed by a form of knowledge is bound to erode over time as it comes to be more widely possessed and eventually absorbed into the infrastructure of civilised society. In fact, the university encourages this very erosion as part of the creative destruction of social capital that constitutes the institution's Vatican face.

If a university aims to maintain the lifelong activity of intelligent but fallible beings – a natural rendering of tenured academic appointments – then quickly spotted truth always has the potential to cost the institution more in the long term than belatedly discovered error. This is due to the temptation for academic innovators to become what economists deride as 'rent-seekers' – people who discourage subsequent development or application of their original insights by making the entry costs too high for new innovators. To be sure, the ordinary institutionalisation of academic disciplines encourages rent-seeking, thereby amplifying 'path-dependency' in the growth of knowledge. For example, what Thomas Kuhn notoriously called a 'paradigm' is simply the conversion of an innovator's conceptual framework into an authorised blueprint for further research in a field that could have been – and probably still could be – addressed from a radically different conceptual framework. That paradigms are so marked in intellectual work reflects the halo effect that easily accompanies the initial generation of a few striking research results.

However, again taking the long view of the intellectual speculator, fetishising priority in research caters to the superstition that the first route into a new field is the only or best route. Of course, if enough people pay long enough lip service to this superstition, it can turn into a self-fulfilling prophecy, at which point it becomes honoured as a 'research tradition' dominated by rituals of pilgrimage and patronage that are very hard to avoid or escape. Thus, a postdoctoral fellowship at the right lab or a letter from the right professor can be the make-or-break moment in a fledgling academic's career.

In 'natural markets', this problem does not arise because the notable success of a new product signals to would-be entrepreneurs the prospect of more efficient means of reaching the same, related, or better ends. Novelty serves as an incentive for creative destruction. To be sure, the legal history of capitalism has increasingly put the brakes on this tendency through the extension of intellectual property rights. But this much decried use of the law to restrict free trade merely follows the lead of academics who mark, if not outright create, their turf by spontaneously generating trademark jargons and tariffs of technique, obeisance to which is paid in the 'literature reviews' and 'citation counts' of journal articles.

The university's role here should be to counteract academics' propensities to pump needless ontological gas into the words and practices they happened to have found useful in advancing the course of inquiry. Conjuring up the law's historic role as the nemesis of monopoly capitalism, we might say that the university functions here as an 'epistemic trust-buster'. There are two general ways of thinking about this function, both of which are designed to counteract specifically discipline-based assessment bodies (i.e. public and private professional accrediting agencies) that exist independently of the universities, but whose members they are deemed qualified to judge. Incentives need to be offered, on the one hand, for academics to translate their research into teaching; and on the other, to vacate their field of research in favour of another. Of course, there are no guarantees that these institutionally induced career shifts will lead to new insights. But that is part of the exhilaration of being a member of the 'creative class': it is less a matter whether you win or lose than enjoying an opportunity to play a game of potentially major social significance.

Ensuring institutional autonomy in an expanding market environment: the ultimate weapon in the Academic Caesar's arsenal

The historically surest strategy for universities to maintain their autonomy in a relatively unregulated knowledge market has been to shift from producing knowledge as a first-order to a second-order good. 'Autonomy' in this context implies an ability to turn the market to one's own advantage, so that rival knowledge producers are forced to compete on one's preferred turf. This is another way to look at Joseph Schumpeter's original definition of entrepreneurship as the 'creative destruction' of markets: Henry Ford was Schumpeter's exemplary entrepreneur because he reconfigured the transport market so that his own product, the automobile, set the standard that rivals had to then meet or surpass. Not only today, but throughout their history, universities have periodically had to 'creatively destroy' knowledge markets in order to overcome challenges to their prime position as authoritative knowledge producers.

At first, the relevance of the Schumpeterian entrepreneur to today's Academic Caesars may not seem so clear. After all, Ford actually produced a first-order innovation on the basis of which he generated a new market standard, which then became the second-order innovation. But on closer inspection, universities prove not to be so different. Take the matter of accrediting primary and secondary schools, both in terms of courses taught and people licensed to teach them. Although universities do not exert much control over day-to-day school practices, nevertheless they have played a major role in defining the foundations and even the logic of instruction of the various taught subjects, which to a large extent mirror those taught in universities. (In the UK, geography is one of the few subjects whose place in the school curriculum was *not* due to university-based initiatives.) Indeed, the proportion of high school graduates who qualify for university is routinely treated as the gold standard of school performance.

Today this last point seems perfectly reasonable, especially given the increasing percentage of each student cohort attending university. However, a quarter-century ago, when at most a quarter of students outside the US attended university, the career trajectories of high school graduates and academic degree holders were much more distinct. Yet even then universities were setting the standard of school performance. In this context, the relevant first-order goods manufactured by universities have been discipline-based textbooks, simplified versions of which continue to make their way into high school classes, with the overall effect of standardising how teachers communicate their subject areas.

To be sure, if the expectation of university attendance by high school graduates continues, then Academic Caesars may be compelled to cultivate a less condescending attitude toward secondary and even primary schools when defining the knowledge content of taught subject areas. In particular, schoolteachers tend to be more sensitive to non-academic – notably ethnic- and religious-based – sources of epistemic authority that students bring from their local environments. In the past, state enforcement of secular education was specifically designed to counter such potential obstacles to national solidarity. Indeed, the disciplinary identity of sociology in the early twentieth century, especially in France and the US, was tied to this project of harmonising epistemic standards across the entire education system, a.k.a. education as a melting pot. However, as universities lose the state's unconditional political and economic support, they will need to negotiate anew their relationship to the local knowledges that are most naturally given voice at the school level.

While the struggle between universities and schools over what knowledge is worth teaching is bound to intensify in the coming years, at least the contesting parties share a common understanding of knowledge as a second-order good, namely, a potentially universal standard of thought and conduct. However, a much more serious threat to university autonomy is posed by knowledge managers who call into question the very existence of knowledge as a second-order good, over which universities might lay *prima facie* claim.

To appreciate the nature of this threat, we need to keep in mind that currently popular phrases for our times such as 'knowledge society' and 'knowledge economy' mainly refer to the opening up of the market to non-traditional manufacturers of knowledge goods, the overall effect of which is designed to diversify the knowledge market, forcing universities not only to spread their resources more thinly but also to confront the sorts of internal tensions that an Academic Caesar normally sublimates. In contrast, institutes devoted purely to research, such as corporate laboratories in the past and today's science parks, operate with fewer encumbrances than universities in need of maintaining a delicate balance between several constituencies: research peers at other universities, campus colleagues from other disciplines, as well as the university's own dedicated review boards to matters of ethics and finance. Similarly, a training centre with reliable access to relevant employers can function more efficiently – at least from the standpoint of student *qua* consumer – than degree programmes that subordinate job training to a systematic presentation of the body of knowledge represented by an academic discipline. Under the circumstances, it is easy to draw the knowledge manager's conclusion that the university has become an obsolete organisation that tries to do too many things at once and hence does them all suboptimally. Thus, the university's longevity comes to be used against its future prospects: The institution has simply become entrenched in its old ways, which renders it incapable of adapting to today's changing market environment. The obvious solution, then, would be to disaggregate the university's functions into organisations focused primarily on either the research or teaching markets.

However, as I have suggested, the knowledge manager's solution is not the main historic strategy that universities have used to reinvent themselves and thereby reassert their autonomy. The successful strategy first became clear in the mid-nineteenth century when Oxford and Cambridge, which were already over 600 years old, had yet even to house scientific laboratories on their grounds, even though major industrial innovation was increasingly tied to research conducted in such facilities and, in any case, had already occurred in factory settings for at least a century. While Oxbridge of course eventually permitted labs to be constructed on their grounds, their principal response to this challenge was inspired by the man who coined the word 'scientist' in English, William Whewell, Master of Trinity College Cambridge, who is nowadays seen as the founder of the historical and philosophical study of science.

Whewell proposed something that we now take for granted: namely, that inventions may emerge in all sorts of non-academic settings but only academics can determine whether these inventions are anything more than lucky accidents. This is because academics – unlike inventors – are devoted to making sure that all of what we know hangs together as a systematic unity, something regularly performed in the curriculum as new knowledge is integrated into existing conceptual frameworks to inform the next generation. In that case, for any invention, the academic wants to know why it works when it does, and especially when it does not work, which in turn provides grounds for improvement – ideally in the disciplined setting of a university laboratory. In this context, Oxbridge could convert its perceived liabilities into virtues: namely, its ideological basis in Anglican theology and its material basis in property ownership. Together they provided grounds sufficiently removed from the mental and physical spaces of industrial innovation to make Oxbridge appear honest brokers of knowledge claims emanating from those sites. Moreover, in positioning Oxbridge as gatekeepers in the otherwise free flow of inventions, Whewell had no intention of stifling that flow. On the contrary, the more disparate the sources of innovation, the more obvious becomes the need to establish common standards for discriminating reliable from unreliable inventions along a variety of dimensions that included not only their theoretical bases – issues that might also concern the government patent office – but also the potential financial and health risks they posed to adopters of the innovations.

It is easy nowadays to overlook the centrality of universities in the institutionalisation of standards of empirical reliability, a.k.a. quality control, in the manufacture and circulation of knowledge products. This development, which explains the strong presence of academics in government regulatory agencies in the twentieth century, was at first strongly resisted in legal and business circles as being against the spirit of a liberal society, in which people should be free to assume their own risks. This strong market sensibility supposed that as long as information about the consequences of adopting an innovation was widely disseminated, anyone capable of participating in public life was mentally equipped to decide for themselves if they should adopt, extend or simply avoid or ignore the innovation. From this standpoint, the idea that universities should normatively mediate society's knowledge flow appeared to be a thinly veiled attempt to reinvent a modern version of clerical oversight on secular affairs. Instead of the Church sanctifying the King's acts, the university lab would now do something similar for politics and business. For classical liberals suspicious of any barriers to free trade, demands that new products pass tests of 'validity' and 'reliability' constructed in academic settings prior to market exposure smacked of what economists call 'rent-seeking', that is, a cost tied exclusively to the ownership, rather than the productive use, of capital – in this case, cultural capital.

So, then, why did the universities manage to retain their market advantage by providing the sort of second-order knowledge goods associated with quality control standards? A theme that emerges from the above account is that universities systematically counter society's centrifugal tendencies with their own centripetal ones. In other words, as society's capacity to alter its knowledge base increases, the threat of fragmentation – indeed, the loss of society's collective memory – also increases. Imagine the character of knowledge in today's society, if our proverbial knowledge manager got his way and the university's functions were disaggregated to teaching-only and research-only organisations. The former would be exclusively oriented toward the labour market, namely, the efficient provision of job-related skills. The latter would be exclusively oriented to a variety of clients for whom new knowledge can increase the value of their goods. The one sort of activity would embed knowledge in people and the other in products, but over time it would be difficult to see what qualifies both activities as oriented towards 'knowledge' *per se*. At that point, knowledge would have become segmented into two discrete markets, one for techniques and another for technologies. The idea of knowledge as the unifying and universalising mode of inquiry epitomised in Max Weber's resonant phrase, 'science as a vocation', would have disappeared. So too would society's sense of self-consciousness. It is rescue from this 'postmodern' condition that ultimately justifies the existence of the Academic Caesar.

Bibliography

Baehr, Peter (1998) *Caesar and the Fading of the Roman World: A Study in Republicanism and Caesarism*, New Brunswick, NJ: Transaction.
Calhoun, Craig (2006) 'Is the university in crisis?', *Society* (May/June): 8–20.

Clark, Burton (1998) *Creating Entrepreneurial Universities: Organizational Pathways of Transformation,* Oxford: Pergamon-Elsevier Science.

Clark, William (2006) *Academic Charisma and the Origins of the Research University,* Chicago, IL: University of Chicago Press.

Collins, Randall (1998) *The Sociology of Philosophies: A Global Theory of Intellectual Change,* Cambridge, MA: Harvard University Press.

Florida, Richard (2002) *The Rise of the Creative Class,* New York: Basic Books.

Fukuyama, Francis (2004) *State Building: Governance and World Order in the Twenty-First Century,* Ithaca, NY: Cornell University Press.

Fuller, Steve (2000) *The Governance of Science,* Milton Keynes: Open University Press.

Fuller, Steve (2002) *Knowledge Management Foundations,* Woburn, MA: Butterworth-Heinemann.

Fuller, Steve (2003) 'In search of vehicles for knowledge governance: on the need for institutions that creatively destroy social capital', in N. Stehr (ed.) *The Governance of Knowledge,* New Brunswick, NJ: Transaction Books, pp. 41–76.

Fuller, Steve (2006) 'Universities and the future of knowledge governance from the standpoint of social epistemology', in G. Neave (ed.) *Knowledge, Power and Dissent: Critical Perspectives on Higher Education and Research in Knowledge Society,* Paris: UNESCO, pp. 345–70.

Lyotard, Jean-François (1983) *The Postmodern Condition* (orig. 1979), Minneapolis: University of Minnesota Press.

May, Robert (1997) 'The scientific wealth of nations', *Science,* 275(5301): 793–6.

Price, Derek de Solla (1963) *Little Science, Big Science,* London: Penguin Press.

Pyenson, Lewis and Susan Sheets-Pyenson (1999) *Servants of Nature: A History of Scientific Institutions, Enterprises and Sensibilities,* London: Fontana.

Schumpeter, Joseph (1942) *Capitalism, Socialism and Democracy,* New York: Harper & Row.

Scott, James (1990) *Seeing Like a State,* New Haven, CT: Yale University Press.

Turner, Stephen (2003) *Liberal Democracy 3.0,* London: Sage.

Wolf, Alison (2002) *Does Education Matter? Myths about Education and Economic Growth,* London: Penguin Press.

5 (Re)producing universities

Knowledge dissemination, market power and the global knowledge commons

Penny Ciancanelli

Introduction

Thirty years ago, financing the production and reproduction of universities in western capitalist societies was largely a national affair and tailored to suit its particular profile of resources, beliefs and ambitions (Readings 1996). Economists' justifications for government's subsidy tended to emphasise, *inter alia*, market failure and the public benefit features of university outputs (Schoenenberg 2004; Stiglitz 1999), including production of expert labour, development of new knowledge (especially in the sciences) and maintenance of their libraries as repositories of cultural, social and scientific knowledge produced in the past (Guedon 2001). The mix of public and personal resources that financed the production of universities reflected national differences in the social structures underpinning capital accumulation (Williams 2000).

The contrast with the current situation is very great. The international context in which nations produce their universities is radically different; deregulation of financial flows and international trade have generated qualitative changes in the fiscal capacities of governments and the perceived relevance of universities. Many economists now emphasise the macroeconomic benefits that arise when university research is more tightly linked to commerce and the 'knowledge economy' (Peters 2001). Researchers have characterised these qualitative changes using a trio of terms: neo-liberalism, globalisation and financialisation (Foster 2007; Epstein 2005), a choice influenced as much by disciplinary focus as by the dimensions of change studied.[1] In this chapter, references to financialisation aim to draw attention to the influence of certain features of finance-led capital accumulation on the *qualities* of the universities being produced in those nations it dominates.

This chapter focuses on the threats posed by financialisation to one 'quality' that has long been central to the production of universities – a system of scholarly communication governed by non-capitalist relations. Originating in the UK and France in the seventeenth century, the system is constituted by the 'free' exchange of ideas, with the primary meaning of 'free exchange' expressed in the idea that scholarly dialogue ought to be politically and ideologically unconstrained (Guedon 2001; Houghton 2002). In addition, there is another meaning, the one expressed in the willingness of scholars to offer their work (as research findings, as referees, etc.) *pro bono*. Thus, the traditional system of scholarly communication can be described as a 'gift' economy in both political and economic terms, with production of the content of academic journals (publication) as a key moment in the exchange of new knowledge (Guedon 2001; Bergstrom 2001; Houghton 2002).

Until the mid-1990s, it could be argued that the overall system had gained as much from globalisation as the universities lost from neo-liberal fiscal policies. This is because knowledge exchange was a beneficiary of the same technological changes that enabled finance-led capital accumulation on a global scale (Henwood 2005; Strange 1998: Ch. 2). The technologies that extended the scale and scope of accumulation also removed the distances (and related time lags and costs) that limited the feasible geography of knowledge exchange (Peters 2001).

The sting in the tail of these benefits only became apparent in the last decade or so, when ownership of publishing companies began to become concentrated in the hands of a few global publishing conglomerates. From the perspective of publishers, the widening of the geography of knowledge exchange, the development of the internet and the increasingly routine digitisation of research content were transforming high-cost, national markets in scholarly content into low-cost, potentially 'global' markets.

Financialisation provided the means to take advantage of the opportunity. Deregulated capital flows were instrumental in the successive waves of mergers and acquisitions that followed construction of global capital markets. Publishing was no exception, including publishers of professional materials (Edlin and Rubenfeld 2004; Munroe 2007). After the dust had cleared, seven multinational firms earned 45 per cent of the $11bn global market in science, technology and medical journals and the price of these journals had risen by 600 per cent between 1985 and 2002 (California Digital Libraries 2003). Operating profits ranged from 25 per cent to 41 per cent (ARL 2007; van Orsdal and Born 2007).

The aim of this chapter is to contribute to debates on these developments by exploring the links between financialisation, commercial dominance of academic publishing and the re/production of universities. The central theme is how commercial intrusion into scholarly communication has thwarted the emancipatory potential of open and free access to the knowledge produced in universities. The discussion is organised into three main sections. The first draws on economists' perspectives on the production of knowledge in market economies. The second is devoted to a case study that illustrates the extent of commercial intrusion into academic publishing and its immediate consequences for the production of universities. The third and final section seeks to situate commercial dominance of academic publishing in the overall context of the qualities of universities produced in nations where finance-led capital accumulation dominates.

Knowledge and its transmission

Market failure is one of the main justifications given by economists for government financing of the production of universities.[2] In conventional perspectives, many types of knowledge production are viewed as a special case of market failure. They are treated as a site of capital accumulation that private investors avoid because it is difficult or impossible to enforce their right to appropriate profits from the sale or manufacture of such items (Stiglitz 1999; Schoenenberg 2004). According to this view, if society wishes to ensure the production of knowledge, it will have to pay directly (in part or in full) or indirectly (via patents or copyrights) for its production (Stiglitz 1999).

Table 5.1 summarises the consumption characteristics of goods and services that are said to affect an investor's ability to enforce his/her rights to appropriate profits from their production.

The preferred focus of private investment will be pure private goods and services, such as shoes, clothes, foods, etc. Rivalry in consumption allows growth in markets; excludability enables enforcement of right to payment. At the other extreme are pure public goods, such as world peace, in which there is little scope for profit since its consumption is non-rivalrous and it is impossible (not to say perverse) to exclude individuals from its enjoyment.

Pure public goods are rare because complete market failure is rare. Some level of production of most goods and services will prove profitable because there will be some element of rivalry or some mechanism of excludability that can be imposed. Many of the goods considered 'public goods' (such as universal primary education) are better classified as 'impure public goods' or 'cases of partial market failure' (Kaul 1999).

For example, the cost price for commercial builders to supply housing may exceed the income earned by the very poor. The market, in this case, partly fails. Housing for the poor could be supplied by a religious charity (a 'club' good) or by governments (a common pool resource). Either approach would imply the willingness of some to subsidise housing for those who lack the purchasing power to access it by themselves. Most economists agree that there are many goods and services vulnerable to underproduction; use of market failure as justification for public provision is essentially ideological, based on ethical rather than technical criteria.

Schoenenberg (2004: 28) suggests that little of the knowledge produced in universities qualifies as a pure public good since '... the public characteristics and cumulativeness of knowledge are not absolute, as the access to and the

Table 5.1 Private versus public goods: what matters to investors?

	Rivalrous	*Non-rivalrous*
Excludable	Pure private good	Club goods (non-rivalrous to members of the club)
Non-excludable	Common pool resource (subject to depletion or congestion)	Pure public good

use of knowledge is limited when the costs of these are high'. Moreover, he argues that the enjoyment of scientific knowledge requires investment (or time and effort) to understand which means it is 'non-rivalrous' only within a limited community. For this reason, the case for government funding ought to be argued in terms of public benefit rather than market failure.

A somewhat different stance is taken by Stiglitz (1999). He focuses on the issue of excludability, arguing that not only is the consumption of knowledge non-rivalrous, it is synergistic, from the perspective of economic development and growth. Open access to the knowledge commons increases the social rate of return from investments in its production. Moreover, on equity grounds, there is no merit in excluding anyone from access to it – whether they can understand it or not. Thus, on grounds of both efficiency and equity, the 'global knowledge commons' is a resource to which all humanity should have access. In this regard, Stiglitz is more faithful to the concept of public goods developed by Samuelson (1954) where 'publicness' has a precise mathematical definition that allows empirical measurement. A good is 'public' if the marginal cost of adding an additional consumer is zero (Holcombe 1997: 11). Stiglitz's (1999, 2004) arguments emphasise this latter feature as a central feature of knowledge *per se*. Since ICT and other technologies reduce the 'cost' of access by the additional consumer to zero, existing knowledge ought to be regarded as a global public good.

The same arguments do not apply to the production of *new* knowledge. Incentives are required to overcome the market failures that regulate what is supplied in capitalist market societies (Schoenenberg 2004; Stiglitz 1999). If society wishes to see new knowledge produced on a regular basis, it must pay for its production. It may do so directly by financing organisations, such as universities, to undertake such production or by providing incentives that enable private investors or philanthropists to do so. The latter is achieved by government enforcement of investors' property rights, through various regimes of intellectual property rights, such as copyright or patents, which ensure that users pay for the use of new knowledge.

Stiglitz (1999) completes his contribution by emphasising the need to distinguish between consumption of already produced knowledge (what he calls the knowledge commons or knowledge *per se*) and the transmission of such knowledge. Many of the services related to the transmission of knowledge have the features of private goods (rivalry in consumption; excludability) and are not subject to total market failure. Table 5.2 identifies common knowledge transmission services, how they are currently provided and the typical mechanisms that are used to exclude or privatise consumption.

In most higher education systems, access to instructional services is conditional on admission, matriculation, and the payment of fees (Johnstone 2003). In addition, universities may offer public lectures as well, controlling access to them by issuing invitations or charging fees. In some parts of the world (e.g. Latin America), universities are also publishers of textbooks and of the academic journals that transmit research knowledge and these are often open-access publications. However, in others (e.g. US, UK, Canada),

Table 5.2 Knowledge transmission services, intermediaries and exclusion
mechanisms

	Transmission mode	Service provider	Exclusion mechanism
Instruction	Lecture	University	Fees or invitation
Instructional materials	Textbooks, etc.	Lecturers and publishers	User charges or copyright charges
Research	Publication	Publisher	Copyright

many of these services are commercially produced and then sold to students,
lecturers and libraries, even though the academics that produced them are
often paid little or nothing in return for the publication of their work.

Schoenenberg's (2004) emphasis on *access to knowledge* as a general factor
limiting its pure 'publicness' leads him to view published research as 'non-
rivalrous' only within a limited community. This would suggest that he views
published research as a 'club' good. Stiglitz (1999, 2004) emphasises the
exclusionary possibilities that arise when transmitting knowledge. This would
imply that he views published research as a 'common pool' resource. Either
way, its status as an impure public good implies that its production can be
organised on a public benefit or commercial basis. Academic journals, for
example, can be produced as a publicly funded 'common pool' resource (e.g.
by national university presses, as in Mexico); as a 'club good' organised on a
cooperative basis by learned societies (e.g. *American Economics Review*), or
as a private 'club good' owned and controlled by for-profit publishers (e.g.
Journal of Applied Financial Economics).

Neither Schoenenberg (2004) nor Stiglitz (1999) fully evaluate the
implications of commercial dominance of knowledge transmission services.
One possible reason may be the tendency to assume that because knowledge
per se and knowledge transmission services can be conceptually distinguished,
they are distinct outputs of distinct processes (e.g. sequentially produced)
rather than joint outputs of a common production process (Navaretti *et al.*
1996). If they are regarded as joint outcomes however, the attractiveness of
investing in knowledge transmission services becomes clear. To the extent
that production of universities is financed by government, charitable bequests
or student fees, others have paid for producing the knowledge encoded in the
media in which it is subsequently published or disseminated.

Following on from this are possible differences in the impact of commercial
dominance of instructional materials versus scholarly communication media.
Commercial dominance of the former concerns communication of 'received'
wisdom; of knowledge produced in the past but whose present consumption
is considered useful. Commercial dominance of the latter (especially academic
journals) is more problematic. Since the system of scholarly communication
is tightly linked to the production of qualities that constitute universities as
distinctive centres of knowledge production, it can be expected to have more
far-reaching consequences (Houghton 2002; Guedon 2001).

While the general features of academic publishing point to its potential as
a site of capital accumulation, some particular features of the US universities

highlight some of the links between the types of universities re/produced and the profitability of academic publishing. These features include a system of job security (tenure)[3] that is tightly linked to publishing in a narrow range of international refereed journals. In addition, the preponderance of public finance for universities is provided by states (rather than the national/federal government); university budgets are subject to debate in state legislatures and the details of annual financial settlements are published in local newspapers. Because most states have only one public university, these universities can mobilise staff (including librarians) to challenge financial settlements; because the settlements are made annually, challenge becomes an institutional feature of the production of universities.

According to Guedon (2001: Ch. 6), the response of state university librarians to the Great Depression was a formative moment. The fiscal crisis provoked by the decade-long depression created strong incentives for librarians to identify those journals whose subscriptions had to be maintained at all costs ('core' journals) and those that could, in an emergency, be dropped. In the post-war period, science-led prosperity offered different reasons for identification of the 'core' journals, this time on a national basis. The task was undertaken in the 1960s by a non-governmental organisation (the Institute for Scientific Information); it decided that the basis for identifying core journals should be the international citation system, the practice of identifying the articles (and the journal in which they were published) that formed the basis of the researchers' knowledge claims. Guedon (2001: 12) emphasises the far-reaching consequences of this development, observing that 'What Garfield did was collapse the entire set of little specialty cores into one big scientific core, the Science Citation Index (SCI) and what used to be a useful tool for making difficult purchasing decisions became a generic concept with universal claims.'

An important consequence of Garfield's work was that producing universities in the US became intertwined with financing the production of a set of 'core journals' since these 'had' to be purchased at any cost. Since the costs of producing the content of academic journals are subsumed within the overall costs of producing universities as centres of knowledge production (Bergstrom 2001), for-profit publishers found themselves in a position to 'free ride' on these investments. From the 1960s forward, the Science Citation Index steered library demand in the US to a narrow range of core journals, because publishing in these had become tightly linked to tenure and promotion (e.g. the production of the national and international status hierarchies that still govern important aspects of group life in scholarly communities and in universities). Libraries came under intense pressure from faculty and departments to purchase these 'core' journals. As a result, a narrow range of 'core' journals came to be regarded as indispensable, to be purchased at any price. There is no doubt that these features of 'free content' and 'core journals' linked to promotion and tenure created such an extreme degree of demand inelasticity that ownership of large numbers of core journals was a nearly risk-free path to high profits.

Commercial dominance of knowledge transmission

In recent years, the entry of for-profit organisations into knowledge transmission markets offers *prima facie* evidence of their potential as sites of capital accumulation. Large, publicly listed corporations sell direct instruction leading to university degrees and large multinational media corporations dominate publication of instructional material and of academic journals. Making money in this way is not new. For example, for-profit corporations have produced vocationally focused instructional services for most of the twentieth century (Noble 1998) and private (for profit) publishers have long been part of instructional and academic publishing. What *is* new is the vast size and scope of the publishing firms and the corresponding scale of the profit accumulated.

Five commercial publishers now own most of the world's 'core' academic journals not owned by learned societies (ARL 2007). They are Reed Elsevier, Candover and Cinven (a private equity group that took over Wolters-Kluwer and Bertlesmann-Springer), Thompson and Wiley. Each of these five grew through take-over of other publishing houses. Kluwer merged with Wolters-Samson in 1987 (creating Wolters-Kluwer, *supra*); Elsevier merged with Reed International to become Reed Elsevier in 1993 which, in turn, took over Lexis-Nexis and Academic Press. There are suggestions that Candover-Cinven may take over Thompson to create the world's largest publisher (Simbanet 2007; Edlin and Rubinfeld 2004; Munroe 2007).

The aim of the discussion in this section is to document the extent to which commercial interests dominate academic publishing, highlighting the level of profitability that has fuelled takeovers and eventual concentration of ownership of core journals by a handful of multinational publishers. The first part of the discussion is devoted to a mini-case study of the 'serials crisis' at a large public university in the US. This is followed by discussion of some of the implications of this crisis for scholarly communication and the production of universities.

Mini-case study of Reed Elsevier and University of California System (2003)

Insights into the consequences of corporate ownership of academic journals can be gained by considering the experience of one of the largest university systems in the world (the University of California) and reports of its library system's experience with the global media group, Reed Elsevier. The University of California system is the company's second largest client, after a consortium of Japanese universities (UCB 2004). The UC system serves more than 208,000 students on 10 campuses and has 121,000 full-time faculty members (UCB 2004).

Reed Elsevier publishes 25 per cent of core science publications and is the largest science, technology and medicine journal publisher in the world. It earned profits of 37 per cent on its publishing business in 2002 (California

Digital Library 2003: 2) and over the period 2000 to 2005, earned an average annual return of 41 per cent on its operations (Simbanet 2007).

UC paid Reed Elsevier $8million in 2002/3 for digital access to circa 1,700 journals and $2million for print copies of journals. This represented 50 per cent of its total budget for on-line journals (UCB 2004). However, the usage of the journals purchased from Reed Elsevier accounted for less than 25 per cent of total usage (UCB 2004). Ten percent of Reed Elsevier journals received 50 per cent of use, an artefact of marketing strategies to increase the yield (e.g. profit) taken from sales to universities (UCB 2004). For example, university libraries are offered portfolio-licensing agreements that resemble cable television packages. Thus, in order to get access to prestigious high-use titles (the analogue to premier league sports or newly released films), the library must subscribe to lower-end, marginal titles comparable to cheap, reality television programmes (Bergstrom 2001; Edlin and Rubinfeld 2004). In 2003, 60 per cent of the system-wide e-journals budget went to only two for-profit publishers, one of which was Reed Elsevier, even though the journals they supply account for only 33 per cent of e-journal use (UCB 2004).

The Association of Research Librarians (ARL 2002), in a study of the cost pressures facing university libraries, singled out the situation at the University of California, as typical of research-led universities. They pointed out that 150 UC faculty served as managing editors of Reed Elsevier journals and a further 964 served on editorial boards. Furthermore, roughly 15 per cent of content of these journals had been written by UC faculty. In other words, even though 'a large portion of what Reed Elsevier sells was created, vetted or enhanced by UC faculty', the university had to buy it back at prices that were becoming unaffordable (ARL 2002; UCB 2004; UCB 2007b).

Further illustration of this trend is evidenced by noting that between 1986 and 2002, expenditures on journals by university libraries in the US increased by 227 per cent but the number of journals purchased increased by only 9 per cent (ARL 2002: Graphs 1 and 2). In addition, a UK Wellcome Trust Study (2003) reported an overall price increase of 204 per cent for UK published journals between 1997 and 2003, adding that the percentage increase in some cases are indefensible. It offered the example of the rise in subscription charges for *World Development*, a journal used extensively in Third World and development studies. The price increased from $250 in 1997 to $1,771 in 2003, an increase of 608 per cent in five years. Both the ARL and Wellcome Trust studies confirm that these price increases are made possible by a few publishers dominating academic publishing. That this rise in price reflects the market power of commercial publishers is suggested by the pattern of price increases in African studies shown in Table 5.3, which reveals that price increases for the core journal owned by the commercial publisher were multiples of those imposed by university presses.

Bergstrom and Bergstrom (2001) developed a method (now widely used in studies of open-access research) to measure the overall benefit of for-profit journals to authors and to the scholarly communication process. They did

Table 5.3 Price increases and ownership of various journals, 1997 to 2003

Publisher	Journal title	Increase
Taylor & Francis	*African Studies*	410%
Edinburgh University Press	*Africa*	87%
Canadian Association of African Studies	*Canadian J. of African Studies*	72%
Indiana University Press	*Africa Today*	44%
Cornell University Press	*J. of Mod. African Studies*	31%
Boston University Press	*Int'l J. of African Historical Studies*	18%

Source: Derived from Zell (2003: 8).

so by devising an average cost per citation (using the Social Science and Science Citation Indexes) and found that cost-effectiveness varies more by type of publisher than by subject matter (e.g. disciplines). According to their research, the average cost per citation is 15 times higher in journals published by for-profit publishers than in journals published by non-profit disciplinary associations (Bergstrom and Bergstrom 2001: 2, Table 1).

Using prices charged by learned societies for journals of equivalent 'impact', they developed estimates of the level of profit achieved by for-profit publishers. They argue that the price charged by learned societies is a reasonable approximation of the cost of producing a journal with those features because learned societies have no motive to charge members more than it costs to produce the journal. If they are right, the gross profit of for-profit publishers can be estimated by comparing the price it charges with that charged by a learned society publisher for a journal of similar impact. An illustration of their results is given in Table 5.4 and points to the significant profitability of core journals.

Research by Soete and Salaba (1998: 10) reinforces the same point, documenting that average subscription prices of science, technology and medical journals are nearly five times higher than those of non-profit journals whilst the average impact factor of non-profit journals is 1.5 greater. Since some for-profit publishers own upwards of 2,000 academic journals, the aggregate profit potential is enormous. Realising this potential is more or less assured by the inelastic demand for core journals.

As the costs of academic journals rise, so does the cost of scholarly communication. Since the latter has historically been regarded as a fixed

Table 5.4 Profit per subscription assuming AER price equals cost to produce

Journal	Individual print sub.	On-line (site licence)
J. Applied Financial Economics (commercial publisher)	£1466	£1393
American Economic Review (learned society)	£ 345	£ 270
Estimated profit on costs	£1121	£1123

Source: Based on data provided by Bergstrom and Bergstrom (2001).

cost of producing universities, the actions of commercial publishers have provoked increases in the fixed cost of producing universities. Under a regime of declining public financing of universities, those fixed costs can be met only by cutting costs elsewhere. Thus, according to statistics compiled by the Association of Research Librarians (ARL 2007), the number of research monographs fell by more than 10 per cent in the period 1986–2006, even though expenditures increased by more than 60 per cent.

Some implications for the production of universities

Clearly, the knowledge base of the universities produced under these financial conditions has changed. Libraries have fewer monographs and fewer journals whose archives are *intact*.[4] In the arts and humanities, this implies that fewer epistemic communities are represented. Interestingly, the commercial dynamic in the social sciences (especially business studies) appears to have worked in the opposite direction. Some estimated 1,700 new journals[5] were created from 1985 to 2005 in business studies alone (Mort 2005). Publishers appear to have acted as venture capitalists, financing the creation of a large number of new journals, perhaps in the hope of creating one of the 'core' social science journals of the future.

Guedon (2001: 42) interprets proliferation (and the absence of serious price rises) as the best clue that '... commercial publishers, despite their vast intellectual resources, have not yet figured out the way to profitably manipulate the social sciences market'. However, from a finance perspective, Guedon's assessment overlooks the possibility that proliferation is an aggregate outcome of a rational response by each publisher to the problem of lacking the information required to manipulate the market. Publishers' investments in core science journals are virtually risk free because their revenue potential is fully understood. In contrast, the fuzzier definition of 'core' journals in the arts and social sciences creates uncertainty; this makes investment riskier. To manage this risk, publishers appear to have created portfolios of journals, spanning disciplines and filling in gaps identified by academic gatekeepers cum journal editors. Thus, a portfolio perspective explains proliferation as the aggregate effect of each publisher's effort to reduce the financial risk.

The consequences of commercial dominance are not limited to increases in the cost of producing universities. Dominance also has the potential to allow for-profit publishers to intrude on scholarly communication in unexpected ways, raising basic questions of control over the process of knowledge production in universities.[6] A case in point concerns how subscriptions to journals are packaged and the reputation of scientists (as measured by the Science Citation Index or SCI) and the universities that employ them. Increasingly, libraries are asked to sign up for multi-year package deals in which publishers provide the desired core journals at a discount, conditional on taking a number of journals that libraries would prefer not to buy.[7] Guedon (2001) argues that these 'big deals' distort the scholarly landscape that confronts researchers. It introduces a bias in their search towards articles in those journals owned by the publisher that dominates their library's science serials collection.

He cites the case of OhioLINK, a deal between Reed Elsevier and a consortium of universities in the state of Ohio. By 2001, Reed Elsevier owned 76.9 per cent of all electronic articles downloaded even though it owned less than 25 per cent of the core journals (Guedon 2001: 37). Since Elsevier's package deal included far more titles than those provided by any other publishers, it stands to reason that there is a higher probability that a chosen article will be from one of Elsevier's journals (Guedon 2001: Ch. 10). With these deals in place at hundreds of universities in the US and Canada, publishers thus influence the rate of use of their articles, which affects the citation rate which, in turn, can influence the impact factor of its journals.

Pity the poor scholars who remain unaware of the commercial forces to which the 'free exchange' of ideas (and his/her reputation) is now held hostage. In the social sciences, they may be forgiven for not understanding that the audience for their research now depends more on how publishers are structuring package deals than on the quality of their work or the editorial policies of the journals for which they write. Those smart enough to publish in journals owned by an oligopoly publisher who, in turn, owns most of the e-content available at the top ten research universities have a greater chance of being read and cited, thereby increasing their chances for tenure and promotion.

A third major implication concerns access to already produced knowledge, what Stiglitz (1999) identifies as the knowledge commons. Because so many core journals are owned by the big publishing firms, these publishers have acquired copyrights to a great deal of the knowledge commons. In the past, university scholars had permanent access to such knowledge because the print-based serials collections were owned and housed in their universities. As the new deals shift library holdings from print to electronic site licences, access to previous issues is not guaranteed. Unlike subscriptions to print copies, site licences provide access to the article, not permanent possession of the journal itself. In the context of electronic journals in the packaged deals, authors' assignment of copyright to a publisher has different consequences. Assignment privatises bits and pieces of knowledge, to no apparent plan or standard. Moreover, when a great deal of the knowledge commons is in private ownership, the 'social' returns from government investments in universities disappear. It becomes, instead, a massive subsidy to private interests and public funding of universities can no longer be justified on grounds of public benefit. It would appear there is no 'middle ground' – public financing to produce universities is justified only if full access to the knowledge commons is guaranteed. Otherwise, there is no economic justification for using public money to produce universities and every reason to oppose it.

Financialisation and universities

Developments in academic publishing are reflective of the more general shift in the financial relations governing capital accumulation and thereby the production of universities. Because there is very little work linking the production of universities to financialisation,[8] the discussion begins with a brief overview of their links. This is followed by a discussion of universities as new sites of capital accumulation. In this context, the experience of university librarians can be viewed as illustrative of the likely path pursued by private businesses in their efforts to commercialise other types of knowledge transmission.

Stagnation and capital flows

When recent changes in the global economy are characterised as 'financialisation' (or finance-led accumulation) important dimensions of change come into view. First, one's attention is drawn to the increased weight of finance and finance-related activities in the (now) open economies of most nations. This imbalance is especially pronounced where corporate finance is market-based (e.g. the UK and the US). Second, one is made aware that the search for higher returns is constituted by relentless comparison of returns from what you are doing to the returns in volatile capital markets or unexploited opportunities in the sectors pried open by neo-liberalism (Foster 2007; Stockhammer 2004; Williams 2000).

Financialisation is attributed, *inter alia*, to stagnation in the rates of return that can be achieved in sectors already dominated by a few large firms (Foster 2007; Magdoff 2006). Its persistence reflects the extent to which financialisation itself provokes slower overall growth because it drives down investment in capital goods (which remain largely physical assets) and the latter generate more employment and related increases in effective demand than do investments in financial assets (Stockhammer 2004; Tobin 1997).

Stagnation does not mean firms (and investors) are losing money; the problem is the opposite. The market power of dominant firms allows them to make substantial profits at little risk. The problem is what to do with the profits. Reinvestment would lower their returns; they already achieve the highest rate of return allowed by the distribution of income and social preferences of the markets in which they operate (e.g. the price elasticity of demand). From a macroeconomic perspective, paying out profits to existing owners (as dividends), would not help; it would merely shift the problem of what to do with the surplus to owners or fund managers, without changing the structure of investment opportunities.

The elimination of controls on cross-border flows of finance capital widened the geography of investment opportunities and offered a way out of stagnation. Deregulation and privatisation made available new sites of capital accumulation or extended the population space of the old ones. These events were made possible by the flows of finance capital from situations in which returns could not be improved to those in which they could (or so they hoped). Thus, capital mobility since 1980 has been associated with successive waves of cross-border mergers and acquisitions that cartelised markets in the commodities that feature in the consumption bundles of households and businesses everywhere (e.g. petroleum, automobiles, agribusiness, telephony, entertainment media and so forth).

It is ironic that the technologies originating in publicly financed university laboratories, whose creation was initially governed by the 'gift exchange', also transformed production processes in finance and science research. In one sphere, money and profit drive the exchange; in the other sphere, peer recognition and status honour. In both spheres, the transmission of knowledge itself plays an essential role in the production and reproduction of the relations that govern their respective sites. Placed in this context, it is not surprising that knowledge transmission was targeted as a site for capital accumulation; the surprise is how long the sector is taking to succumb entirely.

Open access, open rebellion and uncertain futures

For at least the past decade, scientists have been working to revolutionise scholarly communication, seeking to transform the worldwide web into a true knowledge commons and to restore the 'free exchange of ideas' as the basis of scholarly communication. Open access has mobilised the support of governments, important non-governmental organisations and leading figures in the science research community. There are 2,500 open access journals in the sciences (about 10 per cent of the world's peer reviewed journals) and this is an important beginning. It is now accepted that publishing can be easily and safely decoupled from evaluation and long-term archiving (Guedon 2001). It is also accepted that scientific knowledge advances further and faster under open access. Indeed, as Swan (2007: 3) argues, 'Research is expensive enough that the world can scarcely afford an antiquated, inefficient and high-cost system of information dissemination.'

The evaluation process, however, remains in the publisher's grip, that is to say, the grip of those academic gatekeepers whose alliance with the very largest publishers secures the publisher's grip. Evaluation via peer review confers legitimacy on knowledge and this legitimacy is central to the related tenure and promotion prospects of the scientists themselves. Stock market investment analysts are betting that the publisher's grip (and profits) will hold, arguing that efforts

> ... to encourage academics to publish research directly on the internet and to encourage the boards of individual journals (who peer review the scientific articles included in the journal) to defect to not-for-profit publishers will fail because barriers to entry enjoyed by the incumbent journals are far too high.
>
> (Gooden *et al.* 2002: 4)

The problem of course is the perverse incentives arising from tying promotion, pay, tenure and research funding to a few journals in each field (Houghton 2002: 15). When academic publishers were small businesses, owning perhaps one or two 'good' titles, these arrangements were not so perverse. However, once transmogrified into 'global' networks, academic publishers have powers over knowledge production that the creators of that knowledge no longer have in themselves. Moreover, as with most multinational firms, globalisation allows most anti-competitive behaviour to slip the leash of national regulation. Publishers are free to engage in periodic reassignment of ownership of journals in different national subsidiaries, thereby evading any effort to regulate them (Edlin and Rubenfeld 2004; Gooden *et al.* 2002).

All of which leads us to the sacred cow of knowledge transmission – producing universities that educate undergraduates between the ages of 18 and 24. Commerce is more than nibbling on the edges of this market. Global publishing giants exert oligopoly control of textbooks and e-learning technologies, such as virtual learning environments (VLE) (Mort 2005). In addition, there has been significant expansion in the number and offerings of for-profit universities and every reason to expect further growth (Waks 2002; Ruth 2006). As profitable as these investments are proving to be, they pale in comparison to the profit potential of student loans. The logic of finance-led capital accumulation means it targets sites where demand is price-inelastic and the service is subsidised in some way. Student loans fulfil these requirements with the added advantage of significant information asymmetries (after all, how well does the average 18-year-old understand debt contracts?), and the emotive bonds of kinship (after all, what kind of parent would prevent their child from investing in education?).

Until recently, debt-financed university education was another peculiar feature of how universities were produced in the US. This is changing as governments in Europe allow universities to charge fees and simultaneously legislate programmes that guarantee the loans students use to pay the fees (Johnstone 2003; Vossensteyn 2004). If developments in the US are any guide to the profit potential opening up in Europe, one can only commend those financial services giants that get into the market early. Exhibiting all the features of other financial services (retail markets, securitisation markets, derivative markets), the largest banks charge students between four and eight percentage points more for money than they pay to buy it (from depositors, say). This provides them with gross profit margins of 100 to 200 per cent. In addition, they charge origination fees and other 'transactions' costs. Lower-cost loans are guaranteed by the government; if a student fails to service his/her debts, the government accepts the debt as its own. The costlier loans are usually guaranteed by the student's parents; if the student fails to service the debt, the parents are obligated to pay it. The risk is minimal and returns on the business are said to average 40 per cent.

The picture of the kind of university being produced by finance-led capital accumulation supplements those constructed from globalisation and neoliberal perspectives. What emerges is a sector in which the job security of academics may be hostage to the package deals negotiated by their cash-strapped librarians. It is one in which most of their students are (or soon will be) in thrall to multinational money lenders. It is also one in which university managers advocate more commercialisation as the answer to financial problems created by commercialisation processes they do not understand or would prefer to ignore (Ciancanelli 2006; Boden and Epstein 2005; Deem 2004).

The financialisation perspective offers a context for understanding the contradictory motivations for and the consequences of commercial intrusion in scholarly communication. It also brings to light the irrational processes, accidents and complex motives that secure its grip. In spite of this, as illustrated by the Open Access movement, there is a belief that the gift economy ought to govern relations between universities and society as a whole. In the words of the Budapest Open Access manifesto, 'An old tradition and a new technology have converged to make possible an unprecedented public good' (Budapest 2002: 1). What this chapter emphasises is that the realisation of this public good is thwarted by the intrusion of commerce into the very heart of scholarly conversation.

Notes

1 Financialisation is a loose concept, deployed by a broad range of heterodox economists and economic sociologists concerned with macroeconomic drivers of investment and employment. The characterisation of economic changes in the closing decades of the twentieth century as 'financialisation' has come to refer to the increased reliance of some developed economies on employment and income derived from the financial services sector (e.g. financial markets, insurance and real-estate, sometimes given the acronym 'FIRE') (Foster 2007; Williams 2000; Stockhammer 2004). FIRE activities are linked to the circulation of claims to value-added in other sectors of the economy.

2 Taxes remain an important source of finance for university systems worldwide. What varies is the mix of user fees (tuition, matriculation fees, etc.), charitable bequests (which are often motivated by tax avoidance) and direct government funding. For an overview, see Johnstone (2003).

3 Unlike job security in other nations, US tenure is a set of employment rights that form part of the individual's contract of employment and is granted to ensure complete freedom in their expression of ideas. The specifics of tenure differ from one university to another and from state-based employment laws. However, tenure is governed by covering laws at federal level of equality of opportunity, health and safety, etc.

4 This creates new commercial opportunities via making available to consumers digitised back issues of academic journals (Swan 2007).

5 There are approximately 26,000 different academic journals in circulation and roughly 3,000 publishers (Gooden *et al.* 2002). The large numbers of new journals created in business and management studies may reflect the fact that until recently these subjects were not considered academic disciplines.

6 Reed Elsevier's involvement in organising arms fairs is not something it publicises in the academic community. It is a sobering thought, however, that in submitting articles, refereeing or serving as an editor of any of its thousands of journals,

one is complicit in the corporate view that arms fairs are a perfectly respectable component of their knowledge dissemination business (see Hill 2007).

7 Librarians at many cash-strapped state universities have accepted deals because they remain the cheapest way to maintain access to core journals. In recent years, many of the top research universities (e.g. Harvard, MIT, California Institute of Technology) have refused the deals, paying more to subscribe to the core journals because doing so restored their control over their collections (Cal Tech 2007).

8 For a recent intervention that considers some related issues, see Besley and Peters (2004).

References

Association of Research Librarians (ARL) (2002) *ARL Statistics 2001–02*. Accessed at www.arl.org/bm-doc/arlstat02.pdf on 10 May 2007.

Association of Research Librarians (ARL) (2007) *Issues Brief*. Accessed at www. arl. org/issuebrief/2007 on 1 May 2007.

Bergstrom, C. and T. Bergstrom (2001) 'Do Electronic Site Licenses for Academic Journals Benefit the Scientific Community?', Working Paper, pp. 1–13. Accessed at www.ucsd/~Tedb/Journals/nature2.pdf on 10 May 2007.

Bergstrom, T. (2001) 'Free labor for costly journals?', *Journal of Economic Perspectives*, 15(4), Fall: 183–98.

Besley, T. and M. Peters (2004) *Performative Epistemologies: The Theatre of Fast Knowledge*, Glasgow: University of Glasgow.

Boden, R. and D. Epstein (2005) 'The absent minded professors or how universities forgot to think: The globalisation of managerialism and the management of globalisation in higher education'. Draft of paper given at ESRC Seminar Series, Geographies of Knowledge; Geometries of Power: Higher Education in the 21st Century, University of Wales, Cardiff, 18–19 January 2006.

Budapest Open Access Initiative (2002) at www.soros.org/openaccess/index.html. Accessed 10 May 2007.

California Digital Libraries (2003) 'STM and Elsevier Publishing Information'. Accessed at www.cdlib.org/ on 15 April 2007.

California Institute of Technology (Cal Tech) (2007) Scholarly communication. www.caltech.edu/scholarlycomm.html.

Ciancanelli, P. (2006) 'Hollow victory: globalisation and the commercialisation of higher education'. Seminar 2/3. ESRC Seminar Series, Geographies of Knowledge, Geometries of Power: Higher Education in the 21st Century, University of Wales, Cardiff, 10 July 2006, pp. 1–15.

Deem, R. (2004) 'The knowledge worker, the manager-academic and the UK university: new and old forms of public management', *Financial Accounting and Management*, 20(2): 107–28.

Edlin, A. and D. Rubinfeld (2004) 'Exclusion or efficient pricing? The "big deal" bundling of academic journals', *ABA: Antitrust LJ*, 72(1): 128–59. Accessed at www.law.berkeley.edu/faculty/rubinfeld on 10 May 2007.

Epstein, G. (ed.) (2005) *Financialization and the World Economy*, Northampton, MA: Edward Elgar.

Foster, J. B. (2007) 'The financialization of capitalism', *Monthly Review*, 58(11), March. http://www.marxsite.com/Finance_Capital.html. Accessed 14 May 2007.

Gooden, P., M. Owens and S. Simon (2002) 'Scientific publishing: knowledge is power', *Report on Media Industry*, Equity Research, Morgan Stanley Europe, 30 September, pp. 1–18.

Guedon, J.-C. (2001) 'Oldenburgh's long shadow: librarians, research scientists, publishers and the control of scientific publishing', www.arl.org/resources/pubs/ mmproceedings/138guedon.shtml. Accessed 15 May 2007.

Henwood, D. (2005) *After the New Economy*, New York: The New Press.

Hill. S. (2007) 'Laying down arms in Guardian Unlimited' (12 June) http:// commentisfree.guardian.co.uk/symon_hill/2007/06/laying_down_armsl.html. Accessed 20 August 2007.

Holcombe, R. (1997) 'A theory of the theory of public goods', *Review of Austrian Economics*, 10(1): 1–22.

Houghton, J. (2002) 'The crisis in scholarly communication: an economic analysis', http://www.vala.org.au/vala2002/2002pdf/16Houton.pdf. Accessed May 2007.

Johnstone, B. (2003) 'Cost sharing in higher education: tuition, financial assistance, and accessibility in a comparative perspective', *Czech Sociological Review*, 39(3): 351–74.

Kaul, I., I. Gruenberg and M. A. Stern (eds) (1999) *Global Public Goods*, New York: Oxford University Press.

Magdoff, F. (2006) 'The explosion of debt and speculation', *Monthly Review*, 58(6): 1–19.

Mort, D. (2005) 'Industry overview'. Accessed at www. irn-research.com on 18 May 2007.

Munroe, Mary H. (2004) *The Academic Publishing Industry: A Story of Merger and Acquisition*, DeKalb, IL: Northern Illinois University Libraries, www.niulib.niu. edu/publishers/ accessed March 2007.

Navaretti, G. B., P. Dasgupta and K. Maler (1996) 'On institutions that produce and disseminate knowledge'. Working Paper, Fondazione Eni Enrico Mattei (FEEM) http://www.feem.edu.it.

Noble, D. (1998) 'Digital diploma mills: the automation of higher education', http:// www.firstmonday.org/issues/issue3_1/noble/ at *FirstMonday: Peer Reviewed Journal on the Internet*. http://www.firstmonday.org/issues/issue3_1/noble/. Accessed 10 January 2007.

Peters, M. (2001) 'National education policy constructions of the knowledge economy: towards a critique', *Journal of Educational Enquiry*, 2(1): 1–22.

Readings, B. (1996) *The University in Ruins*, Cambridge, MA: Harvard University Press.

Ruth, S. (2006) 'Learning: a financial and strategic perspective', *EDUCAUSE Quarterly*, 29(1): 22–30. www.educause.edu/apps/eq/eqm06/eqm0615. asp?bhcp=1. Accessed 20 May 2007.

Samuelson, P. (1954) 'The pure theory of public expenditure', *Review of Economics and Statistics*, 36(4): 387–9.

Schoenenberg, A. (2004) 'Are higher education and academic research a public good or a public responsibility: review of the economics literature'. Council of Europe Conference on Public Responsibility for Higher Education and Research, 23–4 September, Strasburg, pp.1–39. www.bologna-bergen2005.no/EN/Bol_sem/ Seminars/040923-24Strasbourg/040923-24_programme.pdf.

Simbanet (2007) 'Report on STM publications'. Accessed at http://www.simbanet. com/publications/report_gstm.htm on 20 May 2007.

Soete, G. and A. Salaba (1998) 'Measuring journal cost effectiveness: ten years after Barschall', University of Wisconsin-Madison Report, pp. 10–13, http://www.library.wisc.edu/prospects/glsdo/costs.html.

Stiglitz, J. (1999) 'Knowledge as a public good', in I. Kaul, I. Gruenberg and M. A. Stern (eds) *Global Public Goods*, New York: Oxford University Press, pp. 308–25.

Stiglitz, J. (2004) 'Towards a pro-development and balanced intellectual property regime'. Keynote Address, Ministerial Conference on Intellectual Property for Least Developed Countries, World Intellectual Property Organisation (WIPO), Seoul, October, pp. 1–17.

Stockhammer, E. (2004) 'Financialization and the slowdown of accumulation', *Cambridge Journal of Economics*, 28(5): 719–41.

Strange, S. (1998) *Mad Money*, Manchester: Manchester University Press.

Swan, A. (2007) 'Open access and the progress of science', *American Scientist online*, May/June. Accessed at www.americanscientist.org on 15 May 2007.

Tobin, J. (1997) 'Comment', in Pollin, R. (ed.) *The Macroeconomics of Savings, Finance and Investment*, Ann Arbor, MI: University of Michigan Press.

University of California (UC) (2007a) *Annual Financial Report, 2004–05*. Accessed at www.universityofcalifornia.edu/finreports/index.php?file=/04-05/pdf/facts.pdf.

University of California (UC) (2007b) *The Promise of Value Based Journal Prices And Negotiations*. Libraries Collection Development Commission (January). Accessed at www.libraries.universityofcalifornia.edu/cdc.htm on 24 March 2007.

University of California Berkeley (UCB) (2004) *Scholarly Publishing-Crisis and Revolution*. Accessed at www.lib.berkeley.edu/collections/crisis.html on 2 May 2007.

Van Orsdal, L. and K. Born (2007) 'Serial wars – open access gains ground, STM publishers change tactics', *Library Journal*, May. Accessed www.libraryjournal.com/article/CA6431948.html.

Vossensteyn, H. (2004) 'Fiscal stress: worldwide trends in higher education financing', *NASFAAJ of Student Finance*, 34(1): 39–55.

Waks, L. (2002) 'In the shadow of the ruins: globalisation and the rise of corporate universities', *Policy Futures in Education*, 2(2): 278–98.

Wellcome Trust (2003) *An Economic Analysis of Scientific Research Publishing* (October), www.wellcome.ac.uk/doc_wtd003978.html. Accessed 10 May 2007.

Williams, K. (2000) 'From shareholder value to present day capitalism', *Economy and Society*, 29(1): 1–12.

Zell, H. (2003) 'The rise and rise of journal subscription prices in African studies', *Africana Libraries Newsletter*, No 111 (June–September), p. 8.

6 New tricks and old dogs?

The 'third mission' and the re-production of the university

Maria Nedeva

Introduction

During the last two decades or so universities around the world have been subjected to unprecedented exogenous pressures for change (Boden *et al.* 2004). These pressures are evident in a number of policy documents as well as observable in structural and ideological transformations (Lambert Review of Business–University Collaboration 2003; Nedeva and Boden 2006). The social uncertainty that pressures on universities have created is also reflected in growing controversies about the changing nature of the university (Etzkowitz 2002; Williams-Jones 2005; Hagen 2002; Martin and Etzkowitz 2000). While the extent to which the universities have responded to these pressures for change is debatable, it is apparent that many in the developed world (and beyond) have been charged with a different set of responsibilities, mainly associated with issues around wider participation, social engagement, and generally contribution to society and economy. This set of disparate activities is commonly referred to as the 'third mission' of the universities.

The rise of the 'third mission' of the universities is a global phenomenon. Governments in a number of countries including the UK, Australia, Sweden, Germany, Italy, Chile, Japan etc. have introduced policy measures to encourage the universities to develop their 'third stream' activities. The ways in which the 'third mission' is promoted vary substantially between countries. It can be backed by sizeable funding streams (as in the UK), supported mainly by discourses of usefulness, or encouraged by relative and absolute decline of public funding (as in Australia). The direction of the transformation in each case, however, is very similar and its essence is expressed by the steering of the universities to contribute systematically towards achieving economic and social goals and objectives.

Implicitly or explicitly, discussions of the third stream activities and the third mission convey certain messages. Here a distinction is made between three messages, namely that these activities are different from the ones already performed by the universities, that these activities are seen to be 'new' (whether they are or not) and that the 'third mission' is commensurate with the other two traditional missions of the universities, namely teaching and research.

In the rest of the chapter the 'third mission' of the universities is unpacked by distinguishing between 'activities' and 'organisational missions' and it is argued that though the 'third stream activities' are not new in themselves, re-framing these as a 'mission' creates new organisational imperatives. Also, the 'third mission' is defined in relational rather than functional terms. Defining the 'third mission' as a demand for interacting externally or establishing relationships with non-academic domains reveals that this process is not about the gradual absorption of new functions into the core of the university but about re-producing it. Finally, it is posited that the re-production of the university via 'third mission' activities can be mapped on a continuum from 'private for-profit university' to 'service provider' and examples of these are described using scenarios. While the evidence draws mainly on the UK, the overall arguments and conclusions have global significance because of the similar conditions and pressures developing in different national and trans-national contexts.

The global push ...

A global push for the increase of the interactions between universities, economy and society has been evident during the last decade or so. On the one hand, rhetoric about repositioning universities as global players in the 'knowledge society' and major contributors to 'economic competitiveness' and 'wealth creation' has come to dominate the policy domain of higher education and other public service domains too (e.g see Kwiek and Dale in this volume). Political expectations regarding the new third stream or mission role of the universities, and by implication the knowledge this can produce, using higher education institutions as 'economic engines' (Williams-Jones 2005), are formalised through policies and in some instances, supported by public funding.

The process of recasting the universities as direct and immediate agents of the 'knowledge society' is global in terms of geography (it can be detected empirically at regional, national and supranational levels) and in terms of its impact on organisations, structures, governance and concepts. It is symptomatic, for example, that recently

> ... national research, technology, and development (RTD) policies in Europe have converged on a number of initiatives aimed at transforming universities into central components of the knowledge infrastructure for innovation.
>
> (Jacob *et al.* 2003: 1555)

Similar developments in policy have been reported outside the European Higher Education Area, most notably in Australia (Biggs and Davis 2002), Chile (Bernasconi 2005), Japan (Yokoyama 2006) and Canada (Landry *et al.* 2006).

Policy documents and high-level reports increasingly refer explicitly to the changing role of the universities. So for example, in the UK, the 2003 Lambert Review of relations between higher education and industry stated that '... there has been a marked culture change in the UK's universities over the last decade ...' and went on to specify that universities are '... actively seeking to play a broader role in the national and regional economy ...' (Lambert Review of Business–University Collaboration 2003: 1). Moreover, the language the Review used to describe universities is reminiscent of descriptions of an industrial firm. Thus, the UK's universities will have to learn to identify better their 'areas of competitive strength'; they are advised to 'develop a code of governance'; and are considered to be in a good position 'to capitalise' on different global trends (Lambert Review of Business–University Collaboration 2003, *passim*).

Moreover, linking universities with issues of development, economic growth and the knowledge society is gaining prominence in documents and policies funded and supported by trans-national organisations (see also Dale in this volume). A simple search of the documents and reports of the World Bank Institute produced 155 papers containing the terms 'universities' and 'knowledge society' – 133 of these were produced during the last seven years or so. In one World Bank paper it is not only argued that the role of universities in Latin America has changed along 'third mission' lines, but the authors also propose that in Organisation for Economic Co-operation and Development (OECD) member countries the '... contribution of universities has developed well beyond applied and contract research ...' and '... borders, roles and division of tasks have become increasingly blurred ...' (Thorn and Soo 2006: 4). In Europe, the re-casting of the role of the universities is incorporated into the broader agenda of the Lisbon Agenda (or the Lisbon Process) which broadly aims to 'make Europe, by 2010, the most competitive and the most dynamic knowledge based economy in the world'. In this context, European universities are expected to provide the impetus for accelerated innovation through industry relevant research and through training the workers of the 'knowledge society'. To achieve that role, universities from different member states are re-aligning higher education degree programmes within the framework(s) provided by the Bologna Process and are encouraged to modernise along the lines suggested by the Commission of the European Community (Commission of the European Community 2006).

In terms of organisational change, the recasting of the universities as key players in the knowledge economy is signalled by the rise of the 'entrepreneurial university'. An impressive body of knowledge about the accelerated change of the universities along commercial lines has emerged during the last decade (Clark 1998, 2001; Etzkowitz 1994, 1998, 2002; Jacob *et al.* 2003; Marginson and Considine 2000; Yokoyama 2006) though some of the analyses have a rather thin empirical base (Deem 2001). Clark argues that there is a growing imbalance between the demands placed on universities and their ability to respond to these, which affects particularly strongly publicly funded universities. This imbalance creates an imperative for what Clark calls 'the entrepreneurial response' whereby universities revisit their functions, re-organise their activities and transform their structures to be able to meet the growing expectations for commercial relevance. The outcome is the 'entrepreneurial university' (Clark 1998). Similarly, Etzkowitz argues that the universities are '… undergoing a "second revolution" … incorporating economic and social development as part of their mission' (Etzkowitz 1998: 832). He goes on to argue that

> … The entrepreneurial university integrates economic development into the university as an academic function along with teaching and research. It is this 'capitalisation of knowledge' that is the heart of a new mission for the university, linking universities to users of knowledge more tightly and establishing the university as an economic actor in its own right.
>
> (Etzkowitz 1998: 833)

Jacob *et al.* define the entrepreneurial university through the structural transformation that the organisation has undergone. Hence, the 'entrepreneurial university' is

> … a university that has developed a comprehensive internal system for the commercialisation and commodification of knowledge. This system includes not just structures such as liaison or technology transfer offices … but also incentives for adjusting lines of study and the allocation of research budgets to the demand in the private and public sector.
>
> (Jacob *et al.* 2003: 1556)

Yokoyama also traces the 'entrepreneurial university' through organisational change affecting university governance, management and funding. The author goes on to identify five different types of entrepreneurial university (Yokoyama 2006: 528).

Marginson and Considine, using 17 case studies of universities in Australia were not surprised '… to find that an entrepreneurial spirit is now sweeping the cloisters'. What did surprise them, however, was '… the speed and extent of the changes now taking place' (Marginson and Considine 2000: 3). The authors posit that a new institutional type of university is emerging and that it is distinguished by the way its purpose is defined, by the advent of its corporate character, by the emergence of new and shadow governance and management structures and the development of 'pseudo-markets'.

This process of re-casting the universities as agents of the 'knowledge society' is also evidenced by shifts of emphasis in theoretical and empirical focus and new conceptual developments. Examples here are provided by the shift from 'science' to 'research' and from 'research' to 'innovation', and by conceptual developments such as the National Innovation/Research Systems (Freeman 1987; Lundvall 1988, 1992; Rip and van der Meulen 1995), the 'Mode 1 – Mode 2' concept of knowledge (Gibbons *et al.* 1994; Gibbons

2000; Nowotny *et al.* 2001) and the Triple Helix concept (Etzkowitz and Leydesdorff 1995; Leydesdorff and Etzkowitz 1996, 1998). While each of these concepts has been subject to critique (Shinn 2002; Boden *et al.* 2004), their policy significance and influence need to be acknowledged (Boden *et al.* 2004).

These global processes of re-casting the universities into new roles are being institutionalised in some countries by directing designated public funding streams to facilitate the interactions between universities and non-academic domains (especially with industry); by re-aligning public HE funding via the incorporation of requirements for external involvement and commercial relevance into the criteria for receiving funding and by institutionalising the emergence of the 'third' institutional mission.

Implicitly or explicitly, discussions of the third stream activities and the third mission tend to convey three key messages: that these activities are substantially different from the ones in which the universities have been traditionally involved; that they are 'new' activities; and that the 'third' mission is commensurate with the other two missions of the universities. How far do these messages stand up to scrutiny?

What is the 'third mission' of universities?

Firstly, existing definitions are explored. Then, using an analytical distinction between 'activities' and organisational 'missions', it is argued that although third stream activities are not necessarily new, re-framing these as a third university mission creates new imperatives. The possibility to define the 'third mission' as a function (or even a set of functions) is also disputed and a 'relational' definition is proposed instead.

Theoretical and policy perspectives on the third mission

While the third stream of university activities have been only very loosely defined, there appears to be a general agreement that these are about the involvement of universities with non-academic domains. Some writers emphasise the requirement for the higher education institutions to provide the conditions for achieving government policies regarding '… regional competitiveness; urban and rural regeneration; lifelong learning and employability; social wellbeing and health; sustainability and environment; and regional decision making' (Jones 2002). Others have discussed the third mission as recognition of the necessity for universities to 'get out', to 'reach out' and increase their involvement and input into '… achieving widening participation and social inclusion, employability, knowledge transfer and wealth generation and cultural contribution' (Floud 2003). The third mission has also been defined as a

> … stream of activities … concerned with the generation, use, application and exploitation of knowledge and other university capabilities outside

academic environments. In other words, the Third Stream is about the interaction between universities and the rest of society.

(Molas-Gallart *et al.* 2002: ii–iv)

Nedeva and Boden discuss the third mission as '… part of the neo-liberal rhetoric of the state for usefulness of science and an expression of the drive for control and immediate application' (Nedeva and Boden 2006: 275). They go on to argue that the third mission is also an expressed attempt of the state to offload some of the responsibility for funding academic science onto non-academic domains, especially industry. This is achieved through encouraging universities to develop facilities and infrastructures which facilitate direct links with industry.

Given the fairly general definitions of the 'third mission' and the 'third level activities' it is not surprising that most authors and policy bodies have placed their emphasis on either its commercial aspects or on the broader social engagement and wider participation agenda. Moreover, the third mission '… is often equated with knowledge transfer narrowly defined as licensing and commercialization of research' (Thorn and Soo 2006); these authors go on to suggest it should also include advanced education.

The UK Higher Education Funding Council for Wales (HEFCW) accord third mission activities a role to '… stimulate and direct the application and exploitation of knowledge to the benefit of the social, cultural and economic development of our society' (Arthur 2004: 4). The Higher Education Funding Council for England (HEFCE), on the other hand, emphasises the commercial aspects of the third stream activities by specifying that HE institutions are funded to '… increase their capability to respond to the needs of business and the wider community, where this would lead to wealth creation'. Moreover, as part of HEFCE's strategic development, the possibility of re-launching the 'third stream' as a *second* mission (after teaching but before research) is under discussion.

There have been attempts to pinpoint the 'third mission' by developing analytical frameworks demarcating the boundaries within which third stream activities can occur. One such attempt is the framework developed by Molas-Gallart *et al.* (2002) in the process of developing indicators for measuring third stream activities. The framework builds upon the distinction between university capabilities and university activities, identifying, on the one hand, knowledge capabilities and facilities, and on the other research, teaching and communication (Molas-Gallart *et al.* 2002: v–vi). The authors identify twelve categories of third stream activities ranging from 'technology commercialisation' to 'non-academic dissemination'. While it is a worthwhile attempt to specify the third stream, so that success and failure can be measured and (possibly) controlled, this framework has some deficiencies. The most obvious one is that it emphasises the commercial side of the third stream activities but fails to account for university interaction with other non-academic domains. Another obvious problem is that the twelve categories are not self-explanatory and lack internal demarcation criteria.

Another attempt to develop a framework for the third stream was made by Arthur (2004: 7). This framework uses as a starting point the two core activities of the universities, namely teaching and research, and translates these in the context of benefits for the economy and benefits for society at large. The result is a fairly balanced list of activities on the intersection between universities and their traditional functions, economy and society. However, this attempt falls into the functionalist trap of confusing function and cause and does not provide demarcation criteria.

Attempts to distinguish the 'third stream' and the 'third mission' often do so through 'defining' by example. Where more serious, analytical attempts to unpack the 'third mission' have been made (usually as part of a broader evaluation and accountability agenda) these build upon functionalist assumptions thus making it difficult to establish inherent demarcation criteria and leaving fuzzy boundaries. Indeed some authors have drawn attention to the potentially serious consequences that the fuzziness associated with the third mission of the universities could have (Jacob *et al.* 2003; Nedeva and Boden 2006).

Is the 'third mission' really new?

The debates around the third stream activities are to a degree framed by an implicit assumption that the contribution of the universities towards the achievement of societal and economic aims is a relatively recent phenomenon that has become particularly visible in the last two decades. Thus, assumptions regarding the novelty of external engagement shape the accounts of the two main camps involved in discussions about the future of the university (Martin and Etzkowitz 2000). On the one hand, there are the 'pessimists' who believe that the future of the university, and even knowledge production as we know it, is under threat as a result of pressures to develop third mission activities. Some 'pessimists' draw attention to the possible loss of university autonomy (Ziman 1991, 1994; Pelikan 1992) while others link the pressures on universities to an overall transformation likely to affect their very capacity to produce knowledge (Nedeva and Boden 2006). The 'optimists', on the other hand, draw attention to the opportunities afforded to the universities in the wake of the so-called 'knowledge society' (Stehr 1994). They see the rise of the 'knowledge society' and correspondingly the third stream activities as a unique opportunity for the universities to become central players both in research and teaching, and training (Martin and Etzkowitz 2000). Novelty also underpins the conceptualisation of the latest transformations of the university in terms of a 'changing social contract' (Guston and Keniston 1994).

Is the set of activities arising in the context of the interactions between the university and non-academic domains really new? Martin and Etzkowitz (2000) argue that the engagement of universities with non-academic domains, and more specifically with industry, is not a new phenomenon and that university functions have always evolved to incorporate new tasks. Examples are provided by the broadening of scholarship to incorporate the creation of new knowledge, and later branching this into 'knowledge for its own sake' and 'knowledge intended to meet societal needs' (Martin and Etzkowitz, 2000: 16). Moreover, the authors assert, historically many universities have gone through periods of close relationships with non-academic domains followed by periods of cooler, more distant links.

Etzkowitz (1997: 141–3) also posits that the third stream activities are not only a phenomenon of the late twentieth century. Indeed, he provides historical evidence that third mission activities were probably more pronounced in the nineteenth century universities than today. Williams-Jones (2005) goes even further to argue that the universities have never been the closed institutions that Merton imagined them to be:

> [the] ... 'Ivory Tower' protected from external influences and conducting research based on the institutional imperatives of disinterestedness, communism, organised scepticism and universalism has always been a myth; ... and ... the reality is that academic research is invariably conducted in and responsive to the larger community.
>
> (Williams-Jones, 2005: 249)

While content with the overall direction of the arguments presented here, it is suggested that if the novelty of these processes is to be discussed usefully, one ought to distinguish between 'third stream activities' and the re-frame of these activities as one of the missions of contemporary universities. When viewed as 'a set of activities' the 'third stream' is not new. There is a long history of a relationship between universities, society and industry.

To begin with, it is apparent that the main 'products' of the university – namely education and scholarship or research – have invariably been found ultimately 'useful'. It is true, however, that this usefulness has either been mediated – through labour markets, for example – or there has been a notable delay between the development of understanding and explanation, and their subsequent application for the achievement of social and economic goals.

Secondly, for the best part of their history universities have been sensitive to the needs of society and economy and even the more basic 'understanding' knowledge that they produce has often been informed by practical problems. Indeed, the very emergence of the university as an institution can be seen as a response to societal needs and imperatives – on the one hand the need for educated clerical intelligentsia, and on the other the need for educated state administrators (Kearney 1970). The emergence and development of the civic universities in the UK is another albeit more recent example of the engagement of the universities with non-academic domains. The civic universities were initially set up with industrial money and their mission statements explicitly stated their intention to contribute to the development of industry by training the workforce and by conducting industry relevant research (Sanderson 1972). During the nineteenth century, universities in Germany, the United States and Japan also experienced similar developments.

For example, in German universities '... engineering departments worked very closely with companies in the mechanical engineering, civil engineering, chemical engineering ...' (Martin and Etzkowitz 2000: 22). However, national differences still remain. Mowery, comparing the economic performance of Britain and the United States, concludes that one of the factors explaining the difference is that universities in the United States have been historically more sensitive to the needs of industry in both education and research terms (Mowery 1984).

And thirdly, throughout most of their history, universities have been directly involved with society and economy. Until relatively recently the direct links between universities and industry happened on an ad hoc basis and usually resulted from the efforts and activities of the so-called 'cross-over' personalities. Newton, for example, worked on the problem of longitude, which was very important for navigation and the Royal Navy, and Marie Curie spent up to half her time working on industrial or industry related problems.

Seen as a set of activities the 'third stream' is not new but, on the contrary, the story of the university is inextricably intertwined with the story of its responsiveness to society and economy. This probably explains, at least in part, the success of the university as an institution and its persistence. What is 'new', however, is the re-framing of this set of activities as the 'third' mission of the university.

There are three substantive differences between the activities of an organisation and its missions. To begin with, missions usually involve a necessary degree of compulsion. In the context of the third mission, this means that universities no longer engage with non-academic domains and contribute to the economy in a serendipitous and unpredictable manner, but are expected to do so. These expectations are normally enforced in some way. Practices in this respect vary. In the UK, the process is promoted by the parallel existence of a public funding squeeze and the designation of public funding to universities specifically to develop the necessary infrastructure for the third mission[2] (Nedeva and Boden 2006). In Australia, financial pressure rather than infrastructure support plays a major role (Biggs and Davis 2002). Providing financial support for the development of third mission capabilities from the public purse also means that imperatives for evaluating and assessing its institutionalisation have developed. This is evidenced by attempts to develop indicators measuring third stream activities (Molas-Gallart *et al.* 2002).

Secondly, re-framing the third stream activities as a third mission makes the expectations for productive involvement with society and economy not only and simply global but also universal. Expectations for direct contribution to the local or global economy, for example, are universal in that they apply indiscriminately to all research fields and types of knowledge, as well as to all universities. These do not account for the specific features of the universities as organisations (whether these are predominantly teaching or research led, for example) or for their specialisation (whether these have competence predominantly in the traditional sciences, new sciences or social sciences and humanities).

And last but not least, re-framing the third stream activities as a mission moves them from the institutional periphery to the very core of the universities. Hence, ensuring that universities contribute to economy and society is presented – and in time becomes – as having (in institutional terms) equal standing as teaching and training, and research. Incorporating another set of activities into the core of the university as an institution demands change of institutional scripts. New rules supporting academic entrepreneurship have started to emerge and incentives encouraging academics to account for the commercial impact of both their teaching and research are being introduced. It is symptomatic, for example, that most universities in the UK have included 'knowledge transfer' among the criteria for promotion.

To summarise, in the specialised literature the 'third stream' and the 'third mission' have been only very loosely defined. There appears to be a broad agreement, however, that these terms refer to a set of activities arising in the context of the interactions between the universities and non-academic domains. A marked tendency to use 'third stream' or 'third mission' in their narrow interpretation as 'knowledge transfer' between universities and industry or as commercialisation of research can also be discerned. We argued that seen as 'a set of activities' the 'third stream' is not new and can be traced almost to the beginning of the university. Re-framing these activities as a university mission, however, creates new imperatives and institutional challenges. But even more importantly presenting the third mission as a set of 'new' activities and/or functions diverts attention from the fact that it creates demands for change of the already existing activities and functions of the university.

A relational definition

At the most general level the 'third stream' can be defined as the set of activities arising in the context of the interaction of the universities with non-academic domains. When re-framed as an institutional mission, however, the emphasis ceases to be on the 'set of activities' and shifts to the 'interactions'. In other words, the third mission of the universities is fundamentally about their fruitful interactions with industry and society – the activities included in the 'third stream' are the means rather than the goal. Thus, if the third mission of the universities is to be understood and at least some of its implications usefully discussed it ought to be defined not in functional but in relational terms. All definitions of the third mission of the universities that were discussed either do not distinguish between activities and missions or equate functions and missions. Here the third mission is defined in relational terms, as the institutional imperative of the university to engage in a variety of exchanges with non-academic domains thus establishing different kinds of relationships with societal and economic/industrial agents.

Presenting the third mission as a new set of activities masks the fact that it is not about the gradual absorption of new functions by the university but it is about dramatically altering the way in which the university carries out its existing activities. The change of the ways in which the existing functions are perceived and the transformation of its traditional activities is achieved by changing the relationships (and type of exchange) in which the university is involved.

In terms of teaching, for example, the third mission creates an overall imperative for a shift from providing social and cultural capital to professional elites to preparing the workers of the knowledge society by equipping them with fairly practical and technical skills and knowledge. Here universities can enter into different types of relationships with social or industrial agents. One type of relationship, for example, is predicated on the exchange of undergraduate degree programmes developed without the direct involvement of users, for funding. While these degrees by necessity will reflect perceived and interpreted user needs the relationship is still usually mediated by labour markets. Another possibility for establishing a relationship is one founded on an exchange of a degree programme or a course developed with direct participation of the user and partially or fully funded by them. There is some empirical evidence that the latter is becoming more widespread (Howells *et al.* 1998; CURDS 2000; HEFCE). This emerging imperative for direct relationship(s) and exchange between universities and non-academic domains is also evidenced by the fact that currently in the UK one of the key ways of assessing the success or failure of universities is judged by surveys of graduate first job destinations.

In terms of research and knowledge the third mission creates imperatives for an overall shift from the universities selling or gifting what they have already produced to the universities producing what can be sold. In particular, this can be seen as consisting of two inter-dependent parts. On the one hand, if the universities are to survive as organisations they need to raise funding streams from non-government sources. In the UK, as well as in other countries, the main source of non-public funding for the universities is industry and the proportion of university funding originating directly with industry has been steadily increasing (HEFCE). Where relationships with industry are concerned, different types of exchange are possible. Thus one possibility is the exchange of 'understanding' knowledge for money. Another possibility is the exchange of routine services, like consultancy, measurement and calibration for money. These obviously would have different implications for the university as an institution – whereas the former does not substantively affect its core, the latter is very likely to create imperatives for organisational change. Even more importantly, public funding streams are being re-aligned to respond to third mission pressures; the UK is an example of this. As a result, the proportion of public funding that reaches universities without prior contractual obligations involving society and economy is progressively decreasing. Consequently, university research is by and large no longer simply informed by 'problems' but rather its directions are shaped by the availability of funding.

What follows from this definition is that the third mission is not commensurate with the other two university missions. While teaching and research are functional and can be defined by a set of activities, the third mission of the universities is relational and cannot be outlined by a set of activities. Incorporating the third mission into the core of the university as an institution is not about the organic absorption of new functions – something universities are very good at – but about a radical change of its existing functions as a result of its transformed relationships.

The third mission, therefore, is about the re-production of the university. Whether the old dog is going to learn the new tricks or the dog will re-produce its 'self' to emerge like a Phoenix from the remains of the university cannot be said.

The re-production of the university

Elsewhere in this chapter, I argued that the 'third stream' or the 'third mission' have been defined only very generally and that seen as a set of activities these are not particularly new. Where clear differences emerge is at the point of re-framing this set of activities as a third mission of the university. It was also suggested that the relational nature of the third mission implies that the imperatives for change it poses are not about the gradual absorption of new functions into the core of the university but about transforming the way into which core university functions are being carried out.

Here I turn my attention to the re-production of the university. The future of the university as an institution and the development trajectories of different universities are uncertain. One might reasonably expect, however, that transformations reaching beyond the 'second academic revolution' and the 'entrepreneurial' universities are likely to occur. These changes are also likely not only to affect the universities but also to have clear implications for the knowledge our societies produce as well as for the conditions of its use.

It is possible, for example, to envisage a situation where, following from demands and expectations for the immediate industrial application of knowledge and for increased direct involvement of universities in wealth creation, public funding for 'understanding' type research reaches sub-critical level. In such a case, universities will either stop conducting research leading to 'understanding' knowledge or, more likely, they will continue to do that using private funding. On the one hand, the second option is a marker of the ultimate success of the 'third stream' and a sign that universities have successfully incorporated the 'third mission' into their core. On the other hand, conducting 'understanding' research using private funding means that the results are a 'private' rather than a 'public' good. This in turn is likely to affect adversely the development of science, the economic value of knowledge, the ability of the universities, and other research organisations to produce 'transforming knowledge' and the rationale for industrial support for research in universities. There are also moral arguments for preserving substantial parts of knowledge as 'public' goods.

How higher education institutions react to the pressures for closer engagement with non–academic domains, or the 'rules of engagement', is likely to depend on the nature of the domain (industry, local community, wider participation etc.), the current position of the university and the type of exchange. Here we focus on the interactions between universities and industry.

In the context of the relationships between universities and industry one possible implication of the third mission is a further differentiation of universities. One line of differentiation is the amount of funding from industry that different universities attract. Here, data already suggests that there is a significant concentration whereby a dozen or so universities account for almost half of the total funding from industry (Howells *et al.* 1998; CURDS, 2000). Another possible line of differentiation is whether the university is teaching-oriented or research-led. Yet another dimension relates to the type of exchange that the universities enter and can be expressed as 'selling what one already has' and 'producing what one might be able to sell'.

Accounting for these dimensions for differentiation, we believe that as a result of the third mission universities could be positioned on a continuum from 'private for-profit universities' to 'service providers'. Naturally the end points of the continuum are 'ideal' types and most organisations will combine features from both. To explicate this point further we offer two scenarios for the re-production of the university.

The private for-profit university

The University of Infinite Wisdom has a long and distinguished history. Being one of the earliest universities in the country it developed through the centuries by gradually, though sometimes belatedly, adapting to the 'outside' world, and its demands and expectation. It acknowledged progress and modern science, developed research capacity and even accepted, at least for some time, that the way in which it uses its funds will be monitored and that its accounts will be subject to public scrutiny.

Through its history, however, the University of Infinite Wisdom always maintained high academic standards in both teaching and research. These high standards translated into an enviable external reputation. The University was respected not only by other academic and research institutions but also by industry. This became particularly important when all universities were expected to interact with industry and to contribute to wealth creation. Many people watched from the sidelines expecting the University of Infinite Wisdom to fail and get into financial problems, to claim exclusivity to attract public funding or to start calling in favours and depending on its historical networks. What happened surprised the sceptics but not the leadership of the university.

As early as the early 1990s the leadership of the university saw that the policy pressure for closer interactions with industry is not necessarily a threat but in fact might be a unique opportunity. The extent to which this were to be an opportunity, however, depended on the positioning of the university and a very specific and clear understanding as to what industry really wants.

In terms of positioning the University of Infinite Wisdom already had a strong research and teaching reputation. What it needed was to develop the research areas yielding the highest economic return for research (and teaching) that the university already undertook. The leadership of the University saw that one such area of research is bio-sciences and started to develop it in strategic manner. Hence, research groups in the bio-sciences were started, PhD schools in the area developed, and undergraduate programmes were set up. Considerable effort was made to attract public funding to support the laboratories including the research infrastructure. Before too long the University started reaping the results – several of the groups established themselves as world leaders in their respective areas. They not only published their work but also started to patent it. Spill-over effects were also visible in other areas of academic enquiry. Ultimately spin-off companies were started by university academics which was of mutual financial benefit to them and to the university.

Hence, the leadership of the University of Infinite Wisdom actively promoted commercialisation of research and academic entrepreneurship from the outset. This, however, was based on the understanding that what industry needs in terms of research ranges from deeper understanding to frameworks for problem solving. What industry might want but is not prepared to pay much for is immediate problem solving. In terms of teaching, it was accepted that industry needs 'thinking' capable employees rather than people with a narrow set of technical skills.

Founding the interactions of the University with industry on such understanding soon led to contracts whereby knowledge intensive large firms supported particular research groups to conduct 'understanding' research. On the teaching side, industrial firms started setting up a number of studentships (particularly at PhD level).

By 2007, through its commercialisation activities, the University of Infinite Wisdom has amassed considerable wealth. In fact the University currently operates as a private university, outside government frameworks and regulations. Having independent wealth, the University can attract the best minds in different areas, to invest in areas neglected by public funding and to counteract state pressures it considers as being detrimental to academic standards in research and teaching.

The University of Infinite Wisdom transformed itself by 'selling what it already had'. Wealth ensures that research at the University continues to be at the forefront and that the reputation of the organisation in academic and industrial circles has in fact increased. Moreover, the University did not need to transform its research practices as part of its third mission – the only thing that changed is the source of funding. While everyone recognises that the

University of Infinite Wisdom has managed to commercialise its research and teaching without considerable organisational implication, few worry about the broader implications of such developments.

Even fewer people have noticed or mention that the University of Infinite Wisdom while preserving its wisdom has transformed its soul – the knowledge it produces is no longer a 'public good'.

Service provider

The University of Prose and Packaging was set up in the mid-twentieth century as part of the expansion of higher education. The University quickly established as a regional player in education and research. Its reputation and relative prosperity were embedded in its engagement with the local community and interactions with local industry. The University of Prose and Packaging, however, was never a global player in teaching or research; it never gained the academic reputation of institutions like the University of Infinite Wisdom.

Towards the end of the twentieth century, the government introduced policies encouraging all universities to compete for resources and to operate along similar sets of requirements. Thus, to attract public funding for research the University of Prose and Packaging had to compete with the University of Infinite Wisdom, whereby one of the criteria was international reputation of research. Another set of pressures required all universities to contribute directly to wealth creation.

The University of Prose and Packaging saw these demands as different and to a degree conflicting. On the one hand, it was apparent from the outset that the University could not compete successfully for scarce public resources for research. On the other hand, the University leadership believed that the University was quite successful in raising funding from local industry and other agents, notably local government.

The University of Prose and Packaging allocated significant internal resources to trying to build its research capacity. In an attempt to achieve this fairly quickly the University started trying to 'buy' research stars. Soon, however, it became apparent that this strategy succeeded mainly in research areas where research performance is still to an extent an individual achievement and does not require costly equipment or other infrastructure. In other words, the University of Prose and Packaging successfully 'imported' academic stars in the social sciences but not in the 'new' sciences. Even in the social sciences and humanities, the 'imported' academics did not make much difference in terms of increasing the standing of the academic unit overall – in fact the University ended up having, in some cases, exceptional researchers in weak departments. It was soon acknowledged that the overall competitive position of the University in terms of 'understanding' research was not much improved.

The University of Prose and Packaging maintained and even developed further its links with local industry. The leadership of the University perceived its strength in being able to provide solutions to industry. In terms of education the University saw its niche in equipping its students with fairly practical knowledge and technical skills.

Because of these choices and its disadvantageous initial position the University of Prose and Packaging started operating as a service provider, mainly but not exclusively for industry. Industrial firms sought interactions with the University based on the exchange of consultancy or routine services for money. In many cases the ensuing contracts were not in recognition of specific competence but because of other considerations – cheaper labour, for example. In terms of research, the University started offering degrees that had been developed with direct input from industry and focusing mainly on the skills needed by employees in particular companies or industrial sectors.

These developments made the University of Prose and Packaging extremely vulnerable and significantly weakened its position in respect to both the state and industry. On the one hand, being under continuous financial pressure, the University was very dependent on public funding for teaching, research and post-graduate teaching and training. On the other hand, because of its failure to develop 'understanding' research capacity, its competitive advantage had diminished even further. One way to compensate was to bring more income from industry for both teaching and research. Thus, in terms of research the University started to provide consultancy or other services moving into the space vacated by the privatised Government Research Establishments and competing with private consultancy firms. More often than not University teams won externally funded contracts on price rather than competence. In terms of teaching, becoming a provider of knowledge and skills specified by industry the University started to compete with other providers.

There was a time when the University of Prose and Packaging had a clear identity and was an organisation respected by the local community and valued by local enterprise. Today, although the University serves local enterprise, its identity is gone and with it its value and the respect it used to inspire.

Conclusion

In this chapter it has been argued that presenting the third mission of the universities as a new set of activities or functions masks the fact that it is not about the continuous and gradual absorption of new activities and functions into the core of the university. On the contrary, the third mission, by demanding the re-casting of the relationships between the universities and non-academic domains, transforms its existing functions, thus re-producing it.

The third mission of the universities, it was argued, is not commensurate with its other two missions, namely teaching and research. The new relationships of the university ensuing from imperatives created by the third mission are outlined by new types of exchange ranging from 'selling the research done anyway' to 'researching into what can be sold'. It was posited that the concrete form that the re-production of different universities could take depends on their current position and can be mapped on a continuum between 'private for-profit university' and 'service provider'.

The scenarios of the two fictional universities that were developed to illustrate the kind of processes that might take place are 'ideal types'. In reality one ought to expect to find some combination between features of the two. Overall though, the message is that one can expect research universities with a high reputation for 'understanding' research, particularly in the 'new' sciences, to be in a strong position to develop their third mission to advantage and amass independent but reproducible wealth. This wealth helps the institution to maintain and even gain autonomy, and to appear unchanged. In fact the 'private university' has transformed its soul in that the heart of its continued success is knowledge as a 'private good'.

Notes

1 The Bologna Accord aims to harmonise the higher education systems of 40 European countries. This would be achieved by creating a single system of degrees, within a specified framework and with a consistent credit and grading system.
2 In the UK the public funding stream to support the development of the necessary infrastructure and to make the activities under the third mission (mainly interactions with industry) self-sustaining is substantial. About £140 million has been allocated through the Higher Education Innovation Fund (HEIF) alone.

References

Arthur, L. (2004) 'Annual report to the Higher Education Funding Council for Wales'.

Bernasconi, A. (2005) 'University entrepreneurship in a developing country: the case of the P. Universitad Catolica de Chile, 1985–2000', *Higher Education*, 50: 247–74.

Biggs, J. and R. Davis (2002) *The Subversion of Australian Universities*, Wollongong Fund for Intellectual Dissent.

Boden, R., D. Cox, M. Nedeva and K. Barker (2004) *Scrutinising Science: The Changing UK Government of Science*, Basingstoke: Palgrave Macmillan.

Clark, B. R. (1998) *Creating Entrepreneurial Universities: Organisational Pathway of Transformation*, New York: Elsevier.

Clark, B. R. (2001) 'The entrepreneurial university: new foundations for collegiality, autonomy, and achievement', *Higher Education Management*, 13(2): 9–24.

Commission of the European Community (2006) 'Delivering on the modernisation agenda for universities: education, research and innovation', Brussels: COM (2006) 208 Final.

CURDS (2000) *Higher Education – Business Interaction Survey*, Report to HEFCE.

Deem, R. (2001) 'Globalisation, new managerialism, academic capitalism and entrepreneurialism in universities: is the local dimension still important?', *Comparative Education*, 37(1): 7–20.

Etzkowitz, H. (1994) 'Knowledge as property: the Massachusetts Institute of Technology and the debate over academic patent policy', *Minerva*, 32(4), Winter: 383–421.

Etzkowitz, H. (1997) 'The entrepreneurial university and the emergence of democratic capitalism', in H. Etzkowitz and L. Leydesdorff (eds) *Universities and the Global Knowledge Economy*, Science, Technology and the International Political Economy Series, London: Cassell Academic.

Etzkowitz, H. (1998) 'The norms of entrepreneurial science: cognitive effects of the new university–industry linkages', *Research Policy*, 27: 823–33.

Etzkowitz, H. (2002) *MIT and the Rise of Entrepreneurial Science*, London: Routledge.

Etzkowitz, H. and L. Leydesdorff (1995) 'The triple helix of university–industry–government relations: a laboratory for knowledge based economic development', *EASST Review*, 14(1): 11–19.

Floud, R. (2003) Universities UK on www.universitiesuk.ac.uk/speeches/.

Freeman, C. (1987) *Technology and Economic Performance: Lessons from Japan*, London: Pinter Publishers.

Gibbons, M. (2000) 'Mode 2 society and the emergence of context-sensitive science', *Science and Public Policy*, 27(3): 159–63.

Gibbons, M., H. Nowotny, C. Limoges, M. Trow, S. Schwartzman and P. Scott (1994) *The New Production of Knowledge: The Dynamics of Science and Research in Contemporary Societies*, London: Sage Publications.

Guston, D. H. and K. Keniston (eds) (1994) *The Fragile Contract*, Cambridge, MA and London: MIT Press.

Hagen, R. (2002) 'Globalization, university transformation and economic regeneration: a UK case study of public/private sector partnership', *International Journal of Public Sector Management*, 15(3): 2004–218.

HEFCE, 'Higher Education-Business and Community Interaction Survey', on http://www.hefce.ac.uk/reachout/hebci/.

Howells, J., M. Nedeva and L. Georghiou (1998) *Academy–Industry Links in the UK*, HEFCE.

Jacob, M., M. Lundqvist and H. Hellsmark (2003) 'Entrepreneurial transformations in the Swedish university system: the case of Chalmers University of Technology', *Research Policy*, 32: 1555–68.

Jones, G. (2002) *The Third Mission Creating a Business Culture for Higher Education in Wales*, Cardiff: Institute of Welsh Affairs.

Kearney, H. (1970) *Scholars and Gentlemen: Universities and Society in Pre-industrial Britain 1500–1700*, London: Faber and Faber.

Lambert Review of Business–University Collaboration (2003) Final Report, December, London: HMSO.

Landry R., N. Amara and I. Rherrad (2006) 'Why are some university researchers more likely to create spin-offs than others? Evidence from Canadian universities', *Research Policy*, 35: 1599–615.

Leydesdorff, L. and H. Etzkowitz (1996) 'Emergence of a triple helix of university–industry–government relations', *Science and Public Policy*, 23(5): 279–86.

Leydesdorff, L. and H. Etzkowitz (1998) 'Triple helix of innovation: introduction', *Science and Public Policy*, 25(6): 358–64.

Lundvall, B. A. (1988) 'Innovation as an interactive process – from user–producer interaction to national systems of innovation', in G. Dosi, C. Freeman, R. Nelson, G. Silverberg and L. Soete (eds) *Technical Change and Economic Theory*, London: Pinter Publishers.

Lundvall, B. A. (1992) *National Systems of Innovation: Towards a Theory of Innovation and Interactive Learning*, London: Pinter Publishers.

Marginson, S. and M. Considine (2000) *The Enterprise University: Power, Governance and Reinvention in Australia*, Cambridge: Cambridge University Press.

Martin, B. and H. Etzkowitz (2000) 'The origin and evolution of the university species', *Journal for Science and Technology Studies*, 13(3–4): 9–34.

Molas-Gallart, J., A. Salter, P. Patel, A. Scott and X. Duran (2002) 'Measuring third stream activities', Final Report to the Russell Group Universities.

Mowery, D. C. (1984) 'Firm structure, government policy, and the organization of industrial research: Great Britain and the United States, 1900–1950', *The Business History Review*, 58(4) (Winter): 504–31.

Nedeva, M. and R. Boden (2006) 'Changing science: the advent of neo-liberalism', *Prometheus*, 24(3), September: 269–81.

Nowotny, H., P. Scott and M. Gibbons (2001) *Re-thinking Science: Knowledge and the Public in an Age of Uncertainty*, London: Polity Press.

Pelikan, J. (1992) *The Idea of the University: A Re-examination*, New Haven, CT: Yale University Press.

Rip, A. and B. J. R. van der Meulen (1995) 'The post-modern research system', *Science and Public Policy*, 23: 343–52.

Sanderson, M. (1972) *Universities and British Industry 1850–1970*, London: Routledge and Kegan Paul.

Shinn, T. (2002) 'The triple helix and the new production of knowledge: prepackaged thinking on science and technology', *Social Studies of Science*, 32(4): 599–614.

Stehr, N. (1994) *Knowledge Societies*, London: Sage.

Thorn, K. and M. Soo (2006) 'Latin American universities and the third mission', World Bank Policy Research Working Paper 4002, August.

Williams-Jones, B. (2005) 'Knowledge commons or economic engine – what's a university for?', *Journal of Medical Ethics*, 31: 249–50.

Yokoyama, K. (2006) 'Entrepreneurialism in Japanese and UK universities: governance, management, leadership, and funding', *Higher Education*, 52: 523–55.

Ziman, J. (1991) 'Academic science as a system of markets', *Higher Education Quarterly*, 12: 57–68.

Ziman, J. (1994) *Prometheus Bound: Science in a Dynamic Steady State*, Cambridge: Cambridge University Press.

Part II

Supplying knowledge

Rebecca Boden

The attempted and ongoing reconstitution of the majority of the world's universities as globalised knowledge-creating corporate actors strutting the stage of the globalised knowledge economy is much in evidence. This organisational repositioning from the realm of the gift economy (Kenway *et al.* 2006) to that of the free market generates readily visible consequences such as the commodification of knowledge, the corporatisation of universities and their massification (for discussions of these consequences see Baskaran and Boden 2007; Boden and Epstein 2006).

These visible consequences are the direct and intended product of the inexorable introduction of an underlying 'industrial-capitalist architecture of knowledge creation on the sector' (Boden and Epstein 2006: 228). An essential aspect of this architecture is the re-positioning of universities as globally competitive marketplace actors capable of profitably selling their teaching and research knowledge products to suitable paying 'customers'. Implicit in this reconstitution of universities as knowledge-trading organisations is a commensurate and commutative transformation of students and the other social and economic stakeholders in higher education's knowledge product into 'customers'. In the new globalised higher education order universities and those they have always benefited are translated into supply–demand actors locked in a binary and dialogic relationship. By such means the 'free' market in knowledge creation and education is framed by a series of supply–demand relationships of a classical, liberal nature.

Of course, a central theme of neoliberalism is that such transformations of essentially non-market contemporary organisations and their would-be 'customers' require very significant exogenously-driven interventions (Rose 1999; Dean 1999; Boden and Epstein 2006). This part of the *World Yearbook* explores the ways in which individual states, transnational organisations and supra-national entities have, on a global scale, sought to effect the re-forming of universities as free market supplier organisations.

Such transition necessitates structural and cultural change on at least four levels: globally regulated marketplaces, quality assurance, control over labour and, finally, participation, partnership and mobility across organisational boundaries in pursuit of innovation and continuous improvement. These are the core characteristics of any globalised business entity and the environment in which they seek to operate. The four chapters in this part (from Spain, Finland, the UK and Australia respectively) explore each of them in turn.

Global regulated marketplaces

There are two possible interpretations of the perceived need for state and supra-national intervention to regulate marketplaces. On the one hand, global capitalism acknowledges that its own practice has a tendency towards anti-competitive behaviour and protectionism: that is, it is an inherent and unavoidable feature of capitalism, which espouses free and fair competition, that actors will seek to maximise their own interests through distinctly unfair and uncompetitive practices. This necessitates intervention to ensure what is usually called a 'level playing field' for open competition. Of course, this does not necessarily deter firms that are active in framing such regulatory regimes from seeking to then covertly undermine them. For instance, in 2007 the world's fourth largest defence firm, BAe Systems plc was accused of paying bribes totalling nearly £1 billion to a Saudi prince in contravention of OECD anti-corruption rules.

In contradistinction, it is possible to see such regulatory regimes as the means by which extremely powerful global commercial interests open up otherwise closed or partially closed markets to 'competition'. The reality, it might be argued, is a very far from level playing field, with well-established commercial actors effectively setting the barriers to market entry so high that others, typically from poorer countries, cannot even leave the locker room.

The World Trade Organisation (WTO) is a supra-national body whose principal aim is the liberalisation of global trade and the regulation of resultant trade agreements. The General Agreement on Trade in Services (GATS), negotiated within the framework of the WTO, has come to play a major role in the globalisation of higher education. In his chapter, 'The constitution of a new global regime: higher education in the GATS/WTO framework', Antoni Verger explores the role of GATS in higher education.

Verger argues that, because GATS promotes trade liberalisation in services, it stimulates the 'consumption' of distance courses and degrees in foreign countries and the development of multinational universities and/or international teacher and researcher mobility. This liberalisation process aims to modify, eliminate and/or harmonise a large set of pre-existing regulations and laws to construct a new global free market in educational 'services'.

In contrast to comparable supra-national bodies such as UNESCO or the World Bank, the WTO has no overt education policy agenda. This would, of course, be beyond its remit of trade liberalisation and its enforcement. Rather, it simply promotes a commercialised and globalised trade in educational services. This approach runs counter to the views of some members of university communities, who argue that HE should be internationalised on a cooperative or partnership basis and that national HE policy should not be subordinated to or conditioned by international trade agreements.

Verger's chapter is framed by two considerations. First is the transformation of universities from a medium for the smooth functioning of markets (by, for instance, providing knowledge and labour as a public good) to being an object of markets. The second consideration is the transition from internationalisation to transnationalisation inherent in the GATS process. He considers these debates and reactions to GATS in the HE sector from a critical political analysis perspective, employing a range of variables (such as ideologies, principles and beliefs) to explain the position of WTO member states to the negotiation of GATS in the area of education.

Quality assurance

Since the rise of Japan as a manufacturing giant in the 1960s and 1970s, corporations globally have become obsessed with issues of 'quality'. 'Quality' is a loose and inherently subjective concept that takes on new meanings in capitalist contexts. 'Quality' is something that has a symbolic value, offered by the supplier to the consumer. It aims to assure the customer that there is minimal and known risk associated with the product or service. Hence 'quality' becomes a matter of 'quality assurance' (QA). This is essential 'oil' in marketplace transactions, with QA regimes offering cheap and cost-effective means for the customer to ensure that they are getting what they pay for. At heart, they not only grease supply–demand relationships but are also reconstitutive of suppliers themselves as they seek to trim operations to suit the needs of QA regimes of control, audit and surveillance.

'Quality' has become a hegemonic meta-narrative of higher education in many countries and globally. In HE such regimes are re-constitutive of the nature of the relationships between the institutions, academics, students and the beneficiaries of knowledge production. In his chapter, 'In quality we trust? The case of quality assurance in Finnish universities', Jani Ursin explores how efforts to implement QA regimes in universities reflect a profound change in university practices and cultures, with a confrontation between the dualistic traditional and the market-oriented cultures at its heart. Ursin argues that some of those involved in the implementation of QA regimes see them as a genuine means to develop the traditional activities of universities but that others consider them, at best, as nothing but an additional burden to be shouldered and, at worst, fundamentally aimed at marketisation and commercialisation.

As might be anticipated, the introduction and shaping of quality assurance regimes in universities has become a core item on trans- and supra-national policy agendas where there are overarching ambitions to create global education markets. After discussing this more global context, Ursin's chapter explores empirically the introduction of internal QA systems in Finnish universities. Ursin employs, following Marginson and Rhoades (2002), a 'glonacal' approach, whereby global trends (in this case international competition in educational markets) are interpreted both nationally and locally. Thus Ursin successfully explores the impact of such global commercial discourses on the re-forming of universities in a local context.

Controlling labour

Production outputs from business in the richer countries are shifting progressively from manufacturing to services. This means that employers need to find more sophisticated and nuanced ways of disciplining workers towards organisations' desired goals because these new production modes are not amenable to more traditional approaches such as direct surveillance, time-keeping regimes and the regimen of the production line.

Consequently, for the past twenty years or more corporate commercial organisations globally have sought new ways to enhance their utilisation of their 'human resources' (workers) to maximise both the volume and efficacy of work outputs. To this end, organisations have increasingly deployed a suite of techniques known collectively as strategic 'human resource management' (HRM). Such techniques aim to ensure a reliable flow of quality assured work outputs of the desired type to meet customer demand.

In seeking to enter and compete in the global educational supply chain, universities, especially in the UK, are increasingly deploying the strategic HRM toolbox to control and direct the work of academics. In his chapter, 'HRM in HE: people reform or re-forming people?', Matt Waring sees the development and use of such tools as synchronous with wider social trends towards increasing, and often institutionalised, individualisation. The core objective of HRM is to individualise the relationship between the employee and the employer, dispensing with collective categories such as class or, in the case of universities, traditional collegiality. Operating in conditions of neoliberalism, the ultimate aim is to make employees individually responsible and accountable for responding and adapting to the risks impinging upon the organisation. Like all neoliberal individual freedoms, this liberty is illusory: the ultimate aim is to encourage and cajole the individual to mould and shape themselves towards the organisation's objectives.

To position themselves in global knowledge marketplaces, universities are coming under increasing national, trans- and supra-national pressure to introduce quasi-market structures and focus on quality management, flexibility and cost minimisation. Pressure is exercised via the introduction of tighter control mechanisms and by allocating funds on a more competitive basis. As a result, it can be argued that the ability of academic staff to control their work is becoming increasingly constrained by a growing bureaucracy, the monitoring of performance and pressure for enhanced productivity. Such changes create the demand for the more effective management of academics.

After discussing the HRM concept and the individualisation of labour in universities, Waring provides a case study of English attempts to introduce a comprehensive approach to strategic HRM incentivised through the use of government funding for universities and aimed at securing an embedded

HR culture. Waring explores debates over the suitability of such overtly individualistic management techniques within a sector built upon the values of collegiality and cooperation. He concludes by arguing that HRM strategies, if successfully implemented, could do lasting damage to HE institutions.

Participation, partnership and mobility

Systems of innovation are a key contemporary mechanism for facilitating endogenous growth in the knowledge economy. They represent attempts to proactively manage and facilitate the innovation process. 'Innovation systems' are designed, amongst other things, to bring together leading researchers and to facilitate knowledge flows between them to produce cutting edge research. They also seek to bring together different 'players' in the innovation system such as government, the academy and industry. If, as Schumpeter says, innovation entails new combinations of existing resources, then this interaction maximises the number of possible combinations and varieties of knowledge. But mobility and the transgression of pre-existing boundaries can also imply threats to organisations anxious to retain workers and maintain intellectual property rights. Despite this, globalised businesses are those that are now and increasingly 'on the move'.

Participation and partnership, and the mobility across organisational boundaries that it implies, are central features of leading innovative businesses in the global knowledge economy. Universities, in seeking to join such innovation systems in pursuit of new customers for knowledge services, must therefore promote mobility and openness as a sector. They are increasingly recasting themselves as 'knowledge transfer' professionals working in partnership with knowledge customers, especially in the private sector. This involves particular kinds of personal academic practice, which may be difficult to achieve and/or control.

Such developments, however, in many ways contradict the closed and competitive spirit that universities have been developing for some time in many states. Despite this, mobility is a key aspect that is reflected in many research policies for universities at institutional, national and regional levels. Such policies promote individual academic mobility and the formation of disciplinary, trans-disciplinary and trans-national networks to support the production of and access to the 'best' knowledge. Knowledge, movement, connections and relationships are understood as tradable assets to be put to work in institutional, national and regional economic interests. Mobility is presented as a desirable attribute in itself and academics are encouraged to develop what Kenway and Fahey, in their chapter 'Policy incitements to mobility: some speculations and provocations', call mobility biographies. I have worked as an 'expert evaluator' on some of the European Union mobility programmes that form the empirical focus of this chapter and can verify the reification and glorification of the 'mobility' of researchers as a good thing in and of itself. Indeed, the EU, under successive Framework Programmes has pursued the creation of the European Research Area through, in part, the sponsorship of such 'human mobility'.

In their chapter Kenway and Fahey explore the way in which mobility is inscribed on national and institutional university policies and consider some of the specific policies and programmes in place at present. Utilising a range of 'travel tropes', metaphors of the researcher as tourist, exile, explorer, stranger and hobo, this chapter offers a critique of the moral agendas associated with such policy imperatives and points to alternative possibilities. It explains the paradoxical potential of institutionalised knowledge networkers to undermine the 'free and fair' flow of knowledge and thus the ontological security and intellectual productivity of the neoliberalised academy. More broadly, it meditates on the relationships between academic mobility, knowledge, power and cultural and economic geography in a world on the move.

It is evident that universities are coming under increasing pressure to recast themselves as commercialised knowledge suppliers in a globalised knowledge economy. The road to such change is likely to be bumpy: no market mechanism is perfect and resistance is evident – as demonstrated by these chapters. These changes will have repercussions for the nature, accessibility and democratisation of the knowledge supplied – for the geographies of knowledge and the geometries of associated power. The future for universities in this regard is far from clearly mapped.

References

Baskaran, A. and Boden, R. (2007) 'Prometheus bound', *International Studies of Management and Organization*, 37(1): 9–26.

Boden, R. and Epstein, D. (2006) 'Managing the research imagination? Globalisation and research in higher education', *Globalisation, Societies and Education*, 4(2): 223–36.

Dean, M. (1999) *Governmentality: Power and Rule in Modern Society*, London: Sage.

Kenway, J., Bullen, E., Fahey, J. and Robb, S. (2006) *Haunting the Knowledge Economy*, London: Routledge.

Marginson, S. and Rhoades, G. (2002) 'Beyond national states, markets, and systems of higher education: A glonacal agency heuristic', *Higher Education*, 43(3): 281–309.

Rose, N. (1999) 'Governing "advanced" liberal democracies', in A. Barry, T. Osborne, and N. Rose (eds) *Foucault and Political Reason*, London: UCL Press.

7 The constitution of a new global regime

Higher education in the GATS/WTO framework

Antoni Verger

Introduction[1]

At the present time, higher education is immersed in a sea of transformations and transitions. The subject of this chapter, the inclusion of Higher Education (HE) in the material scope of the World Trade Organisation (WTO) and in the General Agreement on Trade in Services (GATS), is closely linked to two of them. The first is the transition of the conception of the university from a *medium* for the smooth functioning of the market to an *object* of the market. The second is the transition from a dynamic of *internationalisation* to one of *transnationalisation*.

The intensification of economic globalisation has pressured universities to expand their functions. Currently, in addition to providing means for the smooth functioning and competitiveness of the capitalist economy, universities and the services they offer are, in themselves, objects and products of this economy. Furthermore, today the operations of many universities do not differ in any way from those of conventional private industry: they merge, take each other over (Rodríguez Gómez 2004) or opt to be listed on stock exchanges (see the 'Global Education Index' compiled by the OBHE).[2]

This process of commodification of HE is part of a dynamic of transnationalisation, which must be distinguished from internationalisation. In the first place, internationalisation of higher education, as opposed to transnationalisation, is nothing new. In fact, the internationalisation of universities was already underway in the colonial period, when empires like those of Spain, France or Great Britain exported institutions of higher education to the colonies. The commercialisation of university education at the international level is not new either – the very first European universities were already in the habit of enrolling foreign students in their courses (Brock 2006). The principal difference between internationalisation and transnationalisation does not have to do so much with the scale of operations as with the way relationships are structured in that scale. Thus, while internationalisation structures the relationships of the university community based on national borders, transnationalisation constitutes circuits of exchange and trade in services that transcend borders, and in which universities, professors and students operate and circulate freely. Transnationalisation materialises, for example, when a university establishes branches in different countries, issues certificates recognised in foreign countries by means of in-person or on-line courses, or freely employs international teaching and research personnel. At present, the dynamics of the transnationalisation of higher education coexist with those of internationalisation in the same way that the dynamics of commercialisation coexist with interuniversity cooperation. Nonetheless, the former (transnationalisation and commerce) are tending to become more prevalent.

Both elements, the growing commodification and the transnationalisation of higher education, lay the foundations for the establishment of a global regime of free trade in education. But this regime is still under construction. GATS is a key legal instrument, probably the most important one, for reaching this goal, since it has the capacity to determine most of the elements that constitute a commercial regime.[3]

This chapter specifically focuses on the process of the construction of a global commercial regime in the area of higher education under the auspices of GATS. In particular, it analyses the reasons why the member countries of the WTO decide whether to become part of this regime through the establishment and consolidation of liberalisation commitments. Although the changes currently manifested in the area of higher education are linked to the development of the global economy and other macroeconomic processes, it is necessary to make use of an agency theory to understand the more complex explanations for these changes. The purpose of this study on the construction of a global trade regime in education is to penetrate the black box of the process in order to reveal some of its constituent mechanisms.

The subject under discussion here is of the utmost importance for various reasons. First, the process is currently happening – the GATS negotiations have been under way almost continuously since the Uruguay Round of the General Agreement on Trade and Tariffs (GATT) from 1986 to 1994. Secondly, the process strengthens the neoliberal restructuring of universities and gives greater legal weight to a series of pro-market measures which, once put in place, are practically irreversible (Kelsey 2003; Robertson and Dale 2003).

The chapter is divided into two sections. The first examines the ways in which GATS contributes to the constitution of a global commercial regime for higher education and the political implications of this process. In the second, the construction of this regime is examined in depth. To this end, the process is explored on a micro level, and the positions of the member countries of the WTO at the moment of negotiating the inclusion of higher education in the GATS are systematised. In this second, empirical, section the intention is to demonstrate that there exist a series of cognitive variables (ideology, principles, beliefs, etc.) that turn out to be fundamental for understanding the positions of the member countries in the negotiation of the educational sector in the GATS and, thus, for understanding the results of these negotiations.

GATS and the regulation of a global HE market

Interestingly, GATS was not engendered with the object of expanding the flow of trade in the area of education, and still less of establishing a global regime of trade in education. The Agreement was driven, in its day, by a grouping of actors with 'offensive interests'[4] in service sectors like banking, insurance and telecommunications. Among these, the roles played by the US Trade Representative, American banks and various neoliberal think-tanks were of particular importance (Altay 2006). These actors, among others, promoted the creation of the Coalition of Service Industries, a lobby whose aim was to insert services into the international commercial regime (Feketekuty 2005) – a goal that was reached in the Uruguay Round of the GATT. At that time, ideational factors and, specifically, the action of several epistemic communities that shared causal beliefs and principles were fundamental in understanding the success of the venture (Drake and Nicolaidis 1992). Although it must be said that the 'idea' of trading services (and promoting the liberalisation of trade in services) would probably not have caught on to the same extent if it had had less powerful promoters.

In the Uruguay Round, in addition to creating the legal structure of the GATS (many of whose chapters were not, incidentally, completed) the first negotiations towards the liberalisation of services were undertaken.[5] The process, however, was not completed there, since the Agreement envisions the realisation of successive rounds of negotiations in order to achieve a progressively liberalised environment for the global trade in services. Thus, since 2000 the member countries of the WTO have been immersed in the second round of the negotiation of services. In 2001 at the Doha Ministerial Conference it was decided that the negotiations of services would be included in a broader round known as the Development or Doha Round. This round will promote, in addition to the liberalisation of services, further liberalisation of trade in industrial, agricultural, fishing, and other products.

The negotiation of services is much more abstract than the negotiation of goods. This is due in part to the fact that services are traded in a more complex manner. Four commercial modes exist for services, each of which can be liberalised separately:

a)   Cross-border supply (some examples of this mode in the field of education are e-learning and distance learning programmes in general),
b)   Consumption abroad (students travel to another country for their education),
c)   Commercial presence (the establishment of educational branches abroad, which involves foreign direct investment operations), and
d)   Movement of natural persons (teaching and research personnel travel to a foreign country to offer their services).

Another indication of the complexity of GATS is that higher education is only one of the more than 160 sub-sectors of services that are being negotiated in parallel by the 150 countries that have signed the Agreement.[6] It should be noted that higher education is the educational sub-sector that is negotiated with the most intensity. This is due to the fact that the education market is developing more strongly at post-compulsory levels. In fact, the only plurilateral request made in the area of education in the Doha Round was focused on 'higher education' and 'other educational services'.[7]

The dilemma of the policy space

Economic globalisation entails the progressive dissolution of spatial barriers and the subordination of the logic of geography to that of production. This phenomenon, known as spatial–temporal compression, is not new, but it is currently manifesting itself with unprecedented intensity (Robinson 2005). As part of this global dynamic, the principal objective of GATS is to contribute to the elimination of barriers to trade in services by the member states of the WTO by means of the establishment of liberalisation commitments.[8] The most significant thing about this process is that the barriers that GATS seeks to eliminate are not strictly of a conventional tariff nature, as with trade in goods. Rather, they are concerned with the rules and regulations of government systems that hinder the transnationalisation of service companies. In the area of higher education, these barrier rules might be taxes on the repatriation of the profits of education companies, stipulations as to what type of judicial personality educational centres must adopt (for example, in some countries for-profit companies are forbidden to provide regulated education), measures for controlling the guarantee of the quality of educational services, tests of financial need, systems of scholarships or subsidies to specific educational centres, etc. These and other measures can be considered, according to the logic employed by GATS, as barriers to free trade that must be eliminated.

The elimination of such perceived barriers depends on the negotiation process and, consequently, on the political disposition of the governments in question. Nonetheless, there exists a group of measures, still undefined, that can be considered 'more onerous than necessary', according to how the agreement is interpreted. These must be eliminated separately from established commitments.[9]

A second objective of GATS is to inculcate the principle of predictability. That is, countries must guarantee that service providers will be able to carry out their activities in a stable environment in which new barriers will not be erected or old barriers re-established once they have been eliminated. To this end, GATS 'freezes' the commitments made, making it extremely difficult to withdraw from or reduce commitments once made.[10] Thus Article XXI of the Agreement establishes that:

a) Members cannot withdraw their commitments until three years after they are made,
b) Notice of the modification must be given at least three months in advance, and

c) Members affected by the modification can file a complaint, as a result of which it may be decided that the country that has modified its list must compensate other countries affected.

As can be seen, GATS blocks a set of regulatory frameworks and, in consequence, leads to situations in which governments can find themselves with a limited capacity for intervention (both in education and in other areas) due to the trade policies of the preceding government.

In short, the race towards free trade in services is a phenomenon that can not only be interpreted economically or commercially, but also politically. As has been shown, the adoption of commitments by the WTO for liberalisation in the area of services limits the policy space of member countries and, at the area of concern here, entails a redefinition of the functions of the state as regulator, provider and financer of education. In consequence, it can hinder the state from solving or ameliorating through educational policies a series of problems in the areas of social cohesion, economic development or education equality (Robertson *et al.* 2002).

GATS and the global educational governance

The regulatory power of GATS together with the sanctioning capabilities of the WTO (Jackson 2002) turn the Agreement into a key element in global educational governance (Robertson *et al.* 2002). The contribution of GATS to global governance is not at all neutral since it consolidates a favourable environment for free enterprise and the expansion of the private sector. According to Gill (2003) GATS and the other agreements of the WTO are principal exponents in the process of the constitutionalisation of neoliberalism, a process by which neoliberal politico-economic ideology is institutionalised in a quasi-legal structure of the state and in international political conformations.

Therefore, the regime for higher education that GATS is seeking to institute belongs to a commercial regime of disembedded liberalism, rather than the one of embedded liberalism instituted by the original GATT. Furthermore, GATS is absolutely consistent with the process of neoliberal restructuring of university systems and with the need to compensate for the effects of the fiscal crisis of governments in the area of higher education. As a result, governments immersed in the present dynamic of global competitiveness, both in the North and the South, may feel that GATS will have beneficial effects on their systems of higher education. For the former, the commercialisation of higher education services promoted by the Agreement implies an ever-increasing source of financing for universities (Larsen *et al.* 2002). For the latter, it can enable them, as the World Bank proclaims (WB 1994; Heyneman 2003), to concentrate scarce public resources at the primary and secondary levels, while the demand for tertiary education by the more well-to-do sectors of the population is satisfied in the transnational education market.

Finally, it should be noted that the regime of trade in education advocated by GATS clashes, in various aspects, with certain agreements and systems of international cooperation, such as those promoted by international agencies like UNESCO or universities themselves.[11] Thus, as the ex-director of the Division of Higher Education of UNESCO, Marco Antonio Rodrigues Dias, himself points out,

> The acceptance of the proposal of the WTO and certain countries to include higher education in the GATS is contradictory to the Paris declaration [*Higher Education in the Twenty-first Century: Vision and Action*].
>
> (Rodrigues Dias 2003: 13)

Ideas for and against the constitution of a regime of global trade in education

GATS does not institute an *ad hoc* commercial regime of services. This is due mainly to the fact that it is a 'flexible' agreement. The principle of flexibility was introduced in GATS during the Uruguay Round, at the time when the Agreement was being designed. In fact, this was the condition *sine qua non* for the acceptance of the insertion of services in the material scope of the WTO proposed by the countries of the South, since they considered that in this area of trade they had nothing to gain, due to their comparative disadvantage in most sectors (Drake and Nicolaidis 1992). The principle of flexibility means that services, unlike other areas of the WTO, will not be liberalised at the same pace in each country – or according to differing degrees of development – but rather, that countries will have the capacity to decide, *a priori*, the pace and level at which they wish to liberalise their different sectors.

The flexibility of GATS, together with other methodological variables, has been singled out by the most powerful countries, those that are more competitive in trade in services, as the principal cause of the slow advance of the liberalisation of services (Khor 2005; EC 2005). This is reflected in a document authored by the President of the Council of Trade in Services, Alejandro Jara, published after a cluster of services meeting held in June 2005. According to Jara, during the meeting a 'considerable number of members' identified the current methodology as part of the problem in the negotiation of services (WTO 2005).[12] But are these the 'real' reasons why there is no advancement towards a global regime of trade in education and other types of services? This empirical study endeavours to examine these reasons in depth and, among other things, to disprove the 'hypothesis' hinted at by Jara.

Commercial positions in negotiations on education

The premise on which the present analysis is founded is that ideational factors are key elements in understanding transformation processes. Numerous analyses of the international system consider ideas as explanatory factors for actors' choices (Ruggie 1982), elements with constituent effects (Wendt 1999) or road maps for decision making (Jackson 1993). This perspective, markedly constructionist, is especially appropriate for the analysis of subjects that are relatively new on the political agenda, like the one dealt with here (Goldstein and Keohane 1993; Haas 2002). It is also appropriate to analyse policy changes related to complex phenomena. In these cases, policy makers use the advice of epistemic communities to define their interests and positions (Evans 2006).

It should be noted that constructivism is not the only theoretical approach to consider ideational factors as explanatory variables of policy changes and processes. The difference to other approaches, such as rationalism or institutionalism, is that constructivism understands that ideas are autonomous sources of influence and ontologically precede definitions of interests (Gofas 2006). On the other hand, rationalism assumes that interests are established beforehand and ideas are confined to acting as focus points in cases where there are different policy options. And for institutionalist authors, ideas are embedded into norms systems that act as mediators between actors' interests and their political behaviour (Goldstein and Keohane 1993).

From the analysis of the empirical data available,[13] a set of models was systematised that represents the different ways of confronting GATS negotiations in the education sector. These are theoretical models and, therefore, the position of a country is not necessarily identified with only one discursive model. In fact, the *real* position of many countries can be the result of the interaction between two or more models. The models are arranged according to the predisposition to liberalise education under GATS. While there exist multiple classifications of ideational factors or intersubjective structures in the literature of the social sciences, the categories used by both Gilpin (1987) and Goldstein and Keohane (1993) in particular were found extremely useful in systematising these models.

Model 1: 'Education is not a commodity'

This first model is subscribed to by countries that reject the establishment of commitments in the educational sector for ethical or moral reasons. It is a position irrespective of cost-benefit calculations or the knowledge of prevalent theories on the subject. Ethic-moral reasons are associated with the category of ideas that Goldstein and Keohane (1993) call *principled beliefs*. Principled beliefs are normative ideas that enable us to distinguish what is proper from what is improper and what is fair from what is unfair. Some countries condition decisions taken in the negotiation of the educational sector of GATS on considerations such as those above – that is, on a set of values or an explicit ideal of education shared by different social sectors. The argument put forth by these countries is that education is a social right and a public asset that should be provided by the state. From this philosophical vantage point it is feared that GATS might undermine the public function of education and its very conception as public. In some cases there is, quite simply, an attitude of rejection to education being negotiated and traded like 'common merchandise'.

Countries with social democratic or leftist governments usually adopt this position. In some of them, civil society has pressured against the establishment of commitments in education, or for the exclusion of education from GATS negotiations entirely (Verger and Bonal 2006).[14]

Model 2: Caution towards adopting commitments

The delegations included in this model also reject making commitments for education, but for other reasons than those mentioned in the previous model. In this case, instead of adopting a critical position for reasons of identity or because of adherence to certain values, the rejection of GATS is based on ambiguities in the text and on the uncertainties that these generate. It must be remembered that GATS is an incomplete agreement and some of its chapters are still being finalised.

The main ambiguities in GATS are found in the definition of the services included in the Agreement, in the rules and systems for national regulation, and in the classification of services. With respect to the first of these, Article I establishes that the Agreement will apply to all services in all sectors except for 'services provided in the exercise of governmental authority', which are defined as '[services] which [are] supplied neither on a commercial basis, nor in competition with one or more service suppliers'. This definition does not clearly exclude public services, since, for example, there are public universities that provide services commercially and in competition with other providers.[15] As a result of this blurred border between the public and the private, those countries that do not want the liberalisation of a particular sector to affect the public sector choose not to make commitments.

A second area that has not yet been finalised in the Agreement is Domestic Regulation (Article VI). Thus, it has not yet been defined which type of national policies can be considered 'more burdensome than necessary' in keeping countries from reaching their objectives. In the educational sector this might affect rules such as the definition of the curriculum by the state, the evaluation of the quality of educational centres or the accreditation of degrees obtained in other countries. For this reason, many countries condition their offers for access to markets on knowing the contents of the disciplines of national regulation. Their logic is fairly obvious: before committing a sector or sub-sector, they want to know exactly what their obligations will be.

Something similar occurs with the classification of services, since it is still not clear what sub-sectors of services are included in the categories of services used in the negotiations. Cases have arisen in which the Dispute Settlement Body of the WTO has ruled that a country has liberalised a service sector when the country in question maintains that it had not included that sector in their list of commitments. This was the case with the USA with online games of chance,[16] which remains ever-present in the minds and the calculations of the negotiators.

With respect to what is known as the GATS Rules, there are also grey areas that relate to their scope and meaning, which have led to the creation of a working group in the WTO on this subject. Nonetheless, unlike the Domestic Regulation group, it is unlikely that its task will be concluded in the current round. The Rules cover three broad subjects:

a) Subsidies (Article XV): in the wording of the agreement it is not clear, among other things, what type of subsidies can be retained by governments for developmental reasons and to which ones the National Treatment rule must be applied;
b) Government Procurement (Article XIII): whilst general and specific obligations do not apply to government contracts some wealthy countries, led by the EU, are pressuring for this no longer to be the case, so that their companies can participate in calls for tenders by foreign governments;
c) Safeguard Mechanisms, which are not defined either, although, in this case, the countries that have a greater interest in their advancement are the less-developed ones.

These measures would permit the establishment of a trial period for the liberalisation process. Thus, if a member is not satisfied with the results of liberalisation and can justify it in a convincing manner to the Council of Trade in Services, it may be allowed to withdraw the commitment.

Finally, the mandate for Evaluation envisaged in Article XIX of GATS has not been applied either. According to this, some WTO resources should be devoted to evaluating the results of the liberalisation of trade in services in order to determine, among other things, to what extent it benefits or harms developing countries. Since these evaluations have not been carried out, there is greater uncertainty for some countries.

Fears such as these are based on *causal beliefs*, that is, on theories and beliefs about cause and effect relationships that guide actors in reaching their objectives (Goldstein and Keohane 1993). In the framework of this model, negotiators' technical knowledge of the contents of the agreement, together with the theories they construct in this respect, are a key mediator variable when trying to understand countries' positions in the negotiation of services. This knowledge, often hypothetical in nature, is not directly related to the world of education. The result of the pre-eminence of these ideas is that delegations choose not to move any pieces in the negotiations so as to avoid making experiments whose consequences are still unknown and which, due to the characteristics of the Agreement mentioned above, would be difficult to reverse.

Model 3: Defensive interests

The third model, like the previous one, is made up of those delegations that refuse to establish liberalisation commitments in the education sector, basing their position on causal beliefs. However, in this case the arguments and theories that the delegations put forward are not centred on the GATS text but rather on the effects of the liberalisation of the education sector that GATS entails.

Negotiators who adhere to this model are concerned with information and knowledge relative to the opportunities and dangers of liberalising the education sector or to the potentials and weaknesses of their national educational service industries. As with the first model, education is conceived of as a sensitive sector, not so much as a matter of moral principle, but because national education systems might be harmed as a result of the adoption of commitments for the liberalisation of trade. This posture is normally associated with governments that subscribe to a programme of economic nationalism. In the definition of this position pressure exercised from the domestic private sector acquires a certain relevancy. Thus, some associations of private universities in different countries have effectively pressured their ministers of trade not to make liberalisation commitments, thereby avoiding international competition. This position can be sustained on mere hypotheses as to the possible effects of competition, although on occasions it is based on the experiences of other countries that have damaged their domestic education sector after liberalising higher education. One of the most noteworthy of these cases was the acquisition of the Universidad del Valle (the second largest private university in Mexico) by Sylvan Learning Systems (an American education consortium), which was made possible as a result of the ratification of NAFTA[17] by Mexico.

On the other hand, many countries in the South have still not developed adequate regulations in the area of higher education. They consider that acquiring liberalisation commitments could render this task difficult in the future and, consequently, the task of controlling the quality of the providers of cross-border education as well.

As with Model 2, some of the countries that adhere to this model do not give a resounding 'no' to the introduction of education into GATS. They might do so in the event that a certain series of conditions were present, like the possession of a more solid regulatory framework or a more competitive education industry.

Model 4: The most instrumental logic

For those that inhabit this fourth model, the decision to liberalise education is not based on ethics, uncertainties associated with the grey areas of GATS or oscillation between the perceived opportunities and dangers of liberalising education. Rather, their decision is clearly based on factors extrinsic to the education liberalisation itself. Among these factors, the results of the negotiations over other areas in the Doha Round are by far the most salient. In the framework of this model we find some developing countries that have no offensive interests in education services at all (or in services in general) but that might liberalise their education sector in exchange for greater liberalisation by other countries of trade in agricultural or textile products. Thus, education in the framework of this model is treated as a bargaining chip, and ideas about education do not carry any weight when explaining the results of negotiations. In cases where such ideas have been developed, educational concerns have ended up totally superseded by interests from other sectors of the economy.

Model 5: Ode to the liberalisation of education

Normally, countries that are close to this last model have already liberalised education in the framework of GATS. They are countries that consider fears of educational liberalisation unfounded, arguing rather that it entails a series of advantages for education systems. Among the most often mentioned of these advantages are the introduction of greater competition in the sector, the attraction of foreign investment, enhanced human resources and expertise to the education system, and the increase in the education offer. In consequence, they feel that the overall result obtained from the liberalisation process is an increase in the quality of education in the home country. In addition, they consider that fears related to the grey areas of the GATS are also unfounded.

According to what can be gathered from their discourse, the dominant rationale is that education is an economic sector that, like so many others, must be liberalised so that the system becomes more efficient and generates more wealth and well-being. Although their arguments are based on certain causal relationships, the foundation of their position is fundamentally ideological in nature. Specifically, the delegations that comprise this model subscribe to a neoliberal ideology.[18] *Ideology* is a broader category than causal beliefs. According to Gilpin (1987), while ideologies provide scientific descriptions of how the world works (as causal beliefs do), they also constitute normative positions on how it should work. In this sense, the governmental delegations framed in the model maintain that free trade is the ideal economic exchange system and that the liberalisation of trade is always desirable. Furthermore, ideologies, unlike theories, represent intellectual commitments or acts of faith that, normally, cannot be refuted by logical argument or empirical evidence (Gilpin 1987).

In describing this model, it should be noted that other country delegations are impregnated by ideology (neoliberal ones or others). What is specifically meant here is that trade negotiators that are close to Model 5 appeal to ideological reasons to justify their position in the GATS and education negotiations.

The majority of countries that have liberalised their education sector did so in the Uruguay Round, when public opinion was focused elsewhere and people were generally uninformed about GATS and its implications. It is probable that if they had established their liberalisation commitments more recently, the political costs of the decision would have been much greater and the decision-making process would have been more controversial. So, it is possible that, at the time, they may have established their commitments for the liberalisation of education in a less thoughtful manner or for reasons similar to those of the previous model (that is, using education as a 'bargaining chip'). Now, however, once these commitments have been adopted and the public debate on the relationship between GATS and education is more heated, they have adopted a rhetoric supportive of liberalisation. In other words, it is plausible to consider that they have rationalised the advantages of liberalisation *a posteriori* and, from what can be gathered from their arguments, based on flimsy empirical evidence.

Table 7.1 systematises the five positions: Each of the models is described according to the type of idea that characterises it, the conception of education held (when this is related to the country's position) and the way in which ideas influence the results of the negotiations.

Conclusions

GATS is the main international legal instrument for the constitution of a multilateral regime for trade in education. This regime will have a decidedly pro-market character since, consistent with the *raison d'être* of the WTO, it is structured around the free market and free trade rules. In addition, it entails the redefinition of the functions of the state in educational matters and the economic and social functions of education.

Nevertheless, this new regime is still under construction, in part due to the flexibility that GATS allows to member countries when consolidating liberalisation commitments. But there exist other factors of greater importance when attempting to explain the irregular pace at which the process has proceeded. The most important of them is that the application of GATS rules to the educational sector is a highly contested. The opposition to GATS usually comes from the education community (public universities, teachers' unions, etc.), but, as we have observed, some government representatives in the WTO themselves also adopt a critical position. This is the main barrier to the constitution of a trade in education international regime because, in order to create an international regime, the parties must share certain principles, aims and values. Currently, several WTO member countries have already made commitments for education under GATS and believe that this will enhance the quality and competitiveness of their education systems. Nevertheless, at the moment, some member countries refuse to adopt some of the GATS rules in the educational sector (above all, to establish liberalisation commitments) because they consider that education is a public asset that should not be partially regulated by free trade agreements. So, there is clearly a non-common understanding among countries in the principles domain of

Table 7.1 Summary of models for the negotiation of education in the GATS

	Model 1	Model 2	Model 3	Model 4	Model 5
Type of factors	Moral principles ('Education is not a commodity')	Causal beliefs (contents of GATS)	Causal beliefs (dangers of liberalisation)	Instrumental, not ideational	Ideology (opportunities derived from education liberalisation)
Conception of education	Public asset provided by the State	Independent conception	Supplied by national providers	Independent conception: a 'bargaining chip'	Scarce asset – merchandise
Result (Yes/No education liberalisation commitments)	No. Liberalisation non-negotiable	No. Necessary condition: that the grey areas of GATS are cleared up	No. Necessary condition: possess an adequate regulatory framework or a competitive domestic industry	Yes or No: Liberalisation commitments in function of results in other areas	Yes

the regime, as well as a lack of convergence on the conditions and the goals that make this regime necessary.

Moreover, there is another important grouping of countries that are reluctant to make GATS commitments with regard to education solely for technical reasons (such as the presence of ambiguities in some chapters of the Agreement or certain loopholes in their own national regulations that could heighten the risks of liberalisation). However, once these questions have been resolved, these countries could be disposed to make these commitments. Another group of countries, with an even more instrumental approach, would be willing to establish commitments for liberalising education under GATS if negotiations advance in other areas (such as agriculture, industrial products, etc.).

GATS was not created with the primary objective of constructing a global regime for trade in education. However, today it is the main juridical tool used to enable the constitution of this regime. Similarly, as we infer from the position of the WTO members, many countries might opt to commit their educational sector to the GATS framework for reasons unrelated to educational objectives. This would lead to an apparently paradoxical process: the construction of a global regime for transnational education without an education rationale, relegating the conception, functions, and objectives of education to background.

The future of education in GATS is as yet not completely known. There are many variables that could influence the outcome of this process. As we have observed elsewhere, it seems that the correlation of forces at the domestic level between critics of GATS and pro-free trade sectors may tip the scales either towards a model of free market educational transnationalisation or towards one structured on other principles, rules and procedures (Verger and Bonal 2006). Nonetheless, if the appeals of some education sectors to exclude education from GATS go unheeded, the regime of free trade in education will sooner or later be established, since the rules of the Agreement itself pave the way for a progressive liberalisation that will be difficult to reverse.

Notes

1 This chapter is part of the project 'Beyond "targeting the poor": education, development and poverty alleviation in the Southern Cone. An analysis of the new political agenda in the region', funded by the Ministry of Education and Science (Government of Spain: ref. SEJ2005-04235).
2 The Observatory on Borderless Higher Education.
3 A regime is defined as a set of explicit or implicit principles, norms, rules and procedures around which actors' expectations converge in a specific area of international relations (Ruggie 1982).
4 In the trade negotiator's jargon, when a country has 'offensive interests' in a sector it is pushing proactively for the international trade liberalisation of this sector.
5 An analysis of the levels of liberalisation in the sector of Higher Education consolidated by the member countries can be consulted in Verger (forthcoming).

6 The complete list of services can be consulted at www.wto.org/english/tratop_
   e/serv_e/serv_e.htm (last accessed 25 January 2007).
7 The collective request was led by New Zealand. See the complete text of the
   request at: www.esf.be/pdfs/Collective%20Requests/Education%20Services.
   pdf (last accessed 10 January 2007).
8 The liberalisation commitments established acquire legal status.
9 In the first section of the GATS it is established that the members must guarantee
   that specific measures relating to licences, technical standards or requirements
   for qualifications are not more trade-restrictive than 'what is necessary to achieve
   the legitimate objectives of the country'. Something similar is established in the
   chapters on subsidies and government procurement.
10 On the other hand, the Agreement includes the possibility that, at any moment,
   countries can add new commitments to their lists, independently of the
   development of the current round of negotiations.
11 It is interesting to point out that the majority of traditional universities foster
   initiatives for cooperation and, at the same time, for the commercialisation of
   educational services. The rules of the WTO can lead one to interpret that certain
   initiatives for cooperation are obstacles to free trade (either because they distort
   market dynamics or because they discriminate against some centres or countries in
   favour of others). Nonetheless, the universities' necessity for obtaining non-state
   funds can be the principal reason why initiatives for cooperation by universities
   are de-emphasised.
12 In fact, from that cluster meeting until the CM in Hong Kong, discussions in
   the area of services were monopolised by the guidelines in which the negotiation
   methodology of the GATS is defined.
13 Specifically, 20 interviews to trade negotiators and four interviews to WTO and
   UNCTAD staff were done.
14 It must be said that there are cases of countries that oppose the introduction of
   education into the GATS for clearly 'anti-commodification' reasons, while they
   are promoting the commercialisation of education by other routes.
15 Post-graduate courses at market prices offered by certain public universities are
   the most widespread example of this.
16 See Gould (2004).
17 North American Free Trade Agreement.
18 Paradoxically, the delegations that most closely approximate this model criticise
   those that sustain positions contrary to the liberalisation of education in the
   GATS as doing so for 'ideological' or 'electoral' reasons.

References

Altay, S. (2006) 'Ideas, private actors and regime creation after US hegemony: the
   case of the GATS'. BISA Annual Conference 2006, Cork, Ireland.
Brock, C. (2006) 'Regulation and accreditation of higher education: historical
   and sociological roots', in *Higher Education in the World 2007. Accreditation
   For Quality Assurance: What is at Stake?*, GUNI. Barcelona: Ediciones Mundi-
   Prensa.
Drake, W. J. and K. Nicolaidis (1992) 'Ideas, interests, and institutionalization:
   "trade in services" and the Uruguay Round', *International Organization*, 46(1):
   37–100.
EC (2005) 'Non paper on complementary methods for the services negotiations.
   Possible elements'. Room Document. Council for Trade in Services – Special
   Session, 13 September.

Evans, M. (2006) 'Elitism', in C. Hay, M. Lister and D. Marsh (eds) *The State: Theories and Issues*, London: Palgrave.

Feketekuty, G. (2005) 'International trade in services. An overview and blueprint for negotiations', Institute for Trade and Commercial Diplomacy, from: www.commercialdiplomacy.org.

Gill, S. (2003) *Power and Resistance in the New World Order*, London: Palgrave.

Gilpin, R. (1987) *The Political Economy of International Relations*, Princeton: Princeton University Press.

Gofas, A. (2006) 'The ideas debate in international studies: towards a cartography and critical assessment', *IBEI Seminar Series*, November 2006.

Goldstein, J. and R. O. Keohane (1993) *Ideas and Foreign Policy: Beliefs, Institutions and Political Change*, New York: Cornell University Press.

Gould, E. (2004) 'The GATS US-gambling decision: a wakeup call for WTO members', *CCPA Briefing Paper. Trade and Investment Series*, 5(4).

Haas, P. M. (2002) 'UN conferences and constructivist governance of the environment', *Global Governance*, 8: 73–91.

Heyneman, S. P. (2003) 'The history and problems in the making of education policy at the World Bank 1960–2000', *International Journal of Educational Development*, 23: 315–37.

Jackson, J. H. (2002) *The World Trading System: Law and Policy of International Economic Relations*, London: MIT Press.

Jackson, R. H. (1993) 'The weight of ideas in decolonization: normative change in international relations', in J. Goldstein and R. O. Keohane (eds) *Ideas and Foreign Policy: Beliefs, Institutions and Political Change*, New York: Cornell University Press.

Kelsey, J. (2003) 'Legal fetishism and the contradictions of the GATS', *Globalisation, Societies and Education*, 1(3): 321–57.

Khor, M. (2005) 'GATS negotiators debate "crisis" in WTO services talks', *TWN Info Service on WTO and Trade Issues* 199, from: www.twnside.org.sg/title2/twninfo199.htm.

Larsen, K., J. P. Martin and R. Morris (2002) 'Trade in educational services: trends and emerging issues', *The World Economy*, 25(6): 849–68.

Robertson, S. and R. Dale (2003) 'This is what the fuss is about! The implications of GATS for education systems in the North and the South'. UK Forum for International Education and Training, 29 May, Commonwealth Secretariat.

Robertson, S., X. Bonal and R. Dale (2002) 'GATS and the education services industry: the politics of scale and global reterritorialization', *Comparative Education Review*, 46(4): 472–96.

Robinson, W. I. (2005) 'Capitalist globalization and the transformation of the state', in R. Little and M. Smith (eds) *Perspectives on World Politics*, London: Routledge.

Rodrigues Dias, M. A. (2003) 'Espacios Solidarios en Tiempos de Oscurantismo'. UPC, Inaugural Course Lecture, Barcelona, 25 September.

Rodríguez, Gómez R. (2004) 'Inversión extranjera directa en educación superior. El caso de México', *Revista Educación Superior*, 33.

Ruggie, J. G. (1982) 'International regimes, transactions, and change: embedded liberalism in the postwar economic order', *International Organisation*, 36(2): 379–415.

Verger, A. (forthcoming) 'GATS and higher education: state of play of the liberalisation commitments', *Higher Education Policy*.

Verger, A. and X. Bonal (2006) 'Against GATS: the sense of a global struggle', *Journal for Critical Education Policy Studies*, 4(1).

WB (1994) *Higher Education: The Lessons of Experience*, Washington, DC: World Bank.

Wendt, A. (1999) *Social Theory of International Politics*, Cambridge: Cambridge University Press.

WTO (2005) 'Initial and revised offers: a factual assessment of the state of play'. Retrieved 27 June 2005, from http://docsonline.wto.org.

8 In quality we trust?

The case of quality assurance in Finnish universities

Jani Ursin

Introduction

Quality and quality assurance are much debated issues in higher education (HE). Quality is not a new consideration in HE, but currently global knowledge economies are posing new challenges to universities which cannot anymore rely on their exception status as educational and social institutions. Rather, they have to react to the emerging commercialisation of higher education, even in national systems which only have public universities and strong government steering policies, such as Finland. The introduction of the European Higher Education Area (EHEA) on the one hand and the expansion of sites capable of producing new knowledge on the other pose challenges to individual higher education institutions (HEIs) which have to find their place in these global HE markets. One way to rationalise one's market position is to ensure the level of educational provision and knowledge production by developing internal procedures and systems for quality assurance (QA).

Efforts to implement quality assurance thinking into universities have, however, proved controversial in universities. Frontline academics can easily see QA as a threat to the autonomy of their work and as changing the power relationships within universities, with the result that quality improvement is reduced to mere ritualistic game-playing. Conversely, QA can, for example, increase the transparency of decision-making in the academy, help develop core activities of the university and bring benefits to students.

Following a discussion of HE QA in the global context and analysis of the complexity of QA as a concept, this chapter explores empirically the introduction of internal QA systems in Finnish universities. The introduction of QA systems is viewed from three perspectives: global, national and local, following Marginson and Rhoades' (2002) 'glonacal' approach whereby global trends are interpreted both nationally and locally. This approach emphasises the simultaneous significance of global, national, and local dimensions in shaping the landscape of national higher education. The chapter focuses on how quality assurance is shaped by the European and Finnish higher education policies and how academics (locally) are interpreting the policy initiatives. The chapter draws upon material generated by a project which studied the introduction of internal quality assurance systems in Finnish universities and academic conceptions and opinions regarding quality assurance. The data were gathered by sending a questionnaire to unit heads (n = 238) and interviewing academic staff and students (n = 25).[1]

Multifaceted concept of 'quality'

Quality is a multidimensional and ambiguous concept (e.g. Vidovich 2004) and one used fairly loosely in HE texts (Brennan and Shah 2000). Several different meanings of 'quality' have been proposed (Harvey and Green 1993; Harvey and Knight 1996; Yorke 2000; Vidovich 2004). Quality can be perceived as excellence, standard setting, exceptional, perfection, consistency, fitness for purpose, value for money, transformation and moral purpose. To summarise these various 'quality' conceptions Knight and Trowler (2000) distinguish Quality Type I and Type II. Type I quality emphasises outcomes, well-specified procedures, hierarchies and low-trust cultures and has a rational view of communication and planning. The Type I meaning of quality 'has an intuitive appeal because it has such affinities with foundational views that have pervaded Westerns academic life since the 17th century intellectual revolutions' (Knight and Trowler 2000: 112).

Quality Type II has focus on processes, creativity, self-actualisation and on communication as sense-making where planning is far from rational. Knight and Trowler (2000) conclude that even though both types can be applied to HE, Type II quality is quality for change whereas Type I is primarily for some maintenance functions. Therefore, it is essential to consider which quality conception can be applied and when.

We can also relate various conceptions of QA to this division between Type I and II quality. The literature distinguishes such concepts as quality assurance, assessment, improvement, management, enhancement, monitoring and control. The differences between these concepts are blurred, but *quality control and monitoring* embody the notion that quality can be externally observed and, if needed, can be intervened in and restricted. Thereby, quality control and monitoring are close to Type I. *Quality improvement and enhancement* on the contrary includes a conscious aim to develop academic activities and thus are associated with Type II. *Quality management, assurance and assessment* have features of both Type I and II as quality is seen not only as an externally steered entity but also as something that can be developed internally. Hence, these latter three concepts are the most neutral ones.

Altogether, it seems that quality assurance has both managerial and academic (in a collegial sense) features: Type I quality relates to the managerial features and Type II to the academic. This idea is also close to Gibbons *et al.*'s (1994) notion of Mode 1 and Mode 2 knowledge production. In Mode 1 the research context is defined in relation to the cognitive and social norms that govern academic science (cf. Quality Type I). In Mode 2, in contrast, knowledge is produced in the context of application. Instead of producing knowledge within the discipline, research in Mode 2 is transdisciplinary and heterogeneous. In Mode 2 new forms of organisation have emerged to accommodate the changing nature of the problems Mode 2 addresses. This will, Gibbons *et al.* argue, also expand social accountability and reflexivity as well as create new forms of quality control (cf. Quality Type II). In sum, Mode 2 science reflects the closer interaction of science and society and the emergence of a new kind of science: context sensitive and an outcome of the contextualisation of knowledge in a new public space, the development of conditions for the production of socially robust knowledge and the emergence of socially distributed knowledge.

Quality assurance in the global context: the introduction of EHEA

There are political and economic imperatives to promote European HE so that it can better meet the growing diversity of the globalised world. QA is an important aspect of this project, even though quality assessment is not a new phenomenon in European higher education. Its roots lie in medieval universities (van Vught and Westerheijden 1994) where quality assessment was either vested in external authorities (the 'French model') or was seen to belong to the self-governing community of fellows (the 'English model'). QA had its impetus in the early 1990s when, after the Maastricht Communiqué, the European Commission financed various projects whose purpose was to analyse European quality assurance practices (e.g. van Vught and Westerheijden 1993). As a consequence, the Council of European Union recommended in 1998 that cooperation in the field of quality assurance needed to be intensified (Council Recommendation 1998).

In June 1999 some 19 European ministries of education signed the Bologna Declaration, the purpose of which was to set up the EHEA by the year 2010. The aim is to increase the competitiveness and attractiveness of European HE in relation to the rest of the world. The introduction of quality assurance in HE is one part of this endeavour. Other objectives include the adoption of a system of easily comparable and comprehensible degrees, the establishment of a system of credits (such as ECTS), and the promotion of mobility.

QA regimes started to proceed faster after the education ministers' meeting in Berlin 2003 where it was agreed that national quality assurance systems need to be developed in order to pave the way for the establishment of the EHEA in the global higher education market. The European Association for Quality Assurance in Higher Education (ENQA) was obliged to elaborate European HE QA practices and to suggest principles which would support the development of national QA systems (Berlin Communiqué 2003). The Bergen Communiqué (2005) pushed this further by adopting the QA standards and guidelines proposed by ENQA and emphasising the importance of the systematic introduction of internal QA mechanisms into HEIs.

With respect to internal quality assurance, ENQA (2005: 6, 15–19) emphasised that HEIs should have both a policy and a culture for the assurance of quality. Thus, institutions should develop and implement a strategy for the continuous enhancement of quality. In practice this means that institutions should

1= have a policy and associated procedures for the assurance of the quality and standards of their programmes and awards;
2= have formal mechanisms for the approval, periodic review and monitoring of their programmes and awards;
3= have a means of assessing students using published criteria, regulations, and procedures which are applied consistently;
4= have ways of satisfying themselves that the staff involved in the teaching of students are qualified and competent to do so;
5= ensure that the resources available for the support of student learning are adequate and appropriate for each programme offered;
6= ensure that they collect, analyse and use relevant information for the effective management of their programmes of study and other activities; and
7= regularly publish up-to-date, impartial and objective information, both quantitative and qualitative, about the programmes and awards they are offering.

These recommendations concentrate primarily on teaching and learning. They emphasise transparency, accountability and comparability of QA systems. The principles recognise the appropriate use of teaching resources and stress the importance of the pedagogical competence of university teachers.

The ENQA recommendations frame and act to converge the quality work of HEIs. In order to assess this convergence effect ENQA undertook research which included six countries (United Kingdom, Lithuania, Norway, France, Sweden and Hungary). According to the results, national HE culture has a strong influence on quality assurance practices (see also Billing 2004). It was suggested that confidence is important in the process of cultural transformation towards convergence in HE systems and policies. The confidence can be gained through a progressive increase in mutual comprehension and in the capacity for interaction between higher education systems at different levels (Crozier *et al.* 2005).

Quality assurance in the national context: the case of Finland

In Finland the development of quality assurance has been rather similar to that in the other Western European countries, even though it has so far been a relatively absent element in Finnish higher education policy. Until the end of the 1970s, 'quality' as an overt consideration did not exist in Finnish HE policy discussions. In the early 1980s decision-makers started to pay attention to 'quality' issues and in the 1990s it was seen as a competitive factor in HE policy. By the mid-1990s quality assessment became a legal obligation of Finnish HEIs. Currently, Finland is committed to the introduction of national and institutional quality assurance systems according to the Bologna Process (Saarinen 2005).

The Finnish Ministry of Education has agreed to support universities in their efforts to pay more attention to quality through management by results. A working group appointed by the Ministry has proposed that HEIs should develop their QA systems so that they:

1= meet the developing quality assurance criteria [proposed by ENQA] of the European Higher Education Area;
2= are part of the operational steering and management system;
3= cover the entire operation of the HE institution;
4= are interrelated as part of the normal operation of the HE institution;
5= are continuous;
6= are documented; and
7= enable the participation of all members of the higher education community in quality work (OPM 2004: 37).

These recommendations are similar to the guidelines proposed by ENQA. The essential difference is that the working group explicitly highlights the implementation of QA systems across the entire field of operations of HE institutions, whereas ENQA primarily concentrates on teaching and learning. The working group also puts more stress on equality in quality work than does ENQA. Altogether, the principles proposed by ENQA and the working group converge in their understanding of internal quality assurance. Since individual Finnish HEIs have the freedom to develop their own QA systems, the question is to what extent the principles suggested by intermediary bodies will be applied as a starting point in elaborating internal quality assurance systems.

The Finnish Higher Education Evaluation Council (FINHEEC) is responsible for carrying out the audits of HEIs. It started the audits with two pilots in 2005. FINHEEC (2005) has produced an audit manual in which the premises, objectives, focus, criteria and consequences of audit are presented. It defines auditing as

> independent external evaluation to ascertain whether a QA system conforms to its stated objectives, is effective and fits its purpose. Auditing does not address the objectives or the results of operations as such but evaluates the processes that the HEI uses to manage and improve the quality of its education and other activities.
>
> (FINHEEC 2005: 31)

Although universities have the autonomy to develop their own quality assurance systems, the Ministry of Education has a major role in determining 'quality' in universities. This arises because of a 'management by results' steering system in which each individual university negotiates their future goals with the ministry. All Finnish universities are publicly funded and these negotiations determine the level of funding. Thus, universities are, more or less, directly accountable to the Finnish government.

Quality assurance as a managerial or academic device?

Morley (2003: 47–66) sees QA as an education political response to the increased risks and global nature of modern society and argues that the state has shifted from promoting intellectual activities to controlling them. Thus, QA is perceived as one device through which to administer everyday university practices. Quality assurance is also a way in which the new managerialism is being introduced into the universities. New managerialism can be understood as the transfer into the public sector of principles and ideologies from the private sector (e.g. Exworthy and Halford 1999). According to Neave (1985), new managerialism highlights the role of the external interests groups and strategic management in HE, supported by assessment systems. In practice this means increased competition between employees, the commercialisation of public sector services and the monitoring of efficiency and effectiveness through the measurement of outcomes and individual staff members (Deem 1998). To satisfy the ever-growing demands of the new managerialism, academic managers have been reorganising, controlling and regulating the work and conditions of academic staff so that activities which once symbolised academic freedom are now becoming indicators of academic performance (Deem 1998; Trowler 1998).

As a consequence of this new order, the relationship between the university, the state and the market has changed. El-Khawas (2001: 111–13) points out that government has a great deal of authority when it comes to QA issues. Neave (1998) however stresses that this increased governmental authority does not necessarily imply the strengthening of direct control by the central authority but rather the growing role of so-called intermediary bodies, such as ENQA on the European level or FINHEEC on the national (Finnish) level. This kind of evaluative state (Neave 1998) is characterised by increased accountability and continuous quality monitoring in all its sectors, including the universities (Dill 1998). Nonetheless, the key question in the process of introducing QA systems into universities is to what extent they reflect the principles posed by the new managerialism and to what degree they accommodate and assimilate to traditional academic values and imperatives. Is quality assurance actually creating a quality-oriented culture or is it enhancing the instrumental nature of quality work (see Yorke 2000)?

Perhaps paradoxically, politicians have acknowledged institutional autonomy in quality issues, arguing that 'the primary responsibility for quality assurance lies with each institution itself and this provides the basis for the real accountability of the academic system within the national quality framework' (Realizing the European Higher Education Area 2004: 21). This means that universities can potentially contribute to how well traditional and market-oriented cultures are able to co-exist in terms of quality assurance.

The consequences of quality assurance

Quality assurance has both intended and unintended consequences. One of the main results is the new division of academic power so that university administrators and managers have more (hegemonic) power than ever before. This 'new managerial class', as Amaral *et al.* (2003) label it, has acquired symbolic and actual power from academics, threatening the latter's collegiality and autonomy (Rinne and Koivula 2005) and increase externally measured and controlled quality assessment that has little or no relation to academic work (Salter and Tapper 2000; Newton 2002b; Morley 2003). As a consequence, assessment practices have bureaucratised and technicised (Barnett 1994). On the other hand, where quality assurance increases cooperation and interaction it can also strengthen collegiality among academics (Hoecht 2006). The risk is, as the UK example shows, that the constant power battles between various interests groups leads to the development of unstable quality assurance cultures (Tapper and Filippakou 2006).

University teachers and researchers have been the most critical of quality assurance regimes (Newton 2000, 2002b; Vidovich 2002). The issue of trust is especially important here. Hoecht (2006) observed that quality assurance increased distrust among academics, leading them to have less confidence in the 'system'. Distrust between academics and administrators of the university may also be increased as a consequence of QA regimes (Biggs 2001; Jones and Darshi de Saram 2005). Heads of the academic departments play a crucial role in averting or attenuating distrust between academics and administrators (Brunotto and Farr-Wharton 2005). Nonetheless, there is an unsolved paradox in quality assessment: it is used in low-trust situations but also *increases* levels of distrust (Power 1994).

The measurement of quality is one of the main challenges related to quality assurance. How is a multi-faceted concept such as 'quality' to be operationalised (Broadfoot 1998; Brooks 2005)? According to Brooks (2005), attention must be paid to methodologically robust assessment practices. This is evident especially in terms of teaching and learning (Jones and Darshi de Saram 2005). Current quantitative-based assessment discourse reduces teaching and learning to an externally steered and pre-determined activity (Broadfoot 1998). Accordingly, this categorical assessment culture shapes teachers' and students' conceptions and ultimately the nature of what 'good' teaching and learning is. Therefore outcome-oriented assessment practices should be complemented by more flexible and empowering modes of assessment which better take into account the basic nature of learning.

Quality assurance can increase the bureaucracy associated with academic work and place a greater focus on assessment activities instead of the fundamental missions of universities – that is teaching and research (Hoecht 2006). Newton (2002b; see also Kinman and Jones 2003) observed that quality assurance burdened university teachers and researchers with various administrative tasks. QA systems may also be too complicated and detailed and therefore be time consuming to maintain (Jones and Darshi de Saram

2005). On the other hand quality assurance has been observed to develop core university activities – although Vidovich (2002) points out that this primarily refers to 'a perception that processes had improved, or at least been better documented' (Vidovich 2002: 396).

The number of assessment bodies and professionals has increased considerably over the last decade. It seems that quality assessment is self-justifying: it produces a need for more assessment (Salter and Tapper 2000; van Thiel and Leeuw 2002). Quality assessment also consumes economic resources. However, it is difficult to estimate the exact costs of QA, but nonetheless the maintenance and development of a QA system demands financial investments (Morley 2003: 61, 66) and its cost-effectiveness is uncertain (Bornmann *et al.* 2006). Strydom *et al.* (2004) state that there is no such thing as an inexpensive QA system, even though they can help to eliminate inefficiencies in work processes.

Newton (2002b; see also Hoecht 2006) observed that academics regarded quality assurance as a game, the roles and language of which they adopt tokenistically to demonstrate their accountability. Newton (2002b) also points out that academics' reactions to quality assurance are diverse: for some it is a game, for others it is a way to develop academic work. Academic leaders have an essential role as QA has strengthened the role of management in all levels of the university (Brennan and Shah 2000; Newton 2002a; Vidovich 2002). The introduction of quality assurance systems, it can be argued, has also brought new opportunities for groups previously marginalised and silenced in the academic community (Luke 1997).

Quality assurance in the local contexts: Finnish universities

I turn now to the question of how quality assurance is perceived in Finnish universities and how academics are reacting to it. According to the respondents in our study, increased discussion about quality at universities was a particular consequence of international pressures to harmonise the European HE systems. This has implications for the national level as well, such that universities are expected to adjust their operations accordingly. The inexorable rise of quality rhetoric was not seen as originating from the academic community itself. Rather, the quality discourse was primarily seen as managerialist in that its origin was outside the university community (see Neave 1985; El-Khawas 2001). Nonetheless, the respondents acknowledged the global concerns behind the quality issues in higher education.

Quality was primarily seen as consistency of operations, meaning that it was based on and embodied a commitment to jointly agreed rules. Quality was also seen in terms of fitness for purpose, i.e. that the efforts matched the goals set. Quality as excellence was associated with research that seeks to achieve the highest possible scientific levels. Quality as consistency and fitness for purpose reflects managerial comprehensions, whereas quality as excellence relates to the traditional academic values (see Harvey and Green 1993; Harvey and Knight 1996).

The main judges of quality came from within university – the academic community and, as far as education services are concerned, the students in particular. Other stakeholders, especially external to the universities such as the labour market and society at large, are influential in determining what quality is. The respondents considered that while the responsibility for academic activities of good quality rests upon the formal structures and decision-making bodies of university, it also belongs to the academic community and its members. These observations reflect the division between managerial and academic conceptions of quality: the managerialist approach highlights the role that external actors play whereas the academic approach emphasises the part played by universities' internal bodies (see Salter and Tapper 2000).

QA was understood by our respondents as primarily quality management and control (see Csizmadia 2006). This view was particularly common among the central administration and faculty staff. Moreover, QA was also seen as a reforming instrument and to some extent as a means to monitor and control academic activities. Quality assurance seemed to have a dual role: on the one hand quality was developed whilst on the other it was controlled and managed (see Biggs 2001).

Most often the QA system was seen to focus primarily on teaching and research and rarely on the service functions, administrative and support services or management of HEIs. Most importantly, QA can be used to reorganise operations where necessary, including for instance descriptions of the activities and exhortations to strive for efficiency. QA systems prioritise the identification and development of essential targets and the making of adjustments perceived as necessary. The concrete components of QA systems comprise various feedback mechanisms and written instructions, as well as instruments and indicators that depict the activities. Some see the introduction of QA systems as enhancing and clarifying academic functions as well as bringing better quality and reliability. It may also have some disadvantages, such as increased demand for human and time resources (cf. Brennan and Shah 2000; Salter and Tapper 2000).

According to the departmental heads who were respondents in our study, QA systems are useful and applicable to academic units. They also stated that, in their own units, as at the university in general, the QA systems had mostly either just been introduced or were still being developed. They also considered that, at their best, QA systems would improve and clarify the units' functioning by increasing reliability, systematic organisation, and transparency (see Brennan and Shah 2000; Newton 2002a). Hence, the departmental heads had aspirations that QA systems would increase spontaneous evaluation and development and enhance operations. At their worst, such systems were considered to take up too much by way of resources and lead to excessive bureaucracy (see Barnett 1994; Morley 2003; Hoecht 2006). It was found that participation in relevant training increased the departmental heads' understanding and generated a positive attitude towards QA systems.

QA and strategic efforts and intent were seen as closely connected, particularly in the sense that while strategies do guide quality work, QA systems also provide the management with information about the success or otherwise of strategy. The respondents expressed a concern that QA may start to have an undue influence on strategic planning. From the central administration point of view, QA was a welcome means of 'steering by results'. At other levels of the universities however, the respondents did not see such effects as desirable because they might lead to increased external control (see Newton 2000; Hoecht 2006).

The development of a QA system calls for motivation and commitment from the whole university community, together with sufficient resources, positive attitudes, and continuing interaction and communication. The respondents stressed the importance of QA systems being sensitive to different disciplinary cultures (see Newton 2002b; Jones and Darshi de Saram 2005).Whilst QA systems were developed in accordance with universities' own starting points, the audit criteria of the FINHEEC were regarded as important mirrors in the process. The main threat perceived from such external audits was that they may make the universities' QA systems overly uniform and insensitive to individual institutions' characters.

It was anticipated that QA systems would come to be a permanent part of the processes aimed at evaluating the performance of universities. However, these systems were judged to be likely to have a more moderate influence on daily practices in the future, after the disruption caused by their introduction had subsided.

Discussion

It seems that, in Finnish universities at least, the managerial and collegial features of QA coexist. Collegial quality assurance includes understanding quality as excellence, quality development and embodying the importance of academic community and collegiality. Managerial quality assurance however comprehends quality as fitness for purpose and consistency, a focus on quality management, monitoring and control, acknowledges the importance of interest groups external to the institution and is outcome-oriented. From the perspective of knowledge production, this observation is interesting. On the one hand, scientific knowledge production is expected to be assured by the means of the traditional university values and norms. On the other, more commercialised quality assurance mechanisms are also emerging and turning scientific knowledge from public good into a more commercialised commodity. The core question, however, is to what extent the two features of QA are contradictory and to what extent complementary.

As such neither of them is good or bad, but the point is to know which approach to use and when. This idea is at the core of holistic quality assurance approaches (cf. Ratcliff 2003). In practice, collegial and managerial quality assurance rarely exists *per se*, but rather in various combinations. For example, the published research findings must conform to academic notions of quality in all regards, yet the actual research and innovation process is characterised by different conceptions of what 'good quality' is. Therefore, a quality assurance system may need to take into account both collegial and managerial features of QA.

Holistic quality assurance demands a strong interaction within and outside the university as well as commitment from the whole university community to quality work. It offers a path to awareness of different conceptions of quality and various goals for quality assurance within the university. Quality assurance cannot be detached from the other academic activities, but rather should be an integral part of core university activities. Quality assurance must also recognise the ever changing needs of global markets and their influence on individual HEIs and academic work.

Major challenges for the future include how to reconcile collegial and managerial QA, how to convince people of the long-term benefits of QA to HEIs, and to what extent universities can learn from each other and from other public and private organisations as regards the development and introduction of QA systems. If QA systems can meet these challenges they can help universities to adapt to the competitive and individualised global knowledge marketplace.

Note

1 This chapter is based on Ursin (2007).

References

Amaral, A., Fulton, O. and Larsen, I. M. (2003) 'A managerial revolution?', in A. Amaral, V. L. Meek and I. M. Larsen (eds) *The Higher Education Managerial Revolution?* Dordrecht: Kluwer Academic Publishers, 275–96.

Barnett, R. (1994) 'Power, enlightenment and quality evaluation', *European Journal of Education*, 29(2): 165–79.

Bergen Communiqué (2005) 'The European higher education area – achieving the goals', Conference of Ministers responsible for higher education, 19–20 May.

Berlin Communiqué (2003) 'Realising the European higher education area', Conference of Ministers responsible for higher education, 19 September.

Biggs, J. (2001) 'The reflective institution: assuring and enhancing the quality of teaching and learning', *Higher Education*, 41(3): 221–38.

Billing, D. (2004) 'International comparisons and trends in external quality assurance of higher education: Commonality or diversity?', *Higher Education*, 47(1): 113–37.

Bornmann, L., Mittag, S. and Daniel, H.-D. (2006) 'Quality assurance in higher education – meta-evaluation of multi-stage evaluation procedures in Germany', *Higher Education*, 52(4): 687–709.

Brennan, J. and Shah, T. (2000) *Managing Quality in Higher Education*. Society for Research into Higher Education. Buckingham: Open University Press.

Broadfoot, P. (1998) 'Quality standards and control in higher education: what price life-long learning?', *International Studies in Sociology of Education*, 8(2): 155–80.

Brooks, R. L. (2005) 'Measuring university quality', *The Review of Higher Education*, 29(1): 1–21.

Brunotto, Y. and Farr-Wharton, R. (2005) 'Academics' responses to the implementation of a quality agenda', *Quality in Higher Education*, 11(2): 161–80.

Council Recommendation of 24 September 1998 on European Cooperation in Quality Assurance in Higher Education (98/561/EC) *Official Journal of the European Communities* L 270/56, vol. 41, 7 October.

Crozier, F., Curvale, B. and Hénard, F. (2005) 'Quality convergence study: a contribution to the debates on quality and convergence in the European higher education area', *ENQA Occasional Papers 7*.

Csizmadia, T. (2006) *Quality Management in Hungarian Higher Education: Organisational Response to Governmental Policy*, Enschede: CHEPS.

Deem, R. (1998) 'New managerialism in higher education – the management of performances and cultures in universities', *International Studies in the Sociology of Education*, 8(1): 47–70.

Dill, D. (1998) 'Evaluating the "evaluative state": implications for research in higher education', *European Journal of Education*, 33(3): 361–77.

El-Khawas, E. (2001) 'Who's in charge of quality? The governance issues in quality assurance', *Tertiary Education and Management*, 7(2): 111–19.

ENQA (2005) *Standards and Guidelines for Quality Assurance in the European Higher Education Area*, Helsinki: Multiprint.

Exworthy, M. and Halford, S. (eds) (1999) *Professionals and the New Managerialism in the Public Sector*, Buckingham: Open University Press.

FINHEEC (2005) *Audits of Quality Assurance Systems of Finnish Higher Education Institutions. Audit manual for 2005–2007*, Tampere: Tammer-Paino. Available online at http://www.kka.fi/pdf/julkaisut/KKA_406.pdf.

Gibbons, M., Limoges, C., Nowotny, H., Schwartzman, S., Scott, P. and Trow, M. (1994) *The New Production of Knowledge: The Dynamics of Science and Research in Contemporary Societies*, London: Sage.

Harvey, L. and Green, D. (1993) 'Defining quality', *Assessment and Evaluation in Higher Education*, 18(1): 9–34.

Harvey, L. and Knight, P. (1996) *Transforming Higher Education*, The Society for Research in Higher Education. Buckingham: Open University Press.

Hoecht, A. Q. (2006) 'Quality assurance in UK higher education: issues of trust, control, professional autonomy and accountability', *Higher Education*, 51(4): 541–63.

Jones, J. and Darshi de Saram, D. (2005) 'Academic staff views of quality systems for teaching and learning: a Hong Kong case study', *Quality in Higher Education*, 11(1): 47–58.

Kinman, G. and Jones, F. (2003) '"Running up the down escalator": stressors and strains in UK academics', *Quality in Higher Education*, 9(1): 21–38.

Knight, P. T. and Trowler, P. R. (2000) Editorial. *Quality in Higher Education*, 6(2): 109–14.

Luke, C. (1997) 'Quality assurance and women in higher education', *Higher Education*, 33(4): 433–51.

Marginson, S. and Rhoades, G. (2002) 'Beyond national states, markets, and systems of higher education: a glonacal agency heuristic', *Higher Education*, 43(3): 281–309.

Morley, L. (2003) *Quality and Power in Higher Education*, Philadelphia, PA: Society for Research into Higher Education.

Neave, G. (1985) 'The university and state in Western Europe', in D. Jaques and J. Richardson (eds) *The Future of Higher Education*, Milton Keynes: Open University Press, pp. 27–40.

Neave, G. (1998) 'The evaluative state reconsidered', *European Journal of Education*, 33(3): 265–84.

Newton, J. (2000) 'Feeding the beast or improving quality?: academics' perceptions of quality assurance and quality monitoring', *Quality in Higher Education*, 6(2): 153–63.

Newton, J. (2002a) 'Barriers to effective quality management and leadership: case study of two academics departments', *Higher Education*, 44(2): 185–212.

Newton, J. (2002b) 'Views from below: academics coping with quality', *Quality in Higher Education*, 8(1): 39–61.

OPM (2004) 'Korkeakoulutuksen laadunvarmistus' [Quality assurance in higher education]. Reports of the Ministry of Education 2004: 6. Helsinki: Yliopistopaino.

Power, M. (1994) *The Audit Explosion*, London: Demos.

Ratcliff, J. L. (2003) 'Dynamic and communicative aspects of quality assurance', *Quality in Higher Education*, 9(2): 117–31.

Realizing the European Higher Education Area (2004) 'Preamble to communiqué of the conference of ministers responsible for higher education', *European Education*, 36(3): 19–27.

Rinne, R. and Koivula, J. (2005) 'The changing place of the university and a clash of values: the entrepreneurial university in the European knowledge society. A review of the literature', *Higher Education Management and Policy*, 17(3): 91–123.

Saarinen, T. (2005) 'From sickness to cure and further: construction of "quality" in Finnish higher education policy from the 1960s to the era of the Bologna process', *Quality in Higher Education*, 11(1): 3–15.

Salter, B. and Tapper, T. (2000) 'The politics of governance in higher education: the case of quality assurance', *Political Studies*, 48(1): 66–87.

Strydom, J. F., Zulu, N. and Murray, L. (2004) 'Quality, culture and change', *Quality in Higher Education*, 10(3): 207–17.

Tapper, E. R. and Filippakou, O. (2006) 'Quality assurance in higher education: thinking beyond the English experience. What are the key issues?'. Paper presentation. The Transformation of Higher Education: International Influences. Boulogne-sur-Mer, 20–22 November.

Thiel, S. van and Leeuw, F. L. (2002) 'The performance paradox in the public sector', *Public Performance & Management Review*, 25(3): 267–81.

Trowler, P. (1998) *Academics, Work and Change*, Buckingham: Open University Press.

Ursin, J. (2007) 'Yliopistot laadun arvioijina. Akateemisia käsityksiä laadusta ja laadunvarmistuksesta' [Universities as quality evaluators. Academic conceptions of quality and quality assurance] University of Jyväskylä. Institute for Educational Research. Occasional Papers 35.

Vidovich, L. (2002) 'Quality assurance in Australian higher education: globalisation and "steering at a distance"', *Higher Education*, 43(3): 391–408.

Vidovich, L. (2004) 'Global–national–local dynamics in policy processes: a case of "quality" policy in higher education', *British Journal of Sociology of Education*, 25(3): 341–54.

Vught, F. A. van and Westerheijden, D. (1993) *Quality Management and Quality Assurance in European Higher Education. Methods and Mechanism*, Luxembourg: Office for Official Publications of the EC.

Vught, F. A. van and Westerheijden, D. (1994) 'Towards a general model of quality assessment in higher education', *Higher Education*, 28(3): 355–71.

Yorke, M. (2000) 'Developing a quality culture in higher education', *Tertiary Education and Management*, 6(1): 19–36.

9 HRM in HE

People reform or re-forming people?

Matt Waring

In a globalised society, where the acquisition and possession of knowledge becomes ever more critical, universities have restructured themselves as sites of knowledge production to take advantage of the market opportunities that arise. Governments worldwide are well aware of the significance of the role of universities as knowledge disseminators, 'where higher education is increasingly seen as an industry for enhancing national competitiveness and as a commodity that can be sold in the global marketplace' (Naidoo 2003: 250). Universities are coming under increasing government pressure to adopt market principles of cost-minimisation, flexibility and quality-enhancement, such is their significance to national economies. For universities the income streams generated are considerable, with the total volume of the global education market estimated at around US$30 billion (van der Wende 2003). In the case of the UK, the nature of the public funding system means that universities are now making decisions about how to operate internationally based on managerial rather than educational considerations (Elliott 1998). National governments are, therefore, playing for big stakes in the market for higher education, resulting in a perceived need to implement new technologies of management 'to undercut the power and control of academics over knowledge production and reproduction' (Naidoo 2003: 250).

Such transformations imply the need for increased attention to be given to the labour elements of universities – the manner and nature of the organisation and control of the academic workforce. 'Human Resource Management' (HRM) is a managerialist technique that has been increasingly utilised in UK universities to facilitate enhanced control over academic labour by implementing systems based on individual performance management.

This chapter is organised as follows. First, I provide a brief outline of the concept of HRM. This is then placed within the wider societal context of neoliberalism. Consideration is given to Beck and Beck-Gernsheim's (2002) concept of individualisation under conditions of globalisation. This is followed by a brief summary of the more recent changes that have occurred in the UK higher education sector. I then present data drawn from a qualitative study that I have undertaken that sought to interrogate the use of HRM in UK universities and discuss the central issues of whether or not the introduction of HRM is people reform in a positive, developmental sense, or if, in fact, we are witnessing a disturbing experiment to re-form people and impose new patterns of behaviour. This is followed by some conclusions.

HRM defined

A comprehensive account of HRM and the ongoing debate surrounding it is beyond the scope of this chapter; however, a brief summary of this particular technology of management is necessary. HRM originated in the US in the early 1980s as a response to increasing foreign competition. Business organisations sought to become more competitive by stimulating their workers to deliver higher quality through the use of 'high commitment work practices'. Under similar competitive pressures in the UK, the arrival of HRM coincided with the election of the Thatcher government with its commitment to reforming industrial relations, privatisation and the promotion of an entrepreneurial and high-technology service-led economy, underpinned with a strong belief in employer-driven decision-making.

Ideologically, HRM emphasises the importance of a tight fit between corporate and HR strategies to achieve a highly committed, high quality and flexible workforce (Guest 1992). Commitment of staff is a central theme in the Harvard model of HRM (Beer *et al.* 1984) and Storey's matrix (1992) notes the implicit belief that staff should be willing to 'go beyond contract'. The successful operationalisation of this strategic approach to HRM requires that the pluralist nature of organisations, and the predominantly adversarial nature of employee relations that traditionally existed in UK organisations, gives way to a more harmonious, unitarist atmosphere. In order to create such an environment, HR work ceases to be seen as a separate activity carried out by a support function, but is rather devolved to line managers who assume a vital role in motivating staff to peak performance. The role of a line manager is to focus on the 'soft' aspects of management – nurturing and developing – rather than monitoring and control. Individual performance management and regular use of staff appraisal are central to the approach. Reward schemes are designed to promote a strong identity with corporate goals and a range of individualised strategies are used, such as profit-related pay, performance-related pay and competence-based schemes.

The debate around HRM tends to focus on whether it can be seen as rhetoric or reality – if it is no more than 'big hat, no cattle' (Fernie 1994: 26). There is empirical evidence to suggest that many HR practices exist in UK organisations (see for example Cully *et al.* 1999; WERS 2004), but whether these are a coherent whole strategy or rather more piecemeal is open to debate (Storey *et al.* 2001). Others have considered the more insidious aspects of HRM. Whilst HRM is ostensibly about mutuality and the need to develop vital human assets in a unitarist environment, there is evidence to suggest that the reality is very different (Legge 1995). It has been suggested that HRM can be seen as a tool for controlling and manipulating the actions of workers through compliance (Willmott 1995) and that, in fact, it is 'a wolf in sheep's clothing' (Keenoy 1990).

The inherently individualistic ideology of HRM runs counter to the long-established notions of collegiality that traditionally existed in universities and has more in common with a neoliberal individualisation discourse.

The societal context of individualisation

HRM evolved as a business response to increasing competition in a globalising environment. Local and global events are interconnected under conditions of globalisation (e.g. Giddens 1991) or, as Held *et al.* (1999: 15) argue, 'globalization can be located on a continuum with the local, national and regional'. According to Beck and Beck-Gernsheim (2002), under such conditions Western society has entered a 'second-modernity' characterised by 'institutionalised individualism'. This 'liberating' process apparently sets people free from the traditional institutions of society. Collective notions such as class, religion, gender-roles and family are no longer relevant, coming as they did out of the 'modern' era that was itself the consequence of the emergence of capitalism.

Increasing individualisation, globalisation, under-employment and the worsening ecological crisis are global forces that require a fundamental questioning of the way we live. Beck and Beck-Gernsheim (2002: 203) contend that we have seen 'the disembedding of the ways of life of industrial society (class, family, gender, nation) without reembedding'. Individuals now exist in a society with few rules and an inherent short-termism, resulting in uncertainty. No longer can one automatically assume support from friends and family or societal norms, as such things are now 'zombie categories' – still with us but increasingly irrelevant in the modern world.

In Beck's (2000) analysis, risk is firmly placed on the shoulders of the individual. For many workers this is a common workplace experience, not least in the UK public sector where there has been a concerted effort to drive down costs through the use of non-standard, flexible and therefore more insecure forms of employment. Sennett (1998) has noted the individualising trend of 'flexible capitalism' where, as organisations become more transient, so too do the people who work in them. As organisations undertake more contracting out and replace jobs with projects so short-termism comes to dominate. Consequently, individuals do not put down roots and begin to lead fragmented lives, fending for themselves. Not all can survive without a strong network of support and this gradual erosion of all that ties people together and out of which grows loyalty and sustainable collective spirit results, Sennett argues, in a 'corrosion of character' (1998: 10).

At the organisational level there is evidence to suggest that employers have attempted to individualise contracts (Brown *et al.* 1998). But Kelly (1998) has questioned this decline of collectivism, suggesting that collective action is subject to cyclical waves in the same way that the economy experiences up- and down-swings. For him, there are signs of a resurgence in collective action within the labour movement. The general consensus that is emerging from many industrial relations academics is that although the world has moved on, and the nature and experience of work has clearly radically altered, the essential tension and conflict at the heart of the struggle between labour and capital remains the same. In fact, recent research by Brown and Oxenbridge (2003) found evidence that collective bargaining is still very much alive and evolving in line with workplace developments.

Whether or not we have seen a process of de-collectivisation and individual-isation or whether we are about to see a surge in collective action, there has undoubtedly been a recent transformation in the conduct of industrial relations (Millward *et al.* 2000). Whilst the situation in the broader public sector has been widely researched (see, for example, Winchester and Bach 1999; Corby and White 1999; Farnham and Horton 1996), so far, little empirical work has been carried out to evaluate the experience of academics. Yet universities have always been unique and heterogeneous institutions with distinctive values and traditions. Therefore, recent British attempts to introduce homogenising HRM systems are likely to have met with a number of ideological challenges, potentially generating tensions and conflicts.

The marketisation of higher education

Following the Education Reform Act of 1988 and the Further and Higher Education Act of 1992 UK HE was radically transformed, starting with the creation of the 'new universities' as independent bodies managed by boards of governors from the old polytechnics to add to the ranks of more traditional institutions. Subsequently, a quasi-market system was created, with competition between the increased number of HE providers. Many have questioned whether a market system, which effectively turns knowledge into a commodity, is an appropriate method of HE delivery (e.g. Lynn Meek 2000). Some writers have argued that a proletarianisation of academic labour has been taking place (Wilson 1991; Willmott 1995; Miller 1995; Farnham 1999), with the massification of HE leading to a de-skilling of academic work and a situation where academics' 'prestige, salaries, autonomy, and resources have been much humbled' (Halsey 1995: 146). Wilson identified a number of trends in HE typical of proletarianised work:

> ... less trust and discretion, a growing division of labour; stronger hierarchies of management control; greater conflict; growing routinisa-tion; bureaucratisation; worse conditions and facilities; above all a steep decline in relative pay.
>
> (Wilson 1991: 251)

Universities increasingly employ staff on casual or non-permanent contracts, leading to the model of a 'flexi-university' (Farnham 1999: 28) where institutions reduce their staffing overheads considerably but the consequence for staff is a 'fractionalisation of the academic profession where divisions of interest can emerge' (Fulton 1999: 29).

The issue of control is clearly a key consideration in the nature of academic work and Wilson (1991: 253), drawing on Thompson (1989), has noted the similarities in traditional academic work to Friedman's notion of 'responsible autonomy'. The increasing focus on HRM and a more assertive style of management challenges this autonomy leading to tension and conflict. Wilson sees a degree of degradation 'in the objective sense that conditions of employment, broadly conceived, have dramatically worsened' (1991: 258). For Wilson, the changes are threatening the traditional notion of universities as independent communities of scholars pursuing knowledge for its own sake. Willmott (1995) argues that the whole thrust of government HE policy has had the effect of intensifying and commodifying the work of academics. In a sense, the organisation and control of the work of academics 'is conditioned, but not determined, by capitalist priorities and disciplines' (1995: 1001). In this analysis, students see themselves as consumers of educational services and academics 'are purveyors of commodities within a knowledge "supermarket"' (Winter 1995: 134). Thus academics may be seen to be losing ideological control of their work due to an increasing individualisation of their working conditions brought about by the marketisation and massification of HE. Such developments have created an employment relationship of growing complexity and diversity and there is evidence of an increasingly managerialist tendency (Deem 1998). Ironically, whilst the very values – harmony and unity of purpose – which traditionally framed universities are those that HRM seeks to engender, these have apparently been eroded by the approach taken by management in HE.

The UK government has long favoured the implementation of individual performance management systems in universities. This was reinforced in 2001 when the Higher Education Funding Council for England (HEFCE), the intermediary body between government and the universities, launched its 'Rewarding and Developing Staff in Higher Education' (RDS) initiative (HEFCE 2001). The RDS was partly inspired by the Dearing (NCIHE 1997) and Bett (IRHE 1999) reports, both of which highlighted the need for better leadership and a more effective approach to people management in universities. These reports suggested that the low priority placed on people management issues acted as a disincentive to staff that could ultimately undermine the government's vision for a world-class higher education sector.

The core idea of RDS was that a percentage of universities' funding would be contingent upon the production of a detailed HR strategy which identified specific and costed HR objectives. It was for institutions themselves to determine priority areas, but HEFCE identified six key areas[1] which had to be addressed, including a focus on individual performance management. In the first period 2001–2 to 2003–4 some £330 million was set aside for RDS (around 4.95 per cent of the total funding for universities in England), with a further £167 million made available to maintain the progress made through to 2006. It was always HEFCE's intention that RDS would have a finite timescale and that, from 2006, all funding would be returned to the core. It was envisaged that by then the HR values promoted by the initiative would be sufficiently embedded in the strategy of HEIs and be self-supporting.

The notion of individual performance management within UK universities remains problematic for many reasons which I address below. Significant is the fact that in many organisations 'people performance is vitiated by the obsession with control and therefore is liable to undermine, rather than contribute to, performance' (Hendry *et al.* 2000: 46). This not only presents a challenge for university managers to counter this perception and demonstrate a genuine commitment to improving individual performance, but also challenges the very values upon which UK universities were originally founded.

Three cases, five themes

This section draws upon fieldwork data from three English HEIs. Staff at all levels were interviewed: lecturers, line and senior managers (including HR directors) and representatives of the academic trade unions. I also undertook some observation and documentary analysis. The initial sample of respondents included the HR director; a member of the senior management team (either deputy or pro-vice chancellor depending on context); the chief academic union negotiator; Deans/Chairs of faculty and then Heads of Department/Institute in the pre-92s; Heads of School/Department and then Section Heads/Line managers in the post-92s. Snowball sampling was used to identify the lecturing staff. A brief pen portrait of each institution follows.

> **Dartmoor:** Initially established as a teacher training college, Dartmoor became a college of higher education in the 1970s and was granted university status comparatively recently. Dartmoor enjoys a reputation for being a small, friendly, student-focused teaching institution with particular strengths in vocational subjects.

> **Wormwood:** Established in the early twentieth century, Wormwood is situated in a large city and has an international research reputation, being a prominent member of the elite 'Russell Group' of universities. The university is renowned both for the quality of its teaching and research and achieved several 5* and 6 ratings in the 2001 RAE exercise.

> **Parkhurst:** Also a prominent member of the Russell Group, Parkhurst was established in the 1960s and has an international reputation for innovation in research. It has academics of world-class standing in its many 5* and 6 rated departments.

Five key themes emerged from the fieldwork data: modernisation; management reorganisation; the role of the head of department; HR strategies and appraisal; and collegiality.

Modernisation

Modernisation was the unifying, and indeed, dominant theme that emerged across all three institutions. It was manifested in a variety of different ways and was progressing in a variable manner according to institution. In all cases there was an underlying current of change that was creating an atmosphere of instability and uncertainty. This was most apparent at Dartmoor, which was embarking upon a huge expansion plan that included a major building project. All respondents at Dartmoor recognised the need to expand its research and consultancy work and to grow student numbers. The challenge this posed to their key strength as a student-focused teaching institution was recognised by all. Some of the newer appointees expressed a concern that they had been appointed on the basis of their research profile in line with the changing university mission but were still required to carry out significant teaching loads. Change was apparent too at Wormwood, which had major expansion plans for its campus, and Parkhurst which was also involved in substantial capital investment plans to upgrade and replace a number of its buildings.

All of the senior managers that were interviewed expressed the view that such developments are essential in the modern era of HE. All agreed that universities had no choice but to become more 'business-like' as it was seen as a matter of survival. As one Wormwood pro-vice chancellor put it,

> ... in the last twelve years we have completely evolved our management processes to ensure that we are a business. We are driven to make a surplus ...

All of the senior managers talked about the challenges of a market system which required a more strategic, corporate approach than in the past. Decision-making, they felt, had to be based on strong financial evidence and loss-making areas would inevitably be under threat. At Wormwood, for example, a strategic decision had been made following the last research assessment exercise to withdraw support for research in a poorly performing department and to make it concentrate purely on teaching.

Management reorganisation

In line with the hegemonic modernisation discourse, reorganisation of management structures was seen as essential in all three institutions. Wormwood had embarked upon a major reorganisation a few years before that coincided with the arrival of a modernising VC tasked with changing the culture of a very traditional university. The new structure strengthened faculties by devolving budgets to that level to be managed by powerful executive deans supported by a management team. The creation of a few such stream-lined 'cost-centres' to replace what was seen as a rather inefficient and outdated system based around departments was justified on grounds of economic and administrative rationality. At the time of the fieldwork a further reorganisation was taking place within some of the faculties to amalgamate a number of smaller departments into schools, with a single head of school and a management team that included a business manager. A similar reorganisation was taking place at Parkhurst, and at Dartmoor a new tier of management had recently been created within schools to support the head of department. The management teams comprised academics and a member of the support staff. One member of staff at Dartmoor spoke for many in expressing a view about this new tier of management:

> There is a lot of ill-feeling about this new line-manager role and most people think this is really a layer of management too far. Most people ignore them anyway, so what's the point?
>
> (Senior lecturer, Dartmoor)

All three universities had powerful executive steering groups centred around the VC, PVCs, registrar and/or finance director and, in two cases, the HR director. These tended to meet regularly (at least once a week) and coordinated the day-to-day running of the university. At Wormwood and Parkhurst some concern was expressed by lecturing staff and some heads over the degree of control given to administrators who were making decisions based on corporate rather than academic criteria. Examples included the setting of increasingly high targets for student numbers on a MBA course – the perception being that this was about maximising revenue and with little concern for academic standards. This concurs with Smyth's (1995) suggestion of a growing separation in HE between those who conceptualise and execute the work and that important decisions are made in elite policy-making units. All of which suggests a rather anti-collegial mindset at the senior management level.

No outright opposition was expressed towards the various management reorganisations and there was a general acceptance of the need for some sort of change and modernisation of management practices. Respondents were certainly frustrated by some of the more bureaucratic processes and a culture of 'form-filling', but blame for this was targeted at external bodies rather than the university itself. There was a strong sense at Wormwood and Parkhurst that whatever management were doing there remained a clear recognition of the primacy of research activity. As long as the academics felt they were able to concentrate on this, and most felt they still could despite the increased pressures, then they were prepared to tolerate, albeit reluctantly, an increasingly business-focused culture. Here, then, are clear echoes of Miller's notion of bargained autonomy 'whereby degrees of at least apparent control are retained by the individual on the implicit understanding that the targets of increased student numbers, more articles or more form filling are met' (Miller 1995: 54).

Role of the head of department

Clearly, the role of head is a key one that has major implications for the experience of work for academics in a department. Many heads actually saw themselves as a kind of buffer between the university's management and the academic staff. For one the role was about nurturing rather than managing staff:

> Just about all the academics in my department are internationally recognised experts in their field so I do what I can to keep them happy – I'm just here to massage their egos. (Head of department, Parkhurst)

The rotational appointment system[2] was also coming under scrutiny. Several heads expressed frustration that their academic careers had to be put on hold for their three-year period of tenure, which was frequently described as 'Buggins' turn'. To some extent the creation of departmental management teams was a response to this and at Wormwood one objective of the HR strategy was to identify potential leaders in order to groom them for future management roles. Academic staff recognised rotationality as a problem, but were strongly opposed to any notion of appointed managers. For them the virtue of the current system was that an academic voice remained at the management table. However, at Wormwood there was one example of an appointed manager being brought in to sort out a problem department:

> They brought in a sort of hired gun ...
>
> (Union representative, Wormwood)

Interestingly, at Wormwood and Parkhurst, whatever the nature of the reorganisation academics continued to feel a strong allegiance to their department, based, as they are, on disciplines. Whether the focus of the management structure was on faculties or merging departments into schools, the academics clearly identified closely with their department. Thus, attempts to alter the identities of academics through this strategy were met with opposition from the academics themselves, and on this evidence, by the heads of department too, in much the same way that Henkel (2000) found.

HR strategies and appraisal

All three universities had an HR strategy in place. At Wormwood and Parkhurst the HR directors had been appointed around the time of the launch of the RDS initiative and completion of the strategy had been their first task. All had come from other HE institutions and had significant experience of the sector. But awareness of the HR strategy in all three universities appeared to stop at the level of head of department. Apart from the union representatives, very few academic staff knew anything about it:

I know nothing about an HR strategy. If we do have one it has no impact on me.

(Senior lecturer, Dartmoor)

Although the strategies emphasised the values of communication and consultation with staff, the evidence suggests they had been written with little of either. At Wormwood it had been left up to departmental heads to decide whether or not to consult with staff. At Dartmoor the strategy had been discussed at various committees including the joint consultative committee (with the union), but not disseminated to all staff. At Parkhurst the HR director saw no need to involve staff in what he saw as strategic decision-making. Academic staff displayed an awareness of certain HR initiatives but there was little or no awareness of the strategy as a whole.

There was, however, significant awareness of staff appraisal regimes, of which experience was variable and largely dependent upon the personality of the departmental head. At Wormwood there was a requirement that heads should carry out annual appraisals, but records were kept in the department so there was little to ensure that they actually took place. One head, who saw far more value in operating in an informal collegiate manner where staff were free to come and see him whenever they wanted, did not bother with appraisals at all. Staff in the department confirmed this, but were concerned for the future as this department was soon to be merged in the latest reorganisation. Parkhurst were in the process of moving from a fairly benign triennial review to a more formal annual process of performance management. The three HR directors all recognised the potential for conflict in trying to quantify academic performance, but also believed it would ultimately provide a more structured career path. Responses in the medical faculties were significantly different as there is a far stronger tradition and, therefore, greater acceptance of performance review and evidence-based professional updating. There is certainly evidence to suggest that the effectiveness and, indeed, acceptance of appraisal systems is dependent upon the cultural background and traditions of particular disciplines. Evidence suggests that resistance to appraisal takes different forms and occurs on several fronts.

Collegiality

Notions of collegiality and the extent to which this and an individualistic approach to people management can co-exist in a university environment were explored at some length. For one HR director there were far too many myths about the past in HE and they saw collegiality as all part and parcel of a general mis-perception of a supposedly glorious past. According to this respondent there was no alternative but to modernise and this meant replacing an outdated informality with formal processes and procedures that were 'fit for purpose'. In fact there were responses at all levels to suggest there might be a degree of harking back to the past with rose-tinted spectacles. However, there was consensus around the idea that collegiality was very much at the heart of a university's ethos and also that it was coming under pressure from an increasingly corporate management style. Definitions of collegiality varied to a degree, but all centred around the idea of shared ownership, working together supportively, informality and a collective will. Most academics felt that it was important to maintain a collegiate approach but the following quote sums up the concerns of many:

> Collegiality? I think we are being restructured away from that.
> (Union representative, Wormwood)

Collegiality was also discussed in terms of the informal social networks of the university, and there was general consensus that the ability to meet informally was being eroded by time pressures; whether it was from teaching loads, research assessment exercise imperatives or attending meetings. Many discussed a time, not that long ago, when everyone was able to meet for coffee or lunch in a senior common room and that it was here where valuable time was spent discussing and sharing ideas. Lack of time emerged as a key concern for staff at all levels and was largely seen as an inevitable consequence of the changes to the sector, but significantly was seen as gradually eroding that which was fundamentally part of the essence of a university.

People reform or re-forming people?

Universities are rather unique environments and, for many, this arises from the traditions of collegiality. Attempts to impose control and order the work of academics through the use of HRM strategies would seem to be challenging that norm. But, to paraphrase Hyman (1987), is it possible to actually have a coherent people management strategy that effectively harmonises with the other business strategies in an area that is normally characterised by ad-hocery (1987: 34)? Models of strategic fit, such as best-practice, best-fit, and the resource-based view (Boxall and Purcell 2003) attempt to theorise the issue, but there is still little consensus, except perhaps that there is no 'one best way', and that the management of so-called 'knowledge workers' is notoriously difficult, if not futile. As Hyman tells us,

> The more complex and sophisticated the workers' knowledge and experience, the more difficult normally for management to prescribe tasks in detail and to monitor closely their performance.
> (Hyman 1987: 39)

It seems clear that the increasing reliance on business-led solutions and their associated control systems are the source of much contention throughout the sector. But as Dearlove (1997: 57) explains 'good academics cannot be told what to do; they defy control; and the kind of creativity required cannot be commanded by an academic master'. It is this kind of autonomy based in the collegial system that academics have struggled to retain in the face of massification and other changes to the HE system. Having established the key themes, I now turn to address whether we are seeing a case of people reform, in the sense of improving the working lives of academics through enhanced HR management, or if indeed there is a more ominous agenda to re-form the identities of academics as individualised neoliberal subjects.

The contention that universities *have* to modernise – the unifying theme in my fieldwork – is in itself very revealing and perfectly in tune with the prevailing neoliberal consensus that informs debate around HE in the UK today. Modernisation has been central to the New Labour reform programme and for universities this has led to the creation of a policy narrative that presents the marketisation of higher education and its associated policies as the only way forward (Wright 2004). Furthermore, as Reed (2005) explains '… modernisation discourse is inherent in neo-technocratic managerialism …' and 'the organisational hybridisation that it has generated has relocated public service professionals in an evermore confusing, threatening and uncertain environment' (Reed 2005: slide 21). That paradox certainly seems apparent for those working in HE and has echoes in my research but, as Wright (2004) points out, this is now presented as the only solution to the problem and challenges to the dominant orthodoxy cannot be countenanced. The seeds of this ideology are, arguably, apparent in the Robbins Report of 1963 and are quite clear in the Jarratt Report of 1985 and the Fender Report of 1993.

The Jarratt Report (1985) was produced for the Committee of Vice Chancellors and Principals and looked at efficiency in universities. According to Kogan (1989: 75) it 'is explicit in its managerialism'. The report saw the reason for universities' perceived inefficiency as stemming from academics who saw their discipline as more important than the well-being of the university. But as Kogan suggests,

> The well-being of the institution is important only because it ensures the good work of the individuals who work in it. Any academic enterprise which does not have powerful academic departments and individual academics who cherish their academic discipline above all else, will be second rate or worse.

> (Kogan 1989: 76)

The CVCP's report 'Promoting People' (CVCP 1993), also known as the Fender report, set out to provide a framework for the development of staff in universities and, like Jarratt before it, was heavily influenced by private sector management trends, with much talk of modernisation, customer satisfaction, teamwork and continuous improvement. A single pay spine was proposed (the genesis of the 2004 pay deal discussed below) with an emphasis placed on rewarding individual performance. The whole tone of the report is extremely revealing, with notions of academia as described by Dearlove and Kogan implicitly dismissed as out of touch with the realities of a modern era. The Fender Report is perhaps not as well known as the Dearing (NCIHE 1997) and Bett (IRHE 1999) reports that followed, but it is important in that it signals a point where HRM rhetoric and managerialism really begin to influence agendas and when the language of the market became the norm for those running HE. By 1997, when the National Committee of Inquiry into HE, under the chairmanship of Sir Ron Dearing, published its report 'Higher Education in the Learning Society' (NCIHE 1997) a fundamental shift in thinking that implicitly accepted that HE could be run along conventional business lines was clearly visible.

The 2004 National Pay Framework (JNCHES 2004) provides the most recent example of the government's neoliberal agenda in this area. Here was a broad national framework for guidance but, significantly, with the flexibility for substantial local negotiation. Although the agreement fell short of the pre-existing system of national collective bargaining over pay and conditions, it did retain some element of national guidance and prevented a complete free-for-all in local pay bargaining and was accepted by a majority of academic staff in a national ballot. Ultimately, through the decentralisation of bargaining, the government had achieved a further degree of individualisation at the level of the institution.

On the basis of this evidence there appears little doubt over the ideology that has informed the UK government's HE reform agenda. This leads to consideration of the particular methods chosen to achieve its aims. The following quote summarises the central issue.

> I think this idea that it's possible to project certain images of personnel management into a university that is not in accord with the way that many people feel about their employment ... it just doesn't fit. It's a bit bizarre actually.
>
> (Dean, Wormwood)

Given that HRM, with its inherent individualism and well-documented weaknesses (see, for example, Legge 1995) is apparently at odds with the very essence of a university, exactly what is the rationale for attempting to implement such an approach? Townley's (1993) Foucauldian analysis of HRM provides a useful starting point as she considers the indeterminacy of an employment contract – the gap between what is promised and what is actually achieved –and how HRM and its various techniques attempts to reduce that space (and the individuals who inhabit it) and render it knowledgeable and governable.

In this sense we can see appraisal systems as a means of turning the individual academic into an 'object of knowledge' which then renders them more manageable and easier to control. The appraisal forms one part of a management process that attempts to standardise and codify the performance of academics (as above, where staff continually referred to audit trails and increased bureaucracy in the name of accountability). Time and again in my fieldwork senior managers talked about the need to create systems of management that provided rationality and accountability and that were presented as the only sensible way to manage in a more corporate era.

Yet, in the Foucauldian sense that Townley adopts, we can see this whole process as one that 'acts to impose order on the inherently undecidable' (Townley 1993: 75). The individualising process that underpins this approach acts as a controlling mechanism, affirming Foucault's concept of power-knowledge. Significantly, this offers a different interpretation to that of Beck, who saw the process of individualisation as a liberating one that offered choices to individuals. Rather, it has greater resonance with the work of Rose and Miller in their analysis of the mechanisms of contemporary political power (1992). In this analysis of the governmentalisation of the state under conditions of neoliberalism, although we are encouraged to make independent choices over the way we organise our lives, those choices are constrained by others. For Rose and Miller this is a very subtle process, 'the delicate construction of a complex and hybrid assemblage ...' (1992: 271), where individuals construct their life-worlds according to a set of relatively standardised forms of individuality and personality. Although such 'narratives and techniques of the self' (1992: 270) are clearly pluralistic and differentiated along various dimensions, under such conditions we all become neoliberal subjects. The use of HRM in HE can therefore be seen as part of this much wider process, in that it offers a tightly constrained freedom that seeks to impose certain patterns of behaviour and modes of action upon the work of academics, justified as being the only possible, rational response to the demands of a globalised HE sector.

Given the importance attached to the modernisation agenda one might justifiably expect the university to strive for effective implementation of the strategy. Yet whilst all three institutions in my study had invested a great deal of time and effort in drawing up their HR strategies, they were clearly only having a partial effect and were not penetrating all levels of the structure. The impression was of a sector in transition, with some aspects of the modernisation agenda having a greater impact than others. As described, there was no outright opposition to the various agendas and in some cases there was support for the formalisation of processes and procedures in areas such as recruitment and selection, working conditions, equal opportunities and action to tackle bullying and harassment. However, there was a clear degree of frustration over ineffective implementation of policy.

This finding does not support those of the two independent evaluations carried out on behalf of HEFCE (Deloitte and Touche 2002; Office for Public Management 2002) which both concluded that there had been a strengthening of the HR function and that HEIs were generally taking a far more professional approach to HR management. Whilst my research does indicate a far greater level of HR activity, it does not support the claims of greater effectiveness. Whether this was to do with academics who were simply not competent in the role of line-managers, is evidence of a more covert form of resistance, or a function of both, is not clear. What was clear, however, was the significant role played by the head of department in affecting the way academics experienced their work. Ultimately, although some of the objectives appear worthwhile and were supported by academic staff, it is the underpinning individualistic ideology that informs the HR strategy which puts it in direct conflict with the prevailing collegiate ethos of a university. Lacking the unitarist conditions upon which HRM theory is based and without the total commitment of staff such an approach cannot be successfully implemented. Ironically, the democratic structures and collegiality that traditionally existed in universities would be far more suited to seeking solutions to the challenges of modernisation, yet it is those very structures and their established traditions which are threatened by the current strategy.

Conclusion

The dominance of the individualisation discourse in universities cannot be under-estimated, coming at HEIs both at the level of the institution (the neoliberal milieu) and of the individual employment contract (HR strategies). However, we are again reminded of Hyman who argues that emerging patterns of labour control contain their own emergent contradictions and that new disciplines imposed on workers can be expected to provoke unpredictable and disruptive forms of revolt (Hyman 1987: 52). The recent industrial action[3] in 2006 in the UK was an explicit and overt form of rebellion, yet the evidence in this research suggests that resistance usually takes a rather subtler form and is variable in its effect. Whether or not strength of opinion is such that it will lead to the mobilisation of more overt forms of resistance as suggested by Kelly (above) remains to be seen. There is far greater acceptance of individual performance appraisal in medical faculties where such systems have long been accepted as a normal part of professional updating. In other areas quite senior personnel such as heads of department are resistant to many of the overtly individualistic policies and act as a kind of buffer between senior management and staff. Clearly, the sort of 'hearts and minds' buy-in that HRM requires if it is to be effectively integrated cannot be taken for granted. Pressure on individual academic staff has certainly increased, but does not seem to signal a transfer of risk in terms of decreased job security for those on permanent contracts, but there is clearly a greater level of insecurity for contract research staff. There is certainly an indication of some of the more insidious aspects of HRM outlined above, where organisations become locked into a cost-reduction approach and seem to want '... workers to be both dependable and expendable ...' (Hyman 1987: 43).

There is a certain irony that universities actually feel the need to control the work of academics, given that the unique nature of academic work requires a high degree of self-motivation anyway. Many academics tend to tolerate less than ideal working conditions and earn significantly less than comparable private sector workers because they are inherently driven to pursue their particular academic discipline. This raises much wider questions as to the role of the university in society today. The government is apparently attempting to re-shape universities into sites of knowledge production, by imposing '... an industrial-capitalist architecture of knowledge creation on the sector' (Boden and Epstein 2006: 225), and to re-form academics into standardised roles by the use of individual performance management and bureaucratic control mechanisms dictated by HR strategies. Yet, the very essence of a university, a view expressed by many in this research, is rooted in the collegial culture as a place where academics come together to share ideas and to further learning and understanding. The universities are, therefore, pursuing a strategy, influenced by a government locked into an ideological policy narrative of modernisation, that is ultimately flawed and unlikely to achieve its aims, but that could have far-reaching implications for the future of higher education.

Notes

1 The six areas identified by HEFCE were:
   a. Recruitment and retention.
   b. Staff development and training – including management development.
   c. Equal opportunities – including equal pay for work of equal value.
   d. Review of staffing needs.
   e. Annual performance reviews – includes individual rewards.
   f. Action to tackle poor performance.
2 In the pre-92s university heads of department were traditionally chosen by democratic election involving all academic staff members. Appointments were usually made on the basis of a three-year rotational system.
3 In the summer of 2006 there was a UK-wide one day stoppage followed by an assessment marking boycott. Union/management relations were seen as generally cordial at all three of the universities, but the industrial action, which was ongoing during this fieldwork, put those relationships under pressure. At Wormwood and Parkhurst the departmental heads who, once again, were pivotal figures, largely refrained from putting staff under pressure to mark work. The management at Dartmoor took a much more confrontational stance, with staff required to indicate whether or not they were prepared to mark, and if they were not, then alternative plans were formulated. This was interpreted by staff as effectively a lock-out and once the action was lifted there was little goodwill or effort made to clear the backlog of work. There was evidence of a lingering resentment of the management's tactics at Dartmoor that was not apparent at Wormwood or Parkhurst.

References

Beck, U. (2000) *The Brave New World of Work*, Cambridge: Polity Press.

Beck, U. and Beck-Gernsheim, E. (2002) *Individualization: Institutionalized Individualism and its Social and Political Consequences*, London: Sage.

Beer, M., Spector, B., Lawrence, P. R., Quinn Mills, D. and Walton, R. E. (1984) *Managing Human Assets*, New York: Free Press.

Boden, R. and Epstein, D. (2006) 'Managing the research imagination? Globalisation and research in higher education', *Globalisation, Societies and Education*, 4(2): 223–36.

Boxall, P. and Purcell. J. (2003) *Strategy and Human Resource Management*, Basingstoke: Palgrave Macmillan.

Brown, W. and Oxenbridge, S. (2003) 'The development of co-operative employer/ trade union relationships in Britain'. Paper delivered to the 13th International Industrial Relations Association World Congress in Berlin, September.

Brown, W., Deakin, S., Hudson, M., Pratten, C. and Ryan, P. (1998) 'The individu-alisation of employment contracts in Britain', Centre for Business Research – University of Cambridge for Department of Trade and Industry.

Committee of Vice-Chancellors and Principals (CVCP) (1993) *Promoting People: A Strategic Framework for the Management and Development of Staff in UK Universities*, London: CVCP.

Corby, S. and White, G. (1999) *Employment Relations in the Public Service: Themes and Issues*, London: Routledge.

Cully, M., Woodland, S., O'Reilly, A. and Dix, G. (1999) *Britain at Work: As Depicted by the 1998 Workplace Employment Relations Survey*, London: Routledge.

Dearlove, J. (1997) 'The academic labour process: from collegiality and professionalism to managerialism and proletarianisation?', *Higher Education Review*, 30(1): 57–75.

Deem, R. (1998) '"New managerialism" and higher education: the management of performances and cultures in universities in the United Kingdom', *International Studies in Sociology of Education*, 8(3): 47–70.

Deloitte and Touche (2002) *Rewarding and Developing Staff in HE: Evaluation of Phases 1 and 2*, Bristol: HEFCE.

Elliott, D. (1998) 'Internationalising British higher education: policy perspectives', in P. Scott (ed.) *The Globalization of Higher Education*, Buckingham: SRHE/Open University Press.

Farnham, D. (1999) *Managing Academic Staff in Changing University Systems: International Trends and Comparisons*, Buckingham: SRHE/Open University Press.

Farnham, D. and Horton, S. (1996) *Managing People in the Public Services*, London: Macmillan.

Fernie, S. (1994) In I. Beardwell, L. Holden and T. Claydon (eds) *Human Resource Management. A Contemporary Approach*, 4th edition, Harlow: Pearson.

Fulton, O. (1999) In D. Farnham (ed.) *Managing Academic Staff in Changing University Systems: International Trends and Comparisons*, Buckingham: SRHE/Open University Press.

Giddens, A. (1991) *Modernity and Self Identity*, Stanford: Stanford University Press.

Guest, D. (1992) 'Personnel and human resource management: can you tell the difference? *Personnel Management*, January: 48–51.

Halsey, A. H. (1995) *Decline of the Donnish Dominion*, Oxford: Clarendon Press.

HEFCE (2001) 'Rewarding and developing staff in higher education'. Reference 01/16, March 2001, pp. 1–24.

Held, D., McGrew, A., Goldblatt, D. and Perraton, J. (1999) 'Rethinking globalization', in D. Held and A. McGrew (eds) *The Global Transformations Reader*, Cambridge: Polity Press.

Hendry, C., Woodward, S., Bradley, P. and Perkins, S. (2000) 'Performance and rewards: cleaning out the stables', *Human Resource Management Journal*, 10(3): 46–62.

Henkel, M. (2000) *Academic Identities and Policy Changes in Higher Education*, HE Policy Series 46. London and Philadelphia: Jessica Kingsley Publishers.

Hyman, R. (1987) 'Strategy or structure? Capital, labour and control', *Work Employment and Society*, 1(1): 25–55.

Independent Review of Higher Education Pay and Conditions (IRHE) (1999) (Committee chaired by Sir Michael Bett). The Stationery Office.

Jarratt Report (1985) 'Report of the Steering Committee for Efficiency. Studies in Universities', London: CVCP.

Joint Negotiating Committee for Higher Education Staff (JNCHES) (2004) 'Framework agreement for the modernisation of pay structures'.

Keenoy, T. (1990) 'HRM: a case of the wolf in sheep's clothing?', *Personnel Review*, 19(2): 3–9.

Kelly, J. (1998) *Rethinking Industrial Relations: Mobilization, Collectivism and Long Waves*, London: Routledge.

Kogan, M. (1989) 'Managerialism in higher education', in D. Lawton (ed.) *The Education Reform Act: Choice and Control*, London: Hodder and Stoughton, pp. 65–81.

Legge, K. (1995) *Human Resource Management – Rhetoric and Realities*, Basingstoke: Palgrave Macmillan.

Lynn Meek, V. (2000) 'Diversity and marketisation of higher education: incompatible concepts?', *Higher Education Policy*, 13(1): 23–39.

Miller, H. (1995) 'States, economies and the changing labour process of academics: Australia, Canada and the United Kingdon', in J. Smyth (ed.) *Academic Work*, Buckingham: SRHE/Open University Press.

Millward, M., Bryson, A. and Forth, J. (2000) *All Change At Work? British Employment Relations 1980–1998, as Portrayed by the Workplace Industrial Relations Survey Series*, London: Routledge.

Naidoo, R. (2003) 'Repositioning higher education as a global commodity: opportunities and challenges for future sociology of education work', *British Journal of Sociology of Education*, 24(3): 249–59.

National Committee of Inquiry into Higher Education (NCIHE) (1997) 'Higher education in the learning society. Findings of the Independent Report chaired by Sir Ron Dearing'.

Office of Public Management (2002) *Development of HR Strategies: Learning from Assessing Strategies and Advising Institutions*, Bristol: HEFCE.

Reed, M. (2005) 'New managerialism and public services reform. From regulated autonomy to institutionalised distrust'. Quote taken from slide presentation of a paper given to annual Employment Research Unit Conference, September, Cardiff University.

Rose, N. and Miller, P. (1992) 'Political power beyond the state: problematics of government', *British Journal of Sociology*, 43(2): 172–205.

Sennett, R. (1998) *The Corrosion of Character*, New York: W.W. Norton.

Smyth, J. (1995) *Academic Work*, Buckingham: SRHE/Open University Press.

Storey, J. (1992) *Developments in the Management of Human Resources: An Analytical Review*, Oxford: Blackwell.

Storey, J. *et al.* (2001) *Human Resource Management. A Critical Text*, London: Thomson Learning.

Thompson, P. (1989) *The Nature of Work*, Basingstoke: Macmillan.

Townley, B. (1993) 'Foucault, power/knowledge, and its relevance for human resource management', in G. Salaman, J. Storey and J. Billsberry (eds) *Strategic Human Resource Management Theory and Practice*, 2nd edition, London: Sage.

Van der Wende, M. C. (2003) 'Globalisation and access to higher education', *Journal of Studies in International Education*, 7(2): 193–206.

WERS (2004) 'Inside the workplace. First findings from the 2004 Workplace Employment Relations Survey', Kersley, B., Alpin, C., Forth, J., Bryson, A., Bewley, H., Dix, G., Oxenbridge, S. London: Department of Trade and Industry.

Wilson, T. (1991) 'The proletarianisation of academic labour', *Industrial Relations Journal*, 22(4): 250–62.

Willmott, H. (1995) 'Managing the academics: commodification and control in the development of university education in the UK', *Human Relations*, 48(9): 993–1027.

Winchester, D. and Bach, S. (1999) *Public Service Employment Relations in Europe: Transformation, Modernisation or Inertia?* London and New York: Routledge.

Winter, R. (1995) 'The University of Life, plc – the industrialisation of higher education?', in J. Smyth (ed.) *Academic Work*, Buckingham: SRHE/Open University Press.

Wright, S. (2004) 'Markets, corporations, consumers? New landscapes of higher education', *Learning and Teaching in the Social Sciences*, 1(2): 71–93.

10 Policy incitements to mobility

Some speculations and provocations[1]

Jane Kenway and Johannah Fahey

Introduction

Bauman argues that 'mobility climbs to the rank of the uppermost among the coveted values – and the freedom to move, perpetually a scarce and unequally distributed commodity, fast becomes the main stratifying factor of our late-modern or postmodern times' (Bauman 1998: 2). Is it possible to argue that mobility is emerging as a 'coveted value' and a 'stratifying factor' in government policies for the university sector and in the university sector itself? In this chapter we consider this question and the possible ways that such mobility might be or might become linked to nation-state and region building policies and practices and to what Mignolo (2003: 160) calls the 'civilization project' of contemporary times – neo-liberalism and the trans-national ideology of the market.

We enter discussions about the commodified and corporatised university sector from an uncommon angle. The starting point is our current research on the national and regional higher education research policy push for the enhanced trans-national mobility of university researchers and the 'mobility biographies' of such researchers (Kenway and Fahey 2006). In this chapter we include students but focus primarily on university researchers. We consider the ways in which 'ideal' mobile university subjects are constructed in selected higher education policies for trans-national mobility. Our interest is in how such policies explicitly and implicitly call into being such ideal university subjects, what sorts of subjects are preferred and the links to the commodification of knowledge and university travel.

We challenge the notions that trans-national mobility is an ideologically neutral policy principle and that such mobility is an unproblematic good in the university sector. Rather, we suggest that it needs to be considered in terms of its links to contemporary geographies of knowledge, geometries of power and various associated commodity formations. We deploy selected travel tropes to unsettle this policy discourse and its associated accepted wisdom about such things as 'knowledge transfer' (European Commission 2000a) and 'knowledge networks' or 'networks of excellence' (European Commission 2007a). In so doing we mainly speculate about some possible emergent tendencies, raise more questions than we are in the position to answer and hence offer this chapter as a provocation for further inquiry.

We begin with a brief discussion of the manner in which mobility is inscribed in national and institutional university policies. Next, we elaborate on some of the policies and programmes that are currently in place, focusing on Europe because it provides the most potent example. We then offer an outline of the travel literature that informs our subsequent speculations about such policies. This literature has a longer lineage and is better developed than that on 'mobility', despite the relatively recent efforts of those who have sought to conceptually and empirically enrich studies of mobility.[2] It therefore provides a more fruitful starting point from which to critically consider policies that promote the mobility of university researchers and students.

Universities on the move

A global policy discourse focused on researcher mobility is evolving which is an increasingly influential driver of university policy more broadly. Together with the notion of the knowledge economy (Kenway *et al.* 2006), 'brain mobility' research has led many nations and regions to compete more intensely for high calibre researchers (e.g. EU Bologna–Bergen Process 2005). The implications of researcher mobility for national or regional techno-scientific knowledge and innovation capacity are a key policy concern (e.g. Nelson 2003 [Australia]; Zweig 2005 [China]; Commander *et al.* 2003 [Germany]). Further, mobility is used as a national marketing tool so as to help to maintain the attractiveness of national university systems for both local and international students.

Most national research policies now seek to harness and exploit researcher mobility through a wide variety of connectivity schemes and practices designed to support and encourage mobility, link mobile researchers to each other, promote knowledge exchange and international cooperation with a view to 'value-adding' and so maximise the national or regional benefits of their mobility (e.g. EU: EUROPA & PLOTEUS; Australia: Advance & UMAP; Universitas 21; ASEM [Asia–Europe Meeting] Education Hub) thus enhancing economic productivity and global economic positioning vis-à-vis competitors.

Student travel of various sorts is increasingly being built into university programmes. For example, students are offered study abroad programmes, student exchange, international work placements, study tours, internships, language tours, semi-recreational study tours, studying a language and studying in another country in that language etc. (Milbourne 2006). And of course students are also travelling to undertake full university programmes. In policy circles, students are usually urged to travel in order to enhance their job prospects in a globally connected work force, their cross-cultural competencies and, thereby, their work skills and employability. The academic and social benefits to students, for example of international and cultural engagement, are also emphasised.

Students and teachers in Europe: Tempus, Erasmus Mundus, and Socrates/Erasmus

The Bologna Process is currently the pre-eminent higher education reform initiative in Europe. In 1999, the Bologna Declaration called for the establishment of a European Higher Education Area (EHEA) by 2010,[3] to enhance and facilitate the mobility of students and teachers, and set up national systems with common key features such as a system of credits and two-cycle degrees (Bachelors and Masters).

Erasmus is the higher education Action of the *Socrates* II programme.[4] It seeks to enhance the quality and build a 'Europe of knowledge' by encouraging trans-national cooperation between universities, boosting European mobility and improving the transparency and full academic recognition of studies and qualifications throughout the European Union. *Erasmus* consists of many different activities but two in particular seek to facilitate cooperation and mobility in higher education. The *Erasmus Mundus* programme supports European Masters Courses that are offered by a consortium of at least three universities in at least three different European countries.[5] The programme enables students to engage in postgraduate study at universities in the EU and at 'third country' (such as Australian) universities. The *Socrates/Erasmus* teacher exchange programme provides funds for university teachers to spend teaching periods of between one week and six months abroad.

Parallel to the Bologna process is the Lisbon process.[6] The Lisbon Strategy (2000) marked the European Council's endorsement of the new EU strategic goal of 'becoming by 2010 the most competitive and dynamic knowledge-based economy in the world' (European Commission 2004: 3). The Council also affirmed that mobility was an essential feature of the knowledge economy. Consequently the European Research Area (ERA) was conceived to facilitate the creation of Europe's knowledge economy by integrating Europe's research efforts and capacities and increasing the coherence and impact of European research.

Researchers in Europe: research networks and Marie Curie actions

A major initiative that supports the creation of the ERA is the EU's Seventh Framework Programme (FP7): the latest of a series of EU-level research actions which runs from 2007 to 2013. One action of FP7 (continued from FP6) is the so-called *Networks of Excellence,* which aim to integrate research at a European level:

> Networks of Excellence are designed to strengthen scientific and technological excellence on a particular research topic by integrating at European level the critical mass of resources and expertise needed to provide European leadership and to be a world force in that topic. This expertise will be networked around a joint program of activities aimed principally at creating a progressive and durable integration of the

research capacities of the network partners while, of course at the same time advancing knowledge on the topic.

(FP6 Instruments Task Force/European Commission 2003: 1)

Networks of Excellence are expected to engage with other research teams and with 'actors beyond the research community and with the public as a whole' in order to 'transfer knowledge' and 'spread excellence' and encourage 'take up activities' (European Commission 2002: 2–3).

The activities of the FP7 programme on 'People' will be within the Marie Curie Actions, which finance mobility activities for science and technology researchers. The Actions include Research Training Networks involving at least three partners (universities, research centres, enterprises and international organisations) from three different countries. These networks aim to 'achieve a critical mass of qualified researchers; and to contribute to overcoming institutional and disciplinary boundaries, notably through the promotion of multidisciplinary research' (European Commission 2007b). Similarly, the Marie Curie Host Fellowships for the Transfer of Knowledge 'will allow experienced researchers to be hosted at universities and research organisations for the transfer of knowledge, research competencies and technology' (European Commission 2007c). Within this scheme, Marie Curie Industry–Academia Strategic Partnerships aim to 'create and develop strategic and durable partnerships between academia and private enterprises (in particular SMEs) through the mutual exchange of experienced research staff' (ibid.). Funding is also available for individual researchers to move both within Europe and internationally, 'for the acquisition of new knowledge to be transferred on their return home' (ibid.). 'Incoming' fellowships for researchers coming from other countries for a 'period of mobility' in the EU are also offered alongside 'outgoing' international fellowships.

Thinking travel

Broadly, the travel literature speaks to different types and times of travelling and travellers, and importantly, different understandings of travel. We group that which is relevant to this chapter into three parts, acknowledging immediately our debt to Caren Kaplan's (1996) *Questions of Travel: Postmodern Discourses of Displacement*.

The most popular genre is the traveller's tale or memoir – 'travel writing' – which has a long and diverse history (Fussell 1982). It is associated with the recorded travel of, for instance, the adventurers and explorers of European empires, the middle and upper classes of Europe in the nineteenth century on their Grand Tours, and the leisurely journeying of the literary diaspora of Euro-America between the World Wars. Despite such diversity, what such travellers' tales have in common is that they tell stories of the individual difficulties, benefits and pleasures of travel. Explicitly or implicitly they point to the ways that travel demonstrates or builds character through, for instance, the conquering of adversity or the discovery of the 'unknown', how it contributes to creativity, broadens the mind, develops international or inter-cultural understanding and opens up opportunities. Distance is seen to offer perspective, difference to offer insight (Kaplan 1996). Travel writing points to the supposed benefits of defamiliarisation.

> The travelling narrative is always a narrative of space and difference. It may not always broaden the mind, but it prods at it. It provokes new concepts, new ways of seeing and being, or at the very least, when old ways of seeing and being have been stubbornly imported into foreign territory, subjects them to strain and fatigue.
>
> (Robertson *et al.* 1994: 2)

According to Kaplan's interpretation of Fussell, the golden age of travel writing was when travel was seen 'as study and vocation' (Kaplan 1996: 53) – 'a record of an inquiry and a report of the effect of the inquiry on the mind and the imagination of the traveller' (Fussell 1982: 39). Mobility policies often deploy such understandings to explain or justify their policy stance particularly with regard to students.

A second body of literature of interest to us is the sociological and anthropological. This is less concerned with individual movement and more with movements and displacements on a larger scale. It is more critical, and asks such questions as who travels, why, on whose terms, in whose interests and with what socio-cultural and political effects? A further related question concerns the respective roles of 'the nation state' and global economic, cultural and ideological dynamics.

Within this broad space of inquiry, travel is recognised as a 'historically tainted concept', which nonetheless retains some analytical purchase. For instance, Clifford acknowledges its 'associations with gendered, racial bodies, class privilege, specific means of conveyance, beaten paths, agents, frontiers, documents, and the like' (Clifford 1992: 110). Even so, Clifford says, 'I hang onto "travel" as a term of cultural comparison, precisely because of its "historical taintedness"' (ibid.). He argues that travel speaks to 'mapped meanings'. As Kaplan (1996: 133) observes, 'for Clifford as for many other critics, the question becomes how to use terms in the full knowledge of their historically laden construction in transformative and admittedly partial ways?'

Trans-national travel tropes are legion in this literature on travel and have been mobilised by major scholars in the fields of sociology, cultural studies and anthropology. These include: the tourist, the vagabond and the stranger (Bauman 1998, 1997); the discrepant cosmopolitan and diasporic (Clifford 1992, 1997); the exile (Said 1994) the nomad (Deleuze and Guattari 1986; Braidotti 1994); and the explorer, the ex-pat, the pilgrim – the list goes on. Such travel tropes or metaphors of mobility are usually deployed to draw out various broad politics associated with diverse forms of travel. The focus here then is on different and differentiated populations of travellers and, importantly, on the material and cultural conditions and consequences of their travels. In line with this literature, we activate certain travel tropes as a way of identifying some of the key characteristics of the university travellers that mobility policies favour and fetishise.

A third literature, which overlaps that above, deploys travel tropes as metaphors for critical intellectual practice. It speaks to both the embodied travels of the intellectual but also to intellectual practices of travel and displacement, dispersion and experimentation. The stress here is on the critical benefits of a travelling intellectual subjectivity. For instance, Hall and Chen (1996) elaborate on the notion of the diasporic intellectual and Said (1994) develops the concept of the exilic intellectual. Such 'categories in criticism' have been influential and have 'engender[ed] specific ideas and practices' (Kaplan 1996: 2). We will elaborate on this point in the final section of the chapter where we consider those travelling intellectuals who adopt critical standpoints rather than taking up the proffered and preferred subject positions of mobility policies.

Of course the literature on travel is not undisputed. We acknowledge for instance that all tropes of travel do normative, critical and ideological work and that some have become highly 'charged' and even rather strained (Kaplan 1996: 22, 24), suffering from what Mary McCarthy calls 'metaphorical inflation' (1971: 706 quoted in Kaplan 1996: 106). Nonetheless travel tropes have provoked considerable and robust debate and whilst such debates are not central to this chapter, we will refer to them in passing. Overall our interest is in which tropes are explicitly or implicitly mobilised in the policies that promote the mobility of university researchers and students, which tropes are silent or silenced and which tropes might be deployed to assist in the development of a more materialist and critical understanding.

Constructing the university traveller in a European geography of knowledge

There is no doubt that policies for mobility are implicated in nation-state and region building practices and their so-called knowledge markets. When commenting on the role of the EU Framework Programmes (such as *Socrates* and *Erasmus*), a European Commission (2003: 11) report states 'all these activities help to project the European academic universe around the world'. Both the *Erasmus Mundus* European Masters Courses and *Socrates/Erasmus* teacher exchange programmes are aimed at developing a 'European dimension' within university academic programmes. For example, the mobility of university teaching staff is viewed as playing 'an essential role in bringing [their] university closer to Europe and in bringing Europe closer to [their] university' (European Commission 2007d). It is not simply the mobility of university teaching staff that is encouraged, but also their capacity to 'add a European perspective to courses' (ibid.) once they have returned to their 'home' institution.

However, the notion that the increased mobility of university students and teachers will create a 'European academic universe' raises questions about the links between travel, geography and knowledge. It leads us to question the assumption that university teachers will share a common, homogenous and coherent idea about what constitutes a 'European' perspective. It also leads us to speculate about the ability of European university students to recognise the 'European dimension' of their academic travels. How does trans-national mobility foster this dimension? And what does a 'European dimension' mean for national identity? Equally, we must remain aware of the difficulties involved in identifying the so-called 'European dimension' of knowledge. What makes knowledge in Europe distinctly European? Does knowledge also have a national identity? In an increasingly global world, is a strictly 'European dimension' of knowledge even possible or sensible?

In EU policy discourse the 'European dimension' seems largely to be understood in mechanistic/administrative and instrumental terms: for example, in relation to comparative guidelines and comparable criteria for research degrees, where joint degrees such as the European Masters could be regarded as an example of good practice. However, if one thinks about this in more socio-cultural and political ways, and particularly in terms of the dominant tendencies associated with neo-liberal knowledge projects, certain ideal travelling university subjects are implied – albeit in subtle and emergent ways.

The 'cosmopolitan' (but European) travelling university subject

If the notions of a 'European dimension' and the 'European academic universe' are thought of in socio-cultural and political terms, both can be seen as an attempt to construct a particular sort of mobile European university subject. The word 'cosmopolitan' derives from the Greek *cosmos* (the world) and *polis* (city). This has been translated as a 'citizen of the world', implying an identification with a world community rather than with a particular nation or people. Of course, this understanding of cosmopolitanism is one of many and there are many different manifestations of cosmopolitanism and values attributed to it as a form of practice and a political possibility. We will return to some of these.

In the EU's policy discourse, however, the mobile university subject is constructed primarily as a citizen of the world of Europe – a Euro citizen. For instance, it is required that a consortium of three universities in at least three different European countries offer any European Masters Course or participate in the Marie Curie Research Training Networks. More broadly, a European Commission report states that mobility 'helps to promote the feeling of belonging to Europe, the development of European awareness, and the emergence of European citizenship' (European Commission 2001: 14). Here mobility is viewed as contributing 'to extending the view of European citizens beyond national frontiers and cultures' (European Commission 2004: 6). Arguably, the inference of these statements is that mobility is also instrumental in the creation of a 'Europe of knowledge', or what might be called a European geography of knowledge.

In the EU's higher education and research policy discourse the European cosmopolitan traveller implied is a deterritorialised, disembodied and disembedded figure who can readily engage in trans-national travel for study, professional development or research. Without difficulty and impediment, this figure can move and, in so doing, transcend their attachment to national borders, taking up an attachment to Europe.

But how does the Bologna and Lisbon policy impulse to enhance and facilitate mobility within the EU through various mobility programmes translate to the experiences of actual university travellers? This question implies a research agenda similar to that proposed by Clifford, who asks, 'how do different populations, classes and genders travel? What kinds of knowledges, stories, and theories do they produce?' (Clifford 1989: 183). This agenda involves a consideration of who travels as a result of these policies, from what roots and along what routes – a consideration of the links between knowledge, nation, identity and travel. There is an emerging body of research that considers some aspects of these questions with regard to European university students. We consider two cursory examples.

According to Amaral and Magalhães 'the number of students in those programmes remains well below the initial target of 10% of the students in the Union' (2004: 85). They also point out that the percentage of European-mobile students in recent times is much less than the number of European-mobile students in the early seventeenth century. They further predict that student mobility is likely to decrease in the future. Given that such a small percentage of students is participating in these mobility programmes, it has been suggested that they cater for a 'privileged minority' (Amaral and Magalhães 2004: 85) and that the Bologna process has been 'designed to permit the emergence of a Euro elite. Therefore [subordinating] the education and training of the mass to that single over-riding end' (Neave 2002: 11). In terms of qualifications, the National Unions of Students in Europe (ESIB) would appear to support such a claim, stating that 'joint degrees [such as the European Masters Course] are very selective, both socially through usually much higher fees and academically through heavy selection procedures. Study places for joint degrees are [also] very limited and are mainly also only offered in a limited range of study fields in second cycle programmes' (ESIB 2007).

These examples suggest that the cosmopolitan Euro student traveller who has so far evolved as a result of EU university policy is no ordinary university student traveller but one with certain educational and class privileges. But we suggest the possibility that, in addition to this, the sort of university student who is likely to increasingly emerge here is a university student 'tourist'.

The student as educational tourist

Bauman calls people who are on the move by choice and who accept few territorial responsibilities as they travel, 'tourists'. 'They stay and move at their heart's desire. They abandon a site when new untried opportunities beckon elsewhere' (Bauman 1998: 92). Bauman's notions of tourist are applied largely to the mobile winners of globalisation, those who are 'emancipated from space' (Bauman 1998: 89–93) because of the resources at their disposal. Educational tourists might in part be thought of as having a spatial emancipation that allows them to accumulate the European educational credentials and experiences that further enhance their educational and class privileges in the labour markets of Europe and beyond.

Actual tourists usually combine leisure and travel in search of 'experience' and it might also be argued that the metaphorical student tourist combines instead *education* and travel in search of experience – the experience of a different culture, people, education system. For the student tourist, educational travel allows for personal development of the sort described by Minh-ha (1994: 21) who says: 'every voyage is the unfolding of a poetic. The departure, the cross-over, the fall, the wandering, the discovery, the return, the transformation'.

Student travel becomes a form of travelling life-stylisation. Such a policy-endorsed view of the student traveller sees educational travel in individualistic, even heroic, romanticised and glamorised ways. But it fails to acknowledge the ways in which student mobility contributes to the accumulation of international cultural and social capital for certain privileged social groupings – 'value-added' to the human capital that they accrue through their educational travels. It also fails to acknowledge the highly selective role of the current university in attending to the needs and interests of this market for distinctively fortunate students.

Further, it misses the manner in which the student experience itself is becoming increasingly commodified, not just within the university system but also in certain university cities through the emergence of a set of student lifestyle industries that are growing up alongside the university system – the night clubs, the bars, the partying and the consumer goods that go with them. Marketing student mobility and lifestyle is becoming intertwined with marketing place (e.g. Manchester's gay village in the UK, see Chatterton and Hollands 2003). This has obvious implications for the so-called authentic 'other' cultures that students are supposed to travel to and immerse themselves in as they develop their 'cross-cultural awareness'. Further, if student tourists become just another set of tourists consuming places and institutions, how do local people react to them? It is widely acknowledged that although 'locals' enjoy the financial benefits of tourists, the intrusions on their own life-styles are not always so welcome. What are the implications here for social cohesion?

At a deeper level, what are the relations of production in the emergence of the student as tourist? When exploring the potential of metaphors of travel, Clifford (via Fussell) and Kaplan both respectively identify 'entrepreneurship' and 'consumer culture' in their descriptions of tourists and tourism. Fussell suggests that the tourist seeks 'that which has been discovered by entrepreneurship ... [they] move towards the security of pure cliché' (1982: 39). In the same vein, Kaplan states '[t]ourism ... is a product of the rise of consumer culture [and] leisure' (1996: 27). She maintains 'tourists are formed through their actions, they are as commodified as the people and places they visit'. The tourist 'travels, crosses boundaries, is freely mobile, consumes commodities, produces economies, and is, in turn, commodified' (Kaplan 1996: 62).

It can therefore be suggested that one of the defining characteristics of student tourists is their relationship to the commodification of mobility, knowledge and experience. Akin to the travellers' tales that we noted earlier, policy makers couch programmes promoting student travel in terms of their potential for enhancing students' labour market opportunities, broadening their minds and thus building intra-European labour markets and socio-cultural cohesion. However, the life-stylisation of student mobility suggests some additional possibilities. Perhaps we see here the early stages of a trans-national student culture premised on the commodification, even the 'secure cliché' of the student traveller. Given trends in the tourist industry, we might also predict that student mobility will become increasingly valorised and niched. This raises question as to the implications for knowledge, teaching and learning.

The researcher as transcendental traveller, jet set intellectual and modernist cosmopolitan

In the first report to propose the creation of a European Research Area (ERA), attention was drawn to making more use in the future, both at national and at European level, of mobility as an instrument for the transfer of scientific knowledge (European Commission 2000a). This included introducing a 'European dimension' to scientific careers, making Europe more attractive to researchers from the rest of the world, encouraging the return of those who have left to complete their training or pursue careers abroad; and bringing together the scientific communities, companies and researchers of Western and Eastern Europe. All laudable aims no doubt.

The report also states that 'greater European cohesion in research [is] based on the best experiences of knowledge transfer at regional and local levels and on the role of the regions in the European research efforts' (European Commission 2000a: 8). Here, we see an attempt to remap the local and the regional, to create a new European geography of knowledge based on 'knowledge transfer'. We also see an attempt by Europe to map the movement of knowledge. As Cresswell (1997: 364) says 'It is not that the State opposes mobility but that it wishes to control flows – to make them run through conduits. It wants to create fixed and well-directed paths for movements to flow through'.

Further, the promotion of 'European' belonging, awareness, citizenship and knowledge is premised on mobility beyond the boundaries of Europe's national cultures; this move is based on the construction of a bounded Europe, but the irony is that you can frame or identify European frontiers by harnessing mobility within Europe or by enticing the best 'brains' from outside. The European Union is keen for Europe to become 'the preferred destination of students, scholars and researchers from other world regions' (European Commission 2004: 5). Europe clearly wishes to harness universities in its bid to become a globally dominant magnet economy and culture. This, of course has to be understood in relation to its competition with the USA (Wyckoff 2005) and increasingly China (Wang 2005).

We need to consider the so-called 'best experiences of knowledge transfer' and to ascertain how they create a new geography of knowledge associated with 'European cohesion'. Indeed, what are the properties of the knowledge to be transferred? The term 'knowledge transfer' is most frequently associated with the commercialisation of scientific and technological knowledge – and its 'path to market'.[7] In this context it can be inferred that the so-called 'best experiences of knowledge transfer' are seen by Europe as those whereby knowledge is transferred from the university research sector to the private business sector and transformed into profitable knowledge. This view of knowledge transfer is seen to underpin Europe's aim to become the 'most competitive and dynamic knowledge-driven economy in the world', a goal, which, it asserts, can only be achieved 'by making Europe more entrepreneurial and innovative' (European Commission 2000b: 2). The implication here is that understandings of 'European cohesion' are primarily based on economic relationships, but whether economic power is sufficient to cohere disparate geographies and nations remains an open question.

If it is the case that knowledge transfer is primarily concerned with scientific and technological knowledge that can be applied and commercialised, then Europe's knowledge mobility programmes will be skewed towards this norm. This may have implications for the overall remit of European research policy with regard to the social sciences and humanities – they may be not only relegated to the margins but also recast in the image of techno-science (Kenway *et al.* 2004). A key question here is how the policy makers associated with the European Research Area understand the relationship between knowledge and travel.

Our interrogation of the policy literature leads us to observe that despite passing reference to the 'content of knowledge', there is a relative dearth of discussion about the kinds of knowledge that readily travels, the knowledge that most and least requires or benefits from travel, how knowledge travels or why it travels in the manner that it does. Indeed, there is little reference to the ways in which knowledge is transformed or otherwise through travel across national, cultural and political boundaries. If Europe is interested in creating new geographies of knowledge then it seems strange that such questions have barely been asked. According to Peyraube 'a knowledge-based society and economy cannot content itself with producing knowledge that is detached and separated from its context' (2005: 5). As the EU's understanding of knowledge is somewhat mechanistic, it fails to take into account precisely the content and context of knowledge transfer. The implicit assumption seems to be that knowledge will readily travel across national borders providing the right incentive schemes and networks are put in place. But what do such mechanistic and behaviouristic policies overlook?

It is instructive here to consider the network metaphor. We suggest the possibility that it gives insufficient recognition to the power geometries of national politics in Europe. The notion of nodes of knowledge within knowledge networks not only implies that the research network is able to trump territorial sensibilities but also that power is relatively equally distributed between those who help to constitute the so-called critical mass of expertise that makes up the network. The geometries of economic and other forms of power associated with this particular geography of knowledge flows remain conveniently under-examined. Many questions remain unanswered about the ways in which knowledge actually 'transfers' between more and less powerful nations within and beyond Europe. This raises concerns about the power dynamics associated with 'regional and local' European knowledge transfer. Further questions arise as to how national power within Europe influences the direction of the movement of knowledge, its angles of inquiry and points of departure and arrival; how the travelling researcher is constructed within this power geometry; and how self-conscious Europe is about the place of its universities in the 'unequal spaces of postcolonial confusion and contestation' (Clifford 1989: 178). As Clifford (ibid.) says:

> Theory is no longer naturally 'at home' in the West – a powerful place of Knowledge, History or Science, a place to collect, sift, translate, and generalize. Or, more cautiously, this privileged place is now increasingly contested, cut across, by other locations, claims, trajectories of knowledge articulating racial, gender, and cultural differences.

We suspect that, in the main, the concept 'knowledge transfer' signifies an inequitable flow of knowledge from central points of power in the European university system to more marginal points – from old to new Europe; and from Europe to, for instance, the global South. Equally we suspect that researchers' travels are closely aligned with such inequitable flows. However, as we indicated earlier, EU policy discourse summons a deterritorialised mobile cosmopolitan European research subject. Within the discourse of techno-scientific knowledge transfer, this figure is constructed as a transcendental traveller. In the interests of Europe's economic imperatives, the transcendental traveller moves along the smooth paths of Europe's knowledge networks, stopping at various nodes to transmit or soak up knowledge – depending on their points of departure. In the process this researcher 'transfers' transcendent 'knowledge' and thus helps to drive 'European research further and faster than ever before' (European Commission 2002: back cover).

Will this figure come to resemble what Pels (1999) calls the 'jet set intellectual'? Jet set intellectuals, he argues, are highly networked individuals who seek out the 'best' (i.e. the most profitable) knowledge, and who channel personal interactions, 'whether on a formal or informal basis', towards techno-scientific 'knowledge transfer'. Their sense of community is predicated on their research and business 'networks' of association. Jet set intellectuals move about under strong economic compulsions, tend to refrain from acting in non-economic worldly affairs, are often silent about history and politics, whilst remaining institutionally connected with the economics of power. The jet set intellectual has few territorial allegiances and is, potentially, a 'free-floating intellectual, whose technical competence is on loan and for sale to anyone' (Said 1994: 47). As Pels further suggests, the jet set intellectual may be mobile, but they touch down only to transit and therefore have only a superficial engagement with their surroundings. They enjoy a form of 'social, [cultural and political] weightlessness' (Pels 1999: 72). Indeed, Pels (ibid.) says:

> The jet set intellectual may well imagine himself a true nomad in body and spirit, 'like a rolling stone', avid for new experiences and new ideas; but often his practical mobility does not extend very far beyond airport lounges which he transits en route towards another international meeting of his peers.

Given this superficial engagement with their wider surroundings and their detachment from grounded cultural and political concerns, the jet set intellectual is unlikely to be concerned about the links between their own itineraries of embodied and intellectual flight and the geometries of power associated with Europe's geography of knowledge – with the national politics of who travels to bestow knowledge and who travels to soak it up, with who is the pilgrim and who is the prophet.

Of course, the heroic knowledge explorer on a quest for the EU is the dominant and preferred researcher subject in EU policy. But another, albeit less dominant subject, is the European cosmopolitan researcher. Through comparative research across Europe's nations (in, of course, at least three countries) this researcher will assist with the bonding-across-borders that Europe requires as it seeks to develop its new knowledge geography of Europe. This figure is not about the links between travel and the transfer of transcendent knowledge but rather the links between travel and cultural transformation. It is about effecting a form of cultural de- and re-territorialisation.

Let us return to the idea of 'the cosmopolitan' and the critiques and refinements it has provoked. Pollock *et al.* (2003: 8) for instance maintain that the dominant notion of

> cosmopolitanism must give way to the plurality of modes and histories – not necessarily shared in degree or in concept regionally, nationally, or internationally – that comprise cosmopolitan practice and history.

They identify different kinds of cosmopolitanism and make a distinction between the cosmopolitanism of 'our times' and the cosmopolitanism of modernity. The latter, 'springs from the capitalised "virtues" of Rationality, Universality, and Progress' (Pollock *et al.* 2003: 6). Is this the version of cosmopolitanism that the EU policy discourse subscribes to? The promotion of a 'European dimension' to knowledge and researchers' careers is viewed as the means to generate the 'critical mass' (European Commission 2006: 4) necessary in Europe's 'cosmopolitan' knowledge economy; but might it also be used to generate a critical *cultural* mass? A danger then is that this particular policy figure, this mobile researcher, is implicitly constructed as a *cosmopolitan courier* of these 'capitalised virtues'. This is one of many possible ways that the travelling university researcher is caught up in what Kaplan (1996: 103) calls 'the politics of cultural production in trans-national modernities and postmodernities'. While researchers may be encouraged to undertake cross-cultural and cross-national research, implicitly this runs the risk of being little more than a form of academic 'sight-seeing' through comparative research but with an underlying implicit mission to deliver epistemological homogeneity. Further, as Dale (2006) argues, comparative studies often screen from view wider forces of globalisation.

In contrast, according to Pollock *et al.*, the cosmopolitanism of 'our times' is constituted by a 'cosmopolitical community' of refugees, peoples of the diaspora, migrants and exiles who have a certain political and ideological awareness as they are 'often victims of modernity, failed by capitalism's upward mobility, bereft of those comforts and customs of national belonging' (Pollock *et al.* 2003: 6). Clearly this 'cosmopolitanism of our times' involves certain geometries of power that Europe's mobile researcher policies are reluctant to engage head on. The surface compensatory mechanisms of such policies do not properly acknowledge the angles of complexity involved with regard to the 'density of overlapping allegiances' and the 'diasporic predicaments' (Kaplan 1996: 125–6) faced by such people. For instance, researchers who take up schemes that allow them to move from Europe's margins to its centres or indeed from Europe to other global centres of intellectual power are, of course, not constructed in policy texts as diasporic or exilic in the terms noted earlier. Rather they are implicitly constructed as pilgrims who are enabled to travel to holy places of knowledge by their European benefactor. To the extent that they are encouraged to return 'home', they are mostly encouraged to return home to Europe (as an unspecific whole) from beyond its borders. The region of Europe is constructed as 'home' from within and without. A more adequate set of policies would be more sensitive to the contexts and scales of the different 'uprootings and regroundings' involved. It would 'attend to the histories, geographies, practices, forms of experience and relations of power that mark [them]' (Ahmed *et al.* 2003: 2).

Concluding questions

Is there any policy place in Europe's new geography of knowledge for the researcher who does not simply fulfil their role in the transfer of knowledge, as discussed above, but also fulfils their intellectual role as critic? Exilic intellectuals are those who critically engage with conventional geographies of knowledge and geometries of power. The notion of the 'exile' is a major trope associated with 'productive estrangement' (Kaplan 1996: 89) and marginal spaces of subversion. In intellectual terms it involves 'ambivalences, resistances, slippages, dissimulations, doubling, and even subversions of the cultural codes of *both* the home and host societies' (Naficy 1993: xvi quoted in Kaplan 1996:104).

Edward Said's metaphorical notion of the intellectual in exile, points to the position a 'cosmopolitical intellectual' 'of our time' might adopt in the EU space.[8] Said used his real-life experiences of physical and emotional dislocation to develop the notion of the intellectual in exile. According to him, '[e]xile for the intellectual in this sense is restlessness, movement, constantly being unsettled, and unsettling others' (Said 1994: 39). In other words, the exilic intellectual lives and thrives in a state of agitated existence. They have little sense of belonging, they seldom feel settled or at ease, are usually out of place, and don't feel comfortably at home. Said (1994: 39) suggests:

> Even intellectuals who are lifelong members of a society can, in a manner of speaking, be divided into insiders and outsiders; those on the one hand who belong fully to the society as it is, who flourish in it without an overwhelming sense of dissonance or dissent, those who can be called yea-sayers; and on the other hand, the nay-sayers, the individuals at odds with their society and therefore outsiders and exiles so far as privileges, power and honors are concerned.

This prompts consideration of who, in Said's terms, amongst Europe's travelling researchers are the 'yea-sayers' and the 'nay-sayers'. According to Said, to be oppositional in this context means that one is 'involved in the study (and to some degree the enhancement) of resistance to all of these totalising ... institutions and systems of thought [,] ... systems that confirm themselves over and over again' (Said 2004: 65). This raises questions about how such exilic intellectuals are placed in European policy's knowledge and power configurations and particularly under what conditions and for what is the travel of 'nay-sayers' funded by the European Union. Indeed, what sorts of 'nay-sayers' do not get or do not seek funding? Questions arise as to whether they must, or at least feel obliged to, present themselves as 'yea-sayers' in order to attract funding. Further questions are raised around the identity and nature of the knowledge networks that exilic intellectuals are involved in and the knowledge that they 'transfer'. Finally, what travellers' tales do they tell about the links between mobility, knowledge, economics, culture, power and alternative political possibilities? Ultimately such questions raise fundamental issues about the relationship between marginality, oppositionality and researcher mobility under the reign of neo-liberalism and the trans-national ideology of the market in the university sector.

Notes

1 The chapter arises from an Australian Research Council (Discovery) grant for the project *Moving Ideas: Mobile Policies, Researchers and Connections in the Social Sciences and Humanities* – Australia in the global context.

2 For instance, in sociology, see CeMoRe (Centre for Mobilities Research) 2007 online; see also the Cosmobilities Network 2007 online.

3 The Bologna Declaration was not a common European policy initiative issued by the Commission, rather it was a bottom-up process, a joint but voluntary commitment undertaken by national governments.

4 *Socrates* I (which ended in December 1999) and *Socrates* II (which started in 2000) are different phases of the same European education programme.

5 Some examples include: European Master of Arts in Media, Communication and Cultural Studies, European Master of Research on Information and Communication Technologies, European Master of Journalism and Media within Globalization: The European Perspective.

6 Unlike the Bologna process, the Lisbon process is being led directly by the European Commission.

7 For a discussion of cross-institutional border movement between the university and industry see Ozga (2006).

8 We are aware that Aijaz Ahmad (1992) critiques Said's notion of the intellectual in exile. He maintains it is a depoliticised, bourgeois term used by Third World elites, such as Said, that erases class relations and undermines the socialist project.

References

Ahmad, A. (1992) *In Theory: Classes, Nations, Literatures*, London: Verso.

Ahmed, S., Castaneda, C., Fortier, A.-M. and Sheller, M. (2003) *Uprootings/ Regroundings; Questions of Home and Migration*, Oxford and New York: Berg.

Amaral, A. and Magalhães, A. (2004) 'Epidemiology and the Bologna saga', *Higher Education*, 48: 79–100.

Bauman, Z. (1997) 'The making and unmaking of strangers', in P. Werbner and T. Modood (eds) *Debating Cultural Hybridity*, London: Zed Books.

Bauman, Z. (1998) *Globalization: the human consequences*, New York: Columbia University Press.

Braidotti, R. (1994) *Nomadic Subjects*, New York: Columbia University Press.

CeMoRe (Centre for Mobilities Research). Online. Avaliable at http://www.lancs. ac.uk/fss/sociology/cemore/cemorehome.htm (accessed 30 January 2007).

Chatterton, P. and Hollands, R. (2003) *Urban Nightscapes: Youth Cultures, Pleasure Spaces and Corporate Power*, London and New York: Routledge.

Clifford, J. (1989) 'Notes on travel and theory', *Inscriptions*, (5): 177–86.

Clifford, J. (1992) 'Traveling cultures', in L. Grossberg, C. Nelson and P. Treichler (eds) *Cultural Studies*, New York and London: Routledge.

Clifford, J. (1997) *Routes: Travel and Translation in the Late Twentieth Century*, Cambridge, MA and London: Harvard University Press.

Commander, S., Kangasniemi, M. and Winters, L. A. (2003) 'The brain drain: curse or boon?' IZA Discussion Paper No 809. Bonn, Institute for the Study of Labor, June.

Cosmobilities Network (2007) Online. Available at http://www.cosmobilities.net/ index.php?id=16 (accessed 20 January 2007).

Cresswell, T. (1997) 'Imagining the nomad: mobility and the postmodern primitive', in G. Benko and U. Strohmayer (eds) *Space & Social Theory: Interpreting Modernity & Postmodernity*, Oxford: Blackwell Publishers.

Dale, R. (2006) 'From comparison to translation: extending the research imagination?', *Globalisation, Societies and Education*, 4(2): 179–92.

Deleuze, G. and Guattari, F. (1986) *Nomadology*, New York: Semiotext(e).

ESIB (The National Unions of Students in Europe) (2007) 'Bologna analysis 2005 – Bologna with student eyes'. Online. Available at www.esib.org (accessed 1 February 2007).

European Commission (2000a) *Towards a European Research Area*, COM (2000) 6 final. Brussels: Commission of the European Communities.

European Commission (2000b) *Challenges for Enterprise Policy in the Knowledge-driven Economy: proposal for a council decision on a multiannual programme for enterprise and entrepreneurship* (2001–2005). COM (2000) 256 final/2. Brussels: Commission of the European Communities.

European Commission (2001) *Draft Detailed Work Programme for the Follow Up of the Report on the Concrete Objectives of Education and Training Systems*, COM (2001) 501 final. Brussels: Commission of the European Communities.

European Commission (2002) *Participating in European Research: Sixth Framework Programme*, Luxembourg: Office for Official Publications of the European Communities.

European Commission (2003) *The Role of Universities in the Europe of Knowledge*, COM (2003) 58 final. Brussels: Commission of the European Communities.

European Commission (2004) *Report on the Follow-Up to the Recommendation of the European Parliament and the Council of 10 July 2001 on Mobility within the Community of Students, Persons Undergoing Training, Volunteers and Teachers and Trainers*, COM (2004) 21 final. Brussels: Commission of the European Communities.

European Commission (2006) *Delivering on the Modernisation Agenda for Universities: Education, Research and Innovation*, COM (2006) 208 final. Brussels: Commission of European Communities.

European Commission (2007a) *FP6 Instruments*. Online. Available at http: // www.cordis.europa.eu/fp6/instr_noe.htm (accessed 30 January 2007).

European Commission (2007b) *Marie Curie Actions: Research Training Networks*. Online. Available at http://cordis.europa.eu/mariecurie-actions/rtn/home.html (accessed 12 June 2007).

European Commission (2007c) *Marie Curie Actions: Transfer of Knowledge*. Online. Available at http://cordis.europa.eu/mariecurie-actions/tok/home.html (accessed 12 June 2007).

European Commission (2007d) *Socrates: Erasmus*. Online. Available at http:// ec.europa.eu/education/programmes/socrates/erasmus/what_en.html (accessed 1 February 2007).

FP6 Instruments Task Force/European Commission (2003) *Provisions for Implementing Networks of Excellence*. Available at http://www.ec.europa.eu/ research/fp6/pdf/noe_120503final.pdf.

Fussell, P. (1982) *Abroad: British Literary Travelling Between the Wars*, Oxford: Oxford University Press.

Hall, S. and Chen, K.-H. (1996) 'The formation of a diasporic intellectual', in D. Morley and K.-H. Chen (eds) *Stuart Hall: Critical Dialogues in Cultural Studies*, London: Routledge.

Kaplan, C. (1996) *Questions of Travel: Postmodern Discourses of Displacement*, Durham, NC: Duke University Press.

Kenway, J. and Fahey, J. (2006) 'The research imagination in a world on the move', in J. Kenway and J. Fahey (eds) Globalising the Research Imagination – Special Issue, *Globalisation, Societies and Education*, 4(2): 261–74.

178 *Jane Kenway and Johannah Fahey*

Kenway, J., Bullen, E. and Robb, S. (2004) 'The knowledge economy, the techno-preneur and the problematic future of the university', in M. Peters and S. Marginson (eds) Special Issue on Higher Education, *Policy Futures in Education*, 2(2): 333–51.

Kenway, J., Bullen, E., Fahey, J. with Robb, S. (2006) *Haunting the Knowledge Economy*, London: Routledge.

McCarthy, M. (1971) 'Exiles, expatriates and internal emigres', *The Listener*, 25 November, pp. 705–8.

Mignolo, W. D. (2003) 'The many faces of cosmo-polis: border thinking and critical cosmopolitanism', in C. A. Breckenridge, H. K. Bhabha and D. Chakrabarty (eds) *Cosmopolitanism*, Durham, NC and London: Duke University Press.

Milbourne, R. (2006) 'Compatibility of varied mobility', *The Australian – Higher Education*, 11 October: 32.

Minh-ha, T. T. (1994) 'Other than myself/my other self', in G. Robertson, M. Mash, L. Tickner, J. Bird, B. Curtis and T. Putnam (eds) *Travellers' Tales: Narratives of Home and Displacement*, London and New York: Routledge.

Naficy, H. (1993) *The Making of Exile Cultures: Iranian Television in Los Angeles*, Minneapolis: University of Minnesota Press.

Neave, G. (2002) 'Anything goes: or, how the accommodation of Europe's universities to European integration integrates – an inspiring number of contradictions', *Boletim da Universidade do Proto*, 10(35): 9–18.

Nelson, B. (2003) *$34.8 million for Australian Brain Gain*, Media release, Canberra, 20 March.

Ozga, J. (2006) 'Travelling and embedded policy: knowledge transfer and higher education', Paper presented at Seminar Series (3) Universities as Global 'Knowledge Corporations', *ESRC series Geographies of Knowledge, Geometries of Power; Global Higher Education in the 21st Century*, Cardiff School of Social Sciences, Cardiff University, Cardiff, 8 November.

Pels, D. (1999) 'Privileged nomads: on the strangeness of intellectuals and the intellectuality of strangers', *Theory, Culture & Society*, 16(1): 63–86.

Peyraube, A. (2005) 'New horizons for research in the humanities', Paper presented at Social Sciences and Humanities in Europe: New Challenges, New Opportunities, conference organized by the European Commission, Brussels, 12–13 December.

Pollock, S., Bhabha, H. K., Breckenridge, C. A. and Chakrabarty, D. (2003) 'Cosmo-politanisms', in C. A. Breckenridge, S. Pollock, H. K. Bhabha and D. Chakrabarty (eds) *Cosmopolitanism*, Durham, NC and London: Duke University Press.

Robertson, G., Mash, M., Tickner, L., Bird, J., Curtis, B. and Putnam, T. (eds) (1994) *Travellers' Tales: Narratives of Home and Displacement*, London and New York: Routledge.

Said, E. W. (1994) 'Intellectual exile: expatriates and marginals', *Representations of the Intellectual: The 1993 Reith Lectures*, London: Vintage.

Said, E. (2004) 'Overlapping territories: the world, the text and the critic', in G. Viswanathan (ed.) *Power, Politics and Culture: Interviews with Edward Said*, London: Bloomsbury.

Wang, L. (2005) 'Higher education in the EU and in the People's Republic of China: a comparative approach', unpublished thesis, Faculty of Education, University of Tampere.

Wyckoff, A. (2005) 'The changing dynamics of the global market for the highly skilled', Paper presented at Advancing Knowledge and the Knowledge-Economy Conference, National Academy of Science, Washington, DC, 10–11 January.

Zweig, D. (2005) 'Learning to compete: China's strategies to create a "reverse brain drain"', Working Paper No. 2, *Competing for Global Talent*, Center on China's Transnational Relations, Singapore Management University, Singapore, 13–14 January.

Part III

Demanding knowledge – marketing and consumption

Susan Wright

Governments in many parts of the world consider the arrival of a global market in higher education as imminent and inevitable. Most western governments are generating strategies to position themselves in this market, either by extracting profit (e.g. from tuition fees) or by attracting the brightest students from around the world to boost their country's highly skilled labour force. Such strategies rest on the logic of the so-called knowledge economy where strong universities and large numbers of graduates are the prerequisites for making profits from ideas rather than manufacturing. Western countries view the knowledge economy as a new global division of labour, and expect that they will stay dominant by mass higher education. Simultaneously, western countries and international agencies like the World Bank also argue the opposite: that by making for-profit higher education available, poorer countries will be integrated into the global knowledge economy and able to develop their way out of poverty. This part explores these contradictory strategies, both by questioning the assumptions underlying national and international policies to create a global market in higher education and by exploring the perceptions and 'demands' of first world, third world and international students, on whom the success of these strategies depend.

Denmark, my current research area, provides a good example of a western strategy for dominance in the knowledge economy. The government's 'Progress, Innovation and Cohesion: a Strategy for Denmark in the Global Economy' (Danish Government 2006)[1] argues that Denmark's continuing status as one of the world's wealthiest countries depends on the performance of its universities. They must be world-ranking and high on international league tables, turn a high proportion of the population into a highly skilled workforce, and be quick to convert 'ideas into invoices', making Denmark a centre for innovation in this global economy. Denmark's strategy is perhaps more blatant than others in the instrumental role it gives to universities, but, as in other countries, universities which were initially thought of as servicing the knowledge economy, are now considered central players in, even drivers of, that economy itself. Governments in most other western countries place similar demands on universities in order to bring this economy into existence and to secure a front-seat position.

It was Robert Reich (1991), Clinton's Secretary for Labour, who argued that economic wealth in future would be generated from ideas, and that countries needed a far higher percentage of their population to be highly skilled 'symbolic analysts' who could create, manipulate, translate and market symbolic versions of reality in globally organised networks and teams. Tony Blair adopted this argument in his 1997 election mantra 'Education, Education, Education', and his target that 50 per cent of the British population should have experience of higher education. In Britain this projection of a global knowledge economy is known as the 'thin air' thesis, after one of the Prime Minister's advisers who claimed:

> The generation, application and exploitation of knowledge is (sic) driving modern economic growth. Most of us make our money from thin air: we produce nothing that can be weighed, touched or easily measured. Our output is not stockpiled at harbours, stored in warehouses or shipped in railway cars … That should allow our economies, in principle at least, to … be organised around people and the knowledge capital they produce. Our children will not have to toil in dark factories, descend into pits or suffocate in mills, to hew raw materials and turn them into manufactured products. They will make their livings through their creativity, ingenuity and imagination.
>
> (Charles Leadbetter, policy adviser to Tony Blair, major author of Department of Trade and Industry's 1998 White Paper *Building the Knowledge Driven Economy*, quoted in Wolf 2002: xii)

Such an image of limitless growth – as there are no bounds to the number of ideas that can generate jobs – ignores Reich's warning that the knowledge economy will be divisive: if half of a country's population has the educational qualifications and personal competences to create wealth from thin air, that still leaves the other half excluded and, argues Reich, in danger of creating social upheaval. Implicit in Leadbetter's argument is also the assumption that if 'our [British/western] children' do not have to extract raw materials or manufacture them, then this work will go on invisibly elsewhere in the world. This introduces a second divisive feature of the global knowledge economy. The assumption is that the west will develop and control the new, clean, high value-added, high-salaried knowledge industries and the rest of the world can have the less profitable, low paid, dirty and dangerous extractive and manufacturing industries.

Research by Phillip Brown, Hugh Lauder and David Ashton (Chapter 11) challenges this idea of a global division of labour. They show how the idea of the knowledge economy is based on human capital theory. That is, a company's profitability depends more on access to intellectual capital than on its ownership of material capital (land, buildings, machines), and that high skills will necessarily attract high wages. Their interviews around the world with government policy makers and senior managers from 20 leading transnational companies show that current policy prescriptions about the knowledge economy fail to grasp what is actually happening. Western countries are indeed expanding higher education with the idea that their highly skilled population will capture and keep knowledge work in their country, and their high wages will then assure continued prosperity. But Brown *et al.*'s research shows that emerging economies, such as China and India, while expanding the production of raw materials and manufacturing, are also investing heavily in their universities. They are producing graduates of the same quality and in nearly the same numbers as the major western countries. Emerging economies see no reason why the west should expect to have a monopoly on ideas and innovations and they are intent on generating their own knowledge-based industries with a global reach. Western-based companies are themselves instrumental in creating these emergent knowledge economies. Following the model of outsourcing manufacturing to cheaper locations, western companies are outsourcing more and more 'knowledge' activities to well-qualified graduates in China and India so as to avoid the high labour costs of the west.[2] Brown *et al.* report how companies are using digital technologies to break their activities down into standardised component parts and outsource them to the cheapest pools of well-qualified labour. A familiar story from manufacturing, this 'digital Taylorism' is now being applied to financial and service industries, and is turning the hitherto tacit and personal knowledge of professional and managerial occupations into codified prescripts. Indeed, a similar 'unbundling' of universities' activities has long been on the cards – not just the privatisation of housing, canteens and cleaning, or the hiving off of student admissions to a national agency, but the breaking down of the academic task into separate contracts for course design, course delivery and marking, which can be outsourced to anywhere in the world (Thorne 1999; Wright 2004: 74; Shore and Wright 2001). The assumption of western superiority in a projected global division of labour, which underpins Denmark's and many other western countries' strategies towards the knowledge economy, is therefore seriously in doubt.

Wei Shen's study (Chapter 12) of the international migration of Chinese students exemplifies some of the flaws that Brown *et al.* identify in the western approaches to the global knowledge economy. Shen provides detailed insight into students' roles and motivations as they contribute to the rise of Chinese hubs in the global knowledge economy. He identifies the vast numbers of Chinese young people, mainly funded by the efforts of their families, who are coming to Europe for university education. Their aims are to acquire three things – the academic knowledge, language competence and work experience – that will enable them to succeed in the growing private sector, and especially in international companies, in China. UK and US universities currently dominate the market in international students. The UK, in a phrase attributed to Robertson, sees such students as 'cheques on legs'. Since 1981, the UK's cash-strapped universities have all become dependent on income from international students to stay afloat. Total fee income from international students is estimated at £1.2 billion a year (Tysome 2005). Shen's research confirms that, while UK universities treat such students as a 'cash cow', they do respond fully to Chinese students' demands for the three elements of the education that they are seeking. France and Germany are interested in international students for another reason. There, higher education is free, and they do not see themselves acting in a global market for income from students' fees. Rather, they are trying to attract the best students from around the world to bolster their own labour force. Yet Shen, and similarly Spurling (2006), show that Chinese students tend to take only a sojourn in the west. Shen reports how the one-child policy in China and the heavy sense of duty to care for parents, as well as the opportunities to succeed in and drive forward China's fast-growing knowledge economy, bring the students back, like the sea turtles they are named after, to their place of origin where they will be the source of new growth.

A second assumption in human capital theory, which underpins western countries' strategies, is that students are to see themselves as making personal investments in their future earning power. This thinking transforms higher education from a public good to a private positional good. Each individual is to take responsibility for investing in their own education, repeatedly throughout their lives, in order to keep themselves employable in this fast-changing global knowledge economy. Universities are then meant to meet the demands of students and to act like businesses competing for consumers in a global free trade in higher education. The dominant subject position offered to students in the UK government's White Paper (DfES 2003) was that of consumer (Tlili and Wright 2005). The subsequent Higher Education Act (DfES 2004) introduced an explicit market into higher education in England for the first time.[3] Universities were to set differential fees for home students for each course (temporarily capped at £3,000 per annum) based on what the market would bear (calculated in terms of demand from students, competition from similar courses, the job market and salary levels for graduates).[4] Through exercising choice, the government's argument ran, student demand would determine universities' offerings and drive up quality.

Rachel Brooks (Chapter 13) explores how 90 English graduates, looking back on their university education, considered what, if any, choices they had exercised. For certain elements of the middle class, going to university is a natural progression from school, and not itself a matter of choice. A minority described their decision to go to university as prompted by a love of learning, but the majority saw it as an economic decision. They did not, contrary to government expectations, make fine-tuned decisions about how prestigious and expensive a university to invest in, with the expectation of reaping a commensurate employment dividend. Instead, they experienced credential inflation and saw a degree as a basic ticket for admission into the labour market. Indeed, some new graduates demonstrated considerable resistance to exercising choice within educational markets, and others embraced institutions lower in the league tables as appropriate for their social background, even equating class differences with differences in academic ability. Far from seeing a market in higher education as opening up new vistas of social mobility in England, this study indicates that both the power to choose and the inclination to do so are not equally distributed across all social groups.

Contrary to the argument that the knowledge economy will be dominated by the west in a global division of labour, Rajani Naidoo (Chapter 14) shows that since 2000 the World Bank has maintained that the knowledge economy is a development tool for pulling the third world out of poverty. Using metaphors that resemble the UK government's 'thin air thesis', the World Bank says knowledge is like light, weightless and intangible, that can easily travel the world. By improving their higher education, the argument goes, poor countries can utilise knowledge and 'leap-frog' over stages in the development process. Naidoo argues that an uncritical acceptance of the high skills thesis for developing countries, where skills polarities are even greater than in western countries, is highly problematic. After years when the World Bank used aid conditions to compel third world governments to disinvest in universities, and when structural adjustment policies pressured such countries to downsize their state administrations, developing countries are now pressed into 'market colonialism'. That is, they are to create the market conditions for private and foreign providers of higher education. Indeed agreeing to free trade in services has been made a condition for some third world countries to join the GATS negotiations. Naidoo sets out a series of issues that need to be researched to establish the validity of the World Bank and GATS' arguments that an unregulated market will lead to the development of high quality higher education, which in turn will spur economic growth and overcome global inequalities. In particular, she suggests that a useful strategy would be to avoid setting up a dichotomy between market and state provision, but to explore appropriate relations between the two, and the role of the state in moderating the market.

The role of international agencies in not only developing free trade in higher education, but providing mechanisms to moderate that market is taken up by Gigliola Mathisen (Chapter 15). The OECD (Organisation for Economic Cooperation and Development), as the international organisation that first propounded the idea of the global market in knowledge (Godin n.d.), initially supported moves to develop free trade in higher education through the World Trade Organisation's (WTO) General Agreement on Trade in Services (GATS). Gradually, however, whilst not necessarily listening to the voices of critics (Kelsey 2003), the OECD became worried that the GATS provided no security against fraudulent companies. The United Nations Education, Science and Culture Organisation (UNESCO) equally questioned how students in the third world could be sure they were investing their precious resources in *bone fide* educational products. Mathisen records how the OECD and UNESCO both took initiatives to try and provide quality controls over, and accurate information about, the global market in higher education. Gradually, and largely through the behind-the-scenes activities of Norway, the two organisations joined forces to develop Guidelines for Quality Provision in Cross-Border Higher Education. This was seemingly an odd partnership, as UNESCO emphasises the decision-making powers of national states rather than the imperatives of global markets. UNESCO also regards the international mobility of students and staff not so much as a means to develop a knowledge economy motivated by trade and profit but to promote an agenda of personal development, mutual understanding and world peace. Mathisen traces how, through a succession of meetings, the international agencies agreed first to establish a list of the educational institutions, whether public or private, recognised by each country, that students could consult on the internet. Second, the Guidelines themselves concerned the measures countries could adopt to assure the quality of education provided by these institutions. Mathisen asks how countries such as Norway can reconcile their support for free trade in higher education through GATS with the UNESCO/OECD Guidelines, seeing as GATS is likely to deem the latter an illegal impediment to free trade. The article ends with pragmatic questions about whether third world countries have the resources to operationalise the Guidelines, and if so, whether they could ever effectively counteract the forces of free trade to be unleashed by GATS.

Gunnar Guddal Michelsen's study (Chapter 16) of higher education in Senegal shows the difficulty of answering Mathisen's questions. In the 1990s, Senegal faced a sudden and unexpected surge in students' demand for higher education both from its own citizens, and from neighbouring countries. Initially, public universities had received relatively high public expenditure but, strapped by structural adjustment, the country had no chance of expanding its universities through public spending, and per capita funding dwindled. Facilities became intensely overcrowded and years of study were invalidated by strikes of staff and students. Moreover the courses were still geared towards students' employment in the public sector, which had been shrinking due to structural adjustment. Students were therefore open for other alternatives. The World Bank supported a reform of Senegal's higher education, on the condition that recruitment to the most over-crowded public university be decreased in favour of fee-based institutions. In ten years, 50 private institutions sprang up, and they were enrolling one in five students by 2003–4. The facilities and working conditions for academics and students were better at the private universities but their courses concentrated on fast-growing and very volatile entrepreneurial parts of the economy. To cope with sudden fluctuations in student demand, private universities recruited staff on a part-time basis from the public universities.

Michelsen reveals how the sudden growth of for-profit higher education overwhelmed the Ministry of Education's attempts to monitor what was going on, let alone regulate institutions and their quality. The Ministry did not have the capacity to keep or update a list of providers as recommended in UNESCO's Guidelines, let alone check them for quality, or provide potential students with accurate information about choices on offer. With echoes of the research agenda suggested by Naidoo, Michelsen argues that if a state like Senegal is to work out its new role, it is important to understand the fast changing nature of private higher education, its inter-relation with, and influence over, the function of public universities, and its effect on the values and standards of the entire system. Michelsen provides a picture of a very complex market. At the time of his study, these companies were mainly local and often set up by people he calls Senegalese academic entrepreneurs (although since then, it seems that western companies may have bought into this market). The founders of private universities were fired by the idea that this peaceful, democratic country could itself become a hub in the international knowledge economy and a regional exporter of higher education. Although there was evidence of students wanting to buy knowledge packages as tickets to a prosperous future, the chapter concludes that most of the 50 private institutions run by Senegalese academics were motivated by wider educational values than just narrow profit maximisation.

In sum, this part shows the roles of international agencies in creating the policies and conditions for a global market in higher education. Yet the strategies of these agencies seem internally flawed and mutually inconsistent. Far from the expectation, exemplified in the Danish strategy, that western countries will dominate a global knowledge economy and that their universities and companies will exploit a new international market in higher education, the chapters in this part project a much more complicated picture. This western argument is itself contradicted by the strategy of the World Bank, which claims that a market in higher education is a route to propel developing countries into the knowledge economy and overcome poverty and global inequalities. There are equally serious doubts about the validity of that argument. Nor are the international agencies that have been promoting the growth of international exchanges in higher education universally in favour of a free market. UNESCO in particular has tried to qualify the free trade agenda of the WTO.

These various ideas of the market in higher education are predicated upon the expectation that providers will act in response to the demand of consumers, yet universities, especially in western countries, are also heavily steered by the demands of governments. In England, where higher education is already constructed as a market, the government still loads universities with a social agenda to 'widen participation' and overcome social and class inequalities. Several European governments expect that by creaming off the world's brightest students, they will add them to their country's labour force. This did not accord with the evidence of Chinese students. 'Home' students in England did not simply exercise choice like consumers in a shopping mall and they doubted that their investment would lead immediately to employment commensurate with their qualifications or generate the so-called graduate premium. Yet in Senegal, where public universities are starved of funds and hemmed in by restrictive practices, new opportunities for both academics and students are opened up by the provision of higher education on a commercial basis. As a regional provider of higher education, could trade in higher education become as important for the economy of Senegal as it is anticipated it will be for Denmark? The part raises many questions about the global divisions that will be generated by a market in higher education. The WTO and OECD project that there are vast profits to be made, especially if academic work in the west is unbundled and outsourced in standardised components to cheaper academic labour in emerging economies. Yet will the UNESCO/OECD Guidelines be strong enough to protect students as consumers, especially in the third world, from fraudulent operators in such a global market?

Notes

1   To formulate and legitimise this strategy the government created a 26-person Globalisation Council consisting of industrial leaders, confederations of Danish industries and employers, five ministers, four academics and three trade union organisations.
2   This outsourcing now includes journalism, where a US municipality outsourced the writing of newspaper reports about its operations to two journalists in India linked to a video of proceedings (Glaister 2007).
3   England is used advisedly, as Scotland has refused to introduce students' fees.
4   A temporary cap on fees for home students at £3,000 per annum was instituted to assuage opposition within the Labour Party, but all the mechanisms for a domestic market in higher education are in place and will come into full operation as soon as the cap is lifted.

References

Danish Government (2006) *Progress, Innovation and Cohesion. Strategy for Denmark in the Global Economy*, The Prime Minister's Office, Copenhagen, May.

DfES (Department for Education and Skills) (2003) *The Future of Higher Education* (White Paper), January.

DfES (Department for Education and Skills) (2004) *Higher Education Act 2004*, Chapter 8, London: The Stationery Office.

Glaister, Dan (2007) 'On the news beat in Mumbai, California', *The Guardian*, 12 May, http://www.guardian.co.uk/print/0,,329836405-111-087,00.html.

Godin, Benoît (n.d.) *The Knowledge-Based Economy: Conceptual Framework or Buzzword?* Working Paper 24, Project on the History and Sociology of S&T Statistics, Canadian Science and Innovation Indicators Consortium, Montreal, Canada.

Kelsey, Jane (2003) 'Legal fetishism and the contradictions of the GATS', *Globalisation, Societies and Education*, 1(3): 267–80.

Reich, Robert (1991) *The Work of Nations*, New York: Vintage Books.

Shore, Cris and Wright, Susan (2001) 'Changing institutional contexts: new managerialism and the rise of UK Higher Education plc', *Anthropology in Action*, 8(1): 14–21.

Spurling, Nicola (2006) 'Exploring adjustment: the social situation of Chinese students in UK higher education', *Learning and Teaching in the Social Sciences*, 3(2): 95–117.

Thorne, M. (ed.) (1999) *Foresight: Universities in the Future*, London: Department of Trade and Industry, Office of Science and Technology.

Tlili, Anwar and Wright, Susan (2005) 'Learn to consume, teach to account?', *Anthropology in Action*, special issue *Politics of Accountability* (ed. D. Brenneis, C. Shore and S. Wright), 12(1): 64–78.

Tysome, Tony (2005) 'Foreign students put off by visa hike', *Times Higher Education Supplement*, 11 February.

Wolf, Alison (2002) *Does Education Matter? Myths About Education and Economic Growth*, London: Penguin.

Wright, Susan (2004) 'Markets, corporations, consumers? New landscapes of higher education', *Learning and Teaching in the Social Sciences*, 1(2): 71–93.

11 Towards a high-skills economy

Higher education and the new realities of global capitalism

Phillip Brown, Hugh Lauder and David Ashton

> Human capital refers to the knowledge, information, ideas, skills, and health of individuals. This is the 'age of human capital' … the economic success of individuals, and also whole economies, depends on how extensively and effectively people invest in themselves.
>
> (Gary S. Becker 2006: 292)

In the developed economies the idea that we have entered an 'age of human capital' is part of a policy mantra that foresees a knowledge-driven economy in which most are in high-skilled, high-waged employment. This chapter will outline the underlying assumptions of this mantra, which in many respects has changed little since the 1960s when human capital theory gained increasing prominence in education and economic policy (Halsey 1961). It will then examine the prospects for the creation of high skills economies in the light of new realities of the global economy. This analysis is based on interviews with senior managers and executives in leading transnational companies and government policy makers in seven countries including China and India. In conclusion we will argue that further investment in education and skills will not deliver high-skilled, high-waged jobs to a majority of workers in the developed economies. Human capital theory does not offer a universal explanation of the relationship between education, jobs and rewards. Indeed, in the early decades of the twenty-first century we may witness the rise of high-skilled, low-waged economies.

Technological evolution and the rise of the knowledge economy

A striking feature of what Grubb and Lazerson (2006) call the 'educational gospel' is the continuity in thinking about economic development and the role of education. It is consistent with a technocratic model of evolutionary social change that has a long tradition in the social sciences. Clark Kerr and his colleagues (1973) highlighted the progressive nature of industrialisation since it depended on a greater role for science and technological innovation that demanded high levels of education and meritocratic opportunity.

While sociologists have been critical of economic theories of human capital because of their emphasis on economic rationality (Fevre 2003), they have shared a similar model of industrial progress that runs through the writings of Comte, Durkheim, Parsons and Bell. Societies are assumed to move from simple to complex divisions of labour driven by scientific knowledge that accelerates the pace of technological innovation. These trends are mirrored in the transformation of the education system – from mass elementary to mass higher education – as the demand for skilled workers increases due to what economists call 'technological bias' which asserts that at the same time that new technologies eliminate some jobs through automation they create new higher skilled employment and up-skill existing jobs (Lauder, forthcoming).

The transformation of work is also assumed to change the relationship between employees and employers. High skills (including individual expertise, knowledge and creativity) are considered to be major assets that determine the profitability of companies, superseding the ownership of land, machines, and material capital. The competition for ideas, knowledge and skills comes to define the new economy because it is no longer ownership of capital that generates wealth creation (Drucker 1993). Consequently, the increase in educated labour is interpreted as a power shift where the prosperity of individuals, companies and nations depends on human and intellectual capital rather than on issues of ownership that defined Marxist accounts of the capitalist system.

The importance of human capital theory to current policy debate is not limited to issues of skills upgrading but to the broader relationship between credentials, jobs and rewards. Investments in education are premised on a political equation of high skills = high wages. The introduction of 'user pays' models for the funding of higher education rest on the human capital view that income reflects the level of skill. Low-skilled workers get low wages because the market value of their labour is limited because other people are able to undertake the same jobs with little formal training. Alternatively, high-skilled workers are assumed to be paid more because they are more productive and have greater market worth.

Globalisation as knowledge wars

The impact of the global economy on the prosperity of Western nations has increased rather that diminished the importance attached to human capital and the idea of a high-skilled, high-waged economy. The Leitch Review of Skills in the UK, when reflecting on the increasing global economic competition, observed that 'skills were once *a* key lever for prosperity and fairness. Skills are now increasingly *the* key lever' (Leitch 2006: 3).

This is premised on the view that globalisation dramatically weakens the power of nation states to manage the economy in the national interest. In the global economy it is no longer possible for Western governments to protect domestic workers from the full force of international competition. The shift of manufacturing jobs to low-cost economies such as China, Poland and Brazil bears testimony to the realities of the new economy. Higher living standards in North America and Western Europe can only be achieved by competing within niche markets for customised goods and services, based on the application of knowledge, skills and entrepreneurial ideas (Jones 1999; Stewart 2001).

Robert Reich (1991) explained the growth in income polarisation in the United States in the 1980s in terms of the relative ability of workers to sell their skills, knowledge and insights in the global job market. He argues that the incomes of the top 20 per cent have pulled away from the rest because of their ability to break free of the constraints of local and national labour markets. The global labour market offers far greater rewards to 'symbolic analysts' or 'knowledge workers' precisely because the market for their services has grown, whereas those workers who remain locked into national or local markets have experienced stagnation or a decline in income.

Reich, amongst others, interprets rising wage inequalities as proof of both the realities of the global labour market and as evidence of the failure of the existing education system (Brown and Lauder 2006). The reason why income inequalities have grown is not explained as a 'structural' problem – that the proportion of high-skilled, high-waged jobs is limited by the occupational structure – but due to the failure of the education system to make a larger proportion of the workforce employable in the global competition for high-skilled, high-waged work.

Thomas Friedman (2005: 230) is also upbeat about what can be achieved by investing in the knowledge and skills of the workforce:

> America, as a whole, will do fine in a flat world with free trade – provided it continues to churn out knowledge workers who are able to produce idea-based goods that can be sold globally and who are able to fill the knowledge jobs that will be created as we not only expand the global economy but connect all the knowledge pools in the world. There may be a limit to the number of good factory jobs in the world, but there is no limit to the number of idea-generating jobs in the world.

It is believed, therefore, that there is now a global auction for jobs. Low-skilled jobs will be auctioned on price and will tend to migrate to low-waged economies such as those in Asian or Eastern Europe, while high-skilled jobs will continue to attract higher wages. These jobs will be auctioned on 'quality' rather than price, including the skills, knowledge and insights of employees. The main bidders for 'quality' jobs are assumed to be today's advanced economies. This offers the potential for countries such as Britain, France and the United States to become *magnet* economies, attracting a disproportionate share of high-skilled, high-waged jobs (Brown and Lauder 2001).

But the technocratic model of an evolutionary shift from physical to mental labour is not limited to the changing relationship between education and the occupational structure within specific societies. It is extended to include the relationship between nation states. The rise of the global knowledge-based economy is believed to remove much of the source of conflict and strife between nations. Trade liberalisation is presented as a 'win-win' opportunity for both developing and developed nations.[1] The territorial disputes that drove nations to war in pursuit of land and material wealth become less important in terms of power, privilege and wealth. According to Rosecrance:

> In the past, material forces were dominant in national growth, prestige, and power; now products of the mind take precedence. Nations can transfer most of their material production thousands of miles away, centring their attention on research and development and product design at home. The result is a new and productive partnership between 'head' nations, which design products, and 'body' nations, which manufacture them.
>
> (Rosecrance 1999: xi)

This shift from *bloody wars* to *knowledge wars* represents the highest stage in evolutionary development as nations compete for ideas, skills and knowledge that contribute to economic advantage by 'out-smarting' economic rivals. Schools, colleges, universities, think tanks, design centres and research laboratories are now on the front line in the search for competitive advantage. This is reflected in current attempts by organisations such as the OECD's PISA studies and the International Education Association (IEA) to develop comparative measures of academic quality and performance, along with global rankings of universities such as that developed by Shanghai's Jiao Tong University (Marginson 2006). It is no longer the qualities of individual students within national systems that are benchmarked, but the quality of these national education and training systems as a whole. As Gordon Brown (2004), Britain's Prime Minister has suggested, '... if we are to succeed in a world where offshoring can be an opportunity ... our mission [is] to make the British people the best educated, most skilled, best trained country in the world'.

A report from the field

What is surprising about policy and academic debates about the impact of globalisation is the lack of detailed empirical evidence. Much of the evidence is derived from consultancy companies that invariably conflate prognosis with prescription in order to profit from their knowledge. It has also been dominated by American writers on management and business issues that have tended to focus on US transnational companies and business interests. While some of this research is excellent, it may limit our understanding of the wider global transformation that is currently in progress.

Much of the debate is also outdated given the pace of change and the fact that globalisation is a process which, assuming further liberalisation of international trade (which is by no means inevitable), will have an increasing impact at the national level as companies exploit new, cheaper and more reliable ways of communicating and working across knowledge, cultural and geographical boundaries.

Our argument is based on research with leading transnational companies at the vanguard of global economic change. The United Nations estimates that there are around 64,000 transnational companies, a rise from 37,000 in the early 1990s. These transnational companies comprise parent enterprises and foreign affiliates which vary in size and influence. The foreign affiliates of these companies generated around 53 million jobs around the world (UNCTAD 2005). General Electric had the largest foreign assets in 2003 with 330 enterprises in the United States and over 1,000 foreign affiliates.[2]

The key role that these firms play in shaping the global economy is reflected in the fact that a third of global trade is due to intra-firm activities where components, products, services and software are sold between affiliates within the same company. Equally, it is estimated that over 60 per cent of the goods exported from China in 2005 came from foreign-owned firms that had moved manufacturing plants to increase profit margins.[3]

Over the last three years we have interviewed 180 senior managers and executives in twenty leading transnational companies in financial services, telecoms, electronics and the automotive sector, to achieve a better understanding of their global corporate strategies and the future of skills. We investigated how transnational companies were globalising their human resources and whether high-skilled jobs were concentrated in the developed economies as predicted within the official discourse. We interviewed the same companies in different countries, often including the 'home' country where the head office is typically found and in two other countries including Britain, China, Germany, India, Korea, Singapore and the United States. We also interviewed government policy-makers in each of these countries to understand their competition strategies in respect to high value inward investment from foreign transnational companies.

Our findings show that there are new global possibilities for transnational companies to define, deploy and develop their human resources in new ways. As a result human resource issues have assumed greater strategic importance because they have come to represent a major source of competitive advantage (Ashton *et al.*, forthcoming). While a global brand does not necessarily represent a global company, many leading transnational companies have realised that the new competition depends on developing the global capacity to integrate people, knowledge, software, networks and other corporate resources both within and beyond the organisation. This challenges much of the established literature on the knowledge economy, which does not adequately grasp the realities of knowledge capitalism or the transformation in the global division of knowledge-intensive work.

To understand why the policy discourse outlined above has failed to grasp the nature and implications of the economic transformation which is now in train we will focus on a number of interrelated issues to explain why this vision of a high-skills, high-wage economy is illusory.

Quality *and* price

Much of the literature has suggested that the comparative advantage of nations depends on their ability to compete on quality or price. We have described how developing economies are assumed to be restricted to price competition for low-skilled, low-value goods and services because they lack the skilled labour and hi-tech capabilities of OECD countries, such as the United States, Germany or the United Kingdom. In turn, to maintain their prosperity, workers and businesses in developed economies must move up the value chain towards the 'quality' end of the market, based on the assumption that the value of knowledge will continue to rise.

But at a time where human knowledge is being taught, certified, and applied on a scale unprecedented in human history, the overall value of human knowledge is likely to decline rather than increase. We are witnessing an increasing polarisation in the market value of different kinds of qualifications, knowledge and occupational roles. If knowledge is the key asset of the new economy the task of business is not to pay more for it but less. There are two aspects to the strategies that companies adopt to pay less for more. The first is by accessing the increasing supply of graduates from across the globe, many of whom will work for far lower incomes than those in the West, either by offshoring or by locating their high-skills work, such as research and development, in developing nations including China and India. The second is by standardising knowledge work through processes that we call Digital Taylorism (see below).

Companies will continue to pay a premium for outstanding 'talent' (however it is defined) as part of the hierarchical segmentation of 'knowledge' work. This has long been a feature of capitalism, but today it has greater significance because the incomes of so many workers in Western economies depend on maintaining if not increasing the market value of what they know. It has also become more significant because the global economy offers employers new ways of reducing costs and raising productivity that were not available until now. A high profile political example is the growth in offshoring in key sectors such as financial services and information technologies. The cost of employing a chip design engineer in the United States is over four times more than a designer in Korea and 10 times or over the costs associated with the same workers in India and China (Brown *et al.* 2006). In financial services, relocations increasingly involve 'front' as well as 'back' office functions, including financial analysis, research, regulatory reporting, accounting, human resources and graphic design.[4] Quality has become price sensitive and labour arbitrage (profiting from differences in labour costs around the world) no longer stops with factory workers and call-centre operatives.

The new competition is based on quality *and* price, enabling companies to raise their game and lower their costs at the same time. While national governments in the developed economies may see the knowledge economy as a way of increasing prosperity, and while there is a tendency in the policy literature to understand competitiveness and productivity as a question of competing for knowledge and skills rather than profits, it is far removed from the way companies understand the new competition which involves getting smart things done at a lower price.

High skills: a declining advantage

The argument that a knowledge-driven economy demands a larger proportion of the workforce with a university education and with access to lifelong learning opportunities has had a major impact on participation rates in tertiary education. In OECD countries, university is no longer the preserve of an elite, whatever the merits of the economic case for expanding higher education. There has been a significant expansion in all OECD countries with the exception of Germany. Canada was the first country to achieve the target of over 50 per cent of people aged 25 and 34 entering the job market with a tertiary level qualification. Korea is not far behind, having engineered a massive growth in tertiary provision since 1991. Germany is the exception due to its continued commitment to the dual system of workplace and off-the-job training.[5]

This expansionary phase is unlikely to end in the near future as most countries benchmark themselves against those with the highest participation rates, although its relationship to employment, productivity and economic growth remains unclear (Ashton and Green 1996). This expansion is consistent with the Western view that low-skilled jobs will be auctioned on price and will tend to migrate to low-waged economies such as those in Asia or Eastern Europe, while high-skilled jobs will continue to attract higher wages. However, this fails to recognise the mass production of well qualified candidates from developing economies that will enable transnational companies to export some of their 'brain' work as well as their 'body' work to low-cost economies.

The collapse of communism, economic integration, and advances in information technologies have brought China, India and Russia along with a number of smaller nations into the global competition for education, knowledge and high-skilled employment. The distinction between 'head' and 'body' nations seems little more than a remnant of economic imperialism that fails to understand that some developing countries have already entered the competition for knowledge intensive, high-tech and high-skilled employment; 'the composition of China's exports has begun to change rapidly, away from reliance on cheap low-margin goods to more value-added manufacturers offering much higher profits'.[6] China and India want to move their cost advantage further up the value chain. As we were told by a government official in Beijing, 'today China is the world's factory, tomorrow the world's competitor'.

In an interview with a senior Indian government official in New Delhi, we discussed India's expansion into manufacturing. This was his response, 'the Chinese have a great advantage when it's mass production. We will not be able to compete with them there ... but increasingly every item is requiring new inputs like design inputs, it's requiring innovation and embedded software. That is our skills advantage, we are moving up the value chain in manufacturing'. It is this attempt to move up the value chain that will transform the global auction for jobs as 'knowledge' workers in the developed economies are no longer immune from price competition with highly qualified workers in low-cost locations.

China had over six times as many students in higher education as the UK and almost as many as the US in 2002, including 600,000 engaged in postgraduate studies. The latest figures suggest that China has now overtaken the US with around 20 million students enrolled in higher education.[7] In India, there has also been a major expansion of higher education with the aim of increasing the participation rate of 18–23 year olds in higher education from 6 per cent in 2002 to 10 per cent in 2007.[8] India's Prime Minister, Manmohan Singh, recently observed that:

> In the next one or two years, the knowledge sector will receive our attention to the extent that it deserves. I do recognise that India has to be the centre, the hub of activity as far as the knowledge economy is concerned. We don't want to miss the chance.[9]

There is little sense of countries such as China, India, Malaysia, Poland or the Czech Republic, being content with doing the 'body' work within the global economy while the 'brain' work is left to the developed economies such as the United States, Japan, Germany and Britain.

Although the quality of education is likely to vary in countries experiencing rapid expansion of educational provision, it is nevertheless the case that Asia is producing more engineers than Europe and North America combined. In the natural and agricultural sciences (including physical, biological, earth, atmospheric, and ocean sciences) Asia is also ahead, although this is not the case for mathematics and computer sciences.

In the United States, close to half of those gaining a doctoral degree in engineering, mathematics and computer science are foreign students. Some of these remain within the developed economies but others return to their indigenous countries, adding to the stock of highly skilled workers (Saxenian 2006). Alone, South Korea graduates as many engineers as the United States and according to recent evidence from a US Business Roundtable report, by 2010 more than 90 per cent of all scientists and engineers in the world will be living in Asia.[10] The World Bank also estimates that Russia has the third highest numbers of scientists and engineers per capita in the world and other Eastern European countries also have a growing proportion of well-educated scientists and IT specialists.[11]

On this evidence, the view that it will take decades for developing economies to compete in the global market for high-skilled jobs has grossly underestimated the speed of educational reform and business innovation in emerging economies including China and India.

Where to think?

Innovation remains a crucial source of competitive advantage as mass customisation has assumed greater importance in virtually all industrial sectors. The demand for constant innovation has also been fuelled by rapid technological advancement and consumer tastes. Over 80 per cent of BMW Minis produced in Britain for the global market are built to customer order, offering a range of over 250 factory-fit options and dealer-fit accessories making every Mini uniquely similar. In the United States the Toyota Tundra sports has 22,000 possible configurations and the Chrysler Dodge Ram is available in 1.2 million variations.[12]

The use of build-to-order where products are only made to the specific requirements of customers is not restricted to the auto industry. Dell computers has established a sophisticated made-to-order business that gives customers the opportunity to build a computer based on a choice of the twenty or so product features including memory (RAM), disk space, modem, processor, screen and software. The same processes are being applied to clothes, watches, sneakers, cosmetics, window-frames and houses. Nike offers customised sports shoes where customers can choose between a range of 'uppers' and 'soles' and have their names embroidered on the back of each sneaker, while the internet company 'customatix' allows you to design your own shoes based on an almost limitless combinations of colours, graphics, logos and materials.[13]

These trends not only highlight the importance of accelerating the development of new ideas and improving on existing ones, but also on reducing the time and cost to get them into the marketplace. To reduce the time from 'innovation to invoice' some companies use 24-hour design teams that work around the clock moving through time zones across Asia, Europe and North America. This is intended not only to reduce the time between invention, application, and market launch, but also to reduce costs, due to lower salary levels in much of Asia. As a senior executive in a German multinational told us, 'we have to drive innovation, we have to be at the leading edge at reasonable cost … we have to try to get higher skills at reasonable cost and high flexibility'.

This is leading companies to give more thought to 'where to think'. Typically, this has led them to question the role of the appropriately named 'head' office as the primary source of corporate brain-power. But where to think is more than a question of finding the cheapest locations, as it reflects a number of other considerations such as the need for a critical mass of people that understand the organisation, or share the collective intelligence necessary for advanced R&D. It is also assumed to reflect the importance of embedded capabilities as innovation rarely depends on the skills of individuals working in isolation but on a culture of mutual collaboration and purpose. However, companies are increasingly experimenting with research, design, market and product development activities in the emerging economies.[14]

Such trends reflect a quality revolution within emerging economies that challenges much of the existing literature on the social foundations of economic performance. It is, for instance, assumed that quality depends on particular 'regimes of production' such as the dual system of workplace and college training in Germany or high-trust relations in the 'third Italy', that are difficult if not impossible to duplicate (Hall and Soskice 2001). But what companies have discovered as they experiment with higher end activities such as research and design in lower cost countries, is that quality may not be impaired and may even be improved, although there are also companies who retreat because they struggle to achieve the standards they require or due to fears about intellectual property rights.

Our studies show that the assumption that hi-tech depends on social sophistication in the form of democratic politics, welfare provision and high GDP per capita, fails to capture the extreme forms of uneven development where the pre-industrial and the post-industrial share the same postcode. There is a tendency to study economic activity from the outside looking in, based on an assumed correspondence between society and economy, but business is being turned 'inside out'. While companies need a decent infrastructure (roads, communications), and supply of well educated and motivated workers, they are able to set up 'oasis operations' (high-tech factories, offices and research facilities in low-spec societies). It is also a mistake to assume that the rapid development especially in China, is at the price of quality. One does not need to spend much time in Beijing, Shanghai or Guangzhou to understand that they are building to compete with America, Japan and Germany rather than other developing economies.

The rise in quality standards around the world is making it more difficult for highly qualified workers in developed economies to shelter from the global competition for jobs. Equally, as the performance gap rapidly narrows, differences in labour costs between developed and developing economies are narrowing far more slowly, apart from in a few hot spots in China and India, and even here there is still a long way to go before the price advantage is seriously eroded. Consequently, companies have greater scope to extract value from international webs of people, processes and suppliers, based on a Dutch or reverse auction where quality is maintained while labour costs go down.

In the late 1990s when we asked a leading German car manufacturer whether they could make their executive range anywhere in the world, the answer was an emphatic 'no'. Today it's an equally emphatic 'yes'. Another car maker, this time from the United States, added, 'If you had asked me 5 years ago I would have said that the skill sets probably are still in the advanced economies but I think that is changing very, very quickly ... The advantage from our perspective is that you are paying those guys anywhere from sort of 12 to 15 thousand dollars a year versus say a European or a US engineer at anywhere from 75 to 95 thousand dollars a year with a whole bunch of benefits as well'.

A leading engineering corporation also told us there has been a significant narrowing in the performance of operations and factories around the world, 'those in emerging countries are catching up fast and this is making it more difficult for plants in the West. It's really a bit of a rat race'. Research in China revealed that many enterprises had adopted the latest high performance management practices which flourish in the context of a highly educated labour force, enabling them to produce high value-added goods at much lower costs (Venter *et al.* 2002). Moreover, a United Nations survey of transnational companies also found that China was the most attractive prospective R&D location in 2005–9, followed by the United States, India, Japan, the United Kingdom and the Russian Federation.[15]

As differences in quality and productivity narrow between operations in different parts of the world, the cost and working conditions of Western employees are no longer the global benchmark. This has been true for various kinds of low-skilled activities in the manufacturing sector for thirty years. But the same may now be true for high-skilled workers in the developed economies as a growing proportion of high-skilled, high-value activities can be undertaken in low-cost locations. In moving inward investment up the value-chain of products and services, transnational companies are not only 'following the business' into rapidly expanding emerging markets, but adopting a deliberate strategy to establish leading edge operations in parallel to those in the developed economies. This not only gives them global flexibility and continuity if there are industrial relations problems or problems of underperformance in a specific regional centre, but it also enables companies to point to their lower cost operations in the emerging economies when negotiating with employees in the West.[16]

Digital Taylorism

While the policy spotlight has focused on the creation of new ideas, products and services, the ability of companies to leverage new technologies to globally align and coordinate business activities has also brought to the fore a different agenda involving the standardisation of functions and jobs within the service sector, including an increasing proportion of technical, managerial and professional roles. As Jay Tate (2001) has observed 'industrial revolutions are revolutions in standardization'.

Standardisation is well understood in manufacturing where the same standard components such as wheels, brake linings, and windscreens, can be made in different factories around the world and shipped for final assembly at one location in the knowledge that all the components meet international quality standards and will fit together. This not only gives companies flexibility but also enables them to reduce costs. The same logic is now being applied to service sector occupations that were previously difficult to standardise because there were no digital equivalents to mechanical drills, jigs, presses and ships, all required to create global supply chains in manufacturing.

The potential to transform work in the service sector, that is work that does not involve physical proximity to the customer, client or patient (although our understanding of what can be done 'remotely' is being transformed by new communication technologies), is inevitably limited so long as knowledge remains in the heads of individuals working in idiosyncratic ways using different computer systems and application software. But the communication technologies that we have today, including the capacity for digital processing, internet capability, and increasing bandwidth (which determines the volume and speed that data, information, or live video can be transferred across a network), have created the realistic possibility of developing global standards that reduce technical complexity and diversity (Davenport 2005).[17]

Through building modular applications, business processes including ordering, marketing, selling, delivering, invoicing, auditing, and hiring, can be broken down into their component parts, which include the unbundling of occupational roles so that job tasks can be simplified and sourced in different ways. In other words, an increasing proportion of managerial and professional jobs that were previously sheltered because they were not tradable are being redesigned, although it is difficult to predict how far this process can transform technical, managerial and professional occupations (Bryant 2006).

Terms such as 'financial services factory' and 'industrialisation' are being applied by leading consultancy companies to describe the transformation of the service sector. Accenture Consulting (2007: 1) is a proponent of 'the concept of industrialization – breaking down processes and products into constituent components that can be recombined in a tailored, automated fashion – to non-manufacturing settings'. Likewise, Gupta (2006) states that 'by componentizing their business processes, the Financial Services firms have begun to look at each component independently of the other components while selecting the best sourcing option (i.e. insourced or outsourced, onshore and/or offshored, etc.). Should the trend continue tomorrow's banks would look and behave no differently to a factory' (p. 43).

It is this form of organisational innovation in the way companies hire, order, market, sell, deliver, distribute, invoice and account, driven by new information technologies and greater choices in terms of where to produce, partner or purchase goods and services that define today's knowledge capitalism. These trends remain in their 'craft' stage resembling manufacturing in the early twentieth century. While it took decades for manufactures to 'lift and shift' through standardisation, the process is likely to be much quicker when applied to service sector employment because the only hardware you need can fit on the average office desk.[18]

This part of our analysis suggests that if the twentieth century brought what can be described as *mechanical Taylorism* characterised by the Fordist production line, where the knowledge of craft workers was captured by management, codified and re-engineered in the shape of the moving assembly line, the twenty-first century is the age of *digital Taylorism*. This involves translating *knowledge work* into *working knowledge* through the extraction, codification and digitalisation of knowledge into software prescripts that can be transmitted and manipulated by others regardless of location.

Anell and Wilson (2002) argue that 'the question of how to extract and distribute knowledge efficiently will not be answered by recommendations about how to build and use human and structural capital. The solution resides in the ability of knowledge firms to extract and translate more or less tacit, personal knowledge into explicit, codified knowledge, into what we call prescripts. Prescripts constitute a form of capital, to be regarded in the same vein as the company's human, structural, social and financial capital' (pp. 7–8).

While there seems little doubt that the extent to which companies can capture the knowledge of those who think for a living is often exaggerated, the problem for 'knowledge' workers was recognised by Harold Wilensky nearly half a century ago when he envisaged a time when the distinction between conception and execution would move further up the occupational hierarchy as new technologies would give senior managers and executives much greater control of the white collar workforce.

> Top executives, surrounded by programmers, research and development men [and women], and other staff experts, would be more sharply separated from everybody else. The line between those who decide, 'What is to be done and how' and those who do it – that dividing line would move up. The men who once applied Taylor to the proletariat would themselves by Taylorized.
>
> (Wilensky 1960: 557)

Whereas the distinction between conception and execution in a period of mechanical Taylorism transformed the relationship between the 'working' and 'middle' classes, digital Taylorism also takes the form of a power struggle within the middle classes, as these processes depend on reducing the autonomy and discretion of the majority of managers and professionals. It encourages the segmentation of talent in ways that reserve the 'permission to think' to a small proportion of employees responsible for driving the business forward.[19] But the loss of autonomy for managers and professionals remains significantly different from the era of mechanical Taylorism, because its digital variety eliminates the need for close, over-the-shoulder supervision. Control is remote because it is built into the software, so that the monitoring of activities is at a distance. Equally, it does not eliminate the importance of employee motivation or the need for good customer-facing skills as the standardisation required to achieve mass customisation still needs customers to feel that they are receiving a personalised service. This may contribute to a continuing demand for university graduates but their occupational roles are far removed from the archetypal graduate jobs of the past.

Creating a 'war for talent'

While the 'official' account of the knowledge economy assumes a linear relationship between education, jobs and rewards, where mass higher education is predicted to reduce income inequalities as people gain access to high-skilled, high-waged jobs, the reality is more complex. In America and Britain the expansion of higher education has been associated with an increase in wage differentials (Mishel *et al.* 2007). This is not only between university graduates and non-graduates but also within the graduate workforce. Frank and Cook (1996) argue that income inequalities are not the result of changes in the distribution of human capital – that some have invested more in their education and training that others – but due to the changing structure of the job market (Brown 2006). Even within 'graduate' occupations those at the top of the occupational pyramid receive a disproportionate share of rewards, in what Frank and Cook call 'winner-takes-all markets'. They argue that changes in domestic and global competition make 'the most productive individuals more valuable, and at the same time have led to more open bidding for their services' (p. 6).

This argument is consistent with that of consultants from McKinsey's who popularised the idea of a 'war for talent' (Michaels *et al.* 2001). They argue that reliance on talent increased dramatically over the last century. 'In the 1900s, only 17 per cent of all jobs required knowledge workers; now over 60 per cent do. More knowledge workers means it's important to get great talent, since the differential value created by the most talented knowledge workers is enormous' (Michaels *et al.* 2001: 2). Whatever the merits of this argument, virtually all those we spoke to in China, Korea, India and Singapore as well as the United States, Germany and Britain believed that they were in a war for talent, which was increasingly global.

Therefore, is the war for talent essential to higher productivity and competitiveness, or can it be explained in terms of positional conflict (i.e. bosses taking a larger share of the profits)? It seems clear that there is a more intense positional conflict within organisations, especially when the emphasis is on shareholder value (Lazonick and O'Sullivan 2000). When the focus is on maximising the returns to shareholders, senior managers and executives need to be aligned to short-term profit maximisation often through share options which require a consistent attempt to reduce costs. Workers that are not defined as top talent will constantly come under pressure to 'prove their worth' within an increasingly global context. We know that in many transnational companies a larger share of the profits is also going to shareholders rather than the workforce, as predicted by pundits of the knowledge economy (Roach 2006). There is also evidence of corporate executives in the United States and Britain gaining massive wage hikes that often bear little relationship to business performance (Bebchuk and Grinstein 2005).

But this is not the whole story because the war for talent also reflects the changing nature of economic competition. The value of a company is not simply determined by the 'value' of what it produces, but by its 'reputational' capital (Brown and Hesketh 2004), or what is commonly referred to as 'branding'. As Samsung, a leading global electronics firm, has observed, 'in the digital era, a product will be distinguished by its brand more than by its functions or by its quality'.[20]

This emphasis on the 'social' rather than the 'technical' facets of business success is also highlighted in the nature of services that include management consultancy and the creative industries. As Alvesson (2001) has suggested, 'the ambiguity of knowledge and the work of knowledge-intensive companies means that "knowledge", "expertise" and "solving problems" to a large degree become matters of belief, impressions and negotiations of meaning. Institutionalized assumptions, expectations, reputations, images, etc. feature strongly in the perception of the products of knowledge-intensive organizations and workers' (p. 863).

Value added in knowledge intensive industries (e.g. consultancy or financial services), stems from branding the company in order to maximise the price of its professional knowledge. But the value of corporate branding is not restricted to the image of the goods or services sold to consumers around the world. It also relates to the workforce. The more corporate value is 'embodied' in the people who work for it, the more companies want to be seen to recruit 'the best' (Brown and Hesketh 2004).

It is assumed that the best graduates gravitate towards the elite universities. This view is actively promoted by leading universities as higher education has become a global business. The branding of universities and faculty members is integral to the organisation of academic enquiry. Claims to world-class standards depend on attracting 'the best' academics and forming alliances with elite universities elsewhere in the world, while recruiting the 'right' kinds of students. Universities play the same reputational games as companies, because it is a logical consequence of market competition.

We can also see how a new global hierarchy is being created that transforms 'national' hierarchies; this is exemplified by recent reforms in German higher education. Until recently it has been based on 'parity of esteem' between universities. To date there has been little difference in the market value of a degree from one German university rather than another. Yet the introduction of 'excellence' reforms is leading more resources to be targeted at a small number of universities. In short, this policy will create an elite in an attempt to lift the profile of German higher education within global rankings of leading universities. In ripping up the level playing field, it will transform the positional relationship between students from different universities. In an attempt to recruit the best and to be seen to do so leading companies will target this elite group, based on the assumption that the most talented students will go to these universities because they are the most difficult to get into. Hence, the idea of a war for talent in Germany is real in its consequences, as a likely outcome will be growing income inequalities between German graduates.

As it becomes impossible for employers to have first-hand knowledge of universities or the quality of their students, reputation (like branding) becomes key. All companies benchmark leading universities around the world based on their own formulations often in conjunction with public rankings of top universities. Despite much talk of greater diversity, the ranking of universities by reputation has made it more important to study at a leading national university with an international reputation. Notions of diversity are being transformed from a concern to recruit from a broad range of social backgrounds within a given national context, towards viewing diversity as the recruitment of foreign nationals as part of the internationalisation of human resource management. In reality, this form of diversity is about recruiting elites from different countries in the global war for talent. To qualify, individuals have to go to the 'best' universities whatever country they live in.

These issues have profound implications for understanding the relationship between education, jobs and rewards, as human capital theory (with its emphasis on technical knowledge) fails to account for positional conflict surrounding shareholder models of corporate governance, or the increasing importance of 'reputational' capital in assessing the differential value of individual credentials and knowledge. Although the relationship between reputation and performance is hazy its consequences are stark, as reputation and performance are woven together through the exercise of symbolic power to define which employees are to be truly valued as exhibiting high potential or outstanding performance. Employees defined as 'top talent' are able to draw on this reputational capital to leverage a better remuneration package whereas other equally well-qualified employees find themselves in a reverse bidding war as companies try to reduce the cost of knowledge.

In short, almost without exception, companies were not only 'segmenting' their educated workforce based on occupational function but also on 'performance' driven by an attempt to reduce the cost of knowledge work, while retaining what they perceived as top talent. Within a context of increasing globalisation, digital Taylorism and the expansion of high-skilled, low-cost workers from developing economies, companies are developing new ways to compete for the best ideas at the same time as delivering them at lower cost. Within this new economy of knowledge, employees are caught in a pincer movement where those defined as 'top talent' are judged to have high market value, while others in the same occupations increasingly find themselves in a cost-driven competition, whether domestic or global.

Conclusions

This chapter challenges the dominant discourse on education in a global knowledge-based economy. We argue that Britain and the United States are not 'knowledge' economies, where the value of knowledge continues to rise, but they are characterised by an economy of knowledge that is transforming the relationship between education, jobs and rewards. This will inevitably lead to claims that education is failing to meet the needs of industry, but the over-riding problem is a failure to lift the demand for 'knowledge' workers to meet the increasing numbers entering the job market with a bachelors degree (Keep 2004).

The disjunction between education, jobs and rewards has profound implications for our understanding of educational opportunity, justice and social mobility. Ernest Gellner (1983) observed that 'modern society is not mobile because it is egalitarian; it is egalitarian because it is mobile' (pp. 24–5). This suggests that the growing evidence of declining social mobility in both the United States and Britain is not simply due to increasing inequalities in opportunity but reflects the transformation of work that we are beginning to capture in this chapter.

The technocratic model of skills upgrading and rising value of investments in human capital is subject to the laws of diminishing returns. Human capital theory does not offer a universal theory of the relationship between education, jobs and rewards, but represents a 'transitional' case in the second half of the twentieth century characterised by educational expansion and a rising middle class.

Today, the 'positional' advantage of many with university credentials is declining not only domestically (as higher education is expanded) but also globally as access to tertiary education becomes more widespread both within and across countries. We predict that the global expansion of tertiary education will lead to downward pressure on the incomes of skilled workers in the developed economies, along with some upward pressure on those in emerging economies. At the same time, there are trends towards 'winner-takes-all' markets, which reveal that people with similar qualifications in the same occupations, organisations and countries will experience increasing polarisation in future career prospects (Frank and Cook 1996).

The trends identified in this chapter raise doubts about the efficacy of economic policies based on educational reform. In much the same way that we have misunderstood the source of social mobility in the developed economies to stem from an extension of meritocratic opportunity rather than changes in the occupational structure, we have also misunderstood the role of high-skilled workers to economic development and national prosperity. There has been a tendency to understand the supply of high-skilled workers as a direct cause of national prosperity rather than a consequence of innovative enterprise (Lazonick 2003) that lifts the demand for skilled workers.

Expanding higher education and raising the skills of the workforce look inadequate given the changes described in this chapter. While the skills of the workforce remain important they are not a source of competitive advantage because many countries, including China and India, are adopting the same tactics. It is how the capabilities of the workforce are combined in innovative and productive ways that holds the key, although high-skilled workers in developed economies will have to contend with the price advantage of university graduates in developing economies. Moreover, if 'permission to think' is limited to a relatively small proportion of knowledge workers, it raises fundamental issues about the role and content of mass higher education. The role of higher education will undoubtedly be subject to intensive political and educational debate as the returns to knowledge decline for many, and when income inequalities are increasingly seen to be divorced from 'meritocratic' achievement.

Acknowledgements

We would like to acknowledge the support of the Economic and Social Research Council of Great Britain (ESRC) who funded this three-year comparative project on 'Global Corporate Strategies and the Future of Skills'. We would also like to thank Susan Wright and Ian Jones for their comments on an earlier draft of the chapter.

Notes

1 See for example, http://www.dti.gov.uk/ministers/speeches/hewitt200904. html.
2 See UNCTAD (2005: Appendix A pp. 267–8). These figures exclude TNCs in the financial sector.
3 See Heather Stewart, 'The West Sees Red', *The Observer*, 12 June 2005.
4 ATKearny Consultants: http://www.atkearney.com/main.taf?p=1,5,1,130.
5 The relative merits of the German dual system and its future have been widely debated. See Brown *et al.* (2001) and Streeck (1997).
6 Report by Richard McGregor in Beijing, *Financial Times*, 4 July 2006, p. 10.
7 Private communication with the Department of Education in Beijing (based on figures for October 2005).
8 India's 'Tenth Plan' for education is focused on increasing access; quality; adoption of state specific strategies; liberalisation of the higher education system; relevance including curriculum, vocationalisation, networking and information technology; distance education; convergence of formal, non-formal, distance and IT education institutions; increased private participation in establishing and running of colleges and deemed to be universities; research in frontier areas of knowledge and meeting challenges in the area of Internationalisation of Indian Education.   http://www.education.nic.in/htmlweb/approach_paper_on_ education.htm.
9 See Rajat K. Gupta (2005).
10 See Tapping America's Potential: The Education for Innovation Initiative (2005) at http://www.businessroundtable.org/publications/publication.aspx?qs=2AF 6BF807822B0F1AD1478E
11 See Maria Trombly (2003).
12 See 'The Challenge of Customization: Bringing Operations and Marketing Together', http://www.strategy-business.com/sbkwarticle/sbkw040616?pg=a ll&tid=230.
13 Michael Chanover 'Mass Customizi-Who? – What Dell, Nike and Others Have in Store for You', http://www.core77.com/reactor/mass_customization.html.
14 But while companies may want to offshore some of their R&D activities there is a constant concern about 'reverse' engineering and technology transfer. The opportunity to extend into new markets of the size of China and India also raises the threat of low-cost competitors able to create competing products or services. This makes multinational companies reluctant to 'share' their state-of-the-art knowledge, technologies and know how, but at the same time they need access to emerging markets and to reduce development costs.

The problem is illustrated in the electronics sector. We were told by a leading multinational company that the Chinese were capable of copying the latest mobile phones in two months. This had led this company to retrench its R&D activities within the home base to protect its product developments for as long as possible. They also launch the same product simultaneously in different countries to gain a lead on the competition even if they can catch up very fast.

15   See UNCTAD (2005).

16   Germany is an obvious example.

17   Davenport identifies various initiatives that have been introduced to standardise and commodify business processes such as the Supply-Chain Operations Reference (SCOR) model that outlines five key steps of plan, source, make, deliver, and return. Another is the Software Engineering Institute's Capability Maturity Model (CMM), and ISO 9000 for quality standards for product development. ISO 9000 is based on the design, development, production, installation, and servicing of products. ISO 9000–9003 were created by the International Organisation for Standardization which is a global consortium of national standard bodies. Six Sigma focuses less on management process and more on the output of the process, especially defect reduction.

18   Combined with offshoring the potential is huge as Suresh Gupta (2006) notes: 'Our research indicates that when used in conjunction with offshoring, componentization can deliver massive benefits. This model assumes three important capabilities: disaggregating (and digitizing) a process into self-contained components and using broadband to ship them offshore; processing each component using best mix of offshore resources and shipping them back to the original location; and reassembling the 'processed' components into a coherent whole' (p. 45).

19   We are grateful to Ian Jones, Innovation and Engagement Officer, Cardiff School of Social Sciences, for the term 'permission to think', which he used in discussion with Phil Brown.

20   Samsung Company Report at http://www.samsung.com/AboutSAMSUNG/ValuesPhilosophy/DigitalVision/index.htm.

References

Accenture (2007) 'Automation for the people: industrializing Europe's insurance industry', http://www.accenture.com/Global/Services/By_Industry/Financial_Services/Insurance/The_Point/Y2007/fsi_thepoint47a.htm.

Alvesson, M. (2001) 'Knowledge work: ambiguity, image and identity', *Human Relations*, 54(7): 863–86.

Anell, B. and Wilson, T. (2002) 'Prescripts: creating competitive advantage in the knowledge economy', *Competitiveness Review*, 12(1): 26–37.

Ashton, D. and Green, F. (1996) *Education, Training and the Global Economy*, Aldershot: Edward Elgar.

Ashton, D., Brown, P. and Lauder, H. (forthcoming) 'Developing a theory of skills for global human resources'.

Bebchuk, L. and Grinstein, Y. (2005) 'The growth of executive pay', *Oxford Review of Economic Policy*, 21(2): 283–303.

Becker, G. (2006) 'The age of human capital', in H. Lauder, P. Brown, J. A. Dillabough and A .H. Halsey (eds) *Education, Globalization and Social Change*, Oxford: Oxford University Press.

Brown, G. (2004) Full text: Gordon Brown's Confederation of British Industry Speech, 9 November. http://news.ft.com/cms/s/eb4dc42a-3239-11d9-8498-00000e2511c8.html.

Brown, P. (2006) 'The opportunity trap', in H. Lauder, P. Brown, J. A. Dillabough and A. H. Halsey (eds) *Education, Globalization and Social Change*, Oxford: Oxford University Press.

Brown, P. and Hesketh, A. (2004) *The Mismanagement of Talent*, Oxford: Oxford University Press.

Brown, P. and Lauder, H. (2001) *Capitalism and Social Progress*, Basingstoke: Palgrave.

Brown, P. and Lauder, H. (2006) 'Globalisation, knowledge and the myth of the magnet economy', *Globalisation, Societies and Education*, 4(1): 25–57.

Brown, P., Green, A. and Lauder, H. (2001) *High Skills: Globalization, Competitiveness and Skill Formation*, Oxford, Oxford University Press.

Brown, P., Lauder, H., Ashton, D. and Tholen, G. (2006) 'Towards a high-skilled, low-waged economy? A review of global trends in education, employment and the labour market', in S. Porter and M. Campbell (eds) *Skills and Economic Performance*, London: Caspian Publishing, pp. 55–90.

Bryant, A. (2006) 'Knowledge management – the ethics of the agora or the mechanisms of the market?', Proceedings of the 39th Hawaii International Conference on System Sciences, pp. 1–10.

Davenport, T. H. (2005) 'The coming commoditization of processes', *Harvard Business Review*, June, pp. 101–8.

Drucker, P. (1993) *Post-Capitalist Society*, Oxford: Butterworth-Heinemann.

Fevre, R. (2003) *The Sociology of Economic Behaviour*, London: Sage.

Frank, R. and Cook, P. J. (1996) *The Winner-Take-All Society*, New York, Penguin.

Friedman, T. (2005) *The World is Flat*, London: Allen Lane.

Gellner, E. (1983) *Nations and Nationalism*, Oxford: Blackwell.

Grubb, W. N. and Lazerson, M. (2006) 'The globalization of rhetoric and practice: the education gospel and vocationalism', in H. Lauder *et al.* (eds) *Education, Globalization and Social Change*, Oxford: Oxford University Press.

Gupta, R. K. (2005) 'India's economic agenda: an interview with Manmohan Singh', *McKinsey Quarterly*, Special Edition: Fulfilling India's Promise, http://www.mckinseyquarterly.com/.

Gupta, S. (2006) 'Financial services factory', *Journal of Financial Transformation*, 18, The Capco Institute, pp. 43–50.

Hall, P. A. and Soskice, D. (2001) *Varieties of Capitalism*, Oxford: Oxford University Press.

Halsey, A. H. (1961) 'Introduction', in A. H. Halsey, J. Floud and J. Anderson (eds) *Education, Economy and Society*, Oxford: Oxford University Press.

Jones, B. J. (1999) *Knowledge Capitalism*, Oxford: Oxford University Press.

Keep, E. (2004) 'After access: researching labour market issues', in J. Gallacher (ed.) *Researching Access to Higher Education*, London: Routledge.

Kerr, C., Dunlop, J., Harbison, F. and Myer, C. (1973) *Industrialism and Industrial Man*, Harmondsworth: Penguin.

Lauder, H. (forthcoming) 'Education, skill bias theory and graduate incomes: a critique and alternative'.

Lazonick, W. (2003) 'The theory of the market economy and the social foundations of innovative enterprise', *Economic and Industrial Democracy*, 24(1): 9–44.

Lazonick, W. and O'Sullivan, M. (2000) 'Maximizing shareholder value: a new ideology for corporate governance', *Economy and Society*, 29(1): 13–35.

Leitch Review of Skills (2006) *Prosperity for all in the Global Economy – World Class Skills* (Final Report), Norwich: HMSO.

Marginson, S. (2006) 'National and global competition in higher education', in H. Lauder *et al.* (eds) *Education, Globalization and Social Change*, Oxford: Oxford University Press.

Michaels, E., Jones, H. H. and Axelrod, B. (2001) *The War for Talent*, Boston, MA: Harvard Business School Press.

Mishel, L., Bernstein, J. and Allegretto, S. (2007) *The State of Working America 2006/2007*, Economic Policy Institute, Ithaca: Cornell University Press.

Reich, R. (1991) *The Work of Nations*, New York: Simon and Schuster.

Roach, S. (2006) 'From globalization to localization', Morgan Stanley, Global Economic Forum, December 14. http://www.morganstanley.com/views/gef/archive/2006/20061214-Thu.html .

Rosecrance, R. (1999) *The Rise of the Virtual State*, New York: Basic Books.

Saxenian, A. (2006) *The New Argonauts: Regional Advantage in a Global Economy*, Cambridge, MA: Harvard University Press.

Stewart, T. A. (2001) *The Wealth of Knowledge*, London: Nicholas Brealey.

Streeck, W. (1997) 'German capitalism: does it exist? Can it survive?', *New Political Economy*, 2(2): 237–56.

Tate, J. (2001) 'National varieties of standardization', in P. A. Hall and D. Soskice (eds) *Varieties of Capitalism*, Oxford: Oxford University Press.

Trombly, M. (2003) 'There's a treasure trove of scientific talent – and lots of government bureaucracy', *Computer World*, 15 September. http://www.computerworld.com/managementtopics/outsourcing/story/0,10801,84874,00.html.

United Nations Conference on Trade and Development (UNCTAD) (2005) *World Investment Report, 2005, Transnational Corporations and the Internationalization of R&D*, www.unctad.org/wir.

Venter, K., Ashton, D. N. and Sung, J. (2002) *Education and Skills in the People's Republic of China: Employers' Perceptions*, ILO/CLMS, University of Leicester.

Wilensky, H. (1960) 'Work, careers, and social integration', *International Social Science Journal*, 12: 543–60.

12 International student migration

The case of Chinese 'sea-turtles'

Wei Shen[1]

Introduction

China is now officially recognised as the largest sending country for international students, with her students spread over 100 countries across the five continents. According to the official statistics of the Chinese Ministry of Education, more than 930,000 students left China to study abroad between 1978 and 2005. The *Global Education Digest 2006* published by UNESCO gives China as the largest source country for students studying abroad, with one out of seven international students coming from China.[2] This provides China with a huge potential human resource but at the same time, it poses challenges and dangers if these students do not return, i.e. the 'brain-drain'. This chapter therefore seeks to analyse the recent trends of Chinese student migration, in the context of both outbound and return migrations. This chapter firstly aims to examine the impact of the increasing influx of Chinese students into major European countries and related economic and social issues. The second aim is to analyse the return migration of Chinese students from abroad, i.e. the phenomenon of the coming home of 'sea-turtles' (as student returnees are called) and the rationale behind this metaphor.

This research is based on the combination of a quantitative data review of Chinese student circular migration between China and Europe and a qualitative inquiry through fieldwork and interviews in the UK, China, Germany and France with various stakeholders, including Chinese students/graduates/returnees, universities, educational agencies, business representatives, and local residents. By using the case studies of the UK, Germany and France, I argue that on the one hand, Chinese students provide substantial financial resources for the receiving countries (as in the UK where education is treated as an export industry), yet they should not be treated merely as 'cash-cows'. On the other hand, the growing economy in China and demands for talents as well as the family kinship (partly) resulting from the 'one-child policy' has led more and more Chinese students (sea-turtles) to return home. The conclusion points to the additional services and policy provisions that are needed to prevent 'brain-drain' and promote a 'win-win' pattern of educational migration.

Chronicle of Chinese students abroad

One hundred and sixty years ago, Yung Wing, a native of Canton, left China to study in the United States of America at the age of 19. That was in 1847 and the Qing Dynasty had started to fall apart. Yung Wing nevertheless returned to China after graduating from Yale College in 1854[3] and consequently persuaded the Qing Government to send 120 young Chinese students to study in America, beginning in 1872. The departure of Yung Wing and his fellow compatriots started the movement to study abroad in contemporary Chinese history.

Although the Chinese Middle Kingdom had sent monks abroad to pursue religious knowledge hundreds of years ago, Wang (2005) argued that Yung Wing was China's 'first real student abroad'. Song (2003) also shared a similar view and divided Chinese students who went abroad into 10 generations:

- 1st generation: Yung Wing and the 120 young Chinese students to USA
- 2nd generation: Chinese navy students to Europe (approximately 100 students)
- 3rd generation: Chinese students to Japan at the beginning of twentieth century
- 4th generation: From 1909, Chinese students to USA financed by money remaining from the huge indemnity in the Boxer Protocol (1901)[4]
- 5th generation: Chinese students to France, self-financed through hard work in France
- 6th generation: Chinese students to USSR in the twentieth century
- 7th generation: Chinese students to Europe (i.e. France) between 1927 and 1937
- 8th generation: Chinese students to Europe and USA between 1938 and 1948
- 9th generation: Chinese students to USSR and Europe between 1950 and 1960
- 10th generation: After the cultural revolution.

Wang (2005) has simplified these detailed definitions into five broader waves of student migration from China and commented on their differentiated roles:

- 1st wave: 1872–1900: young Chinese students and navy students – among those returned, railway specialists, diplomats, journalists and navy officers, the backbone for the 'Self-Strengthening Movement' in China
- 2nd wave: 1900–27: Chinese students to Japan and France, and the first group to the USSR – those revolutionists who brought back the 'New Cultural Movement'
- 3rd wave: 1927–49: Chinese students to Europe and the USA – among them were Nobel Prize Winners as well as missile and satellite experts

- 4th wave: 1949–65: destinations USSR and socialist countries in Eastern Europe – trained as the core of the Chinese Communist Party
- 5th wave: 1978 – present: the largest wave of student migrants spread around the world, overtaking the total of the previous four waves – the vital source for China's progress towards modernisation.

It is clear that Chinese students played important roles in the history of Chinese development and their outbound migration is strongly associated within the international relations and political economy of China and the rest of the world. For example, after the establishment of New China in 1949, China set up a number of student exchange programmes with the USSR and Eastern European (socialist) countries, such as Eastern Germany (DDR), Czechoslovakia, Poland, Hungary, Romania, Bulgaria and Albania; only a very small number of students were sent to Western Europe and other Asian countries. In 1956 this 'Eastern wave' reached its peak and, with the deterioration of Sino-USSR relations in the 1960s, the outbound Chinese student migration to the USSR almost ceased but was diverted to other Western countries (Song 2003; Wang 2005).

In this chapter, I focus on the last wave of Chinese students going abroad, i.e. the post-1978 period. It is possible to divide them into several sub-groups:

1978–89: Post-Cultural Revolution and Open Door Policy: economic and export zones were mushrooming in China, and the door for overseas education was also opened for Chinese students.

1989–2001: Post Tian-An Men: many Chinese university graduates gained a chance to breathe 'new and fresh air' by studying abroad. Self-financing students were growing in large numbers.

2001 – present: Post 9/11: the terrorist attack in America and the consequent difficulties in obtaining US visas led to further diversification of the destinations for Chinese students. The majority of students were self-financed, via parents' savings, loans or other personal resources.

After more than one and a half centuries of pursuing education and learning abroad, more than 460,000 Chinese students could be found in 103 countries across the world in 2002. North America was still the favourite destination for Chinese students followed by Europe and Asia (Figure 12.1).

There are many reasons for studying abroad and several push and pull factors involved. One of the major pull factors is language immersion, as seen from Kirkbride's original 'Foreign Study Plan' in 1923.[5] The push factors include the inadequate provision of tertiary education in China (such as the limited range of subjects taught, the shortage of programmes and the lack of higher education institutions) and the highly competitive university entrance examination. One or a combination of these factors push or sometimes

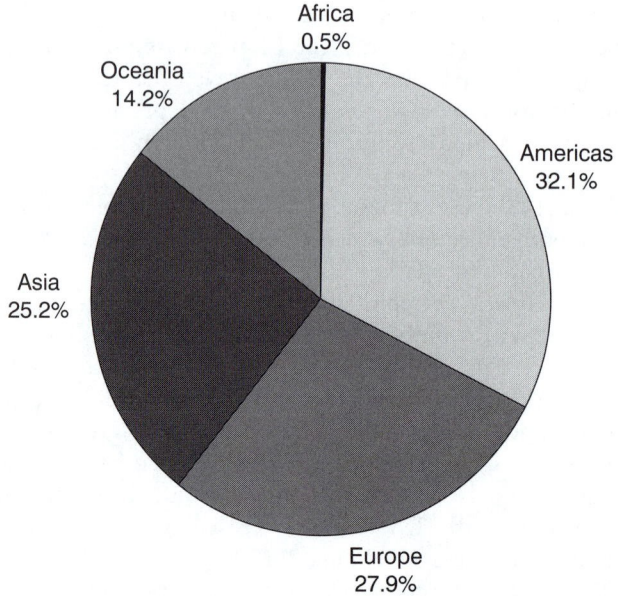

Africa
0.5%

Oceania
14.2%

Americas
32.1%

Asia
25.2%

Europe
27.9%

Figure 12.1 Distribution of Chinese students in the world (Source: Chinese Ministry of Education Annual Work Report 2005)

force Chinese students to seek educational opportunities outside their own country. This can also be regarded as an 'exit option' for these students to go abroad.

On the other hand, some talented students in both developing and developed countries are attracted to the research expertise of foreign institutions and they therefore are pulled to study abroad. In addition, the financial aid offered by foreign governments, institutions and other sources, the experience of living, studying and working in a foreign land, and the exposure to new cultures, languages and traditions are all important pull factors for globalising education. Chinese students are subjected to a combination of these push and pull factors. Due to China's vast population, it is very difficult to pass the university entrance exam, especially for access to top universities. As the income level in China is growing, more and more Chinese families can afford for their children to study abroad if they do not pass the university entrance exam to elite Chinese universities. The prestige of foreign qualifications is very helpful in securing a decent job in China. After China's entry to the World Trade Organisation (WTO), there was an even higher demand for internationally oriented and competent human resources, and this pushed more parents to send their children abroad. Scholarships from Western countries, in particular from the United States, have also attracted many Chinese students to conduct research and studies abroad. However, the majority of Chinese students abroad are nowadays self-financed, as study abroad has been widely seen as an 'investment in the education and future' for most Chinese families.

Chinese students in Europe

Europe now sees an increasingly diverse flow of Chinese migrants, and Chinese students in particular are flocking to Europe.[6] On the one hand, for some European countries, like the UK, the inflow of foreign students (from outside the European Union) represents a very important financial income for the higher education and related sectors. On the other hand, in many other European countries, like France and Germany, higher education is offered either free of charge or at a very modest level and there is no difference between home/EU and international students. There is a large influx of Chinese students in both cases (see both Table 12.1 and Figure 12.2). Note that some data are missing, as indicated by a zero in Table 12.1 – an indication of the lack of comprehensive and comparable data on international student migration.

The United Kingdom, Germany and France are top of the league table for Chinese students in Europe. In this chapter, two case studies of the UK (where foreign students pay fees) and Germany/France (where higher education is free to foreign students) are used to illustrate the impact of Chinese student migration to Europe.

Table 12.1 Chinese students in tertiary education in selected European countries (OECD)

Country/Year	1998	1999	2000	2001	2002	2003	2004
Austria	428	405	407	407	389	527	732
Belgium	...	684	643	716	815	1,062	1,566
Czech Republic	6	10	10	8	6	10	16
Denmark	121	139	125	153	375	1,042	1,139
Finland	479	583	817	1,007	1,026	1,107	1,308
France	1,081	1,934	2,111	3,068	5,477	10,665	11,514
Germany	5,017	5,355	6,526	9,109	14,070	20,141	25,284
Greece	...	...	...	0	13	10	11
Hungary	19	33	...	41	57	73	88
Iceland	6	5	9	9	10	10	11
Ireland	40	55	54	105	159	645	0
Italy	110	101	84	117	124	204	276
Luxembourg	0	0	...	...	0	0	0
Netherlands	...	169	182	410	813	1,371	1,957
Norway	165	157	156	205	238	316	468
Poland	25	32	37	34	39	37	51
Portugal	...	...	43	0	0	53	60
Slovak Republic	...	0	1	2	2	2	1
Spain	127	125	175	183	215	289	390
Sweden	657	635	630	593	670	868	1,141
Switzerland	352	372	426	431	478	674	741
Turkey	52	67	70	84	83	103	107
United Kingdom	2,877	4,249	6,158	10,388	17,483	30,690	48,494

Legend: 0 = Missing; ... = Negligible
Source: OECD Statistics Database: http://stats.oecd.org/wbos/default.aspx

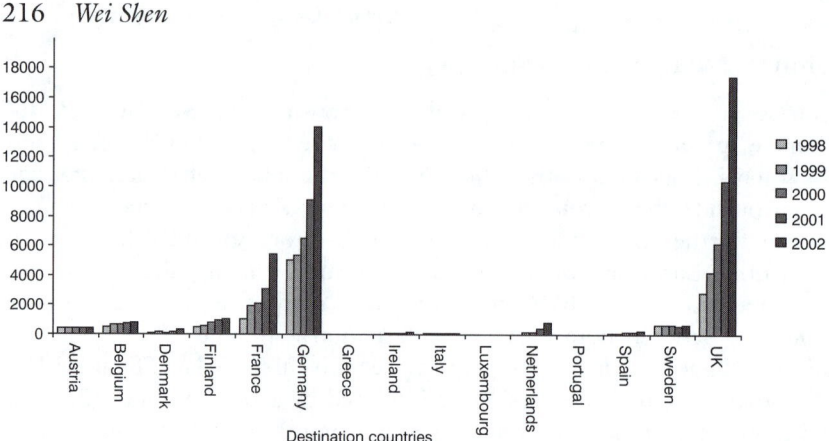

Figure 12.2 Chinese students in Europe (1998–2002) (Sources: OECD education statistics online database)

United Kingdom case study

The United Kingdom represents a key destination for Chinese students in Europe. It has brought huge financial contributions for the UK education sector and economy in general. However, there are social and immigration issues that need to be addressed. In this case study, I will illustrate both financial and social implications of Chinese student migration and address the necessity of policy improvement.

For the UK, the international education sector is regarded as 'extremely attractive' (British Council 2004) and this country has so far been very successful in luring Chinese students to its educational establishments. As mentioned earlier, foreign students have brought important cash income to educational institutions and the national economy. With its advantages of language, academic reputation and history, the United Kingdom benchmarked its excellence in learning in the People's Republic of China from the very beginning. Its main advantages can be summarised as: the shorter course duration, courses taught in the English language, a relatively safe living environment and healthy economy.

Education and other related services and products are among the fastest growing sectors for export earnings. In the UK alone, the Higher Education Statistics Agency calculated that in 2002–3, the total of 270,000 EU and non-EU students was worth over £1.5 billion in fees, and together with their living costs while in the UK, foreign students contribute over £3 billion gross per annum to the UK economy.

In April 2006 the BBC (British Broadcasting Company) raised the calculation for 2006 dramatically. International students, who are charged higher fees than their British counterparts, are estimated to bring in about £4 billion a year to UK universities and about £10 billion to the economy as a whole. Universities UK (2006) has an even higher figure for 2006, claiming that higher education institutions are worth £45 billion to the UK economy. Higher education export earnings are worth about £3.6 billion and Universities UK forecasts that by 2020 the international education market could be worth £20 billion to the UK economy alone.

In 2004, the United Kingdom overtook the USA as the single most popular destination for Chinese students. The number of Chinese students attending UK higher education institutions increased dramatically in the past decade. Among the 100 nationalities represented at University College London, the number of Chinese students has increased from 50 to 590 over the last decade! LSE performed even better: a decade ago there were 18 students from Mainland China and now there are 22 times as many.[7]

It proves to be difficult to estimate the exact number of Chinese students in the UK. Correspondence with the Chinese Embassy in 2006 suggested that there were in the region of 70,000 Chinese students in higher education in the UK in the academic year 2005/6. This was almost double the number recorded in the official HESA statistics (Figure 12.3). Most Chinese students pursue studies in economics and business subjects and they are spread in universities from Aberdeen to York.

While generating huge financial gains for the British education sector, this mass inflow of Chinese students has a deep socio-economic impact on the society. The following are some of the implications that were reflected from the current literature and interviews with universities, families and students in the UK.

Financial contribution

As mentioned above, international students contribute greatly to the income of UK higher education and to the local as well as national economy. Chinese students form a great share of this financial contribution by paying nearly

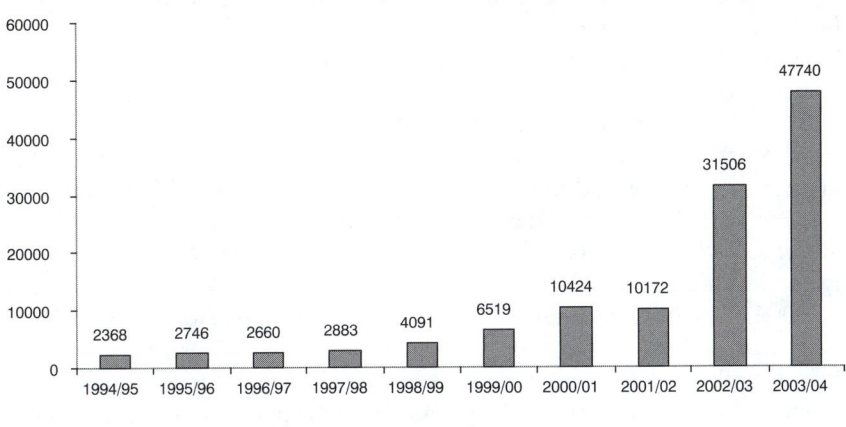

Figure 12.3 Historical record of Chinese students studying at higher education institutions in the United Kingdom (Source: Higher Education Statistics Agency 2004–5)

£800 million to the UK economy for studying and living expenses as shown in a recent Chatham House survey. The official registration number of Chinese students is around 43,000 students within the UK higher education system during 2003–4 and over 90 per cent of them are self-financed.

A Chatham House survey[8] of the Top 100 UK universities shows that students from Mainland China contribute at least £300 million just in terms of tuition fees, an increase of more than 30 per cent on the previous academic year (£223 million for 2002/3). This gives a substantial income for British universities, and for those facing financial crisis this is an important source of economic relief. British universities operate on contributions from government grants and students' tuition fees. In some extreme cases, the contribution from Chinese students is equivalent to as much as 29 per cent of the government grants, as is reported to be the case for the University of Essex as shown in the Chatham House report. Furthermore the income generated by living expenses such as housing and other forms of consumption by Chinese students amounts to a staggering £479 million, which brings the total contribution by Chinese students to the UK economy to £779 million in just one year. This amount will certainly rise again as international students' tuition fees and living costs increase every academic year. Therefore it is not surprising that the *New Statesman* (March 2004) called Chinese student migration, the migration that nobody objects to.

Immigration policy

Compared with other OECD countries, the UK has a relatively high stock of international students. In order to retain this competitiveness, the UK government has implemented a series of changes to promote faster and more efficient immigration procedures. Visa or entry clearance is the main obstacle for Chinese students and Asian and African students entering the UK. Up till now, the two main criteria for the issuance of a visa have been the intention to leave the UK after the studies are completed, and the possession of sufficient financial resources.

Since 1999, a series of policy changes has aimed to increase the UK's share of international students. Among these changes are greater flexibility in entry procedures and more streamlining of visa services. The number of Chinese students who have made visa applications with the intention to study in the UK almost doubled between 2001 and 2004/5. According to the Education Section of the British Mission in China, 19,632 visas were issued in 2004. A substantial number of visa applications are also being refused (approximately 20–30 per cent per year according to Chinese media and the British Embassy). This outcome is mainly attributed to the fake documents supplied by the applicants and misleading conduct by student recruitment agencies. Under the new policy, visa processing centres were also established in China. Students are no longer required to have an interview and in many cases judgements are based solely on the documents supplied by applicants. This change does in one way speed up the process, but it also omits the chances for students to offer clarifications and explanations unless so requested by the visa officer. On the other hand, as mentioned earlier, some British institutions, especially language schools and pre-university colleges, may choose to place economic profits over teaching quality. These schools and sometimes fake institutions not only harm Chinese students, their families and the image of UK education but create various problems of illegal student migration.

Recently the UK government implemented new legislation which allows students to gain work experience in the UK. However, the permits are mainly sector based and only cover students in medical, ICT and some other science subjects. A new scheme will allow nationals from outside the European Education Area, who have graduated from higher or further education establishments in the UK in certain physical sciences, mathematics or engineering and who have obtained good grades, to remain in the UK for 12 months after their studies in order to pursue a career. The revised Highly Skilled Migrant Programme (HSMP) has placed more emphasis on age and UK experience and reduced the earning requirements, giving more young graduates the possibility to work in the UK.

The aim of this kind of policy adjustment is twofold: it makes a more attractive education package for international students, and it is part of the UK government's strategy to retain international intellectual assets for the UK's economy. There have also been regional initiatives, such as the 'Fresh Talents' scheme in Scotland, to enhance the education package and attract more international students to study and work in Scotland after graduation.

Access to quality education

Through fieldwork and interviews with local UK residents it became clear that several university towns are starting to worry about local students' access to education, especially in the popular and highly ranked universities. Seduced by the rich prospects offered by international tuition fees, many UK universities (including Cambridge, Oxford and other elite universities) have substantially increased quotas for international students, including, of course, those from China. Naturally there may be less space left for home students, especially where there are restraints on expanding teaching facilities, buildings and equipment, due in part to a lack of government funding or sponsorship. In individual classes, where well over 60 per cent may be students with limited English language skills, there are real fears among UK students and their parents that this will inevitably slow down the class teaching quality, both in speed of delivery and depth of content and intellectual rigour.

Competition among universities

Competition between universities for student recruitment can impact negatively, in the so-called 'race-to-the-bottom'. Most British schools use agents in China to help to recruit students. The competition among them is fierce and bitter. It follows that for marketing and economic interests some agents, together with schools and/or universities, choose to ignore or at least lower academic requirements. As a result, many under-qualified candidates are recruited which eventually leads them to drop out and seek illegal employment in the UK.

Social issues

For most Chinese student migrants, it is the first time that they have lived independently abroad, away from home, from the close-knit family support and the unspoken shared values and cultural norms. They may well lack the ability to integrate and adapt to these new surroundings, which sometimes seem hostile to newcomers. This will cause not only academic problems, but also social tensions, posing serious security threats to the community. Interviews with Chinese students showed that a few (younger) students also find themselves in trouble (e.g. as victims of crime or bullying). The wealthier students from China undoubtedly suffer from increased robbery, quite high levels of bullying, and threats to personal safety. It is not only computers and equipment that are targeted. The passport itself is one of the most attractive acquisitions to thieves and gangs. These criminal organisations, often international in scope, will recycle them as part of organised illegal immigration.

With the tendency for younger Chinese students to go abroad, there has been vast concern over their safety in the UK, and accidents are frequently reported by Chinese media, with the result that there is public pressure to better regulate the education market for young Chinese students from both countries.

UK students, who are charged tuition fees on top of taking out student loans, have an average debt of over £12,000. Many are forced to take part-time employment while studying, in order to supplement their increasingly limited income. But these very same jobs are now sought by in-coming international students. To take a part-time job helps defray what are to them huge living costs when compared with costs in their home country. So in a very immediate and visible way, we see more pressures on local residents in university towns within the scarce and often tense labour market.

Germany and France case studies

Although much fewer than in the UK, Germany and France still host a substantial number of Chinese students and both experienced a dramatic jump in the past decade (as shown in Figures 12.4 and 12.5 respectively).

According to interviews with DAAD (German Academic Exchange) and the French counterpart EduFrance, the priority for these countries, in contrast with the UK, is not quantity but quality. This can be explained by the fact that educational institutions do not benefit financially as much as their counterparts in the UK. Tuition fees at public universities and institutions in both countries are very low compared with the UK and they do not

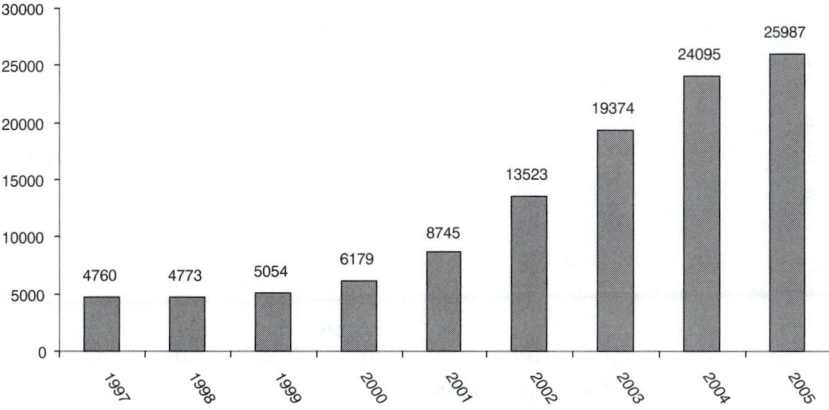

Figure 12.4 Chinese students in tertiary education in Germany (1997–2005) (Source: Wissenschaft weltoffen – http://www.wissenschaft-weltoffen.de/index_html (May 2007))

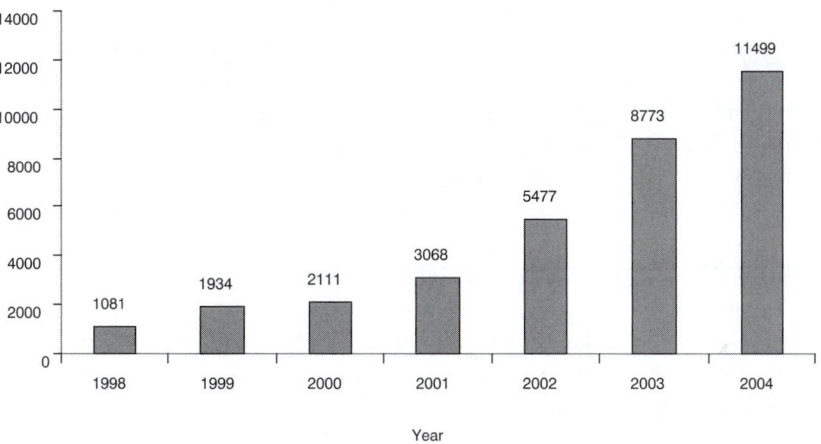

Figure 12.5 Chinese students in tertiary education in France (1999–2004) (Sources: OECD Education Database (1999–2002), French Ministry of Education (2003–4))

differentiate between German / French / EU and Chinese / international students. There was a strong increase between 2001 and 2002, which was largely due to the security situation and tightened visa procedure for the USA after the September 11th attack. The decline of foreign students in the USA has now been reversed, after several years of weakness since September 11th and yet the number of Chinese students in Germany and France continues to climb. A survey by the Institute of International Education suggested that American colleges and universities have increased the intake of foreign students by 8 per cent during autumn 2006 compared with the year before. As the decline is ending in the USA, other countries in Europe are also working hard to attract Chinese students and the result is tangible. There has been a sharp rise in Chinese students in France and Germany and the Chinese student population has increased more than 10 times in the past decade.

Both Germany and France address the importance of cooperation between their own and Chinese universities as a means to control the quality of Chinese students. Germany has furthermore introduced the DAAD Akademische Prüfstelle (APS Certificate), an academic screening process to identify students qualified to study in Germany. France stresses its elite education and the so-called *grande ecoles* in order to attract talented Chinese students to study business, engineering and other subjects in France. French elite colleges and some universities also work in partnership with French industries to provide scholarships for Chinese students, such as the N+I initiative (engineering programme with industrial partnership).

Through interviews[9] with Chinese students and graduates of French business schools, it is also interesting to see that many students have acquired French language skills or work experience with French companies before going to study in France. Most of the interviewees had studied either languages or business and economics before they came to France but there were also a few students with engineering and science backgrounds (such as computing and automation). A few students studied French as their major at the university because of the romanticised image of France, its culture, language and literature. French was also seen as an additional, helpful asset for when the student sought to enter the job market, as many people already spoke English, which is widely taught in China from primary school onwards and throughout university education:

> I majored in French because my interest in literatures and French literature is quite famous. I have already studied English therefore I have the base for self-studies, no need to study further. On the contrary, I thought French would be an added advantage. (Miss D., Joint Bachelor Degrees in French and Economics)

There are also family reasons for studying French:

> My second foreign language at the university was French. The reason I chose it is because my grandfather. He could speak French but unfortunately died very early and left a notebook in French. I found the book very interesting and I wanted to study French in order to understand the content of it. I did not know why he spoke French, but he was in the 'secret service' and I could not tell you more about it. (Miss H., BSc International Economics and Finance)

Those students who did not choose French as their university major share the view that a language (such as French) is just a tool for the business world, while business studies provides the knowledge and skills that are the keys for finding a suitable job:

Before I went to university, I thought French is a very nice language and France is a country with a lot of cultures and history, but eventually I could not resist the temptation of real life and chose to study finance by the recommendation of my school teacher. (Miss W., BSc International Finance)

Many students worked for multi-national companies (MNCs) before going to France. Many French language major students therefore had the opportunities to intern for French companies and organisations (French Embassy and *Le Monde* etc.). Most of them then continued to work for French companies after their studies. For non-French major students, they usually embark on their career in their specialised fields.

This shows the importance of the cultural and language factors in students' decision making about where to study abroad. Many students show a great appreciation of French culture and language that leads to their eventual decision to study abroad. In this case, for those students, it was the natural choice to study in France, this was different from the consumerism of higher education in the UK, where students chose it because of the English language advantage and the short duration of the course.

As we can see from the comparison of different European countries and their reaction to the competition in the global education market, the UK and France and Germany have very different aims behind their strategies for attracting foreign students, and especially when recruiting Chinese students. Whereas some higher education institutions (for example, in the UK) seek to attract high fee-paying foreign students as an essential part of their income, to keep their institutions economically viable, this is not a concern for Germany and France. Instead, the governments of Germany and France and even increasingly smaller countries like Denmark (which has started to charge fees for international students but at the same time offers scholarships for top foreign students) are more interested in the accumulation of foreign talents with the intention of attracting and keeping the best brains from around the world to help develop their own economies. Until recently, the UK made it a condition of visa applications that students would leave the country on the completion of their studies, but this is changing. The new procedures and rules for obtaining visas, which are intended to enable students to stay and work in the UK, show that the UK, like Germany and France, is concerned to attract the best students internationally and keep them as part of their highly skilled labour force. However, many European companies and universities are increasingly aware of the importance of Chinese students' value as the agents for business collaborations between China and respective countries in Europe. This is also reflected in the alumni services by various European countries, notably the UK and the Netherlands, where Chinese graduates are regarded as 'good-will' ambassadors and 'friends for life'. Nevertheless, there is still fear of 'brain-drain' in China and the next section will examine the validity of this worry and look at the recent trends in return migration of Chinese students.

Hope for a win–win future – brain circulation

In a publication from the Chinese Academy of Social Sciences – *Global Political and Security Report 2007* – it stated that China has the biggest diaspora community and the greatest number of scholars abroad, which may pose a serious threat of 'brain-drain'. Indeed, since China's deregulation of 'exit–entry immigration policies', thousands of Chinese students have left China to go abroad. As the sending country, China is concerned about the enormous outflow of students, which could result in huge potential loss, in terms of both financial and human capital.

The Chinese government is increasingly aware of the importance of her students abroad. For China, student return migration has become a 'calculated strategy' by the national government (Zweig 2006) to accumulate skills, knowledge, networks and financial resources abroad. Growing student migration from China will certainly affect China's ability to integrate into global markets.

Figure 12.6 shows the increasing returning rate of Chinese students from Europe, the USA and elsewhere. Out of the 380,000 students since the economic reform who went from China to study abroad, more than half of them, over 180,000 students have returned to China so far; the return rate is increasing by 13 to 15 per cent each year. These returnees are given the nick-name *Hai Gui* or in English, 'sea-turtles'. This phrase nicely sums up the characters of returnees which are similar to the biological behaviour of real sea-turtles: they are born on the sea-shore, leave the land and go out to sea when they are still young, but when they are grown up, they return to their original shore to fertilise and produce their young.

There are different factors and stakeholders influencing the circular migration:

- *Government:* The Chinese government is very keen to have returnees come back to the homeland. Efforts are also made at the municipal level, and cities like Shanghai have set up overseas recruitment agencies and programmes targeted at highly skilled returnees. Incentives from central to local government are given to returnees, such as financial, tax and administrative support.

  There has also been a change of governmental attitudes and propaganda towards returnees. Chinese leaders have regarded returnees highly: President Hu talked of their 'outstanding historical role' and Vice Premier Zeng said they were 'irreplaceable'.

- *Business and private sector:* China is a giant market that no major multinational corporations can afford to ignore. European companies are investing more and more capital and business in China. China does not have a lack of people, with a population of over 1.3 billion. But these multinational corporations need skilled employees, especially on the managerial levels, who understand both Chinese local culture and Western business practices. Certain sectors in China are desperately

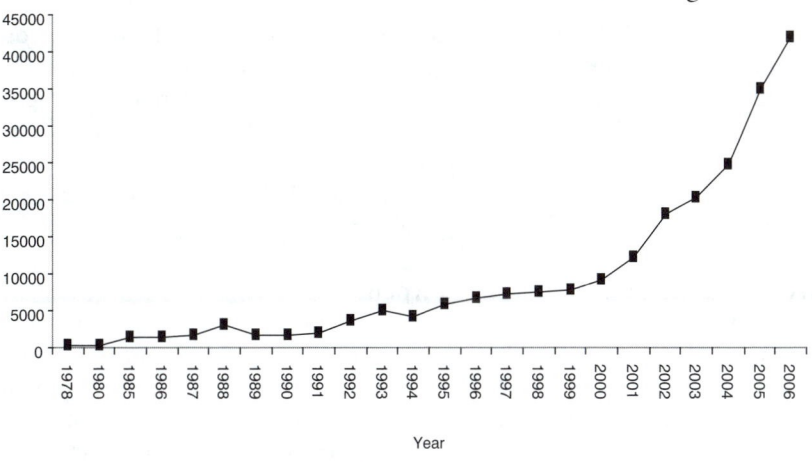

Figure 12.6 Return of Chinese students from abroad (1978–2003b) (Source: China National Statistics Bureau (2000–6))

looking for excellent brains – this is evident in the case of accountancy. Strikes by overworked staff and the continual search for new talent are now top headaches for the Big Four accounting firms. Some companies have already initiated programmes to attract Chinese students, for example the Rolls-Royce China Programme on Purchasing and McKinsey's Asia House in Frankfurt.

• *Personal level:* Family ties and personal relations to China are important factors in Chinese students' return migration. The majority of current young and middle-aged members of the work force in China are the only child in the family because of the 'one child policy'. Most Chinese people have strong family kinship and China's birth control 'one child policy' gives a higher level of responsibilities and attachment for returnees in relation to their family. Thus it is not surprising to see that their family is a major factor in students' decisions to return.

Here are three interviewees' explanations for their return decisions:

• China's potential and confidence in the Chinese economy:
'China is changing, it is changing so fast, but I am outside! I am very frustrated, I do not want to be an outsider, I want to be part of this history, and I want to join the revolution!'
• Family factors also play an important role for many returnees:
'My father was in the emergency room twice when I was in Paris, but none of my family, even my mum told me about this! I simply cannot live and work like this abroad! They gave me everything (what they did not have during the cultural revolution) and as a single child in the family, I have my responsibilities and it's against our tradition to leave my parents alone …'
• The restrictive procedure for labour migration and work permit in EU:

'You know, the 9/11 incident happened when I was in France, so you simply could not imagine or plan anything. Certainly, I and my Singaporean and other classmates had thought about working for Danone or others, but later we feel things have changed a lot (after 9/11). This is especially true for the students of MBA LUXE (Luxury Brand Management) and greater impact for MBA IMHI (International Hospitality Management) because they are related to the hotel industry.'

As we can see from the earlier accounts of students in France, equally important in the considerations of returnees are their career strategies and the potentials they see, as well as their hope and confidence in the Chinese economy. Many of the returnees view China's current economic development as a historical moment that they could not miss. Upon return, returnees still maintain strong links with their hosting countries of study, either by working for a multinational corporation from that country, or by maintaining personal and social links.

Another concern is the lack of training for returnees. Many 'sea-turtles' do not have enough or, worse, any working experience since they went to study abroad before or immediately after finishing their first degrees. They also could not find any training opportunities in Europe due to immigration restrictions and limited time. The lack of practical working skills, either at home in China or abroad, decreases their competitiveness in the labour market. Officials from the Chinese Ministry of Education have openly expressed their discontent with the way the British government treats Chinese students, which I would call a 'fast-food or no-frills' service – treating students as cash cows, not providing them with any training, and kicking them out once they finish their studies. This has resulted in the returnees having difficulty in finding jobs back home in China. Luckily, the UK government has realised the importance of working with their counterparts in China. A high-level expert team was sent to China at the end of 2005 to explain about the newly developed Five Year Strategy for Asylum and Immigration and a new points-based system for visas. The British Embassy highlighted this action by saying it underlines the importance of China to the UK on migration issues.

Conclusions

The unprecedented speed of globalisation has accelerated the demand for human talents in both developing and developed countries. In the global knowledge society, education is the key to economic prosperity and growth. Arising out of the globalisation process in the contemporary world economy, we have also seen the growing internationalisation of education, through the mobility of students and academics, and multiple and satellite campuses around the globe. Education has become an emerging export industry for many countries. The global trade in educational services has grown very fast in the past few years. Different from other trade, overseas education is traditionally supply driven, i.e. the clients (the students) are driven to the place where good and high quality education is available.

Compared with other economic migration categories, student migrants are not only big money spenders, but are also on a limited short stay with few family attachments in the host country. No wonder the market of international education has intensified, with competitors from both industrialised countries like the USA, the UK, Western Europe and from growing economies like Thailand, Malaysia and Central and Eastern Europe.

There is very limited data and research devoted to this field of migration and mobility within the internationalisation of education. The case of Chinese students in Europe clearly illustrates the important economic, social and political impact of student migration between the sending and the host countries and how this migration can be transformed from a migration that nobody objects to, to a migration that could circulate and be mutually beneficial. To maximise the benefits and create a win-win situation, China and Europe need to develop a more coherent and pro-active scheme and work with different stakeholders such as the universities and the private sector.

In recent years, there has also been an increase in two-way traffic in student flows between China and Europe. More European students are going to study in China and Confucius Institutes have been established in Europe and other parts of the world to promote Chinese culture and education. In this regard, more academic research and policy reviews are needed to encourage and facilitate such mutually beneficial global cooperation and in so doing, create a platform of 'education sans frontiers'.

Notes

1 I am grateful for the friendly support and useful feedback I have received from the ESRC Seminar Series on 'Geographies of Knowledge/Geometries of Power: Global Higher Education in the 21st Century' in Gregynog, Wales, in 2006/7.
2 UNESCO Institute for Statistics: there are 2,500,000 international students studying abroad, 14 per cent (350,000) are from China. http://www.uis.unesco.org/TEMPLATE/pdf/ged/2006/GED2006.pdf.
3 For more details about Yung Wing see http://en.wikipedia.org/wiki/Yung_Wing.
4 After the First Opium War, the Qing Empire signed the Boxer Protocol or 1901 Treaty with the Eight-Nation Alliance which included a huge indemnity of 450 million taels. Later, the Qing Government used part of the indemnity refunded by the United States to send Chinese students to the USA.
5 The act of studying abroad originated at the University of Delaware. In 1923, Professor Raymond W. Kirkbride sent a group of eight students to Paris, France. At the time, the concept of students studying in a different country was incredibly unconventional. Kirkbride's programme was originally named the 'Foreign Study Plan'. For a time, study abroad was seen as an option primarily for foreign language students. For more details about study abroad see http://en.wikipedia.org/wiki/Study_abroad.
6 See details at BBC website: http://news.bbc.co.uk/1/hi/world/asia-pacific/3590998.stm.

7 More information can be found at London School of Economics and Political Sciences (May 2007): www.lse.ac.uk/collections/meetthedirector/ppt/Peking_ University_presentation_final.ppt.

8 Chatham House (2004), 'Deus ex MA China: are mainland Chinese students saving Britain's universities?'

9 A total of 60 interviews were conducted in Shanghai (with Chinese graduates and returnees from France) and in Paris (with Chinese students/graduates who are currently studying and working in France).

References

Battling for brains, *The Economist*, 23 Sept. 2004. http://economist.com/world/ europe/displaystory.cfm?story_id=E1_PNNDPQD.

Special Report on Emigration, *The Economist*, 26 Sept. 2002.

Where is the ideal place for overseas returnees? – Ten Chinese Cities in Focus, *Human Resources Market*, 2005.

140,000 Chinese students return from overseas, *China Daily*, 8 April 2002.

Chinese studying abroad top the world, *Beijing Daily*, 18 June 2002.

Abella, M. I. (2003) 'Global dimensions of the highly skilled migration', GTZ Conference on Migration and Development, Berlin, 20–21 October 2003, International Labour Office (ILO).

Accrington, S. (2002) 'Job migration is draining Silicon Valley', *Mercury News*. Available at http://www.siliconvalley.com/mld/siliconvalley/business/columnists/ 4310498.htm.

All-China Youth Federation (Overseas Scholars Division) (2004) *Search for Hai Gui – A Report on the Survey of Study Abroad and Return of Chinese Students*, Beijing: Elite Reference.

Ammassari, S. and Black, R. (2001) 'Harnessing the potential of migration and return to promote development: applying concepts to West Africa', Sussex University, Sussex Migration Working Papers, 1.

Archaimbault, C. (1952) 'En marge du quartier chinois de Paris', *Bulletin de la Société des Etudes Indochinoises*, 17(3): 275–94.

Bhagwati, J. (2004) *In Defense of Globalisation*, New York: Oxford University Press.

British Council, Universities UK and IDP Education Australia (2004) *Vision 2020: Forecasting International Student Mobility*, London: British Council.

Castles, S. and Miller, M. J. (2003) *The Age of Migration: International Population Movements in the Modern World*, 3rd edition, Basingstoke: Palgrave Macmillan.

Cervantes, M. and Guellec, D. (2002) *The Brain Drain: Old Myths, New Realities*, Paris: Organisation for Economic Cooperation and Development. www. oecdobserver.org.

Chatterton, P. (1999) 'University students and city centres – the formation of exclusive geographies', *Geoforum*, 30: 117–33.

D'Costa, A. P. (2004) 'Globalisation, development, and mobility of technical talent – India and Japan in comparative perspectives'. UNU World Institute for Development Economics Research, Research Paper 62.

De Wenden, C. (2004) 'L'Union Européenne face aux migrations', *Migrations Société*, 16(91): 69–75.

Edwards, R. and Edwards, J. (2001) 'Internationalisation of education: a business perspective', *Australian Journal of Education*, 45(1): 76–89.

Findlay, A. M. and Stewart, E. (2002) *Skilled Labour Migration from Developing Countries*, 45th edition, Geneva: International Labour Office.

Ghosh, B. (ed.) (2000) *Return Migration*, Geneva: International Organisation for Migration.

Giese, K. (2003) 'New Chinese migration to Germany: historical consistencies and new patterns of diversification within a globalised migration regime', *International Migration*, 41(3): 156–85.

Graeme, H. (2003) *Migration and Development: A Perspective from Asia*, Geneva: International Organisation for Migration (IOM).

Guerassimoff, C. (2003) 'The new Chinese migrants in France', *International Migration*, 41(3): 136–54.

Haines III, V. Y. and Saba, T. (1999) 'Understanding reactions to international mobility policies and practices', *Human Resource Planning*, 22(3): 40–51.

Hantrais, L. (1999) 'Contextualisation in cross-national comparative research', *International Journal of Social Research Methodology*, 2(2): 93–108.

Holzmann, R. and Münz, R. (2004) *Challenges and Opportunities of International Migration for the EU, Its Member States, Neighbouring Countries and Regions: A Policy Note*, Stockholm: Institute for Future Studies.

International Organisation for Migration (IOM) (2003a) *Migration Policy Issues*, Geneva: IOM.

International Organisation for Migration (IOM) (2003b) *World Migration 2003*, Geneva: IOM.

International Organisation for Migration (IOM) (2005) *World Migration 2005 – Costs and Benefits of International Migration*, Geneva: IOM.

Iosifides, T. (2003) 'Qualitative migration research: some new reflections six years later', *The Qualitative Report*, 8(3): 435–46.

King, R. (ed.) (1986) *Return Migration and Regional Economic Problems*, London: Croom Helm.

Laczko, F. (2003) 'Understanding migration between China and Europe', *International Migration*, 41(3): 5–19.

Larsen, K. and Vincent-Lancrin, S. (2003) *The Learning Businesses: Can Trade in International Education Work?*, Paris: Organisation for Economic Cooperation and Development. http://www.oecdobserver.org.

Leavey, H. (2004) 'China's students flock to Europe', *BBC News*, 24 August.

Li, F. L. N., Findlay, A. M., Jowett, A. J. and Skeldon, R. (1996) 'Migrating to learn and learning to migrate: a study of the experiences and intentions of international student migrants', *International Journal of Population Geography*, 2: 51–67.

Liang, Z. and Morooka, H. (2004) 'Recent trends of emigration from China: 1982–2000', *International Migration*, 42(3): 145–64.

Lowell, B. Lindsay and Findlay, A. M. (2001) *Migration of Highly Skilled Persons from Developing Countries: Impact and Policy Responses (Synthesis Report)*, Geneva: International Labour Office (ILO).

Luo, K. (2005) *China Cross-Border Migration Study*, Shanghai: East China Normal University.

Luo, K., Huang, P. and Chen, Z. (2004) 'Chinese migration and talent flows in economic globalisation', University of Cologne, Department of Geography Working Paper 2.

Ma Mung, E. (2000) *La diaspora Chinoise, géographie d'une migration*, 1st edition, Paris: Ophrys.

Mahroum, S. (2002) 'The International Mobility of Academics: The UK Case', Doctoral thesis. Hamburg: Bundeswehr University (published in 2003 by Dissertation.Com).

Mairie de Paris (2005) *EduParis*, Paris: www.eduparis.net.

Mangen, S. (1999) 'Qualitative research methods in cross-national settings', *International Journal of Social Research Methodology*, 2(2): 109–24.

Mayor of London (2005a) *Study London – Launch Your Career at the Centre of Opportunity*, London: www.studylondon.ac.uk.

Mayor of London (2005b) 'Overseas students', *Student Londoner. News from the Mayor of London*, April 2005. www.london.gov.uk/mayor/education/docs/newsletter_apr05.rtf.

Ministère de l'Éducation Nationale (2002) *Accord franco-chinois de coopération éducative singé le mars 2002*, Paris: MEN.

Ministère de l'Éducation Nationale (2004) *Reprères et réfénces statistiques*, Paris: MEN.

Ministry of Education, China (2003) *Annual Review of Education*, Beijing.

Monro, A. (2004) 'A migration that nobody objects to', *New Statesman*, 1 March. http://www.newstatesman.com/200403010024.

Nania, S. and Green, S. (2004) *Deus ex M.A. China: Are Mainland Chinese Students Saving Britain's Universities?*, London: The Royal Institute of International Relations.

Nyberg-Sørensen, N., Van Hear, N. and Engberg-Pedersen, P. (2002) 'The migration-development nexus: evidence and policy options', *International Migration*, 40(5): 49–73.

O'Connor, K. (2005) *International Students and Global Cities*, Loughborough: Loughborough University. http://www.lboro.ac.uk/gawc/rb/rb161.html.

Ortiz, J. (2004) 'International business education in a global environment: a conceptual approach', *International Education Journal*, 5(2): 255–65.

Pan, L. (ed.) (1999) *The Encyclopaedia of the Chinese Overseas*, Cambridge, MA: Harvard University Press.

Pieke, F. (2002) 'Recent trends in Chinese migration to Europe: Fujienese migration in perspective', *IOM Migration Research Series*, 6, Geneva: IOM.

Pieke, F. (2004) 'Chinese globalisation and migration to Europe', University of California, San Diego, The Centre for Comparative Immigration Studies Working Paper 94.

Quan, Yu and Teck, Hoon Hian (2003) 'Catch-up growth based on international talent mobility in an idea-based world', SMU, Singapore, Economics and Statistics Work Paper Series 11. https://mercury.smu.edu.sg/rsrchpubupload/1798/Quan-Hoon-Talentmobility-D7.pdf.

Salt, J., Singleton, A. and Hogarth, J. (1994) *Europe's International Migrants – Data Sources, Patterns and Trends*, London: HMSO.

Sassen, S. (ed.) (2002) *Global Networks, Linked Cities*, London: Routledge.

Shen, W. (2005) 'Chinese student migration to the UK', *Asia-Europe Journal*, 3(3): 429–36.

Skeldon, R. (1996) 'Migration from China', *Journal of International Affairs*, 49(2): 434–55.

Smith, M. P. and Guarnizo, L. E. (eds) (1998) *Transnationalism From Below* (Comparative Urban and Community Research, 6), New Brunswick, NJ: Transaction Publishers.

Song, J. (2003) 'A hundred years of relay waves of studying abroad', *Technology Daily*, 15 Feb. 2003. http://www.cas.ac.cn/html/Dir/2003/02/15/7140.htm.

Sopemi (2001) *Trends in International Migration*, Paris: Organisation for Economic Cooperation and Development (OECD).

Sopemi (2002) *Trends in International Migration*, Paris: Organisation for Economic Cooperation and Development.

Sopemi (2004) *Trends in International Migration*, Paris: Organisation for Economic Cooperation and Development.

Taylor, P. J. (2004) *World City Network: A Global Urban Analysis*, 1st edition, London: Routledge.

Tremblay, K. (2002) *Student Mobility Between and Towards OECD Countries in 2001 – A Comparative Analysis*, Paris: OECD Directorate for Education (Indicators and Analysis Division).

UBS (2004) *Research Focus: China and India*, Zurich: UBS AG (Wealth Management Research).

United Nations Development Programme (UNDP) (2003) *Human Development Report 2003, Millennium Development Goals: A Compact Among Nations to End Human Poverty*, New York: UNDP.

Universities UK Media Release (11/05/2006) 'Universities boost value of "UK plc" says report'. http://www.universitiesuk.ac.uk/mediareleases/show.asp?MR=454

Van den Berg, L. and Russo, A. P. (2004) *The Student City: Strategic Planning for Student Communities in EU Cities*, Aldershot: Ashgate.

Van Hear, N. and Nyberg-Sørensen, N. (eds) (2003) *The Migration-Development Nexus*, Geneva: International Organisation for Migration.

Wang, H. (2005) *Returning Times*, 1st edition, Beijing: Central Compilation and Translation Press.

Waters, J. (2003) 'Flexible citizens? Transnationalism and citizenship amongst economic immigrants in Vancouver', *The Canadian Geographer/Le Géographe canadien*, 47(3): 219–34.

Wattanavittukul, P. (2002) 'Hai gui: the sea-turtles come marching home'. Online. Available at http://www.apmforum.com/columns/china19.htm [accessed 15 October 2004].

Williams, A. (2005) 'International migration and knowledge', University of Oxford, Centre on Migration, Policy and Society Working Paper 17.

Xiang, B. (2003) 'Emigration from China: a sending country perspective', *International Migration*, 41(3): 21–48.

Xiang, B. (2005) *Promoting Knowledge Transfer through Diaspora Networks: The Case of People's Republic of China*, Oxford: University of Oxford, Centre for Migration, Policy and Society.

Yao, L. (2004) 'The Chinese overseas students: an overview of the flows change', 12th Biennial Conference of the Australian Population Association, Canberra, Australia, 15–17 September.

Zhang, G. (2003) 'Migration of highly skilled Chinese to Europe: trends and perspective', *International Migration*, 41(3): 73–97.

Zweig, D. (2006) 'Learning to compete: China's strategies to create a "reverse brain drain"', in C. Kuptsch and E. F. Pang (eds) *Competing for Global Talent*, France: International Labour Organisation, pp. 187–213.

13 Government rhetoric and student understandings

Discursive framings of higher education 'choice'

Rachel Brooks

Introduction

Over the past two decades, the notion of 'choice' has played an important rhetorical role in UK education policy. The 1988 Education Reform Act introduced a broad raft of measures aimed at increasing parental choice within compulsory schooling, while similar changes were brought about in the post-compulsory sector under the auspices of the 1992 Further and Higher Education Act. Since then, although changes from Conservative to Labour governments have resulted in some modifications to the way in which parental/pupil preferences are expressed and taken account of, 'choice' has remained a central plank of education policy. Despite this continuing commitment to increasing consumer choice within education, there is now a large body of research that has demonstrated that many of these policies have served to exacerbate social inequalities. For example, studies have shown that the 'power to choose' is not distributed equally across all social groups, while in some areas, where there is high parental demand, it is the schools and colleges that often end up doing the 'choosing'– acting, in effect, as what Tomlinson (2001: 49) calls a 'crude mechanism for social selection'.

In engaging with these debates, this chapter first outlines some of the characteristics of the dominant political discourse in the UK with respect to higher education. In particular, it focuses on: the largely economic function of a university education; the normalisation of higher education as a post-18 route; and the alleged benefits of 'choice' within diverse educational markets. The chapter then goes on to explore the extent to which this discourse is evident in the narratives of young adults, themselves, as they describe their reasons for going on to higher education and the decision-making processes within which they engaged. In doing so, it draws on life history interviews with 90 young graduates from a range of different higher education institutions (occupying notably different market positions), five years after they graduated. It considers the ways in which these young adults discursively framed their accounts of 'choosing' higher education institutions, and their post-graduation reflections on the nature and impact of these choices. On the basis of this evidence, it contends that understandings of, and decisions about, higher education are informed by dominant political discourses in relation to the economic function of higher education and its place in a normalised conception of youth transitions, but that government rhetoric about 'choice' has not been as widely embraced.

Analysing policy discourses about higher education

In 1996, Lord Dearing was asked to review the funding mechanisms for the British higher education system. In his report, published in 1997, he outlined what he believed to be the four main purposes of the higher education system (National Committee of Inquiry into Higher Education 1997). The first of these focuses very much on the development of the individual: higher education should 'inspire and enable individuals to develop their capabilities to the highest potential levels throughout life, so that they grow intellectually, are well-equipped for work, can contribute effectively to society and achieve personal fulfilment' (section 5.11). The second purpose outlined by Dearing emphasises the importance of increasing knowledge and understanding for their own sake and applying them to the benefit of wider society. Thirdly, higher education's contribution to shaping a democratic, civilised and inclusive society is emphasised. Finally, Dearing believed that higher education should 'serve the needs of an adaptable, sustainable, knowledge-based economy at local, regional and national levels' (ibid.).

Within the academic literature, it is possible to identify a wide range of putative purposes of a national higher education system. Indeed, Williams (1997) outlines five discrete discourses. At one extreme are the 'academic traditionalists' in whose discourse academic freedom – to choose which students to accept and what programmes of study to offer them – is central. At the other extreme is the discourse of the 'utilitarian trainers', who believe that national economic success is intimately linked to the production of skilled graduates.[1] Some of these divergent discourses are captured in Dearing's account. However, in the decade since his report was published, government documents have tended to marginalise the non-economic functions central to Dearing's conceptualisation of the university system. Indeed, the role of higher education in underpinning a successful globalised economy has come to dominate policy discourse. This is made clear in the strategic plan for higher education, published by the Higher Education Funding Council for England (HEFCE) in 2006. This claims explicitly that the wider economic context in the UK has changed significantly since the Dearing Report: 'global competition has intensified and high level skills and knowledge have become ever more central to the UK's economic success' (HEFCE 2006: 4). This putative shift is then used to justify the strong economic focus that underpins the rest of the plan.

This focus is evident in other key documents that outline the government's understanding of the purpose of higher education in the twenty-first century. Indeed, the first sentence of the executive summary of the 2003 White Paper *The Future of Higher Education* (DfES 2003) makes this clear: 'Our higher education system is a great asset both for individuals and the nation.

The skills, creativity and research developed through higher education are a major factor in our success at creating jobs and in our prosperity.' It then immediately goes on to suggest that, even at the individual level, the most important gains are also economic: 'The benefits of higher education for individuals are far-reaching. On average, graduates get better jobs and earn more than those without higher education' (DfES 2003: 4). The implications of this economic positioning of higher education are spelt out in the White Paper and in various other related policy documents. Indeed, the HEFCE strategic plan for 2006–11, mentioned above, sets out a very detailed set of prescriptions for sharpening universities' economic focus and for increasing business involvement in higher education. For example, even in relation to its aim of achieving excellence in teaching and learning, one of the five specified targets to ensure this aim is met is that the proportion of higher education institutions reporting high levels of employer involvement in their curriculum increases to 80 per cent by 2009 (HEFCE 2006: 16).[2] Furthermore, over the period of the plan, the higher education sector as a whole is expected to secure year-on-year increases in the total contributions for third stream activity (i.e. related to business and the wider community, rather than teaching and research). It is also the case that recent moves towards expanding the UK higher education sector have been predicated upon economic arguments. The 2003 White Paper, for example, states that 'The economic case for expanding the provision of higher education is extremely strong … National economic imperatives support our target to increase participation in higher education towards 50 per cent of those aged 18–30 by the end of the decade' (DfES 2003: 57).

The second discourse explored in this chapter is the shift towards the normalisation of higher education as a post-18 destination. The government warns that 'there is a danger of higher education becoming an automatic step in the chain of education – almost a third stage of compulsory schooling' (DfES 2003: 60). Despite this caveat, the model of degree-level education constructed in the White Paper tends to assume that almost all young people will pass through higher education. Indeed, a few pages earlier in the same document, we are told that the target of 50 per cent participation by 2010 is linked to the government's wider aim of preparing 90 per cent of young people for higher education or skilled employment (DfES 2003: 59). This is predicated upon the assumption that a substantial majority (80 per cent, by the government's calculation) of new jobs over the next ten years are likely to be in higher level occupations, and that they are therefore likely to be filled by those who have been through higher education. What the government's warning seems to refer to, more accurately, is the assumption that higher education will continue to be based on the traditional three-year honours degree. Instead, while it appears that, for the vast majority of young people, higher education will become a 'normal' post-18 transition, its defining features may well be different – encompassing more work-focused, two-year foundation degrees, and easier progression from vocational programmes into university-level study. Indeed, this is articulated clearly in the HEFCE strategic plan:

> We will work to improve the prospects for progression into and through higher education for *all learners*. In particular, we will work with the DfES and the LSC [Learning and Skills Council] to make the routes into and through higher education clearer, more coherent and more certain for learners on vocational programmes.
>
> (HEFCE 2006: 19, italics added)

Alongside this emphasis on the further expansion of higher education and the key economic function of universities is a strong commitment to a 'choice' agenda within the sector. This is something that has characterised New Labour's approach to public services more generally and has perhaps been played out most fully in relation to the health sector (Crinson 2005; Newman and Vidler 2006) and compulsory education (Gorard *et al.* 2003). As noted above, there has been a high degree of continuity between the policies introduced by the Labour government in the UK, and those of its Conservative predecessor. The former Prime Minister, himself, has been at the forefront of championing such reforms. In June 2006, for example, Tony Blair gave a speech on 'Twenty-first Century Public Services' in which he argued that, in contemporary society, people want services to be organised around them, tailored to their specific needs and available at a time and place convenient to them. He went on to contend that 'market mechanisms, choice, the encouragement of a range of different providers of a service, incentives, partnerships with private and voluntary sectors – have a key role to play' (Blair 2006). In relation to education, in particular, he has argued that, since 2001, New Labour has worked to open the system up to new influences and introduced 'the beginnings of choice and contestability' – aiming for 'a market in the sense of consumer choice, not a market based on private purchasing power' (Blair 2005).

In relation to higher education, more specifically, this choice has been articulated through a series of measures intended to increase the transparency of the sector, and enable 'consumers' or potential students to make more informed comparisons between institutions. These measures have included: the introduction of a National Student Survey in 2005, and the rapid manipulation of results into a 'league table' format; an ongoing commitment to the research assessment exercise (for the medium term at least); and strong encouragement for higher education institutions (HEIs) to develop a more diverse higher education sector. This last point is articulated clearly within the 2003 White Paper:

> In the face of increasing competition and more demanding stakeholders, HEIs need to build on their strengths and seize opportunities. As autonomous bodies they have considerable freedom to do this … A

diverse sector, made up of a variety of universities and colleges with a range of missions, is vital if the needs of all stakeholders is to be met.

(DfES 2003: 31)

However, the identity of the 'consumer' is perhaps less easily identifiable within higher education than compulsory education. In the latter, 'choice' policies are aimed clearly at parents and pupils (and, less commonly, at local communities). Within higher education, however, the 'stakeholders' referred to above encompass a significantly wider group, including employers as well as potential students and their families. Whether we can assume a commonality of purpose amongst all stakeholders is discussed further in later sections of this chapter.

Research methods

This chapter draws on evidence from 90 adults in their mid-twenties, recruited for a project on 'Young Graduates and Lifelong Learning', funded by the UK's Economic and Social Research Council. Although our interest was primarily in how our respondents' experiences of higher education had affected their attitudes towards and experiences of learning in the years after completion of their first degree,[3] we also sought to explore the extent to which their decision-making processes about education had changed over the nine years or so since they went about choosing the course and institution for their undergraduate studies. As a result of this, our young adults provided us with considerable detail about their motivations, beliefs and influences at the age of 18–19, in the late 1990s when they were making decisions about higher education.

Most of our respondents had graduated in 2000 and all had studied at one of six different higher education institutions – chosen to reflect different 'market positions' (an Oxbridge college, a college of the University of London, a nineteenth-century redbrick university, a 1960s campus university, a post-92 university and a college of higher education).[4] Respondents were recruited through a mailing sent out by the alumni offices of the six institutions and adverts on 'Friends Reunited' (a UK-based internet site that aims to 'reunite' old friends from school, college and university). As Table 13.1 demonstrates, we recruited 15 graduates from each of the HEIs but, overall, more women than men. In-depth, life history interviews were conducted with the sample between September 2005 and January 2006. These were wide-ranging and typically asked about their 'learning histories' (from as far back as they could remember), their experiences of work (paid and unpaid), and their social lives, through school, college and university and into full-time work. Two focus groups were then held with a sub-sample of the respondents (10 young adults from all HEIs apart from Oxbridge), to discuss cross-cutting issues that had emerged from an initial analysis of the transcripts of the individual interviews.

Table 13.1 Gender of respondents, by higher education institution attended

Higher education institutions (placed in order of typical league table position)	Women	Men
Oxbridge	8	7
London	8	7
Redbrick	10	5
Campus	14	1
Post-92	11	4
College of Higher Education	7	8
TOTAL	58	32

Note:
In this table and the discussion that follows: 'Oxbridge' refers to a college of the University of Oxford or the University of Cambridge; 'London' refers to a college of the University of London; 'Redbrick' refers to a civic university founded between 1850 and 1960; 'Campus' refers to a university founded in the 1960s; 'Post-92' refers to a former polytechnic which assumed university status as a result of the 1992 Further and Higher Education Act; and 'College of Higher Education' refers to a college which does not have formal university status, but offers degree courses.

The following sections of the chapter draw on this data to explore the extent to which the young graduates' narratives can be seen as congruent with the discourses outlined above, namely: the importance of higher education's economic function; the normalisation of higher education as a post-18 destination; and the value of 'choosing' within diverse educational markets. As most of our respondents began their undergraduate courses in the late 1990s (many in 1997), their decision-making processes will not have been informed by the policy documents discussed above. However, the aim of this chapter is to explore the extent to which the young graduates' reflections on their higher education at the time of interview (2005–6) reflect (or contest) current policy discourses. In the sections that follow, all respondents are referred to by pseudonym only. When quoting directly from one of the young adults, I also give their job title at the time of interview, and the type of higher education institution they attended.

The economic function of higher education

The academic literature has subjected to critical scrutiny government predictions about future skills requirements and questioned many of the assumptions upon which much higher education policy (in the UK and elsewhere) is based. Livingstone (2002), for example, provides strong empirical evidence to suggest that in the US, at least, there is a large over-supply of knowledge workers relative to the number of jobs that are available to workers within the 'knowledge economy'. He argues that policymakers, industrialists and educationalists have misread the market for high-level analytical skills and goes on to claim that while there may be other valid reasons for expanding the provision of higher education (and other high-level forms of learning), ensuring an increasingly large labour force to meet the demands of the knowledge economy is not a convincing one. Within the

UK, similar arguments have been made – on the basis that the expansion of higher education has, in practice, done little to benefit the economy (Ainley 1994; Brown 1997) and that many graduates feel over-qualified for the jobs they are doing (Keep and Rainbird 2002). What is less clear from the research conducted to date is the extent to which government discourses about the economic imperatives for higher education are taken up by young people and inform decisions about their post-18 pathways.

Across our sample as a whole, respondents outlined several different motivations for progressing to higher education. Some (albeit a small number) described their 'love of learning' and how they would have been very reluctant to give this up at the age of 18:

> It was just purely because I wanted to learn something new. (Sarina, communications co-ordinator, Campus)

> ... because I enjoyed it. It never occurred to me that this is what I need to do to get on in life. It was just, I liked learning, so I learnt. (Margaret, administrative support officer, Redbrick)

However, in the vast majority of cases, the transition to higher education was explained in relation to one of two main factors (or, in some cases, both). Firstly, many of the young graduates described university as largely an assumed transition, which had required little thought or conscious 'choice' (other than in relation to what subject would be studied, and the institutions to which one applied). This assumption is discussed further, below, in relation to debates about the normalisation of this particular post-18 route within government policy. Secondly, a large majority of the respondents made explicit reference to what they perceived to be the economic benefits of gaining a first degree. However, to most of our respondents, these economic benefits were configured rather differently from those outlined by government ministers, discussed previously.

On the basis of their work in Australia, Dwyer and Wyn (2001) contend that, as a result of the mass expansion of higher education, young people now experience uncertainties on graduation that have previously been associated with the end of compulsory schooling. More specifically, they suggest that young people are 'sold' higher education on the basis of a promise of lasting professional employment and that those who fail to secure this kind of job are likely to experience acute disappointment. However, those in our sample did not assume any such automatic correspondence between gaining a degree and securing high status professional jobs. Indeed, there appeared to be widespread recognition that, for many jobs, a degree was merely a 'basic minimum', which would need to be supplemented with further education, training or work experience after graduation. Thus, a degree was seen to be necessary if one wanted to avoid low skilled and 'dead end' types of job, rather than automatically paving the way to professional employment or the kind of high skilled jobs outlined in the 2003 White Paper. Josephine, who had attended Post-92, described well this type of reasoning, which was common across the sample:

> As much as I didn't use my degree to get me somewhere higher straightaway ... I wouldn't have got through the door without a degree ... I guess more and more it's like that because more and more people are having degrees, aren't they? So it's not so much a unique thing anymore – but without it you're kind of a bit stuffed because you don't even get in [the door].

For these young adults, there seemed to be little recognition of 'new' forms of graduate employment – either those related to a shift to a new 'high skills' economy emphasised by government ministers (DfES 2003) or the types discussed by Purcell and Elias (2004).[5] Instead, their more pessimistic reading of the labour market was grounded in a belief that employers were increasingly raising the qualification levels required for particular jobs (without an associated upgrading of the jobs themselves) in response to the 'over-supply' of graduates. Thus, as Aapola *et al.* (2005) have argued, remaining in education may not necessarily be a personal preference but a consequence of the new demands of the service sector or, as Brown *et al.* (2000) maintain, while graduates may be making themselves more employable by gaining a degree, this may not lead to the kinds of jobs historically associated with a university education.

It is also notable that even difficulties in securing employment immediately after graduation had not stimulated our respondents to rethink the purpose of their higher education. Of our 90 respondents, twelve had experienced unemployment on graduation and a further 31 moved into a temporary (rather than permanent) job. For a small number of this group, such experiences did prompt some questioning of whether their education had been worth it. Overall, however, there was conspicuously little regret at having pursued a degree. Indeed, in line with the argument developed above, almost all implied or stated explicitly that they considered their higher education to be a basic minimum and that what was more important was consolidating this with relevant experience and/or learning post-graduation.

> There are so many good people out there with degrees, who are all the same, and if you only have one degree then employers would say 'Ah, this person has two ... which makes him stand out'. And so I've ... tried to collect as many education things as possible now, just to make myself stand out ... (Carlton, solicitor, Redbrick)

Thus, despite widely publicised government proclamations about the value of a degree, its association with significantly higher lifetime earnings and its increasing importance to a knowledge-based economy (DfES 2003), relatively few of our respondents believed that it offered more than a 'basic minimum' within a competitive graduate labour market. While seeming to reject such government rhetoric out of hand, there was – perhaps surprisingly – a notable absence of any critical reflection about the ways in which these putative rewards of higher education are emphasised in national debate. Indeed, alongside widespread pessimism about a degree providing a pathway to professional employment was a seeming acceptance of the inevitability of credential inflation and the necessity to compensate, specialise and 'gain the edge' (in a largely individualistic and competitive manner) post-graduation. Nevertheless, while our respondents appeared largely sceptical about these putative rewards of higher education, their narratives did also indicate a high degree of congruence with government discourses about the broad purpose of higher education: the economic function of a university education was clearly privileged in their accounts.

A normalised pattern of transition?

Despite the government's aim to make higher education an increasingly common destination for British young people, the 2003 White Paper also recognises some of the barriers to achieving this, citing MORI research that 59 per cent of young people from the four lowest social classes did not plan ever to go to university, and almost half the sample had never thought about doing a degree. The academic literature on young people's decision-making processes about higher education also clearly highlights stark social inequalities (Reay *et al.* 2005; Walkerdine *et al.* 2001). Certainly, among some working class young people there is no assumption that university is a 'logical' next step after schooling, and little evidence of the normalisation of higher education as a post-18 destination. Archer (2006), for example, points to the ways in which higher education is both classed and masculinised; she also provides evidence of the ways in which some young men and young women from working class backgrounds feel excluded from the sector as a result of perceptions of cultural difference. Indeed, she goes on to argue that for working class women, in particular,

> Higher education participation is predicated upon the recognition of a position of inferiority and a subsequent investment in 'change'. Hence, some women's resistance to participation might also be read as part of their resistance to wider discourses of derision surrounding working class femininity.
>
> (Archer 2006: 81)

Nevertheless, the narratives of the respondents in our sample suggested that, for many of them, higher education had been seen as an unremarkable and largely assumed post-18 destination. Previous research has highlighted assumptions of this kind amongst the upper middle classes (Reay *et al.* 2005; Pugsley 2004), with familial experience of university life to draw upon. However, in our project, similar assumptions were evident across all social classes. Indeed, many respondents who were the first in their family to progress to higher education described it as a natural route, following on logically from their sixth-form studies:

> It was taken as given at my school, I think most people went. And my parents encouraged me, because they didn't [go to university themselves] … It was never a choice of, I was never thinking 'Oh, I won't go'. (Lucia, journalist, London)

> It was just something that had to be done … Never considered not going to college, just assumed I would. (Julia, nurse, Post-92)

Clearly, there are still many young people for whom higher education is far from an assumed destination. Indeed, the recently published plans to require all young people to participate in education and training until the age of 18 (DfES 2007) are motivated primarily by a concern to reduce the number who leave school at 16 and enter jobs with no training and few prospects. Moreover, compared with other European countries, the UK also fares poorly. For example, 71 per cent of the relevant cohort in Finland enters tertiary education, compared to 46 per cent in the UK (CERI 2002). A greater proportion of young people go on to tertiary study in Sweden, Iceland, Poland, Norway, the Netherlands and Spain than in the UK. Nevertheless, the evidence from this project would suggest that, as a result of the rapid expansion in the number of higher education places over the last 20 years, and the consequent increase in the age participation index from 14 per cent in 1986 to around 42 per cent in 2004/5, for many young people, higher education has become part of an assumed educational trajectory, in a way that would not have been possible two decades ago. Indeed, these trends appear to have had a significant impact on young people's perceptions, across a range of social groups and geographical areas such that, for many in our sample, including a considerable number from working class backgrounds, progression to higher education was seen as very much part of a 'normal' youth transition. While these perceptions may help to realise the government's aim of increasing the higher education participation rate, they also raise questions about the status of those who do not go on to degree-level study and, in particular, whether they will be further disadvantaged.

'Choice' and decision-making

In line with the findings of other recent studies of university choice, in this project there was considerable variation in the decision-making processes of the young people involved and, specifically, in the extent to which they believed they had engaged with processes of educational 'choice'. Differences were apparent in both respondents' inclination to engage with choice processes, as well as their capacity to do so. While there is now a substantial body of research pointing out the very unequal playing field upon which young people make their decisions about whether or not to go on to university (Archer *et al.* 2003; Brooks 2005; Reay *et al.* 2005), our study indicates that stark differences are apparent even amongst a sample constituted entirely of graduates. Firstly, respondents exhibited clear differences in their knowledge about the stratification of the higher education market, and about differences in status and reputation between institutions. Although the variation in knowledge encompassed quite a broad spectrum (and thus bears more resemblance to Pugsley's (2004) typology of 'thrusting', 'trying' and 'trusting' choosers,[6] rather than Ball *et al.*'s (2002) dichotomy between 'embedded' and 'disconnected' choosers[7]), those who had a very fine-grained understanding of subtle differences between higher status institutions can be contrasted with those who, at the time of their higher education choices, were unaware of any differences in status. For example, Kyla, who had attended a post-92 university for her degree, described how she had been aware of the superior reputations of Oxford and Cambridge but had considered all other institutions broadly similar:

> Everyone knows about Cambridge, Oxford, but when you're talking about Leicester versus [Post-92], I didn't know there was a difference. Didn't know there was a difference at all – but apparently there is … I remember someone saying 'You go to [Post-92], you get a mickey mouse degree'. (Kyla, alumni services and development co-ordinator, Post-92)

Other respondents described how they had been aware of the structure of the higher education market at the time of their university application, but had believed that their own choices were very limited:

> I know it's not as glamorous as the big London ones or Oxford, Cambridge. That's to be expected. I never had ambitions, coming from, I would have put myself as working middle class, the lower echelon, because my family couldn't afford the tuition fees to put me through these schools like Eton … Yes, there are quite a few people who are there, they earned it, they've got the knowledge and educational kudos to get there, but I've never possessed that … I'm very realistic about how I can perform. (Ivan, training and development executive, College of Higher Education)

Here, Ivan indicates that he was concerned about the lack of 'social fit' between his own modest upbringing and the background of the privileged students that he expected to find at more 'glamorous' universities. However, towards the end of this extract, this social unease becomes conflated with concern about a lack of academic fit; he moves swiftly from talking about class differences to, what he perceives to be, parallel differences in academic ability.

For some of the graduates in our sample, higher education had radically affected the nature of their engagement with educational markets and, in particular, their response to perceived status differences. Indeed, a significant proportion of the young adults reported that their views about institutional reputation had changed during their time at university. Some had become conscious of the hierarchical nature of the higher education sector for the first time, while others, who had previously been aware of such distinctions between universities, had come to perceive these differences as more significant. Indeed, many came to share Brown and Lauder's (2006: 50) assertion that 'increasing inequalities in occupational rewards and career prospects place a premium on gaining access to internationally recognised schools, colleges and universities'. A considerable number of respondents in this group then went on to explain how such changing perceptions had influenced their decisions about post-graduation learning (see also Brooks and Everett 2008):

> I started applying to do my Master's the following year, whilst I was in this job, and I looked at different unis. I looked at Birmingham, Warwick, Reading and Leicester. So I kind of picked those because I thought they were better, I suppose, than Post-92. (Rhian, researcher, Post-92)

Here, we see some evidence of a higher education facilitating greater engagement with processes of educational choice. For another group of respondents, however, although issues related to the status of higher education institutions had become more apparent during their undergraduate studies, they chose to embrace the lower status of the institution they had attended.

> At the time it didn't occur to me that there was this class thing and even now, I know that there is this class structure there and that certain establishments are viewed as being better, but to me that's rubbish. I was proud to say I was at [College of Higher Education] ... League tables don't mean a thing to me. I couldn't care less. (Michael, PhD student, College of Higher Education)

> I was very proud to be at university there, very proud to be at [College of Higher Education] even though initially I may have thought about the fact that it was a bit of a lower standard than others, but at the end of the day I still feel passionate about it. (Jason, medical sales rep, College of Higher Education)

Evidence from Michael and Jason and others like them provides further support for those who have argued that the power – or even the inclination – to choose is not distributed equally across all social groups. Moreover, Michael's disdain for league tables and his embrace of what he perceived to be a 'lower status' institution, suggests that mechanisms designed to enhance consumer choice, in higher education and elsewhere, may well be rejected by particular groups for a variety of social reasons (see also Brooks 2006b).

Conclusion

In this chapter I have considered some of the main themes invoked by the UK government's discourse on higher education. In particular, I have highlighted: the emphasis placed on the economic function of higher education (and contrasted this with the significantly broader view of the purpose of a university education contained within the Dearing Report of only a decade ago); the increasing normalisation of higher education as an assumed post-higher education destination for a large proportion of the population; and the importance of exercising individual choice within a diverse education market. In an attempt to explore how widely these official discourses have been taken up by those who have recently moved through the higher education sector, I have drawn on life history narratives from 90 UK graduates from a range of different institutions. These suggest some significant variation. We have seen from the data discussed above that, although young graduates' views about the dominant economic role of higher education broadly corresponded with those propounded by the UK government, they differed considerably in the detail: acceptance of the need for a first degree was driven, not by a belief in a recent shift to a knowledge-based economy but, in contrast, by a recognition of the impact of credential inflation and the need for the 'basic minimum' of a degree, to avoid unskilled, low level work. While understandings of and decisions about higher education appear to be informed by dominant political discourses in relation to the economic function of higher education and its place in a normalised conception of youth transitions, government rhetoric about 'choice' has not been as widely embraced. In this study, at least, some young graduates demonstrated considerable resistance to 'choosing' within educational markets. Important questions thus remain about whether we can assume that all those who have the power to choose also have the inclination to do so.

Acknowledgements

This chapter draws on work carried out for the 'Young Graduates and Lifelong Learning' research project, funded by the ESRC (award number RES-000-22-0662). I am grateful to Glyn Everett, who conducted the majority of the fieldwork, and to all the young adults who gave up their time to be interviewed for the project.

Notes

1 The other three discourses identified by Williams are those of: the 'marketeers' who believe that government should have a residual role in deciding on the size and purpose of HE through its control of finance; the 'liberal meritocrats' who argue that an individual has a right to education if he or she is adequately qualified (and place less emphasis than academic traditionalists on the right of the higher education institution to decide who is or is not selected for entry); and

the 'access movement', which aims to prioritise provision for groups historically excluded from universities.

2 The importance of furthering links between universities and their local business communities has also been emphasised by the former Prime Minister (Blair 2007).

3 The take-up of learning in the years after graduation is discussed in more detail in Brooks (2006a) and Brooks and Everett (2008).

4 The term 'redbrick' usually refers to UK universities founded between 1850 and 1960, particularly large civic institutions. 'Post-92' refers to former polytechnics that assumed university status as a result of the 1992 Further and Higher Education Act.

5 Purcell and Elias (2004) distinguish between four different types of graduate job: 'professional' (defined as jobs for which access has historically been through an undergraduate degree programme, e.g. lawyers); 'modern' (where an undergraduate degree became the normal route into the occupations at the time of the last expansion of HE in the 1960s, e.g. primary school teachers); 'new' (where the route has recently changed and is now mainly via an undergraduate degree programme, e.g. marketing and sales managers); and 'niche' (in areas of employment where most workers do not have degrees but in which there are niches for which graduates are sought, e.g. hotel managers).

6 'Thrusting' choosers are typically familiar with the HE field and can deploy significant social capital, while 'trusting' choosers are first generation university entrants with little knowledge of the HE market. 'Trying' choosers are located between these two extremes, having some level of awareness of the educational market.

7 'Embedded' choosers are typically those who come from families with experience of higher education and who are aware of fine distinctions between HEIs. 'Disconnected' choosers, in contrast, are often unaware of status differences between institutions and have no familial experience of higher education upon which to draw.

References

Aapola, S., Gonick, M. and Harris, A. (2005) *Young Femininity: Girlhood, Power and Social Change*, Basingstoke: Palgrave Macmillan.

Ainley, P. (1994) *Degrees of Difference. Higher Education in the 1990s*, London: Lawrence and Wishart.

Archer, L. (2006) 'Masculinities, femininities and resistance to participation in post-compulsory education', in Leathwood, C. and Francis, B. (eds) *Gender and Lifelong Learning: Critical Feminist Engagements*, London: RoutledgeFalmer.

Archer, L., Hutchings, M. and Ross, A. (2003) *Higher Education and Social Class: Issues of Exclusion and Inclusion*, London: RoutledgeFalmer.

Ball, S., Reay, D. and David, M. (2002) '"Ethnic choosing": minority ethnic students, social class and higher education choice', *Race, Ethnicity and Education*, 5(4): 333–58.

Blair, T. (2005) *Speech on Education*, given at 10 Downing Street on 24 October 2005 www.pm.gov.uk/output/Page8363.asp (accessed 29 March 2007).

Blair, T. (2006) *21st Century Public Services Speech*, 6 June 2006 www.pm.gov.uk/output/Page9564.asp (accessed 29 March 2007).

Blair, T. (2007) 'Keeping universities up to the mark', *The Telegraph*, 15 February.

Brooks, R. (2005) *Friendship and Educational Choice: Peer Influence and Planning for the Future*, Basingstoke: Palgrave.

Brooks, R. (2006a) *Young Graduates and Lifelong Learning*. End-of-award report for the ESRC. Available at: www.esrcsocietytoday.ac.uk (accessed 14 May 2007).

Brooks, R. (2006b) 'Young graduates and lifelong learning: the impact of institutional stratification', *Sociology*, 40(6): 1019–37.

Brooks, R. and Everett, G. (2008) 'The impact of higher education on lifelong learning', *International Journal of Lifelong Education*, 27(3).

Brown, P. (1997) 'Cultural capital and social exclusion: some observations on recent trends in education, employment and the labour market', in Halsey, A. H, Lauder, H., Brown, P. and Wells, A. (eds) *Education, Culture, Economy, Society*, Oxford: Oxford University Press.

Brown, P. and Lauder, H. (2006) 'Globalisation, knowledge and the myth of the magnet economy', *Globalisation, Societies and Education*, 4(1): 25–57.

Brown, P., Hesketh, A. and Williams, S. (2000) 'Employability in a knowledge economy', *Journal of Education and Work*, 16(2): 107–26.

Centre for Educational Research and Innovation (CERI) (2002) *Education at a Glance: OECD Indicators*, Paris: OECD Publications.

Crinson, I. (2005) 'The direction of health policy in New Labour's third term', *Critical Social Policy*, 25(4): 507–16.

Department for Education and Skills (DfES) (2003) *The Future of Higher Education* (Cm. 5735), Norwich: The Stationery Office.

Department for Education and Skills (DfES) (2007) *Raising Expectations: Staying in Education and Training Post-16* (Cm. 7065), London: The Stationery Office.

Dwyer, P. and Wyn, J. (2001) *Youth, Education and Risk: Facing the Future*, London: RoutledgeFalmer.

Gorard, S., Taylor, C. and Fitz, J. (2003) *Schools, Markets and Choice Policies*, London: RoutledgeFalmer.

Higher Education Funding Council for England (2006) *Strategic Plan 2006–11*, http://www.hefce.ac.uk/pubs/hefce/2006/06_13/ (accessed 28 March 2007).

Keep, E. and Rainbird, H. (2002) 'Towards the learning organization?, in Reeve, F., Cartwright, M. and Edwards, R. (eds) *Supporting Lifelong Learning, Volume 2: Organizing Learning*, London: RoutledgeFalmer.

Livingstone, D. W. (2002) 'Lifelong learning and underemployment in the knowledge society: a North American perspective', in Edwards, R., Miller, N., Small, N. and Tait, A. (eds) *Supporting Lifelong Learning, Volume 3: Making Policy Work*, London: RoutledgeFalmer.

National Committee of Enquiry into Higher Education (1997) *Higher Education in the Learning Society (The Dearing Report)*, London: HMSO. www.leeds.ac.uk/educol/ncihe (accessed 3 April 2007).

Newman, J. and Vidler, E. (2006) 'Discriminating customers, responsible patients, empowered users: consumerism and the modernisation of health care', *Journal of Social Policy*, 35(2): 193–210.

Pugsley, L. (2004) *The University Challenge: Higher Education Markets and Social Stratification*, Aldershot: Ashgate.

Purcell, K. and Elias, P. (2004) *Seven Years On: Graduate Careers in a Changing Labour Market*, London: The Higher Education Careers Services Unit.

Reay, D., David, M. and Ball, S. (2005) *Degrees of Choice: Social Class, Race and Gender in Higher Education*, London: Trentham Books.

Tomlinson, S. (2001) *Education in a Post-welfare Society*, Buckingham: Open University Press.

Walkerdine, V., Lucey, H. and Melody, J. (2001) *Growing Up Girl: Psychosocial Explorations of Gender and Class*, Basingstoke: Palgrave.

Williams, J. (1997) 'The discourse of access: the legitimation of selectivity', in Williams, J. (ed.) *Negotiating Access to Higher Education: The Discourse of Selectivity and Equity*, Buckingham: SRHE and Open University Press.

14 Higher education

A powerhouse for development in a neo-liberal age?

Rajani Naidoo

Introduction

In the context of the knowledge economy, higher education has been positioned by influential international organisations and powerful governments as one of the most important powerhouses for development and as an essential prerequisite for developing countries to escape a peripheral status in the global economy. While policy pronouncements abound, there is relatively little recent theoretical or empirical work which can be drawn on to contribute to an adequate understanding of the relationship between higher education and development. In this chapter, I hope to contribute to the development of a research agenda by challenging some of the assumptions underlying global policy shifts pertaining to higher education in developing countries. I will begin by raising questions about the underlying assumptions and unintended consequences of the current focus on higher education as an engine of development. I will then illustrate how these difficulties may be compounded by the implementation of a neo-liberal paradigm which advocates the entry of foreign and private providers through the operation of a global higher education market. In the final section, key issues about the development of a research agenda relating to capacity building of higher education in developing countries will be presented.

The links between higher education and development

Hegemonic ideological, political and economic forces associated with globalisation and the knowledge economy have positioned higher education in developing countries as a crucial site for social and economic development. This marks a dramatic transformation in the long-held policy that there should be little investment in higher education in developing countries since it was believed that higher education achieved few social returns compared with lower levels of education (Task Force on Higher Education in Developing Countries 2000). The view that has emerged in the 1990s from powerful governments and international organisations is that quality higher education, as an incubator for social and economic change, is central to decreasing the disparity between rich and poor nations. In the context of the knowledge economy, the ability of a country to compete successfully in the global context is seen to rely on the production of higher value-added products and services, which are in turn dependent on knowledge, especially scientific and technological knowledge, and on continual innovation (see, for example, Castells 2001). The rationale is that in a context in which knowledge-related products and services are valued at a premium, the ability to generate, utilise, access and transmit information rapidly across the globe will enable developing countries to utilise knowledge to 'leap-frog' over intermediate developmental stages and improve their positions in the global economy (Castells 2001). The World Bank's World Development Report exhibits an almost evangelical belief in the power of knowledge and states that 'knowledge is like light. Weightless and intangible, it can easily travel the world, enlightening the lives of people everywhere. Yet billions of people still live in the darkness of poverty – unnecessarily' (International Bank for Reconstruction and Development/World Bank 1999). In this context, higher education in developing countries has been positioned as a crucial site for the production, dissemination, and transfer of economically productive knowledge, innovation and technology (Carnoy 1994). Higher education institutions in developing countries are also expected to impart to students the skills, knowledge and dispositions related to innovation and the ability to 'learn how to learn' in tune with the demands of a changing global economy. According to the World Bank 'Higher education has never been as important to the developing world as it is now. It cannot guarantee rapid economic development but sustained progress is impossible without it' (Task Force on Higher Education in Developing Countries 2000: 19).

While this new-found appreciation of the importance of higher education in developing countries is to be welcomed, what is of concern is the implicit positioning of higher education by international organisations and governments as a panacea for decreasing the economic gulf between high and low income countries. Many of the assumptions appear to be based on an underlying faith that increasing and improving higher education will automatically lead to social and economic development. In addition, the possible unintended consequences of a focus on higher education are swept aside in policy discussions. I will briefly outline three areas of concern as illustrations of this phenomenon.

The first danger is that the intense focus on higher education as a site for transformation has the effect of reducing the multifaceted and historically constituted social, political and economic difficulties faced by developing countries. Specific internal factors are absent from such depictions, as is the more complex interaction between domestic conditions and external constraints, including the stratified structure of the world economy. The focus on higher education as an engine of change, taken together with the expectation that the strengthening of higher education should follow western models of reform, reflects a type of modernisation theory which emerged in the midst of the logic of the Cold War context in the social sciences in the United States and which offered an alternative to conflict and revolutionary models of national transformation (Miyoshi and Harootunian 2002). Within modernisation theory, western nations are perceived to be the ultimate measure of progress below which other nations are placed at various levels of hierarchy. While the modernisation school of thought has been criticised for its ethnocentric and a-historical stance (see, for example, Roberts and Hite 2000), the notion that developing countries are expected to 'catch up' with western nations by generally replicating western political, economic and social models of development remains highly influential. The focus on an internal social institution like universities as a site for transformation in the absence of an understanding of the interaction of social, political and economic factors at the global and national level is a limited one. In addition, analysts such as Ordorika (2006) have warned that productivity-driven higher education reforms emanating from western countries have homogenising effects and negative consequences for the developmental agenda of universities in low income countries.

A second difficulty is that when particular levels of education suddenly emerge and then disappear from development discourses and policies, they appear to ebb and flow in line with what is currently fashionable rather than in accord with evidence. It is therefore possible that the perception of higher education as a motor of development will result in a diversion of policy attention, and indeed funding, from other levels of education. There are indications that while primary and higher education remain an important topic in many African countries, secondary education appears to have dropped off the policy radar. Shurmer-Smith (2000: 37) has indicated that the privileging of higher education over primary education in India is indicated by the fact that the Indian government spends a minuscule amount on primary education as compared with its heavy investment in higher education. Clearly, given the interdependence of the different levels of education, a strategy that bifurcates, rather than joins up, the different levels of education is bound to be problematic.

Third, the faith in higher education as a motor of development relies heavily on the high skills thesis which states that for nation states to remain competitive in current economic conditions, a change in the nature of skills and its relationship to productivity is required. Higher levels of skill within the workforce in advanced economies are perceived to be a basic pre-requisite for economic activity to shift from the old Fordist and Taylorist paradigms into a new high skills mode of working. The argument is that the emphasis on value-added production through innovation and changes in technology require a configuration of skills that is at a substantially higher level and of a more generic kind than the technical competences required to perform specific occupational roles (see, for example, Dore 2000; Brown *et al.* 2001). However, this thesis, which is intimately linked with the role of higher education in development, has come under criticism by researchers who have pointed out that even in high income countries, high performance production systems and high skills regimes are not all-pervasive and widely distributed (see, for example, Kraak 2004). They assert that in reality in most countries Fordist mass-producing manufacturing, as well as low-skill labour intensive production, exists alongside high-skill production techniques. Other analysts such as Keep (1999) go further to argue that Fordist and post-Fordist modes of production continue to flourish in advanced economies particularly in the United States of America and the United Kingdom as they are based on the expansion of low-skilled, low-cost jobs which give a certain competitive advantage. According to these analysts, the reality of high-skill production strategies is that it only occurs in a few sectors in the leading advanced economies. If this is the case in advanced economies, then the uncritical acceptance of the high skills thesis for developing countries, where skills polarities are even greater, is highly problematic. Indeed, as Ashton (2004) has pointed out, the incorporation of a low skills development strategy may be viewed positively in developing countries since it could lead to labour intensive forms of employment and help alleviate mass unemployment (Ashton 2004). A development strategy built around the interlocking potential of low, intermediate and high skills to allow for greater variability and unevenness is thus a persuasive one (Kraak 2004) and has implications for a mixture of investment strategies in higher and other levels of education.

The global restructuring of higher education

While an understanding of the concerns raised above and a tempering of the utopian vision of higher education is necessary, at the same time the importance of higher education to the economic, political and social development strategies of all nation states is clearly beyond dispute. The strengthening of higher education in developing countries in the context of appropriate macro social, economic and political policies is therefore extremely important. However, what is also clear is that there are many obstacles to achieving this vision. There is, for example, compelling evidence that policy decisions by powerful global regulators such as the World Bank have contributed to the systematic under-development of higher education (Samof and Bidemi 2004). It is reported, for example, that the World Bank called a conference of African Vice Chancellors in Harare, Zimbabwe in 1986 with the intention of persuading them to close down universities in independent Africa (Mamdani 2006). When this was not successful, the World Bank embarked on a strategy of conditional aid which compelled governments to disinvest in higher education. The origins and specific features of the difficulties facing universities in developing countries such as the colonial and post-colonial origins of the university system, the effects of structural adjustment policies, international pressures on developing countries to downsize the state as well as political and economic instability are important to take into consideration in devising contemporary policies (see Sawyerr, undated). The World Bank has reported that university systems in many developing countries are in crisis. They are characterised by increasing demand, a lack of basic physical resources such as classrooms, a small number of skilled and committed academic and administrative staff and the absence of academic resources such as journals and basic scientific equipment (Task Force on Higher Education in Developing Countries 2000).

Despite the multifaceted causes for the weak condition of higher education, the solution proposed by powerful international organisations and western governments has been for governments to create the necessary market conditions for foreign and private higher education institutions to operate in developing countries. These prescriptions can be seen to be closely related to the neo-liberal restructuring of higher education in advanced economic states.

The transition of neo-liberalism from a theory of economic behaviour to its widespread adoption as a framework for governing society has been well documented (see, for example, Peters 2001). Bourdieu (1998) has referred to neo-liberalism as 'doxa', by which he means an unquestionable orthodoxy that operates at all levels of society, from individual perceptions and practices to state policy, as if it were the objective truth. At the most basic level, neo-liberalism rests on the assumption that market competition is an essential prerequisite for a democratic society. The state develops into what Cerny (1990) has termed the 'competitive' state which sees its primary objective as one of fostering a competitive national economy by promoting and maximising returns from market forces in international settings while abandoning some of the core functions of the welfare state. However, unlike classical liberalism with its central philosophy of the freedom of the individual from state interference, neo-liberalism envisions a positive role for the state in facilitating the workings of a market and in developing institutions and individuals that are competitive and responsive to market forces (Olssen *et al.* 2004).

While neo-liberalism developed in the west and operated mainly at a national level, it has also gained ascendancy in the rest of the world. The pressures applied by powerful international organisations such as the World Bank, the International Monetary Fund (IMF) and the World Trade Organisation (WTO) on developing countries to roll back state provision, deregulate domestic markets and open up to international trade and competition have been well documented. More recently, institutions such as the World Bank have moved away from aggressive policies of economic liberalisation to a more subtle and critical role in the global embedding of neo-liberalism (Griffin 2006). Fine (2004) has characterised the World Bank's current stance as the recognition that both markets and institutions are important and that both must be the targets of economic and social policy. This enables the Bank to address both economic and social policies, particularly around issues of good governance. While market solutions are still perceived as central to effective development strategies (Kempner and Jurema 2002), the negative conception of the state's role in development has now been replaced by a more positive conception of the state in creating the appropriate conditions for the market to function. Rather than directing or providing public services, the state is expected to act as a facilitator for global market integration. These pressures on developing countries can be seen to match a vision of world order promoted by advanced capitalist countries which is based on a template of limited state intervention and a minimally regulated global market as the most effective and efficient guarantee of economic growth.

The global restructuring of higher education may be seen to be following neo-liberal paradigms. In many high income countries, the 'social compact' that evolved between higher education, the state and society over the last century (Marginson and Considine 2000) has been eroded. These changes may be seen to be part of a broader policy shift away from the Keynesian welfare state settlement towards a neo-liberal one which introduced mechanisms of the market and new managerialism into higher education. Researchers such as Dill (1997), Deem (2001) and Naidoo (2003a) have indicated how the development of quasi-markets linked to managerialist frameworks in higher education have altered relations within and between institutions as well as the nature of rewards and sanctions in academic life. The assumption of such frameworks is that competition within and between higher education institutions for limited resources will produce a more effective and efficient higher education system and that new managerial modes of governance which measure, compare and evaluate academic work will improve the performance of academics.

Neo-liberal market oriented reform, particularly in the form of privatisation and commercialisation, has also been implemented in developing countries. Researchers have noted that as a result of debt obligations and conditionalities attached to loans and structural adjustment programmes, international bureaucracies particularly the Bretton Woods institutions act as 'parallel governments' (see Torres and Schugurensky 2002). A diagnosis of the problems faced by developing countries and the prescriptions to solve them are often imposed on developing countries by high income countries and powerful organisations such as the World Bank. In relation to higher education, public spending has in general been discouraged, regulation is perceived as a market barrier while competition, privatisation, user fees and the attraction of private and foreign providers has been encouraged. The WTO's trade liberalisation agreement, the General Agreement on Trade in Services (GATS), which comprises a set of multi-lateral rules, has included higher education as a potential service sector. A major aim of the GATS is to identify and break down barriers to trade in higher education by reducing state regulation over higher education (Knight 2003). The effects of the GATS is therefore likely to accelerate the trends transforming developing countries into important new markets that can be invested in by private and foreign providers operating on a global scale.

Asymmetrical trade in higher education

The above trends are likely to create the conditions for the operation of a global market of higher education. The neo-liberal restructuring of higher education in high income countries is likely to reform academic values and pedagogic and research relationships to comply with market frameworks. Rationales for the provision of cross-border higher education include the development of cross-cultural and cross-national links between countries, capacity building in developing countries and in a historical context, the nurturing of allies during the cold war period (see Altbach 2002). However, the rationale that appears to be in ascendance in the light of fiscal and other pressures impacting on higher education institutions in high income countries appears to be that of revenue generating at the institutional level and the generation of trade surpluses at the national level (Larson *et al.* 2002; Larson and Vincent-Lancrin 2003).

Strong regulation, as well as the relative saturation of the higher education market in industrialised countries in the context of enormous financial pressures has led to universities in high income countries viewing developing countries as important new markets. In addition, the development of a global higher education market is aided by an influx of new providers. The profitability of learning has resulted in the rise of non-university providers including global consortia involving governments and corporations (CVCP 2000). Commentators have noted that the amount invested and the number of participants involved in non-public sector providers such as corporate universities is at least equal to levels in the traditional higher education sector (see, for example, Paton and Taylor 2002). The market in learning has also attracted for-profit private institutions which has coincided with the relaxation of state regulation in a number of countries over the recognition of degree granting institutions (see Naidoo 2003b). Developing countries have become important destinations for these new providers and the sector is growing in Africa, Jordan, Malaysia, Vietnam, China, Thailand and Indonesia. The Philippines, for example, has the most established for-profit sector in Asia (Philippines Commission on Higher Education 2003). The sector is also growing throughout Latin America with for-profit institutions constituting approximately 44 per cent of all institutions in Brazil (McCowan 2004). The factors that have been mentioned above have also led to e-learning being perceived as a viable learning mode and online courses and providers of virtual higher education are likely to view developing countries which have the required infrastructure as lucrative markets.

Proponents of a global market in higher education have argued that global competition in higher education will lead to better quality, greater responsiveness and lower costs since developing countries will be able to exert consumer choice and choose the most appropriate providers and programmes relevant to their needs (Tooley 2001; Vincent-Lancrin 2005). However, studies conducted on the relationship between the local and the global in the European context indicate that these may be based on a number of factors including amongst others finance, knowledge and technology, oligopolies and state power (see, for example, Amin and Thrift 2004). This is likely to be even more so in the case of developing countries. Theories attempting to explain the stratification of the global economy such as world systems theory (see, for example, Wallerstein 2004) or the categories of 'core', 'semiperiphery' and 'periphery' used by Payne (2005) indicate that countries exist in a complex web of global power relations which result in different degrees of national self-determination and an unequal exchange of goods and services. In this scenario, high income countries will be positioned as providers of educational products. Developing countries, with the exception of rapidly growing economies such as India and China, will not be in a position to participate in this global market as providers of higher education and will instead be cast in the position of vulnerable consumers.

The terms under which many developing countries participate as consumers in the global market of higher education is also likely to be constrained by the operation of international organisations which set the 'rules' of the global marketplace. Clearly, the weighted voting in the IMF and the World Bank favours rich countries. However, concern has also been expressed about unequal relations of power in relation to the WTO, where negotiations rather than voting provide a basis for policy decisions and agreements. Many developing countries argue that the negotiation process is controlled by the developed economies, in particular the United States, Japan, the European Union and Canada (see Robertson and Dale 2003). In addition, reports of exclusion from key negotiations and bullying and 'rough treatment' have also been made (Jawara and Kwa 2003). In addition, writers such as Mundy (1998) have reported the rise of 'defensive' and 'disciplinary' forms of educational multilateralism. She notes how advanced countries have begun to heighten their involvement in forms of multilateralism that equip them with the defences to compete more effectively in a global marketplace while at the same time shutting out developing countries. Chossudovsky (1998: 37, cited in Arocena and Sutz 2005) has aptly coined the term 'market colonialism' to characterise the relations between high and low income countries in a context of neo-liberalism. This term refers to new forms of economic and political domination which advanced capitalist-led international agencies and countries unleash onto the governments and citizens of developing countries through what they portray as the 'neutral' interplay of market forces in the global arena.

While the implementation of a neo-liberal market framework and the influx of foreign and private providers may bring benefits, there are also numerous pitfalls. A major concern is that the building of indigenous capacity in higher education may be stalled and that governments will be prevented from steering higher education systems towards the attainment of key developmental goals. The operation of international organisations such as the WTO is likely to rupture the relationship between governments and national systems of higher education in developing countries (see Robertson *et al.* 2002). Prescriptions such as the 'most favoured nation treatment' rule which seek to eliminate barriers to trade and which require equal and consistent treatment of all foreign partners may mean that foreign and for-profit providers could be eligible for the same grants and subsidies as national public providers. GATS could therefore result in a curtailment of government ability to fund or strategically direct national systems of higher education (Kelk and Worth 2002). Governments in developing countries may also lose leverage in the face of a heavy reliance on foreign providers who are likely to exert a direct influence on the terms of provision and an indirect effect on the development of policy. In addition, as shown above, international organisations such as the IMF and the World Bank have the potential to diminish the capacity of governments to steer higher education by exerting pressure on governments to reduce state regulation and allow a more free interplay of market forces. While this raises complex questions for all countries, it has been argued that the protection of the social, political and cultural functions of higher education, encapsulated in the notion of the 'public good', is particularly important in countries which have undergone social transformation and where democratic dispensations may be fragile (see, for example, Singh 2002; Badat 2001). Further dangers, as I shall show in the following sections, are present when we scrutinise possible effects on teaching and research.

Proliferation of irrelevant and low quality programmes

The influx of new providers who perceive higher education mainly as an income-generation activity may lead to a proliferation of low-quality programmes in developing countries, particularly those with weak regulation. The assumption that the operation of a global market will secure quality (see, for example, Tooley 2000) has been undermined by evidence that the proliferation of for-profit higher education has led to an increasing number of low-quality 'diploma mills' (Knight 2003). A further argument against the assumption that the market will control quality is the fact that demand is not merely related to quality but also to cost. An illustrative example is presented by McCowan (2004) who has indicated that a number of institutions that are widely regarded to be of low quality in Brazil have achieved growth simply because there is no geographical or financial alternative for large numbers of the population. In addition, skilful branding and advertising can enhance demand even when quality is low, particularly in the case of students and families who do not have the requisite cultural capital to decode corporate advertising strategies.

Pressures on public and not-for-profit private higher education institutions in high income countries may also lead to a decline in the quality of the learning experience offered to students in developing countries. The increasing hierarchisation and stratification of higher education systems in high income countries as a result of government policies which are reconfiguring systems in a marketising milieu are likely to be reproduced in the relationship between high and low income countries. The relative saturation of the higher education market, as well as strong regulatory frameworks governing provision in high income countries may lead to universities' protecting the quality of core on-campus provision in their home countries while viewing developing countries with weak regulation as mass markets for lower cost learning (see, for example, Noble 2002; Altbach 2002). In addition, in a neo-liberal context, the use of information and communications technology which can benefit learning by helping students learn at their own pace and by creating virtual communities of learners across geographic distances may simply become another tool for the global commodification and standardisation of higher education. In addition, many virtual learning providers, who have made the required investment in e-learning including heavy investment in the technological infrastructure, become keen to expand their numbers of virtual students in order to spread their costs by borrowing mass production techniques to deliver teaching and assessment.

The reduction of costs by public institutions as well as private and virtual providers operating in developing countries may be achieved primarily by focusing on scale rather than quality or relevance. The temptation will therefore be to disseminate off-the-shelf standardised products and generic content produced in the providing country which may be irrelevant or inappropriate to the context of developing countries. The above developments have resulted in commentators from the developing world, such as Moja and Cloete (2001), warning that weak regulation and the perception of higher education as a lucrative global export may lead to developing countries becoming mass markets for the dumping of low quality knowledge, similar to the way that they have been dumping grounds for out-of-date medication and other industrial products. Concerns have been raised that this form of teaching may erode the role of higher education as a reservoir of national culture, may displace local knowledge and may channel forms of cultural imperialism, particularly from the United States of America and the United Kingdom.

These strategies are also likely to result in pedagogic and assessment procedures which may be detrimental to developing high level intellectual skills, necessary for successful participation of Southern states in the global knowledge economy. There is, for example, likely to be a large reliance on learning resources which simply provide information to students. Commentators on the type of high quality learning required for the knowledge economy specify that while first order learning may be open to standardisation, more advanced second order learning is unpredictable and requires exposure to uncertainty and risk taking (Seltzer and Bentley 1999). Such learning requires pedagogical relationships of interaction and trust and the space for teachers to adjust what they do to the needs of students, as well as group interaction, which develops social and interpersonal skills. In addition, research on effective learning has indicated the importance of using a variety of feedback mechanisms to help students learn in a developmental way, rather than applying summative assessment systems such as computerised multiple choice tests. However, the requirements mentioned above are unlikely to be met since many providers base their provision on a mechanistic model of learning predicated on the need to deliver information quickly and cheaply to students.

Under such conditions, students may become alienated from the learning process. This may result in a loss of responsibility for their learning, an instrumental attitude and little tolerance for the expansion of study beyond the routine. Learning for them may be transformed into a process of digesting and reproducing an unconnected series of short, neatly packaged segments of information. Rather than gaining access to powerful forms of knowing and knowledge, many students in developing countries may therefore receive an education that has been reduced to narrowly defined core competencies which may stunt their intellectual development and affect their disposition and motivation towards lifelong learning.

Research dependency

In his address to the Conference of Commonwealth Education Ministers in December 2006, Mahmood Mamdani, who worked in higher education institutions in Africa before taking up a post as Professor of Government at Columbia University in the United States of America, spoke eloquently of the need for research to be an integral component of higher education in countries with a recent colonial past. His argument was that, without the capacity for research, a country cannot be in a position to make meaningful choices. In his view, the failure to develop a local research base would mean that both problems as well as solutions would come to resemble 'ideologically defined off the shelf offers' (Mamdani 2006). Furthermore, the development of a strong research base is also crucial if developing countries are to compete in a global knowledge economy.

However, the dominance of western hegemonic research models and concerns as well as assessment systems for research in developing countries which generally emulate the criteria in high income countries may serve as a barrier to national research strategies which aim to explore an optimum relationship between the developmental role of the university and the wider internationalisation role generally ascribed to higher education.

In their extensive research on partnerships between African and western institutions, Samof and Bidemi (2004) have noted that academic partnerships are often one-sided. Their conclusions are that researchers from high income countries frame, organise and validate the academic enterprise which positions research partners from developing countries as research dependent. The development of a global market in higher education based on performance and productivity measures set by western universities and encapsulated in global league tables acts as a powerful mechanism that not merely places national systems of higher education in a global hierarchy but also compels universities in developing countries to meet the same criteria (see Ordorika 2006). In addition, pressures for the marketisation of research, including the greater prioritisation of research for commercial development (McSherry 2001), have also been applied to developing countries. Latin American researchers have indicated that the development policies promoted by international organisations led to the displacement of research for the generation of knowledge by an 'exaggerated adaptation to market demands' (Orozco 1998, cited in Arocena and Sutz 2005). Researchers from developing countries have also argued that the 'triple helix' model developed in the context of high income countries which advocates relations between universities, industry and government may not be appropriate to all higher education institutions in all developing countries. The suggestion is that in national contexts where industries are unwilling to fund research and development and may not have sufficient capacity to utilise research findings, it is crucially important for higher education institutions to develop strong relationships with other stakeholders including public sector and community organisations (see, for example, Arocena and Sutz 2000; Subotzky 1999). The standardisation effect of hegemonic models on higher education systems in developing countries and commodifying tendencies therefore have the potential to drive universities in developing countries away from research that contributes to national social, economic and political developmental goals. In addition, given the infrastructure needed and the amount of time required to realise the returns on financial investments, foreign and private providers, particularly for-profit ones, have not shown a great deal of interest in engaging in research investments (Teixeira and Amaral 2001).

In addition, little interest has been shown in offering programmes to build indigenous research capacity such as research degrees at postgraduate level or doctoral level work. In a marketised higher education system, fee-based Masters and postgraduate Diploma programmes based primarily on coursework hold the promise of economies of scale. In addition, there are indications that institutions have begun to shorten the length of programmes and reduce pedagogical contact so as to reduce provider costs and make programmes appear more attractive to students who wish to obtain a degree in as short a time as possible. Marginson (2001) has argued that such courses are often hard to distinguish from undergraduate courses and may in fact be augmenting credentialism rather then developing national capacity through the training of new generations of indigenous researchers.

Towards a research agenda

One of the major difficulties for researchers and policy makers is that there are few theoretical models or empirical datasets to interrogate the relationship between higher education and development in low income countries. Clearly, in a globalised world, such work will need to incorporate an analysis of the changing relationship between high and low income countries as well as an analysis of the impact and responses to the global restructuring of higher education along neo-liberal lines. Frameworks such as the 'glonacal agency heuristic' developed by Simon Marginson and Gary Rhoades, which emphasise the simultaneous significance of global, national and local forces, offer a powerful conceptual frame (Marginson and Rhoades, 2002). What is needed, however, is to link such theories to broader theories of development, including some of the important concepts of Amartya Sen. His 'human capabilities' concept, which measures development by the capacity of people to do and be what they value, as counterposed to merely focusing on narrow measures of income, offers important possibilities (Sen 1999). A critical appraisal of development theories such as 'dependency' and 'world systems' theory, which acted as important correctives to theories of modernisation, but which emerged under very different economic, social and political contexts, needs to be conducted to determine to what extent they have purchase under changing contemporary conditions. For example, new power relations and webs of interdependencies have been created by the movement of China and India from poor countries to rapidly growing economies. Bach and colleagues (2006) for example, have put forward the thesis that China's movement from a 'command and control' to a regulatory state has given it the potential to set clear market rules at home and leverage its own market to export these rules internationally. In addition, within developing regions themselves there may be a replication of unequal core–periphery relations. A policy debate has emerged for example on the role of China in Africa with some observers labelling China as a 'new colonialist power' while others refer to China's activities as South–South collaboration against western dominance. In addition, work such as that of Robinson (1998) and Sklair (2001) on the emergence of a transnational class, which includes the appropriation of elite fractions of developing countries, must also be taken into consideration.

Theoretical and empirical interrogations of the consequences of linking higher education to neo-liberal models of development is also required. It is important to recognise and incorporate shifts in neo-liberal thinking within such analyses. Fine (2004), for example, has argued that that older models of neo-liberal economics which treated economic and social phenomena as if they were equivalent to a perfectly functioning market has been superseded by a new type of development economics. This new approach, while retaining the principle of methodological individualism, perceives markets and the economic as imperfect and puts forward the need for the inclusion of the social and the non-economic. It is also important to restate that there is a lack of evidence to support the assumption that an unregulated market will lead to the development of high-quality higher education. Research conducted in other sectors shows no inverse relationship between strong trade regulation and economic growth, particularly given the case that this is routinely practised by rich western nations. Analysts from developing countries have therefore argued that the presumption of openness in all areas of the economy is not only untested but forecloses some development strategies that have worked in the past and others that could work in the future. Indeed, countries which are held up as models of rapid economic growth, for example, the East Asian emerging economies, initially followed a 'developmental state' strategy by subverting neo-liberal market principles and retaining protectionism in many areas of the economy (Subotzky 1999).

A useful research strategy may be to avoid setting up market and state provision as alternative and dichotomous arenas but rather to research the evolving relations between the two. Research which focuses on how policy can shape the relationship between the domestic and foreign sectors in order to build capacity is vitally important. This is particularly important given evidence that the assumption that public universities by their very nature will automatically contribute to capacity building is likely to be misplaced. Research on the role of universities in industrialised, developing and transitional countries has indicated that universities have played multiple roles, sometimes contributing to the transformation of societies and at other times reproducing unequal relations in society and often doing both simultaneously (Brennan *et al.* 2004). Studies need to be conducted on how policy and regulatory frameworks may be able to foster collaboration, competition or functional differentiation between domestic, foreign, public and private providers and which functions of the higher education system need to be publicly funded and protected. In addition, closer attention needs to be paid to the implementation of new regulatory mechanisms which are evolving to shape the operation of markets in higher education and to protect higher education through rules and sanctions. However, it would also be useful to focus on the extent to which market forces may be shaped through incentives so that institutions contribute to developmental goals. An argument that has been presented in the South African context is that just as publicly funded universities are urged to become more entrepreneurial, foreign and private providers could also be required to contribute to the public good (Kruss and Kraak 2003). In addition, Arocena and Sutz (2000) in the context of Uruguay have also suggested that developing countries go beyond the state–market dichotomy and make room for 'bottom-up' processes and associative networks in an attempt to include social actors who are generally excluded.

Finally, however, perhaps the most important area for research is the extent to which low income countries are able to exert self-determination in the building of capacity in higher education in their own countries. Research needs to be conducted and disseminated on possible alternative models of linking higher education and development and alternative models of transnational partnerships. Countries need to be free to deviate from neo-liberal models and follow variable pathways depending on particular domestic conditions and developmental trajectories. An updated and critical analysis of the extent to which higher education policy is influenced by dominant countries and organisations and the impact of such policies on capacity building in higher education needs to be undertaken. It may also be necessary to develop better defence mechanisms to resist such pressures, particularly through greater engagement and collaboration amongst developing countries themselves.

References

Altbach, P. G. (2002) 'Knowledge and education as international commodities?' *International Higher Education*, 28: 2–5, The Boston College for International Higher Education.

Amin, A. and Thrift, N. (eds) (2004) *Globalisation, Institutions, and Regional Development in Europe*, Oxford: Oxford University Press.

Arocena, R. and Sutz, J. (2000) 'Interactive learning spaces and development policies in Latin America', DRUID Working Chapter No 00-13. www.druid.dk/wp/pdf_files/00-13.pdf (accessed 10 June 2007).

Arocena, R. and Sutz, J. (2005) 'Latin American universities: from an original revolution to an uncertain transition', *Higher Education*, 50: 573–92.

Ashton, D. (2004) 'High skills: the concept and its application to South Africa', in McGrath, S., Badroodien, A., Kraak, A. and Unwin, L. (eds) *Shifting Understandings of Skills in South Africa: Overcoming the Historical Imprint of a Low Skills Regime*, Pretoria: Human Science Research Council Press.

Bach, D., Newman, A. L. and Weber, S. (2006) 'The international implications of China's fledgling regulatory state: from product maker to rule maker', *New Political Economy*, 11(4): 499–518.

Badat, S. (2001) 'Transforming South African higher education: paradoxes, policy and choices, interests and constraints', Paper to the Salzburg seminar symposium on Higher Education in Emerging Economies, Salzburg, 7–11 July.

Bourdieu, P. (1998) *Acts of Resistance: Against the Tyranny of the Market*, New York: New Press.

Brennan, J., King, R. and Lebeau, Y. (2004) *The Role of Universities in the Transformation of Societies: Synthesis Report*, London: Association of Commonwealth Universities and the Open University.

Brown, P., Green, A. and Lauder, H. (2001) *High Skills: Globalisation, Competitiveness, and Skill*, Oxford: University Press.

Carnoy, M. (1994) 'Universities, technological change and training in the information age', in Salmi, J. and Verspoor, A. M. (eds) *Revitalising Higher Education*, New York: Pergamon/IAU Press.

Castells, M. (2001) 'Information technology and global development', in Muller, J., Cloete, N. and Badat, S. (eds) *Challenges of Globalisation: South African Debates with Manuel Castells*, Cape Town: Maskew Miller/Longman.

Cerny, P. G. (1990) *The Changing Architecture of Politics: Structure, Agency and the Future of the State*, London: Sage.

Chossudovsky, M. (1998) *The Globalisation of Poverty: Impacts of IMF and World Bank Reforms*, New York: Zed Books.

CVCP (2000) *The Business of Borderless Higher Education: United Kingdom Perspectives*, London: Committee of Vice-Chancellors and Principals.

Deem, R. (2001) 'Globalisation, new managerialism, academic capitalism and entrepreneurialism in universities: is the local dimension still important?', *Comparative Education*, 37(1): 7–20.

Dill, D. D. (1997) 'Higher education markets and public policy', *Higher Education Policy*, 10: 167–85.

Dore, R. (2000) *Stock Market Capitalism: Welfare Capitalism – Japan and Germany versus the Anglo-Saxons*, Oxford: Oxford University Press.

Fine, B. (2004) 'Examining the role of globalisation and development critically: what role for political economy', *New Political Economy*, 9(2): 214–31.

Griffin, P. (2006) 'The World Bank', *New Political Economy*, 11(4): 572–81.

Gumport, P. J. (2000) 'Academic restructuring: organisational change and institutional imperatives', *Higher Education*, 39(1): 67–91.

Hall, M. (2001) 'Education and the margins of the network society', in Muller, J. Cloete, N. and Badat, S. (eds) *Challenges of Globalisation: South African Debates with Manuel Castells*, Cape Town: Maskew Miller/Longman.

International Bank for Reconstruction and Development/World Bank (1999) *World Development Report: Knowledge for Development*, Washington, DC: World Bank.

Jawara, F. and Kwa, A. (2003) *Behind the Scenes: Power Politics in the WTO*, New York: Zed Books.

Keep, E. (1999) 'UK's VET policy and the third way: following a high skills trajectory or running up a dead end street?', *Journal of Education and Work*, 12(3) 323–46.

Kelk, S. and Worth, J. (2002) *Trading it Away: How GATS Threatens UK Higher Education*, Oxford: People and Planet.

Kempner, K. and Jurema, A. L. (2002) 'The global politics of education: Brazil and the World Bank', *Higher Education*, 43: 331–54.

Knight, J. (2003) 'GATS, trade and higher education: perspective 2003 – where are we?', Observatory on Borderless Higher Education Report, January.

Kraak, A. (2004) 'Rethinking the high skills thesis in South Africa', in McGrath, S., Badroodien, A., Kraak, A. and Unwin, L. (eds) *Shifting Understandings of Skills in South Africa: Overcoming the Historical Imprint of a Low Skills Regime*, Pretoria: Human Science Research Council Press.

Kruss, G. and Kraak, A. (eds) (2003) *A Contested Good?: Understanding Private Higher Education in South Africa*, Boston, MA: Boston College Center for International Higher Education and 'Perspectives in Education', South Africa.

Larson, K. and Vincent-Lancrin, S. (2003) 'The learning business: can trade in international education work?', *The OECD Observer*, 235, December.

Larson, K., Martin, J. P. and Morris, R. (2002) *Trade in Educational Services: Trends and Emerging Issues*, Paris: Organisation for Economic Co-operation and Development.

Levis, K. (2003) 'Universities online. The new business model?', Paper presented to Universities Challenged: New Strategies and Business Models Conference, London, 4 December.

Levy, D. (2003) 'Expanding higher education capacity through private growth', Observatory on Borderless Higher Education Report, January.

Mamdani, M. (2006) 'Higher education, the state and the marketplace', Talk presented to the Conference of Commonwealth Ministers of Education, Cape Town, South Africa, 12 December.

Marginson, S. (2001) 'Knowledge economy and knowledge culture', Paper for National Scholarly Communications Forum, ANU, 9 August.

Marginson, S. and Considine, M. (2000) *The Enterprise University: Power, Governance and Reinvention in Australia*, Cambridge: Cambridge University Press.

Marginson, S. and Rhoades, G. (2002) 'Beyond national states, markets, and systems of higher education: a glonacal agency heuristic', *Higher Education*, 43(3): 281–309.

McCowan, T. (2004) 'The growth of private higher education in Brazil: implications for equity and quality', *Journal of Education Policy*, 19(4): 453–72.

McSherry, C. (2001) *Who Owns Academic Work: Battling for Control of Intellectual Property*, Cambridge, MA: Harvard University Press.

Miyoshi, M. and Harootunian, H. D. (eds) (2002) *Learning Spaces: The Afterlives of Area Studies*, Durham, NC: Duke University Press.

Moja, T. and Cloete, N. (2001) 'Vanishing borders and new boundaries', in Muller, J., Cloete, N. and Badat, S. (eds) *Challenges of Globalisation: South African Debates with Manuel Castells*, Cape Town: Maskew Miller/Longman.

Mundy, K. (1998) 'Educational multilateralism and world (dis)order', *Comparative Education Review I*, 42(4): 448–78.

Naidoo, R. (2003a) 'Repositioning higher education as a global commodity: opportunities and challenges for future sociology of education work', *British Journal of Sociology of Education*, 24(2): 249–59.

Naidoo, R. (2003b) 'A comparative survey of the criteria and process for the use of the title "university" across six countries', Paper commissioned by the Higher Education Policy Institute, Oxford.

Naidoo, R. and Jamieson, I. M. (2004) 'Knowledge in the marketplace: the global commodification of teaching and learning', in Innes, P. and Hellsten, M. (eds) *Internationalizing Higher Education: Critical Perspectives for Critical Times*, Springer/CERC.

Noble, D. F. (2002) 'Rehearsal for the revolution', in Robins K. and Webster F. (eds) *The Virtual University*, Oxford: Oxford University Press.

Olssen, M., O'Neill, A.-M. and Codd, J. (2004) *Education Policy: Globalisation, Citizenship and Democracy*, London: Sage.

Ordorika, I. (2006) 'Commitment to society: contemporary challenges for public research universities', Presented at UNESCO Forum on Higher Education Research and Knowledge, 29 November.

Orozco, L. E. (1998) 'La reforma de la educación Colombia: balance crítico', in Mendes, C. (ed.) *Autores Associados*, 269–91.

Paton, R. and Taylor, S. (2002) 'Corporate universities: between higher education and the workplace', in Williams, G. (ed.) *The Enterprising University*, Buckingham: SRHE/Open University Press.

Payne, A. (2005) *The Global Politics of Unequal Development*, Basingstoke: Palgrave Macmillan.

Peters, M. A. (2001) *Post-Structuralism, Marxism and Neoliberalism: Between Theory and Politics*, New York: Roman and Littlefield.

Philippines Commission on Higher Education (2002) Higher Education Statistical Bulletin.

Roberts, J. T. and Hite, A. (2000) *From Modernisation to Globalisation: Social Perspectives on International Development*, Oxford: Blackwell.

Robertson, S. and Dale, R. (2003) 'This is what the fuss is about! The implications of GATS for education systems in the North and the South', Globalisation and Europeanisation Network in Education, http://www.genie-tn.net (accessed 20 August 2006).

Robertson, S., Bonal, X. and Dale, R. (2002) 'GATS and the education service industry: the politics of scale and global re-territorialization', *Comparative Education Review*, 46(4): 472–96.

Robinson, W. I. (1998) 'Beyond nation state paradigms: globalisation, sociology and the challenge of transnational studies', *Sociological Forum*, 13(4): 561–94.

Samof, J. and Bidemi, C. (2004) 'Promise of partnership and continuities of dependence: external support to higher education in Africa', *African Studies Review*, 47(1): 67–199.

Sawyerr, A. (undated) 'Challenges facing African universities: selected issues' Association of African Universities www.africanstudies.org/ChallengesFacing AfricanUniversities. pdf (accessed 10 June 2007).

Seltzer, K. and Bentley, T. (1999) *The Creative Age: Knowledge and Skills for the New Economy*, London: Demos.

Sen, A. (1999) *Development as Freedom*, Oxford: Oxford University Press.

Shurmer-Smith, P. (2001) *India: Globalisation and Change*, London: Arnold.

Singh, M. (2001) 'Reinserting the public good into higher education' *Council for Higher Education Discussion Series*, 1: 7–22.

Sklair, L. (2001) *The Transnational Capitalist Class*, Oxford: Blackwell.

Subotzky, G. (1999) 'Alternatives to the entrepreneurial university: new modes of knowledge production in community service programs', *Higher Education*, 38(4): 401–40.

Task Force on Higher Education in Developing Countries (convened by UNESCO and the World Bank) (2000) 'Higher education in developing countries: peril and promise'. http://www.tfhe.net/report/overview.htm (accessed 10 June 2007).

Teixeira, P. and Amaral, A. (2001) 'Private higher education and diversity: an exploratory survey', *Higher Education Quarterly*, 55(4): 359–95.

Tooley, J. (2000) *Reclaiming Education*, London: Cassell.

Tooley, J. (2001) *The Global Education Industry: Lessons from Private Education in Developing Countries*, 2nd edition, London: Institute of Economic Affairs.

Torres, C. A. and Schugurensky, D. (2002) 'The political economy of higher education in the era of neoliberal globalisation: Latin America in comparative perspective', *Higher Education*, 43: 429–55.

Vincent-Lancrin, S. (2005) 'Building capacity through cross-border tertiary education', Observatory on Borderless Higher Education Report, April. http://www.obhe. ac.uk/products/reports/pdf/March2005.pdf (accessed 9 June 2007).

Wallerstein, I. M. (2004) *World Systems Analysis: An Introduction*, Durham, NC and London: Duke University Press.

15 Shaping the global market of higher education through quality promotion[1]

Gigliola Mathisen

Introduction

This chapter will explore how multilateral organisations[2] have contributed to the shaping of a global market of higher education. Organisations such as the World Trade Organisation's General Agreement on Trade in Services (GATS), the United Nations Educational, Scientific and Cultural Organisation (UNESCO) and the Organisation for Economic Cooperation and Development (OECD), each represent different approaches to higher education. Each of these international organisations has translated its approach into its organisational structures and practices. Multilateral initiatives in some cases promote a market in higher education. In other cases, initiatives can be seen as reactions to this growing global market, which seek to challenge a narrow instrumental approach to higher education. Several initiatives represent attempts to limit the global market by establishing quality requirements, thus attempting to restrict liberalisation.

This chapter demonstrates that policies on higher education at the global level were first characterised in market terms through the World Trade Organisation's service agreement (GATS). Gradually, unregulated trade in higher education services was seen to pose potential threats. The risks of the market were seen to imply a deterioration of higher education and a reduction in quality. The logic of the market could not secure the quality of higher education and 'protect students and other stakeholders from low-quality provision and disreputable providers' (UNESCO/OECD 2005). This recognition generated processes for promoting quality and was built into new initiatives that UNESCO developed jointly with the OECD. This extraordinary collaboration was given expression through a set of guidelines established for structuring the market. The three organisations that are the centre of attention in this chapter played an important role, separately or together, in shaping the global market for higher education and in creating conditions for markets to develop. How the three multilaterals interacted will be illustrated through the example of Norway and its efforts to support initiatives to shape the global market of higher education. Interestingly, Norway seems to have a double strategy towards higher education. On the one hand, Norway had a long practice of stressing public governance in major sectors such as higher education and declaring education as a public good. On the other hand, Norway approves broad commitments to GATS, which makes higher education subject to trade within a system where many national regulations are considered obstacles to trade (Mathisen 2006).

This chapter is based on data collected from the public documents concerning the policy processes that are described. The account of the UNESCO/OECD process is in particular based on documentary material from the early discussions, through the drafting phases and onwards to the concluding document of the process. The elaboration of GATS is built on research carried out in an earlier study of Norwegian higher education initiatives in GATS (Mathisen 2006). These documents are complemented with meeting reports scheduled by the Norwegian representatives in charge of international activities in higher education (Norwegian Ministry of Education and Research 2004). First hand data has been gathered through observing a meeting with the Ministry of Education and Research in 2002,[3] and a research seminar on GATS and higher education organised by the Ministry of Education and Research together with researchers in 2005.[4] In addition, informal discussions with representatives from the ministry working closely with GATS, UNESCO and OECD processes have taken place in events related to researchers at my department. The multilateral processes are not very transparent which sometimes causes difficulties in establishing the relevant actors and an accurate sequence of events.

New actors and new perspectives – multilaterals in higher education

Higher education is increasingly located and understood within the frame of a global market. As higher education providers reach beyond national boundaries, this requires new levels of governance through, among others, the multilateral level. Multilateral organisations, some with other goals as their main priority (Halvorsen 2004), have included policies on education and research among their activities, some even awarding them top priority in their strategies. Research has shown that decisions at national level are often connected with and largely correspond to multilateral and international organisations' policies (Mathisen 2005a). The global context challenges national institutional givens whose previous strategies may become outdated overnight (Bjørkelo 2003). The approach in this chapter is to treat multilateral organisations as different from each other and built for diverse purposes; the multilaterals' governing structures and the power they constitute offer different practices that come to be reflected in their governing policies. Thus, some of these global organisations have the opportunity to discipline and sanction states, while others do not have enforcement powers and are left with weaker instruments such as recommendations, advice regarding best practice and guiding principles.

The rise of the global education market is characterised not only by the re-working of existing institutions but also by the entry of new providers, and by forces of market liberalisation that can be traced back to certain multilateral organisations. The global higher education market can be considered both a consequence of multilateral policy and a response to challenges posed by market liberalisation. Hence, the expansion of higher education is closely linked to the presence and policies of both the multilateral organisations who maintain that liberalisation is beneficial to higher education and those who challenge such a narrow definition of knowledge. Parallel questions emerge from the potential drawbacks of a free market, especially regarding what forms of quality assurance are suitable for cross-border education. Who should be in charge of promoting international quality in higher education? And is international quality assurance capable of controlling and regulating new forms of education? These questions also emerge because cross-border education complicates quality assurance through the encounter of two or more national education systems, each possessing a specific history, priorities, and resources (Mathisen 2005b). Given that the engine of trade in education, the WTO/GATS, is not capable of providing a tool for promoting the quality of the services it advocates, other forums such as UNESCO have been held up as an alternative for promoting the development of countries' quality systems. However, many would argue that stipulating quality requirements restricts the market and could be interpreted as an obstacle to trade.

The multilateral organisations and their prospects for action

The multilaterals investigated in this chapter have institutionalised higher education in different ways depending largely on whether they perceived knowledge as a private or a public good.[5] Nevertheless, they possess different instruments to put in force their policy. At one end of this spectrum, higher education has come to be defined as a service within GATS, and is influenced by the new framework the agreement represents. GATS classifies four ways a service can be traded, termed as four 'modes of supply'. The four modes are classified as cross-border supply (distance education), consumption abroad (students studying abroad), commercial presence (foreign universities in a host country), and presence of natural persons[6] (teachers, professors, researchers working in a host country on a temporary basis). These four modes are applied to every service sector covered by GATS. Here, higher education not only takes on a new manifestation by being seen as a service potentially operating in a market, but is also characterised as being part of an extensive and complex trade system. Such a definition of higher education is in line with the frequently applied concept of the knowledge economy as a rationale that increasingly has come to be accepted worldwide. GATS' organisational frame for higher education services is that of a legally enforceable agreement with a high level of obligation on member states. The organisation of the WTO possesses clear judicial procedures for settling disputes between members and the possibility to discipline noncompliant members.

At the other end of the spectrum, UNESCO brings into play the idea of cross-border education, a broader concept that is not necessarily understood in terms of the free market and its economic profit. It seems rather as if UNESCO proclaims a knowledge-concept that takes into consideration the value of national cultures, non-profit internationalisation, and higher education as a public good. UNESCO attempts to build initiatives reflecting this approach. This implies that UNESCO respects a country's national sovereignty and national quality systems, sooner than supporting convergence and standardisation through UNESCO's establishing its own apparatus for quality promotion. UNESCO has announced that it does not see its task as the establishment of a global system of quality assurance forcing countries to adjust to the same standards (Roberts 2005). Rather, the organisation attempts to be a meeting place for stakeholders at the national and regional level and to be a forum initiating debate. Nevertheless, it is most likely that in the construction of norms and guidelines to cope with the issue of quality assurance, UNESCO will give direction to a 'solution' to the problem of unmonitored trade in higher education. Conventions are the strongest instruments available to UNESCO. In the field of higher education, UNESCO has established a number of regional conventions covering the recognition of qualifications. The UNESCO Regional Conventions on the recognition of qualifications are legally binding instruments when ratified by member states. The conventions represent a strong commitment for member countries to implement the measures in the conventions into national practices. Much weaker than a Convention, UNESCO's two other instruments are a Declaration, and lastly Guidelines. Guidelines merely define general principles for action, to be taken up by any nation state that is interested and whose national authorities have the capacity to implement them.

The third organisation is the OECD whose members 'share a commitment to democratic government and the market economy'. The organisation proclaims the benefit of economic growth, and sets out how progress can be achieved in different sectors such as in higher education. The OECD has for a long time influenced member countries' science and technology policies, research policies and higher education policies. The organisation early promoted a closer link with higher education and its direct economic benefits to society. Concerning global higher education, the OECD initially addressed higher education within the framework of the knowledge economy and approved trade in higher education as a means for reaching these goals. It appears that the organisation attempted to connect higher education to its economic potential as an industry, which was to some extent reflected in the events/forums they came to organise for pushing forward policies on trade in higher education. The organisation's instruments are first to develop policy recommendations, which are not enforceable but which are often received as policy prescriptions by member states. The OECD also writes reports on individual countries, highlighting strengths and weaknesses in particular sectors of the economy, and defines best practice for member states to follow. Like UNESCO, the OECD depends on moral pressure for its recommendations to be implemented, but whereas UNESCO's challenge is to create consensus among a constituency, which spans rich and poor nations in all five continents, OECD's membership of wealthy countries makes it more possible to generate an expectation of conformity. The OECD found itself short of instruments for implementing a global policy on quality in higher education and looked for a collaboration partner. As a result, the initiatives taken by the OECD in our example cannot be explored separately but must be seen together with the efforts of UNESCO to formulate policy initiatives regarding the global market of higher education.

Creating boundaries for the global market through quality promotion – the role of WTO, UNESCO and OECD

To identify what role the WTO, UNESCO and OECD played in the core processes of this account, a description of their activities is required.

The demands for trade in higher education

In the 1990s, several countries, including Norway, had taken the first step under the GATS process of making commitments to include higher education in the negotiations over trade in services (WTO 1998). In the early years of the GATS process little attention was paid to any possible drawbacks in transforming higher education into a trade in services, but from 2000, when the negotiations began in earnest, the debate on the consequences of the liberalisation of higher education also started. As attention increasingly was given to the supporters of the liberalisation of higher education, the critique and analysis of the consequences of trade were mobilised. Questioning the consequences of a global market in higher education generated efforts to organise the global market of higher education especially regarding quality. Quality became important to protect consumers and other stakeholders, as well as securing fair access to knowledge globally.

Mobilising global quality initiatives within UNESCO

Several issues that appeared on the quality agenda after 2000 were already included in UNESCO's work. The background for the processes that developed through UNESCO was the fact that cross-border education and trade in higher education generated a need, stated at the UNESCO expert meeting in 2001, for global quality initiatives. There were fears that unmonitored free trade would be an invitation for fraudulent operators, especially in parts of the world where there was little or no consumer protection and potential students did not have reliable information on which to judge where and how to invest in their education and their future. Subsequently, the preliminaries of the 'Guidelines for Quality Provision in Cross-border Higher Education' were launched at an expert meeting in 2001 organised by the UNESCO Division of Higher Education along with other UNESCO offices. The 'Expert Meeting on the Impact of Globalization on Quality Assurance, Accreditation, and the Recognition of Qualifications in Higher Education'[7] declared its support for establishing a UNESCO Global Forum on the International Dimensions of Quality Assurance, Accreditation, and the Recognition of Qualifications. The meeting concluded with a draft outline of an Action Plan for the establishment of the Global Forum, which in turn came to represent the preliminary workings of the Guidelines.

The Global Forum was intended to serve as a platform for dialogue connecting issues such as quality assurance, accreditation, and the recognition of qualifications. The participants in the Global Forum agreed on the need to build bridges between education and trade in higher education services, to create a dialogue between academic and market-based values. UNESCO, WTO and OECD should act as complementary organisations and discuss with each other both cultural and commercial aspects of trade in higher education (Uvalic-Trumbic and Varoglu 2003). Initially the integration of UNESCO, WTO and OECD perspectives could be seen as an attempt to draw benefits from the different worlds the organisations inhabited by overcoming their different starting points. Overall, the three organisations had common interests to coordinate their initiatives, instead of making independent initiatives going counter to efforts to organise the global market.

UNESCO proceeded with the process of taking into account the new developments of cross-border higher education such as the presence of new providers. At various levels these matters were discussed also under the scope of the regional conventions. During meetings arranged by UNESCO together with its constituencies it was agreed that UNESCO's existing conventions on cross-border higher education needed to be revised to cope better with the challenges ahead in the global market for higher education.[8] The revision of the regional conventions did not rule out the development of Guidelines, rather these were thought to exist side by side. Interestingly, the issue under discussion was whether the UNESCO conventions, as regulatory tools, were able to complement other international agreements such as GATS (Uvalic-Trumbic 2004). This implies that there was a desire among UNESCO's constituencies to shape the global market of higher education and embrace alternative tools and frameworks to GATS. The advocates of this perspective supported the view of reducing obstacles for cross-border higher education using conventions, agreements, and multilateral frameworks outside the trade policy regime. However, the possibility of creating a tool that would complement GATS' service agreement was not straightforward. The GATS has several benefits compared with UNESCO's conventions. Perhaps most important is the legal commitment it represents for member countries. In addition, it benefits from the power of being integrated into a large trade system committing countries to higher degrees of liberalisation. But the legality and large scale of GATS was also a potential weakness since service negotiations over one area were often restricted and constrained due to lack of progress in other key trade areas.

In line with a Resolution initiated by Norway and presented at UNESCO's General conference in 2003, UNESCO was to join the OECD in taking a leading role in quality promotion.[9] The joint initiative with OECD to create guidelines would have a non-binding status and contain principles for actions recommended to governments, higher education providers, quality assurance and accreditation agencies, information centres on recognition, and professional bodies (OECD 2005). The joint working group addressing the Guidelines on Quality Provision was to be chaired by Norway (Norwegian Ministry of Education and Research 2005). There was a great deal of consensus on the policy objectives that the Guidelines should address. The consensus had gradually been achieved through the workings of UNESCO's First Global Forum on Quality Assurance, Accreditation and Recognition of Qualifications (October 2002), the UNESCO/Norway Forum on Globalization on Higher Education (May 2003) and the OECD/ Norway Forum on Trade in Educational Services (November 2003). In accordance with the decisions taken in the 2002 Global Forum, UNESCO would focus on three tasks: standard-setting, capacity-building and clearinghouse functions. The standard-setting activities consisted of three elements: the establishment of the Guidelines for Quality Provision in Cross-border Higher Education, a review of the regional conventions and research on the concept of 'public good' (Uvalic-Trumbic 2004). The work on the Guidelines appeared to incorporate a long tradition of practice reflected in the UNESCO conventions although the new instrument of the Guidelines would have a status independent of the regional conventions.

Addressing the OECD as UNESCO's partner in formulating the guidelines

At an early stage in UNESCO's arenas for discussing alternative actions to discipline the market and what can be considered the early stages of the preparation of the Guidelines, the OECD was not mentioned as an active partner. At this stage the OECD seemed devoted to analysing and encouraging trade in services. The risks of trade in higher education were expressed in UNESCO's workings on 'Globalization Impacts on Higher Education', but not the fact that the OECD would play a role in constructing the Guidelines. Nevertheless, at a later stage in the process the two organisations were invited to develop the Guidelines within the framework of a UNESCO tradition. Although acknowledging the different entrance points and attitudes supporting higher education globally, the two organisations for different reasons found each other to be appropriate collaborators.

Understanding how the OECD appeared on the scene as UNESCO's collaborator on this process needs some attention. Within the OECD, the idea of developing Guidelines was launched in 2003 by the governing board of the Centre for Educational Research and Innovation (CERI) as a continuation of the conferences and subsequent initiatives that they had developed on trade in higher education (OECD 2005).[10] In an OECD tradition, the Directorate for Education carried out analyses, created statistics, undertook reviews, and formulated policy on higher education. Responsibility for further work was eventually transferred to the OECD's Education Committee, now put in charge of overseeing the implementation of the Guidelines. This confirms the significant status the work on Guidelines eventually achieved but also reflects that the OECD already had developed initiatives and knowledge on the issues, which eventually came to correspond with the UNESCO-based initiatives.

A process that was developed more or less in parallel to UNESCO's initiatives was the forum jointly organised by OECD/CERI, the US Department for Education, the US Department of Commerce, the US National Committee for International Trade in Education (NCITE), and the US Centre for Quality Assurance in International Education (CQAIE)[11] in cooperation with the Office of the US Trade representative and the US Department of State and the World Bank. The first forum was held in May 2002 in Washington (OECD 2002) and was followed by the second forum arranged in Norway (OECD/Norway 2003). The third and last forum was held in Australia in 2004 (OECD/UNESCO 2004), before the GATS negotiations were supposedly scheduled to be completed in 2005. The initial organisers and sponsors largely represented a view in favour of trade in higher education, which seems to have been reflected in the discussions. Nonetheless, these forums proved to be a crucial arena for developing a dialogue between the cross-border education stakeholders. They also served as an arena for developing initiatives and an engine for processes such as UNESCO's activities on quality. It was at the OECD/Norway Forum on Trade in Educational Services, held in Norway in 2003, that a working group to deal with the question of 'Guidelines' was set up. Ahead of the Forum, the suggestion that OECD should collaborate with UNESCO had been addressed and confirmed in an OECD/CERI Governing board meeting.[12] The background for how this collaboration came about is not so obvious and is difficult to discern and understand, especially considering that the OECD had not been brought into the initial stages of formulating UNESCO's Guidelines (UNESCO 2001).[13]

The OECD forums were central to the creation of the coalition initiated by Norway – the Contact Group on Education Services – claiming to discuss opportunities for delivering proposals in future service negotiations. This group consists of countries[14] that are strikingly different economically and politically, but which share an interest in increasing trade in services. Their common interest is the higher education sector especially related to cross-border education; trade in education services and how to secure quality in education originating from another country. The Contact Group formed with a view to preparing joint proposals in the WTO/GATS negotiations. Norway played a central role in creating this coalition, at the same time as Norway was one of the countries supporting the development of Guidelines in UNESCO. By way of explanation, the former Norwegian Minister of Education and Research argued that the Norwegian WTO policy must be aligned with national policy (Clemet 2003). As mentioned earlier, Norway's attitude towards cross-border higher education is somewhat ambiguous and attempts to incorporate both a strategy for pushing forward higher education trade negotiations,[15] as well as ambitions for supporting principles promoting quality in global higher education (Sørensen 2005).

Preparing the guidelines for quality provision in cross-border higher education

Returning to the progress of the Guidelines, UNESCO's and OECD's work on developing the Guidelines was organised in three phases, each resulting in a preliminary draft stating the policy objectives and how the Guidelines should address quality. At an early stage, the drafting of the Guidelines was an inclusive process. All member states in UNESCO and OECD together with other stakeholders[16] were invited to participate in developing the Guidelines. Draft meetings were chaired by Norway[17] together with vice-chairs from South Africa and India (OECD 2005). Norway gave both financial and administrative support to UNESCO to develop this role. This was part of Norway's commitment to develop alternative and supplementary initiatives to those structuring the global market of higher education.

The follow-up meeting on UNESCO's action plan, *UNESCO/OECD Guidelines on 'Quality provision in Cross-Border Higher Education'* in April 2004 was an attempt to outline the international initiatives on quality in cross-border higher education at a global level. The process rapidly developed from an early draft and gradually became clearer on the objectives and the means to achieve them.

The first phase in the process resulted in an initial draft (First Drafting session), where attention was given to the need to 'establish an international database listing all degree-granting higher education institutions that are recognised within each country' (UNESCO/OECD 2004a). The database would include all recognised higher education institutions operating in a country whether they were public/private, not-for-profit/for-profit or national/foreign. Hence, a university branch campus of a foreign university would have to be recognised by the receiving country in order to be included on that country's list of providers. However, if a higher education provider's foreign campus activities had already been recognised by the sending country, it would automatically be included in the list of the receiving country too (UNESCO/OECD 2004a). The decisions formulated in the first draft reflect the importance of national authorities in determining quality assurance and accreditation, and the value of preserving cultural diversity in education systems. However, in the preparation of the final document it became evident that UNESCO's definition of Cross-Border Higher Education, which only covered two (student mobility and institutional mobility) of GATS' four modes of providing educational services, was not comprehensive enough. Consultations led to a broader definition of cross-border higher education that came to include 'teacher, student, programme, institution/provider or course materials across national jurisdictional borders' (UNESCO 2005). If UNESCO had not been able to integrate the necessary measures into the definition of cross-border higher education, it could have quickly risked jeopardising its role in promoting quality.

At the Second Drafting meeting held in Tokyo in October 2004, it was decided to separate the development of an international information tool for recognising higher education institutions from the adoption of the Guidelines themselves (UNESCO/OECD 2004b). There was a consensus to establish a 'searchable portal' at international level, to carry out a 'pilot study', and to create a 'list of recognized higher education institutions' which would only be updated at the national level. In a different but related process, Norwegian bureaucrats attending the UNESCO/OECD Forum on Trade in Educational Services in Australia in October 2004 also stressed the importance of the Guidelines for Quality Provision and the Information Tools – the global database on nationally approved providers (Levy 2005). Norway was signalling that the efforts made to advance trade in higher education should also recognise the work on the Guidelines.

The collaboration between UNESCO and OECD on the Guidelines resulted in a final document, which was approved in December 2005 (UNESCO/OECD 2005). The impact of these Guidelines is still unknown and 'it has been emphasised that the effectiveness of the guidelines will depend on strengthening the remit and capacity of national systems to assure quality' (Verbik and Jokivirta 2005).

As far as the Norwegian attitude is concerned, a high ranking representative of the Norwegian Ministry of Education and Research has claimed that the Guidelines will not be in conflict with GATS as long as they do not contradict the agreement.[18] How this could be interpreted is not so apparent since the Guidelines seem to have been established in order to limit trade in higher education. To a certain extent, such a statement might be said to express a lack of reflection over the possible effects of the Guidelines, along with an ambiguity between treating higher education as a public good and as a subject for free trade, which is inherent in Norway's policy. Although the initiatives are presented as good intentions it is not clear how these processes will materialise in practice.

Another obstacle for the impact of the Guidelines is that not all governments pay attention to quality assurance processes. This has been particularly evident in trade negotiations where there seems to be a great distance between the education group and the trade group from the different ministries of the same country (Stella 2006). Therefore, the issue of quality is not straightforwardly integrated into the negotiations about education services.

Conclusion

The chapter started by distinguishing between three multilateral organisations and their approaches to the global higher education market. Throughout the chapter, it was also acknowledged that these organisations were equipped with different instruments for action, which influenced their ability to enforce their goals. The starting point was the way WTO/GATS contributed to the prominence of trade in higher education. This attitude to higher education gradually met with critique, which counteracted the position that knowledge should be a service, bought and sold on an unregulated market. The global responses were eventually expressed through the creation of boundaries for that market. The OECD had several initiatives in global higher education prior to the decision to join UNESCO, but the lack of instruments and legitimacy required the OECD to cooperate with another organisation. Although not being included in the first phases of UNESCO's work, the OECD managed to be incorporated in the process and contributed to the construction of the Guidelines. Through the configuration of the Guidelines, UNESCO and OECD agreed on a solution to promote quality in global higher education under the circumstances of a compromise. From the outside, it seems as if the framework, the traditions, and the practices already developed within UNESCO conditioned the process. At this point, UNESCO seemed to capture additional dimensions and to have the ability to reflect issues with a global reach in the application of the Guidelines.

The ambiguous role of Norway has been given particular attention. The country took initiatives in both UNESCO and OECD, which were important in the creation of the Guidelines. Yet these initiatives both supported a system to promote free trade in higher education and supported collaboration between UNESCO and OECD on the formulation of Guidelines to limit trade. Seemingly, Norway attempted to merge these two processes through the Contact Group on Education Services and attempted to integrate both a strategy for trade as well as requirements of quality in global higher education. As pointed out earlier, most likely the framework through which GATS operates will not correspond with the Guidelines.

How the Guidelines of UNESCO and OECD will work in countries' higher education systems is uncertain. A test for the multilateral interaction will be to observe how the Guidelines are put into practice and implemented. In most policy processes, the implementation stage is the decisive phase providing substance and meaning to an issue. Will UNESCO's national diversity approach, which attempts to secure the rights of each country to define their own quality system, tip the scale? There are several possible scenarios to the question of how the Guidelines might be applied. One possible scenario is that the Guidelines will successfully serve the role of an instrument to regulate the market of higher education. The Guidelines have the potential to secure minimum quality requirements in cross-border education and prevent the entry of spurious providers into the market. As such, they could be considered a barrier against the liberalisation of higher education and, therefore, a second scenario is that, under GATS' rules, the Guidelines and their associated instruments may be deemed to constitute an obstacle to trade in higher education. Alternatively, a third scenario is that countries do not have the administrative capacity to develop the Guidelines' instruments for the recognition of providers and the monitoring of quality. If they remain unimplemented, the existence of these supra-national Guidelines may merely serve to deflect dissent and even lend legitimacy to the continuing globalisation of the higher education sector.

Notes

1 The chapter has benefited from my participation in the research group 'Globalisation and its disorder' at the Dept. of Administration and Organisation Theory, University of Bergen from 2002 to 2005 and the work of the members of the group (leader Tor Halvorsen, Tom Skauge, Gunnar Guddal Michelsen, Birthe Bjørkelo, Cecilia Roberts).

2 Multilateral organisations are international organisations consisting of multiple member countries. They vary in terms of structure, financial circumstances, size, and mission, and their ability to discipline their members through various instruments.

3 Meeting on Norwegian GATS negotiations arranged by the Ministry of Education and Research in 2002.

4 Fottland, Håkon (2005) *Dissemination of Knowledge in a Globalized World: Research about GATS and Education*, Final report, SEMUT, University of Tromsø.

5 The multilaterals' different ways of institutionalising higher education seem to mirror the contradiction between knowledge as a private good versus knowledge as a public good.

6 Mode four has been of interest to developing countries, although developing countries are reluctant to liberalise this category through GATS (UNCTAD 2005).

7 The meeting bought together the Presidents of regional committees, intergovernmental bodies in charge of the application of conventions on the recognition of studies and degrees in higher education from the Arab states, Asia and the Pacific, Africa, Europe and northern America, and Latin America and the Caribbean. The meeting also brought together individual scholars from these regions as representatives active in this field; International Association of Universities (IAU), International Association of University Presidents (IAUP), International Network of Quality Assurance Agencies in Higher Education (INQAAHE), European Network of Quality Assurance (ENQU), European Students Information Bureau (ESIB), European University Association (EUA) (Uvalic-Trumbic 2002).

8 A revision should address 'issues of recognition of cross-border higher education provision, strengthening mechanisms to assure quality and emphasising reliable, transparent and coherent criteria for the assessment of qualifications' (Uvalic-Trumbic 2004: 153).

9 This mandate, which will be discussed later, was achieved at an Expert meeting in 2001 for UNESCO to collaborate with 'other international organisations'.

10 The project on Guidelines within the OECD was supported financially by three contributors through their respective ministries, Australia, Japan, and Norway (OECD 2005).

11 Actually, in 1999, The CQAIE initiated the National Committee for International Trade in Education (NCITE), 'a collective voice on trade issues for U.S. higher education and training. NCITE advises the Office of the U.S. Trade Representative (USTR) on the upcoming round of World Trade Organisation (WTO) negotiations related to the General Agreement on Trade in Services (GATS), as mandated by the Uruguay Round'.

12 OECD/CERI Governing board meeting on 29–30 October 2003: 'Enhancing Consumer Protection in Cross-border Higher Education'.

13 The lack of transparency in such policy processes adds to difficulties in achieving information on how the collaboration was established.

14 Consisting of representatives from Argentina, Australia, Chile, Egypt, India, Japan, Jordan, China, New Zealand, Poland, Senegal, South Africa, Thailand, Turkey, Uruguay and Norway.

15 Norway, together with the US and Kenya, has been criticised for putting forward requests to South Africa to negotiate higher education. The South African Education minister, attending a Norwegian conference in 2003, responded that education should not be bought and sold (Asmal 2003) expressing the request as an inappropriate enquiry. Norway chose to withdraw its request and not pursue the intended line and South Africa chose to exclude education from the service negotiations.

16 Higher education institutions, student associations, quality assurance and accreditation agencies, recognition agencies, academic staff associations, professional bodies, private sector, and other international organisations.

17 Chair Jan Levy, Senior Advisor, Ministry of Education and Research, Vice Chairs Mala Singh, Higher Education Quality Committee of the Council on Higher Education, South Africa and Stella Anthony, Australian Universities Quality Agency (OECD 2005).

18 Statement by the Deputy Secretary Stig Klingstedt at the NFU (Norwegian Association for Development Research) seminar Dissemination of Knowledge in a Globalized World: Research about GATS and Education, 21 April 2005.

References

Asmal, K. (2003) 'Education – a common good? Knowledge in the era of GATS'. Presentation at the Conference on Policies and Models for International Cooperation in Higher Education, Norwegian Centre for International Cooperation in Higher Education.

Bjørkelo, B. (2003) *The Power of Learning in the Global Age – The World Bank and the Environmental NGOs*. Master thesis, Dept. of Administration and Organisation Theory, University of Bergen.

Clemet, K. (2003) 'Globalization and higher education: implications for North–South dialogue'. Opening address at the UNESCO/Norwegian Ministry of Education and Research Conference, Oslo, Norway, 26–27 May.

Fottland, Håkon (2005) *Dissemination of Knowledge in a Globalized World: Research about GATS and Education*, Final report, SEMUT, University of Tromsø.

Halvorsen, T. (2004) 'Europe and the world – the need for a sustainable North–South policy'. Paper presented at the 16th Annual Conference of the European Association for International Education, Torino, Italy, 15–18 September.

Levy, J. (2005) 'Quality audit in Norway'. Presentation at the Policy Forum on Accreditation and the Global Higher Education Market, IIEP, Paris, 13–14 June.

Mathisen, G. (2005a) 'Chasing quality: WTO and UNESCO. Multilaterals at work', in Halvorsen, T., Mathisen, G. and Skauge, T. (eds) *Identity Formation and Knowledge Shopping. Education and Research in the New Globality*, Bergen: Norwegian Centre for International Cooperation in Higher Education.

Mathisen, G. (2005b) *Kunnskapsformidling gjennom GATS: Norge og utviklingsland*. Article prepared for the research seminar 'Dissemination of Knowledge in a Globalized World: Research about GATS and Education', 21 April, Bergen.

Mathisen, G. (2006) *Alienation of Higher Education. Investigating Norwegian Initiatives on the General Agreement on Trade in Services.* Master thesis, Department of Administration and Organisation Theory, University of Bergen.

Norwegian Ministry of Education and Research (2004) *Reporting on Meeting Attendance in International Forums.*

Norwegian Ministry of Education and Research (2005) *Norges reviderte tilbud i tjenetsteforhandlingene i WTO.* June.

OECD (2002) *Forum on Trade in Educational Services,* Washington, DC, 23–24 May.

OECD (2005) *Guidelines for Quality Provision in Cross-border Higher Education.*

OECD/Norway (2003) *Forum on Trade in Educational Services. Managing the Internationalization of Post-secondary Education,* Trondheim, 3–4 November.

OECD/UNESCO (2004) *Australia Forum on Trade in Educational Services. Building Capacity for Education through Cross-border Provision,* 11–12 October, Sydney, Australia.

Roberts, C. (2005) 'Does UNESCO have a role to play? Ensuring quality in higher education; challenging multilaterals', in Halvorsen, T., Mathisen, G. and Skauge, T. (eds) *Identity Formation or Knowledge Shopping? Education and Research in the New Globality,* Bergen: SIU.

Stella, Anthony (2006) 'Quality assurance of cross-border higher education', *Quality in Higher Education,* 12(2), November: 257–76.

Sørensen, O. (2005) 'GATS and education: an insider view from Norway', *International Journal of Higher Education,* 40: 7–9.

UNCTAD (United Nations Conference on Trade and Development) (2005) 'Trade in services and development implications'. Note by the UNCTAD Secretariat. http://www.unctad.org/en/docs.cld71_en.pdf; https://kalender.uib.no/exchweb/bin/redir.asp?URL=http://www.unctad.org/en/docs/c1d71.en.pdf.

UNESCO (2001) *Expert Meeting on the Impact of Globalization on Quality Assurance, Accreditation and the Recognition of Qualifications in Higher Education,* Paris, 10–11 September.

UNESCO (2005) *Guidelines for Quality Provision in Cross-border Higher Education,* Division of Higher Education.

UNESCO/OECD (2004a) *Guidelines on Quality Provision in Cross-border Higher Education – First Drafting Meeting,* 5–6 April, Paris.

UNESCO/OECD (2004b) *Guidelines on Quality Provision in Cross-border Higher Education – Second Drafting Meeting,* 14–15 October, Tokyo.

UNESCO/OECD (2005) *Guidelines on Quality Provision in Cross-border Higher Education – Drafting Meeting 3,* 17–18 January.

Uvalic-Trumbic, S. (2002) 'Globalization and quality in higher education: an introduction', in Uvalic-Trumbic, S. (ed.) *Globalization and the Market in Higher Education. Quality, Accreditation and Qualifications,* Paris: UNESCO.

Uvalic-Trumbic, S. (2004) 'UNESCO conventions on the recognition of qualifications'. In *Quality and Recognition in Higher Education. The Cross-Border Challenge,* OECD/CERI.

Uvalic-Trumbic, S. and Varoglu, Z. (2003) *Survey of the 2002 Breaking News: and the UNESCO Global Forum on Quality Assurance, Accreditation and the Recognition of Qualifications,* Observatory on Borderless Higher Education Report, April 2003.

Verbik, L. and Jokivirta, L. (2005) *National Regulation Framework for Transnational Higher Education: Models and Trends,* Observatory of Borderless Higher Education.

WTO (1998) 'Education services. Background note by the Secretariat', Council for Trade in Services.

16 The rise of private higher education in Senegal

An example of knowledge shopping?

Gunnar Guddal Michelsen

Introduction

While private higher education was absent or marginal in many countries until one or two decades ago, it is today gaining prominence everywhere. Senegal represents an interesting illustration of the phenomenon of private higher education growth. It exhibits in a concentrated form many of the common features found in the literature on private higher education: a rapid and unplanned growth over a short period of time, the proliferation of demand-absorbing providers and concentration in academic fields associated with the new liberal political economy, and a diminishing role of the state in higher education. As in many other parts of the world, the significant role private higher education is playing in Senegal was quite unanticipated (cf. Levy 2002). Indeed, the fact that one in five students in Senegal by the year 2003–4 was enrolled in a private institution came as a surprise. It is evident that the emergence of a subsector consisting of around 50 institutions will have profound effects on the system of higher education in Senegal.

Although this development corresponds quite well with the visions of an important reform agent like the World Bank and to a large degree is welcomed by the current Senegalese government, the roles private higher education is beginning to play in Senegal are rather undirected and uncoordinated. There is no real central vision and little steering. Regulation is weak and the attempts to establish a more coherent regulatory framework have not yet led to anything concrete. Furthermore, there is little or no coordination between the traditional public system of higher education and the emerging private sector. Yet, if we refer to the literature on the recent private higher education growth, the Senegalese case is not atypical. With regard to how the state is handling this issue, Daniel C. Levy, in a paper analysing the phenomenon of private higher education growth internationally, has for instance pointed out that 'the state finds itself scurrying to catch onto what is happening outside its direction, things it often regards as having gotten out of hand' (Levy 2002).

What seems to be lacking, then, is a good understanding of the phenomenon of private higher education. This understanding is needed before we engage in normative discussions of what the roles of private higher education and state policy on this issue should be. Given the proportions the phenomenon of private higher education is taking in numerous countries today, it is important to address this issue. One reason is that private higher education is not growing as an isolated sector outside the public universities. On the contrary, it is profoundly influencing the functioning of public higher education institutions and the values and standards of the entire system of higher education. Another reason is that in an age where knowledge as a factor in economic and social development is getting more and more important, the state needs to elaborate a policy covering all parts of the education system. What the roles and responsibilities of private higher education in this system should be and in particular how to integrate private and public institutions into a coherent system, will need attention.

Based on empirical research carried out in partnership with colleagues at the Université Cheikh Anta Diop de Dakar (UCAD),[1] the aim of this chapter is to present a better understanding of the phenomenon of private higher education in Africa, notably through an analysis of the case of Senegal. First, I will place the Senegalese case in a comparative perspective by looking at how recent literature identifies some common features in the development of private higher education and how it explains the spurt in the expansion of both institutions and enrolment in private higher education in Africa. I will then explain the background to the growth of private higher education in Senegal and describe its features and the emerging roles it plays. In the concluding section, I discuss whether the expansion of private higher education in Senegal reduces knowledge to a commodity – is the surge of private higher education an expression of knowledge shopping?

Common features of private higher education

In an international perspective private higher education is not anything new, as it has existed for a long time for instance in the USA, Japan and Latin America. In earlier periods private institutions were often for the elite, as in the USA, or had a religious mission as in Catholic parts of Europe and in Latin America, or were established with civil society or non-profit purposes. Today's wave of new private higher education institutions appears to be a demand-absorbing growth (Levy 2002: 5). It is market driven rather than government designed.

Traditionally, sub-Saharan Africa, in a similar manner to Western Europe, has relied entirely on public higher education. Compared with other regions of the world, the expansion of private higher education is quite recent in sub-Saharan Africa. According to many observers, the growth of private higher education in Africa has taken place mainly in Anglophone countries and Francophone countries have been slow to expand their private sector (World Bank 2002: 54). Given the dearth of available data and the paucity of literature on private higher education in Africa (Thaver 2003: 54), there are reasons to believe that such claims reproduce assumptions in the English language literature and reflect a lack of sources written in other languages, rather than being based on what is actually happening on the ground. In fact, a quick search for available data from Francophone countries indicates that these countries do not 'lag behind'. Côte d'Ivoire, for instance, has some 35,000 students enrolled at about 120 different private higher education institutions (*Fraternité Matin* 2004); that is about one in three of the total number of students in the country. In Senegal, 20 per cent of the students are enrolled in private institutions. That is a figure at the same level as Kenya (Ngome 2003: 360), which is considered a 'pioneer' in private higher education development in Africa. In Cameroon, the number of students in private higher education institutions amounted to 6,000 compared with 60,000 in the public sector in 1999/2000.[2] It has been reported that the private sector represents a similarly growing and vibrant component of the overall system of higher education in Francophone countries like Madagascar, Togo, Benin, and Congo (Edee 2003: 596; Guedegbe 2003: 180; Mbemba 2003: 254; Stiles 2003: 408). What this brings to the fore is that we need more and better research and documentation of the phenomenon of private higher education across the language zones in Africa. Thus far, it is only for South Africa that a comprehensive literature on private higher education exists (cf. Maldonado *et al.* 2004).

According to Roger King, the fastest-growing form of private higher education is for-profit institutions – education 'regarded as a commodity for which individuals are prepared to pay a price that enables a profit to be made by investors' (King 2003: 3). Internationally, the University of Phoenix is the most famous example of this trend. It experienced a growth in enrolment from 25,000 to 213,000 between 1995 and 2004 (University of Phoenix web site, Sept. 2004).[3] Although the importance of publicly listed corporations like Phoenix University and other virtual universities is increasing, for-profit institutions are not the only form of private higher education on the rise in Africa. What dominates the scene in many parts of the world is small and diverse private higher education bodies, and especially an upsurge in Christian and Islamic religious organisations. This is the case in sub-Saharan Africa and is a feature observed more widely in Africa (Sawyerr 2002: 39; Thaver 2003: 55). In a comparison of six Anglophone countries in Africa, Bev Thaver reported that 'institutional types with a religious–moral focus dominate' (2003: 59). However, she also noted a movement in the direction of a greater presence of for-profit institutions with an emphasis on business courses (Thaver 2003: 55). And in an important country such as South Africa, for-profit provision largely dominates the country's private sector (Levy 2003: 21).

A consequence of the strong market orientation of commercial institutions is that such institutions, as Levy has formulated it, 'rarely assume or claim to assume academic elite roles complete with doctoral education, basic research, large laboratories or libraries, or mostly full-time academic staff' (Levy 2002). Their sensitivity to market signals means that commercial institutions tend to mount courses for which employment avenues are clear and sure. In particular in the post-structural adjustment period in sub-Saharan Africa, with a generalised crisis in the state and public administration, traditional employment avenues have been more or less closed. Instead, a series of new trajectories for attaining elite positions, outside the traditional public sector avenues, have emerged in African societies in recent years (Banégas and Warnier 2001: 7).

In this context it is not strange that a common observation is that the new private institutions concentrate their offer on fast-growing entrepreneurial fields in the private sector economy (Levy 2003: 19–20; Sawyerr 2002: 36; Teferra and Altbach 2004: 34). The courses taught are typically in such areas as business and commerce, accounting and management, marketing, human resource management, media studies, tourism, information technology, and secretarial science. These areas are often only partially or insufficiently taken care of by traditional public institutions. One reason is that many public universities do not deign to undertake the role of offering 'academically light' courses (Levy 2002). Another is that public universities in many countries traditionally have been oriented towards the needs of the public sector and have not altered this orientation despite the political-economic changes of recent years.

Characteristic of the new private sector is also the use of part-time academic staff (Levy 2003: 26). Academic staff are typically recruited from public universities. The implication of this in practice, and acutely so in Africa, is that full-time faculty are moonlighting (Thaver 2003: 57). This is certainly affecting public universities in a number of ways. An obvious effect of moonlighting at private institutions is that research and academic publishing is suffering. Another, but less clear effect, is that it may contribute to changing the identity of the academic profession away from classical academic ideals.

The use of part-time academic staff in private higher education institutions is closely related to the volatile market situation in which new private institutions are operating. To survive, private institutions have to be capable of making rapid changes in the courses they offer according to the demand expressed by students. While faculty normally is the core actor at traditional public universities, students are the privileged actors at commercial private higher education institutions. Attention is given to knowledge transfer and to the creation of attractive knowledge packages while the knowledge production function of higher education is marginalised. The focus is on student satisfaction and on attracting new students to the institutions. Faculty are not only 'squeezed' from below by the demands of the students, but also from above. Managers and owners rather than faculty are the ones who set the goals and content of courses at private higher education institutions (Levy 2003: 28).

A final aspect that needs attention is what Philip G. Altbach has called the 'multinationalisation' of private higher education (1999: 10). What this means is that academic institutions increasingly are establishing links, branches, and collaborative arrangements with institutions in other parts of the world. However, according to Altbach (1999: 10), this is a trend which flows mainly in one direction – from the North to the South.

284 Gunnar Guddal Michelsen

Public system crisis as a factor of private growth

There are many factors that have been instrumental in the rise of private higher education in Senegal. A main reason, however, is current weaknesses in the system of public higher education in Senegal. Thus, to explain the surge of private higher education in Senegal, we first have to look at the state of public higher education in the country.

Compared with many other developing countries, current public expenditure on higher education as a share of total current public expenditure on education as a whole has been relatively high in Senegal (cf. World Bank 2002: 190–4). Nevertheless, public higher education in Senegal has been troubled by a continuous series of problems since the 1980s.

An important part of these problems has been linked to underlying structural features. Senegal experienced a continuous negative economic growth rate measured by GDP per capita between independence in 1960 and 1993. During the same period there was a strong growth in the number of students from around 4,000 at the end of the 1960s to 16,000 at the end of the 1980s. As a result, resources per student were dwindling (MEN 2004: 10; Rectorat 2004). This situation provoked a crisis which led to confrontations between the university community and the government. Since the late 1980s up to today, strikes every year among staff and students have undermined the working conditions on campus. In both 1988 and 1994, the study years were invalidated because of strikes.

In addition to structural and political problems, public higher education has been struck by problems of very low internal efficiency. Failure rates of between 50 and 70 per cent are common. Thus, there are high rates of withdrawal and repetition.

Another feature of the Senegalese system of higher education and research is its intensely centralised structure. In the study year 2003–4, more than 90 per cent of the students in the public system were enrolled at Université Cheikh Anta Diop de Dakar (UCAD). The second public university, Université Gaston Berger de St.Louis (UGB), was established in 1990. However, its intake of new students has been strictly limited by severe limitations on its capacity to house students in its student hostels. In contrast, UCAD has in recent years accepted all who have passed the baccalaureate (secondary school leaving certificate). Thus, UCAD has experienced a growth which has been almost exponential in the last few years, while the growth in enrolment at UGB has been rather slow. As of March 2004, UCAD had 37,605 students while UGB only had about 2,900 students. The result is that UCAD has become a completely overcrowded institution. The government appears not to have been capable of implementing any measures which in the short or medium term would provide a solution to the problems of overcrowding. Plans to establish up to ten regional university centres (*centres universitaires régionales*), by 2005, have not yet been implemented, even though the buildings for the first one in Bambey are more or less ready to be taken into use.

The rapid growth in the number of students at UCAD (Figure 16.1) is a result of demographic changes and, equally importantly, a decision by the government after the change of regime in 2000 that all school leavers were eligible for scholarships. In addition, it should be mentioned that public universities in Senegal do not charge any student fees. The government was therefore widening opportunities for school leavers and creating a growth in demand that could not be absorbed by the public universities alone.

Concerning the types of programmes offered at UCAD, the institution displays a pattern that is common in Africa: a concentration of students in arts, law and social sciences. The Faculty of Arts and Social Sciences (FLSH) alone has 43 per cent of the total number of students enrolled at UCAD, while the Faculty of Law and Political Science (FSJP) has 16.7 per cent and the Faculty of Economics and Management (FASEG) has 10.9 per cent (Figure 16.2). In contrast, the five schools offering technical and professional training like the School of Librarianship (EBAD) and the School of Engineering (ESP) only enrol 5.5 per cent of the students at UCAD.

Considering that since the 1980s Senegal has gone through a series of structural adjustment reforms which have shifted the political economy of the country in a neo-liberal direction (Cissé and Daffé 2002: 53), it is apparent that the distribution of students between UCAD's faculties and schools is out of touch. During the two decades after independence the country was building up its public service and expanding the sector of state-owned companies. Since 1986, the recruitment of candidates to the public sector has been fairly limited (Diagne and Daffé 2002: 228). While university graduates in the social and political sciences could look forward to a bright future in the 1960s and 1970s, the reality is quite different today. Today, Senegalese students often talk of UCAD as a 'factory of unemployment' (*usine de chômeurs*).[4]

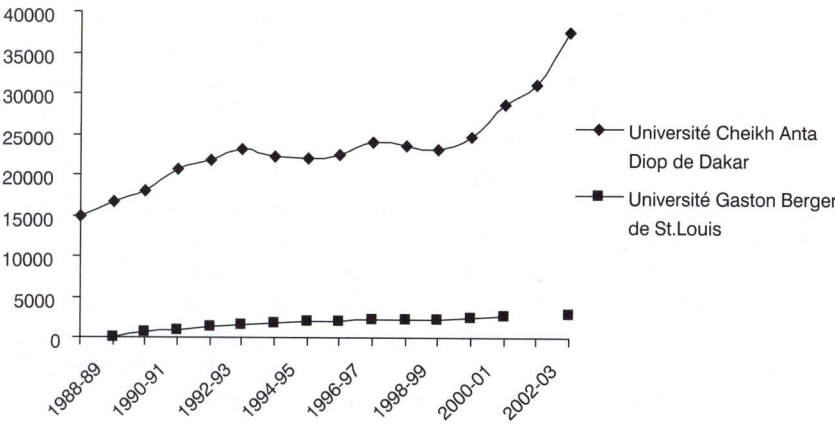

Figure 16.1 Growth in enrolment in public higher education in Senegal (Source: Rectorat UCAD)

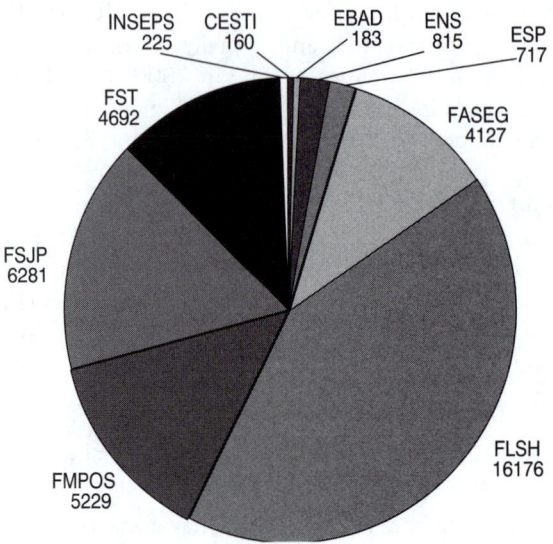

Figure 16.2 Distribution of UCAD students between faculties, schools and institutes (Source: Rectorat UCAD)

All in all, public higher education in Senegal is riddled with a number of problems which can explain why many young Senegalese would be open to other alternatives. Next, I will describe the phenomenon of private higher education in Senegal. I will provide an overview of the roles private higher education is taking and point to some of the positive factors underpinning the growth of the private sector.

The state and private higher education in Senegal

The first private higher education institution in Senegal was founded in July 1992. This institution, the Institut Supérieur de Management (ISM), was founded in a legal vacuum. To create a private higher education institution in Senegal was not illegal, but nor was there any proper legal framework authorising or regulating it. The ISM was established with no other legal backing than a letter from the Minister of Education encouraging the initiator to go ahead with the project (Interview 10 April 2004).

Although no proper legislation existed to regulate private higher education in 1992, it should be mentioned that a law passed in 1991 (*loi 91-22 du 16 février 1991*), whose purpose was to regulate technical schools and vocational training, encouraged private initiatives. Another law passed in 1994 (*loi 94-82 du 23 décembre 1994*) provided private education (in general) in Senegal with a legal status. Thus, we can identify a process in the early 1990s where the issue of private initiatives within the Senegalese education system appeared on the political agenda and became the object of legal regulation.

However, it was only in May 1995 that the first official document appeared which provided private institutions within higher education with something like a regulatory framework. At the initiative of an association of private higher education institutions (*Collectif de l'enseignement supérieur*), a 'framework agreement' (*accord cadre*) was reached with the state. This defined as higher education those institutions recruiting students with a baccalaureate diploma or equivalent qualification recognised by Senegalese authorities and which offered education at post-secondary level. The framework agreement was only supposed to be a temporary arrangement. Due to the fact that the state and the association of private institutions have been unable to reach a consensus concerning important issues such as the minimum number of permanent staff required, a projected decree, which was supposed to establish a more permanent regulatory framework, has not yet been issued (Interview 21 July 2004).

As a consequence of the lack of a decree, the Ministry of Education is only giving the private higher education institutions a temporary authorisation (*agrément provisoire*). This authorisation has to be renewed every year. Renewal of the temporary authorisation requires that the institution submits two reports every year. The first one at the beginning of the school year has to specify the composition of the staff, student enrolment, the percentage of foreign students and their sex distribution, the courses taught, the level of student fees, and how the institution is equipped. The second report at the end of the year specifies the success rates (Interview 21 July 2004). Today, this system of compulsory reporting constitutes the basis of a quality assurance system for private higher education in Senegal.[5]

However, the efficiency and adequacy of the current system of quality assurance can be questioned. Today, the responsible department within the Ministry of Education, the Direction de l'Enseignement Supérieur, appears to lack the necessary manpower resources to follow up and make use of all the data it is collecting through the reports from the private institutions. Furthermore, quite a few institutions were absent from the list of authorised institutions in 2003, including some institutions which definitely cannot be accused of being situated at the low end of the quality scale.[6]

According to the projected decree, the idea is to run periodical evaluations of the private institutions every fourth year (Interview 21 July 2004). Based on the results from this periodic evaluation, the authorisation to stay in business would either be renewed or withdrawn. The responsible body for the future quality assurance system is conceived of as a commission consisting of academics and administrative personnel.

Concerning accreditation, there is as yet no national system in Senegal. Two solutions are emerging, however. One is to use the interstate accreditation body CAMES (Conseil Africain et Malgache de l'Enseignement Supérieur) which traditionally has been responsible for accreditation of academics and academic programmes within the public system in the former French colonies in Africa. Lately, many private higher education institutions in Francophone Africa have sought recognition from CAMES. The second solution, which appears to be the preferred solution for the private higher education institutions in Senegal, is to seek recognition through institutional collaboration with recognised institutions mainly in France and North America. As the founder and managing director of one institution pointed out in an interview with us (Interview 10 April 2004), this means that standards have been imposed upon private Senegalese institutions from abroad. This appears to have contributed to raising the average standard within the Senegalese private sector to a fairly acceptable international level. In addition to these two main solutions for the accreditation problem, some institutions are also making use of the ISO norm, notably the two business schools ISM and Institut Africain de Management (IAM).

Although leaders of the private higher education institutions we interviewed asserted that their graduates in general have met few problems about being accepted when they wanted to continue at universities abroad, the private institutions have no coordination with or recognition from the public system within Senegal. On the contrary, leaders at almost all of the institutions we visited reported a lack of recognition and the impossibility of entering into collaboration with the public system. The private institutions accept diplomas from the public system, but the public system refuses to acknowledge qualifications from the private sector. The fact that the public universities in Senegal organise their education according to the traditional French degree system also prevents exchanges, which a credit based system would have allowed.[7]

The birth of the private sector

1992 was a year which not only marked the appearance of the first private higher education institution in Senegal, ISM, but also several others like Sup'Info and the Institution Sainte-Jeanne d'Arc. The following year saw the creation of five or six other private higher education institutions. What characterised the situation in Senegal in 1992–3 was that UCAD was in turmoil due to repeated strikes over several years among students and teachers. In addition, the only institution offering management education in Senegal, the inter-state school CESAG, was experiencing a serious crisis. As an answer to the problems in the public system, the government in association with the World Bank launched a comprehensive reform of higher education. One of the targets specified in the contract between the government and the World Bank was to bring the enrolment of students within private institutions up to 14 per cent of the total enrolment in Senegal (Interview 21 July 2004). Likewise, the World Bank reform aimed to reduce the number of students at UCAD from 22,000 in 1994 to 15,000 in 2000. Reorganisation of UCAD in 1994 also led to the creation of some fee-based entities inside UCAD such as the Institut Supérieur de Gestion (ISG), Institut de Formation en Administration et en Création d'Entreprises (IFACE) and Ecole Supérieure Polytechnique (ESP) (which also has non-fee based activities).

Thus, the emergence of private higher education in Senegal in the early 1990s was linked both to the crisis of the public system, and to public policy favouring the growth of private higher education. However, there was yet another factor that should not be underestimated. There was an emerging demand for private higher education and the kinds of programmes the sector was offering. Several of our interviewees reported that the creation of their institutions was in answer to an increasing demand. The business school ISM's founding director was for instance working as managing director of the Senegalese employer's association prior to the creation of his institution. In this position he experienced the increasing demand among Senegalese employers for people with business and management skills around 1990 (Interview 10 April 2004). Increasing demand for education in information technology was an equally important reason for the creation of Sup'Info in 1992 (Interview 16 March 2004). Thus, the notion of private higher education growth as demand-driven, as referred to above, appears to fit quite well with the case of Senegal. The more profound reason, however, is that the emergence of a new demand for private higher education was linked to structural changes of the Senegalese political economy from the mid-1980s (cf. Cissé and Daffé 2002).

Accelerating growth

Although many of the institutions existing today can be dated back to the early 1990s, the growth in student enrolment has to a large degree taken place since the late 1990s (Table 16.1). The figures are far from accurate, particularly concerning the early years, but provide an adequate overview of the development.

The size of private higher education institutions in Senegal varies a lot. While the smallest institution (Immaculée Conception) had only 34 students, the biggest (Université Dakar-Bourguiba (UDB)) operated with 1,029 students enrolled in 2003 (DES 2004). The average private higher education institution had 268 students. In terms of size, the institutions can be divided into three different groups: one third of the institutions had an enrolment between 34 and 112 students; a little more than a third had an enrolment between 142 and 306; and the last group, adding up to a little less than a third, had between 398 and 1,029 students enrolled. As the figures in Table 16.1 clearly indicate, there has been a rapid expansion of the private sector in the last two years. There are some new institutions, but the existing ones are expanding significantly.[8] The conclusion we can draw from this is that the sector is consolidating while continuing its rapid growth. It is only a matter of time before one or several of the private institutions will surpass in size the second public university in Senegal, UGB.

The roles of private higher education in Senegal

In Senegal, the private sector is first and foremost assuming the role of undertaking short (2–3 years) post-secondary, job-oriented and technical education. Ninety per cent of the students enrolled in private higher education are taking courses supposed to make them ready for the labour market after

Table 16.1 Number of institutions and enrolment in the private sector

Year	Number of institutions	Enrolment
1994		500
1999	31	5,000
2003	48	8,500
2004	40	13,000

Sources: DES 2004; Interviews 6 March 2003, 21 July 2004; Ndiaye 2002: 360; Tamba 2004.

2–3 years (DES 2004: 4). There is a high concentration of programme offerings in the fields of management, accountability, finance, international business and secretarial training. Most of the institutions offering these fields of study are quite small and specialised. These are fields of study which are only offered to a very small extent, or inadequately, by public institutions.

Another important type of programme offering is information technology; there are some quite specialised and technically oriented institutions like Institut Supérieur d'Informatique and Sup'Info, but also quite a few which are combining information technology with other fields of study such as management.

Some of the biggest and most prestigious institutions are specialising within business administration (bachelor and master), notably ISM, IAM, Hautes Etudes Canadiennes et Internationales (HECI) and Suffolk University.

There are equally some institutions which are aiming at a university status with programme offerings in more classical fields of study such as mathematics, economics, law, sociology, medicine, science and the humanities. However, the ways the programmes are set up are typically giving them a more job-oriented profile than is found within the public system. The two institutions with the broadest university-like programme offerings are UDB and Université du Sahel. In addition to these, we can add Suffolk University's Dakar branch, ISM (calling itself 'Université Internationale') which has programmes up to the doctoral level, and the Université El Hadj Ibrahima Niasse which concentrates on medicine.

In contrast to the observation by Thaver from six African Anglophone countries referred to above, the presence of institutional types with a religious–moral focus is fairly insignificant. On the Department of Higher Education's list of institutions with temporary authorisation there is only one institution with such a focus, namely the protestant organisation Institut Biblique Parole Vivante. In addition, there are two Catholic organisations: Institution Sainte Jeanne d'Arc and Complexe d'Enseignement Saint Michel. These are however concentrating in fields like accounting, management and marketing. During the first years of private higher education in Senegal the Catholic organisations played an important role as they were among the pioneers offering short job-oriented types of education. Catholic organisations also have a long history within private primary and secondary education in Senegal.

In general, private higher education in Senegal is basing its existence on student fees. It is receiving no support or funding from the state. Thus, the sector is bound to be sensitive to market signals. However, the term 'for-profit' appears somewhat limiting when trying to discern what is going on within private higher education in Senegal. Our empirical studies give rise to some doubt whether the for-profit category should be applied as widely as it often is. The reason is that the term for-profit suggests that the main motivation of those behind such institutions is a narrow-minded search for profit. We found that the motivations of the leaders in the sector were linked to a much wider set of values. Rather than for-profit, we can ask whether entrepreneurialism is not a better term to understand what drives the current expansion of private higher education in Africa. Nevertheless, this does not undermine the main conclusion that the emerging field of private higher education in Senegal, as in Africa in general, appears to be distinguished, and increasingly so, by its business orientation and a strong market-related discourse.

Concerning the ownership of private higher education institutions in Senegal, our impression is that, for the most part, it is locally based. All the biggest institutions, at least, are owned by local entrepreneurs. The typical account we came across was the history of an individual with a strong vision or inspiration which he sought to realise through creating his own private institution. Despite the local entrepreneurialism of Senegalese private higher education, Altbach's thesis on the 'multinationalisation' of private higher education still has a bearing. As discussed in the section on regulation, Senegalese private higher education institutions are systematically seeking to establish alliances and links with overseas institutions.

There are not many foreign-based institutions, and the few that have been established are rather small. The US-based Suffolk University had less than 80 students, the Moroccan-based HECI around 200, and the French-based ETICCA less than 80 students. Nevertheless, foreign institutions such as Suffolk University and HECI are considered as some of the most prestigious in Senegal. The level of their student fees is prohibitive for most Africans who therefore rather go for a locally based alternative at an affordable price.[9] While Suffolk University and HECI are operating with student fees at around F CFA 6 million and F CFA 2 million per year respectively, locally based institutions such as IAM and UDB are operating with student fees at around F CFA 800,000 and F CFA 400,000 respectively.[10]

When it comes to academic staff, the picture is the same in Senegal as internationally: the academic staff is overwhelmingly part-time and paid by the hour. According to the Department of Higher Education, most of the staff are either junior staff possessing a doctoral degree (*Assistants*) or post-graduate students at UCAD. There are about 1,200 teaching jobs within private higher education in Senegal (DES 2004: 4). Although the general picture is one of part-time staff, we can observe a development where the biggest and most established institutions are setting up core groups of permanent academic staff members.

Characteristics of the student population

Gender and the public–private paradox

A very interesting feature which struck us when visiting various private higher education institutions in Senegal was the equal distribution of enrolment between the sexes. The Department of Higher Education's statistical overview, with figures from 35 of the 40 institutions with a temporary authorisation in 2003, confirmed this impression. This overview shows that female students make up 50 per cent of the total number of students in the private sector (DES 2004: 4).[11] In comparison, in the public sector only 29 per cent of students are female. These figures are not unique for Senegal, but mirror the trend within higher education in Africa generally. Although there is a paucity of reliable statistics on this issue, available data from private institutions in various African countries indicate that the percentage of female students is around 50 per cent while the female student enrolment in public institutions often is between 20 and 30 per cent (Sawyerr 2002: 40). According to Sawyerr, the explanation for this 'paradoxical' difference can be located among factors such as 'the generally lower entry requirements in the private institutions, their concentration on the "softer subjects" in the humanities and the vocational area, and the greater flexibility of their programming' (2002: 40). However, more systematic research needs to be undertaken to get a clear picture of differences in gender balance and explanations of such differences.

Senegal as an exporter of educational services

Another striking feature concerning the student population within Senegal's private higher education sector is the high proportion of foreign students. No statistics have been published about the global situation. However, the general message from the institutions we have been in contact with is that the proportion is from about one-third to a majority. Furthermore, there are in general between 15 and 25 nationalities represented at the various institutions. These are mainly other Francophone Central and West African countries. When we looked more closely at the figures, it was revealed that most of the foreign students came from the small Central African country Gabon.[12] At the Université du Sahel, there were more Gabonese than Senegalese students in 2004 (Interview 13 April 2004). At IAM, the Gabonese constituted the second largest group, but still the number of Gabonese amounted to 209 out of a total of 547 students in 2003 (IAM 2004a). Other groups of foreign students were much smaller, with the biggest being the groups from Congo (14), Chad (14) and Cameroon (11).

The high share of foreign students within private higher education in Senegal depends very much on students from one specific country. Nevertheless, the idea that Senegal can become a regional export nation of education services is now growing stronger. Reasons that have been evoked to explain this phenomenon are that Senegal still has a reputation in Francophone Africa of being a pole of excellence; it is a peaceful, democratic country with a vibrant civil society and cultural scene; and the climate is very stable and pleasant (Interview 10 April 2004; IAM 2004b). Last but not least, many Senegalese private higher education institutions appear to deliver an education of a fairly good international standard at a price of only a fraction of what it costs to study in North America or Europe: 'at the price of a flight ticket to the USA' as one of our interviewees expressed it (Interview 10 April 2004).

Social background of the students

Senegal is a country where close to 50 per cent of the active population works in agriculture (Diagne 2002: 97), 58 per cent of households are hit by poverty (1995 figures) (Diagne *et al.* 2002: 21), and 62 per cent of the adult population is illiterate (2001 figures) (PNUD 2003: 240). As the system of scholarship and student aid in Senegal is reserved for students studying within the public system, it is only to be expected that the sons and daughters of the richest part of the population are heavily over-represented within private higher education.

Data from our survey at three private higher education institutions confirm this assumption. Of the students 66.8 per cent had a father whose education level was post-secondary. Nevertheless, 10 per cent had a father who had not attended school at all. When looking at the Senegalese students in isolation (57 per cent of the total), this figure amounts to 14 per cent. Concerning the profession of the students' fathers, 44.9 of the students had a father working as a senior executive and 17.9 per cent had a father exercising a liberal profession. Only 5.3 per cent had a father working in agriculture.

Although we cannot deduce directly from these figures the economic status or level of wealth/poverty of the parents, the data can be used to indicate that the level of socio-economic inequality is not significantly different from that seen in public higher education or upper secondary education. Figures from 2001 show for instance that among the poorest two quintiles of the Senegalese population the gross enrolment ratio in upper secondary education (*lycée*) was as low as 2.2 per cent compared with 53.1 per cent for the richest quintile (MEN 2004: 98).

Despite prohibitive student fees for the poorest parts of the population, two reasons can be given to explain how some students from poor families still are making it into private higher education. The first is financial help from more affluent relatives. The relatives do not necessarily have a high level of education but may be working abroad in countries like France or Italy. The second explanation, even though this can only partially explain it, is that some students enrolled in private higher education institutions are enrolled in public higher education too. They are thus receiving student aid from the state. Our survey confirms this phenomenon, as 11.2 per cent of the respondents confirmed that they were also enrolled in a public institution.

Is it all about knowledge shopping?

This chapter has focused on the phenomenon of the emergence of a private sector within higher education. Through a short review of the international literature and a country study of Senegal, a series of features have been highlighted. The international literature as well as the case of Senegal show that the emergence and rapid expansion of private higher education has been unexpected. Although the Senegalese government's attitude towards private higher education has in general been positive, public authorities as well as public universities typically respond to this phenomenon in a reactive rather than a proactive way.

Beyond the skeleton of a regulatory framework established in the mid-1990s, the government has as yet not been able to establish a proper regulatory framework with an appropriate system of quality assurance and accreditation. It has left it to the traditional public universities themselves to organise their relationship with the new private sector. As a result there has been no coordination or mutual recognition between these two parts of the system of higher education in Senegal. This is very much related to hostility in important parts of the traditional university community. It also reflects the lack of attention higher education receives from policy makers in Senegal and, we can add, in Africa in general. All attention is directed towards the realisation of the UN millennium goals of education for all and equality between boys and girls; thus, the focus is on primary education. There are not many signs of preparing Senegal for participation in a global knowledge society and economy through an active policy of higher education.

Concomitant with the absence of an adequate policy of higher education, the growth of private higher education in Senegal appears to follow its own trajectory. Private higher education in Senegal was born in a situation characterised by a legal vacuum concerning the role of private institutions within higher education. The situation was equally characterised by a deep crisis in the public system which has worked as a negative factor favouring the growth of private higher education. A positive factor favouring its growth was undoubtedly the World Bank-sponsored reform programme launched in 1994.

The emergence and the growth of the sector comply quite well with the observations found in the international literature of demand-absorbing growth. The appearance of a private sector in Senegal can be seen as an answer to political-economic change following structural adjustment programmes undertaken since the mid-1980s. The political-economic change brought with it an increased demand for the skills needed by private business. The role of private higher education in Senegal has been to fill this need. It is also characteristic of private higher education in Senegal that it is job-oriented in its programme offerings and that it is organised in such a way that it can readily change to adjust to a volatile market. Thus, the staff is predominantly part-time. Nevertheless, we can perceive the contours of a development where the private sector is consolidating in Senegal. The fact that the biggest and most established institutions now are creating a core of permanent staff members and some have even created their own doctoral school and research centre is emphasising this.

These are development traits which suggest that the emergence and growth of private higher education in Senegal does not necessarily imply that knowledge is being reduced to a commodity. Although their job-oriented programmes appeal to students inclined to buy knowledge packages as tickets to a prosperous future, the conclusion I draw from the study of private higher education in Senegal is that the sector is taking seriously the identity formation function of higher education. Excluding the existence of diploma mills, among the other approximately 50 private higher education institutions which currently can be found in Senegal, the general impression is that there is much emphasis on supervision, giving assistance to students, and the creation of specific institutional cultures. The motivation of the founders of various private higher education institutions, institutions which are predominantly controlled by Senegalese people, refer to a much wider set of values than narrow profit maximisation.

The analysis of the student population shows several interesting traits which can be used partially to support the knowledge shopping hypothesis, but which partially does not fit it. Indeed, the high share of foreign students at Senegalese private higher education institutions can be used as an indicator of the emergence of a market for higher education. On the contrary, the equal gender distribution and the fact that a certain share of the students (although only quite small) comes from backgrounds with parents with few means despite prohibitive student fees does not quite fit with the assumption that the arrival of private institutions means that higher education is left to the play of market forces.

It seems that private institutions have acquired an important role within higher education in Senegal. They fill important needs when it comes to the supply of knowledge and skills required by the Senegalese society and economy today, which are not taken care of by the traditional public system. In a situation where the main public university, UCAD, is completely overcrowded, the private sector constitutes an alternative for many students who otherwise would have been excluded from higher education. What appears to be needed now is a proper regulation of the private sector and coordination with the public sector in order to make it into a coherent national system.

Notes

1 The study of private higher education in Senegal has been conceived and carried out in close collaboration with Dr Falilou Ndiaye and Dr Bacary Sarr within the framework of the project group GHERA Senegal. In 2003 and 2004, open-ended interviews with leaders at ten private institutions and four fee-taking institutions within the public system were carried out together with my partners. In 2004, a quantitative study on identity formation patterns among students at private institutions was carried out in collaboration with a sociology student at UCAD,

Papa Amadou Diawara. The project was financed by the Norwegian Research Council's programme 'Globalization or Marginalization?'. Editor's note: The late Gunnar Guddal Michelsen wrote this chapter in 2005 and presented it at the Third Conference on Knowledge and Policy, University of Bergen, 18–20 May 2005. Any references to the present refer to that time.

2   http://www.ambafrance-cm.org/html/camero/ensrech/prive.htm, November 2004.

3   109,784 out of a total of 213,074 students as of May 2004 were attending via the Internet through the University of Phoenix online campus.

4   Amadou Diop, at the Statistical Office at UCAD, was most helpful in making available the statistical material for Figures 16.1 and 16.2

5   Nevertheless, in addition to the compulsory reporting, in 2003, the Ministry of Education also carried out a campaign of visiting all private higher education institutions with a temporary authorisation in order to contribute to the improvement of the quality within higher education in Senegal. During this campaign covering 40 institutions, the Ministry collected information about administrative concerns, the students, financial concerns, and the staff.

6   Three of the institutions which our research team visited – the Dakar branch of the US-based Suffolk University, ITECOM and Sup'Info – did not appear on the list.

7   In 2003, UCAD's vice-chancellor launched a process aiming to establish a credit system based on the model used by the Bologna Process in Europe. It should also be mentioned that UCAD's vice-chancellor in 2004 stated in the press that the private sector's contribution to Senegalese higher education had to be recognised as necessary and positive.

8   Travelling around Dakar in January 2005, the surge of private higher education in Senegal is noticeable in the form of the expansion of existing buildings. Some of the institutions about to expand their existing campuses are ISM, IAM and Université du Sahel, while Université Dakar-Bourguiba finished a new building in 2004.

9   The locally based alternatives are not necessarily of a worse quality than the foreign, but they are run essentially with local staff. UDB, which probably has one of the lowest, if not the lowest, school fees in Senegal is known as an institution that produces some of the country's best candidates in their fields and is inventive in its organisation and in its programme offering.

10   F CFA 1 = €0.00152449, thus in euros the school fees for Suffolk University, HECI, IAM and UDB are €9147, €3049, €1220, €610 respectively. The reason why Suffolk University is so expensive compared with the others is that it is functioning as a delocalised American institution, notably by flying in staff from the USA.

11   The enrolment figures from around a dozen institutions are lacking in this material. But as we have had interviews with leaders at some of these institutions and looked at the profile of the others, it is still reason to believe that the sex distribution lies around 50–50.

12   Gabon is a country with less than 2 million inhabitants but with rich oil resources. Thus, a combination of lack of an appropriate offer within many fields of higher education nationally and a state which can afford to equip many students with scholarships to study abroad has led to many Gabonese students going to Senegal.

References

Altbach, Philip G. (1999) 'Comparative perspectives on private higher education', in P. G. Altbach (ed.) *Private Prometheus: Private Higher Education and Development in the 21st Century*, Boston: Boston College Center for International Higher Education and Greenwood Publishing.

Banégas, Richard and Jean-Pierre Warnier (2001) 'Nouvelles figures de la réussite et du pouvoir', *Politique africaine*, 82: 5–21.

Cissé, Fatou and Gaye Daffé (2002) 'L'ajustement interne: une politique coûteuse et inefficace', in A. Diagne and G. Daffé (eds) *Le Sénégal en quête d'une croissance durable*, Paris and Dakar: Karthala and CREA.

Diagne, Abdoulaye (2002) 'Les réformes après le changement de parité du franc CFA: 1994–2000', in A. Diagne and G. Daffé (eds) *Le Sénégal en quête d'une croissance durable*, Paris and Dakar: Karthala and CREA.

Diagne, Abdoulaye and Gaye Daffé (eds) (2002) *Le Sénégal en quête d'une croissance durable*, Paris and Dakar: Karthala and CREA.

Diagne, Abdoulaye, Sabiou Kassoum and Salif Sada Sall (2002) 'Nature et sources de la croissance', in A. Diagne and G. Daffé (eds) *Le Sénégal en quête d'une croissance durable*, Paris and Dakar: Karthala and CREA.

Direction de l'Enseignement Supérieur (DES), Ministère de l'Education (2004) *Enseignement Supérieur, Etat de lieux et enquêtes statistiques*, Dakar.

Edee, Emmanuel A. B. K. M. (2003) 'Togo', in D. Teferra and P. G. Altbach (eds) *African Higher Education: An International Reference Handbook*, Bloomington and Indianapolis: Indiana University Press.

Fraternité Matin (2004) 'Enseignement supérieur privé: les fondateurs menacent', Abidjan, 20 July.

Guedegbe, Corbin Michel (2003) 'Benin', in D. Teferra and P. G. Altbach (eds) *African Higher Education: An International Reference Handbook*, Bloomington and Indianapolis: Indiana University Press.

IAM (2004a) Rapport d'entrée pour l'année académique 2003–2004, Dakar, Sénégal.

IAM (2004b) Plaquette d'information 'C'est déjà demain'.

King, Roger (2003) *The Rise and Regulation of For-Profit Higher Education*, London: Observatory on Borderless Higher Education, December.

Levy, Daniel C. (2002) *Unanticipated Development: Perspectives on Private Higher Education's Emerging Roles*, Albany: PROPHE, Education Administration and Policy Studies, State University of New York, April.

Levy, Daniel C. (2003) *Profits and Practicality: How South Africa Epitomizes the Global Surge in Commercial Private Higher Education*, Education Administration and Policy Studies, University at Albany, State University of New York, Program for Research on Private Higher Education.

MEN (2004) *Rapport sur l'Enseignement Supérieur au Sénégal, 2004*, Dakar: Ministère de l'Education Nationale, Direction de l'Enseignement Supérieur.

Maldonado, Alma, Yingxia Cao, Philip G. Altbach, Daniel C. Levy and Hong Zhu (2004) *Private Higher Education: An International Bibliography*, Chestnut Hill, MA and Albany, NY: Center for International Higher Education, Lynch School of Education, Boston College and Program for Research on Private Higher Education (PROPHE), University at Albany.

Mbemba, Gaspard (2003) 'Congo (Brazzaville)', in D. Teferra and P. G. Altbach (eds) *African Higher Education: An International Reference Handbook*, Bloomington and Indianapolis: Indiana University Press.

Ngome, Charles (2003) 'Kenya', in D. Teferra and P. G. Altbach (eds) *African Higher Education: An International Reference Handbook*, Bloomington and Indianapolis: Indiana University Press.

Programme des Nations Unies pour le développement (PNUD) (2003) *Rapport mondial sur le développement humain 2003. Les Objectifs du Millénaire pour le développement: Un pacte entre les pays pour vaincre la pauvreté humaine*, Paris: Economica.

Rectorat (2004) *Statistiques*, Dakar: Université Cheikh Anta Diop, Rectorat.

Sawyerr, Akilagpa (2002) 'Challenges facing African universities. Selected issues', Paper. Accra: Association of African Universities.

Stiles, James (2003) 'Madagascar', in D. Teferra and P. G. Altbach (eds), *African Higher Education: An International Reference Handbook*, Bloomington and Indianapolis: Indiana University Press.

Teferra, Damtew and Philip G. Altbach (2004) 'African higher education: challenges for the 21st century', *Higher Education*, 47: 21–50.

Thaver, Beverley (2003) 'Private higher education in Africa', in D. Teferra and P. G. Altbach (eds) *African Higher Education: An International Reference Handbook*, Bloomington: Indiana University Press.

University of Phoenix web site, http://www.phoenix.edu/mediarelations/index. aspx (accessed 10 September 2004).

World Bank (2002) *Constructing Knowledge Societies: New Challenges for Tertiary Education*, Washington, DC: World Bank.

Part IV

Transnational academic flows

Fazal Rizvi

An increased level of transnational mobility of people, knowledge and capital is one of the key characteristics of contemporary globalisation. Developments in transport technology have enabled more people to travel than ever before. The new digital media has allowed them to remain in touch with each other. Financial exchanges can now take place instantaneously. All this has transformed people's social imaginaries about how they are connected to the rest of the world, and what life options are available to them. The global integration of economic activity has intensified flows not only of capital but also of ideas and ideologies – people's sense of themselves, their desires and aspirations.

These developments have had a profound impact on higher education. Following Appadurai (2001), we posit that the globalisation of higher education is marked by a variety of flows – of academic staff and students, knowledge and the techniques of higher education management itself. Over the past two decades, we have witnessed an exponential growth in the number of international students, and the emergence of a global market in higher education, which has permitted national systems in a number of countries, such as the UK and Australia, to remain financially viable, and even pursue strategies of growth. Tuition fees paid by international students, for example, now generate almost one-fifth of the annual revenue of Australian universities. These students, from a wide variety of national backgrounds, have altered the cultural landscape of the universities, leading them to re-consider their fundamental purposes and re-structure their governance structures.

The globalisation of higher education has not only been shaped by student flows, however. It has also involved enhanced flows of university teachers and researchers, as they have increasingly become tied to global knowledge networks. Both governments and intergovernmental organisations such as the OECD have actively promoted such networks, arguing that the global knowledge economy demands international research and development (R&D) collaboration and its commercialisation. UNESCO, on the other hand, has viewed flows of researchers across the developed and developing countries as one way of overcoming the persistent problems of 'brain drain'. Offshore campuses and programmes have also encouraged cross-border flows of academics.

In this part, we are concerned to address the nature and volume, as well as sources and drivers, of cross-border flows in higher education. We want to consider how these flows are facilitated, what are their outcomes, and how they can be utilised in ways that are educationally and politically productive. Flows, it should be noted, are never smooth. The global markets are structured by student flows, for example, in ways that are uneven and asymmetrical across nations. Some nations are primarily exporters, while others are largely importers, while others still are predicated on the principles of bilateral exchange. Flows inevitably also create disjunctures – local effects that differ in different contexts. This part explores the differential impact of such global flows on universities, higher education systems and research forms, as well as the issue of how such flows impact on the people caught up in them.

The use of the term 'flows' here is deliberate, and, as a metaphor, is designed to highlight the various dimensions of the new global cultural economy of which higher education is clearly a part. This economy can only be understood in terms of complex, overlapping, disjunctive flows, which, as Appadurai (2006: 183) points out, 'cannot any longer be understood in terms of existing center–periphery models, even those that might account for multiple centers and peripheries'. In this way, the idea of flow underscores the importance of political agency. It refers to 'things not staying in their places, to mobility and expansion of many kinds, to globalization along many dimensions' (Harrenz 2006). Flows 'are not objectively given relations which look the same from every angle of vision, but rather that they are deeply perspectival constructs, inflected very much by the historical, linguistic and political situatedness of different sorts of actors: nation-states, multinationals, diasporic communities, as well as sub-national grouping and movements ...' (Appadurai 2006: 185).

Consistent with this view, Simon Marginson, in Chapter 17, suggests that higher education now involves a continuing interplay of global flows and is shaped in global, national and local dimensions simultaneously. Universities are now located within a complex and constantly evolving web of relationships connected to international agencies, governments and national systems, institutions, disciplines, professions, e-learning companies, NGOs and other agencies. While most of the work universities do remains nation-bound, Marginson argues, this work is increasingly affected by the emergence of certain global systems, constituted by various multilateral arrangements that require national systems to conform to the various accords, conventions and protocols. The Bologna Accord, for example, requires 'harmonisation' in such areas as degree structures in Europe, while the UNESCO/OECD protocols on recognition and quality assurance represent another example of an emerging global multilateralism in higher education policy, which is both driven, at least partly, by increasing flows of students and academics and, in turn, encourages further flows.

Drawing on data from the OECD and recent European literature and US sources, Marginson examines a range of questions concerning cross-border flows of academics. He asks whether these are becoming more frequent; if so, whether this is leading to a qualitative change in the worldwide configuration of academic labour; and whether some or all nations are converging in a global academic career system. If such a system is indeed developing, then this, Marginson maintains, has major implications for the preparation and deployment of academic labour at the national level, and for the traditions and rules governing faculty labour and careers.

Marginson's analysis of these questions shows that in so far as there is a global element in the academic labour market, it is deeply shaped by 'an Anglo-American linguistic and cultural hegemony in higher education'. US higher education not only provides stratified opportunities for mobile scholars, its ideologies and structures are also mimicked in a range of diverse ways. While the global reach of the American and, to a lesser extent, British higher education, is considerable, Marginson suggests, these do not entirely eliminate the national labour markets and career systems. Rather, he concludes, it 'residualises them on the global scale, in the longer run tending to weaken the reproduction of national traditions'. This of course more profoundly affects developing nations where capacity is already relatively weak (Altbach 2002). This global residualisation also at least partly explains the on-going problem of 'brain drain' that results from the flow of the most talented scholars and researchers from the developing countries to the United States in particular.

While Marginson's analysis addresses issues of the emerging global academic labour markets, the chapter by Terri Kim examines patterns of academic mobility in comparative and historical terms. She argues that the transnational mobility of academics and knowledge workers is not new, and shows how academic mobility was highly prized in, for example, the early medieval universities in Europe. During the late nineteenth and early twentieth century, there was a considerable amount of scholarly exchange between German and Japanese and American universities. The inter-war period was marked by cross-Atlantic academic movements from Europe to the United States. In each of these periods, Kim argues, academic flows were driven not only by considerations of how knowledge was best produced and disseminated but also by a range of economic and political factors, which led academics to seek opportunities abroad. The period between the first and second World Wars, for example, witnessed a specific pattern of academic mobility and knowledge transfer, with many German and Austrian scientists, mostly Jewish, fleeing to the UK and the USA to escape Nazi persecution. This mobility was structured around both push and pull factors, and took place through various academic and professional networks.

Kim suggests that in the contemporary period of globalisation the scale and speed of cross-border academic mobility has been facilitated by an economic ideology promoted vigorously by national governments, transnational corporations and international organisations alike. This ideology celebrates the liberalisation of economic activity and seeks to eradicate national policy restrictions on the movement of not only capital but also labour. However, while organisations such as the World Trade Organisation continue to advocate the removal of barriers to labour mobility, national governments pursue highly selective policies as to the type of academics they welcome. Guided by a new discourse of knowledge economy, they recognise that knowledge is produced and commercialised through a complex network of cross-border linkages, and therefore make strategic assessments about whom they should seek to recruit. Kim provides a detailed analysis of the various categories of academics that are considered desirable for their talents within an increasingly fierce globally competitive market. In this way, she concludes, the contemporary patterns of academic mobility 'are increasingly multilateral and multidirectional in both coordinated and uncoordinated manners in the global expansion of knowledge economy'.

The drivers of cross-border flows are not only economic, however. They are also cultural and political. Crucial, for example, are the strong diasporic networks which encourage mobility, and which provide a supportive environment for managing the complex social processes associated with it. If we resist the temptation of theorising mobility in a naturalistic and linear fashion then transnational academic labour markets are not merely located within a global economic space but are also linked to the restructuring and extension of networks of money, technologies, people and ideas and to their articulations with real spaces at different scales. In this way, transnational diasporic networks articulate relations of power and meaning. To understand the cultural politics of these networks, we need to realise how academic identities are increasingly linked to transnational communication circuits, which spread out across social and national boundaries, which allows people to think about being affiliated with more than one place at once. The assumption that there is a one-to-one relation between territoriality and belonging can perhaps no longer be entirely sustained.

Recognising some of these theoretical insights, in Chapter 19, Welch and Zhen demonstrate how Chinese-born academics around the world represent an 'intellectual diaspora'. Based on interviews with Chinese-born academics at a research university in Sydney, Welch and Zhen explore the ways in which these academics work within the diaspora, by maintaining communication and collaboration at a global level. They examine patterns of communication and the factors that impact on their formation and sustainability. Their research supports the mainstream research on the so-called 'diaspora option', which suggests that the exodus of the highly skilled from developing countries need not necessarily be viewed negatively, but as a potential resource to be mobilised by the country of origin (Meyer and Brown, 1999). In light of the deepening interconnectedness of the world, especially the research world, scientific diasporas thus represent a new way of representing mobility, as strategically constituted, dynamic and therefore always relational.

The chapter by Britez and Peters also focuses on the social networks that have been created by increased levels of cross-border mobility. But for them this mobility is not only physical but also virtual. Following Castells (1999), they argue that informational technologies have enabled the emergence of a new space of organisation for dominant activities of the world: from 'a space of places' to a 'space of flows', with the digitalising of different types of text, thus the convergence of different media, facilitating the processing and transferring of information. This has changed the cultural landscape within which higher education now takes places. This landscape is characterised by new social and cultural formations, and by new political possibilities for the internationalisation of higher education.

The dominant mainstream view of internationalisation of universities, they observe, is based on a range of neo-liberal precepts, which emphasise the view of international mobility of students, in particular, primarily as a strategic economic resource or a source of revenue for institutions. One of the fundamental problems with this neo-liberal view, they argue, is the lack of its reflexive engagement with the potential consequences and complex dynamics of increasing transnational mobilities. In light of our growing global interconnections, they discuss an alternative view of internationalisation of higher education, forged around what they refer to as a 'cosmopolitical vision of the university', which has a greater potential for realising some of its historic tasks concerned with the creation of globally aware citizens. In the final part of their analysis, they ask: what kind of 'cosmopolitan selves' is a project of university cultivating, and how can 'cosmopolitical' learning be facilitated by mobility, both real and virtual?

The idea of virtual mobility is the theme of the final chapter in the volume by Cope and Kalantzis. In recent years, labour mobility is increasingly virtual. Workers in India, for example, program software applications, transcribe medical dictation online, chase credit card debtors, and sell mobile phones, diet pills, and mortgages for companies based in other countries around the world. According to Aneesh (2005), while these Indian citizens continue to live in India, their skills and labour clearly migrate abroad. He calls this phenomenon 'virtual migration', highlighting the need to examine the emerging 'transnational virtual space' where labour and vast quantities of code and data cross national boundaries, but the workers themselves do not.

Cope and Kalantzis argue that the modern universities are at the cusp of a major revolution in higher education, resulting from the developments in digital technologies, which have the potential of displacing print as the primary means of access to the knowledge of academics and as the dominant medium for the delivery of instructional content. Digitalisation, they argue, is not only changing the textual forms of representation, but is also giving rise to new social forms, which they refer to as the 'social web', a term they use to describe the kinds of relationships to knowledge and culture that are emerging in the era of pervasively interconnected computing. Digitalisation is transforming the nature of cross-border flows, both of people and of knowledge, and of the relations between the two. If this is so then Cope and Kalantzis ask: what, then, are the impacts and potentials of these changes on two of the fundamental missions of the university: knowledge formation and teaching?

References

Altbach, P. (2002) 'Centers and peripheries in the academic profession: the special challenges of developing countries', in Philip Altbach (ed.) *The Decline of the Guru: The Academic Profession in Developing and Middle-Income Countries*, Boston College, Chestnut Hill, pp. 1–22.

Aneesh, A. (2005) *Virtual Migration*, Durham, NC: Duke University Press.

Appadurai, A. (ed.) (2001) *Globalization*, Durham, NC: Duke University Press.

Appadurai, A. (2006) 'Disjuncture and difference in the global cultural economy', in H. Lauder, P. Brown, J. Dillabough and A. H. Halsey (eds) *Education, Globalization and Social Change*, Oxford: Oxford University Press, pp. 179–88.

Castells, M. (1999) 'Flows, networks, and identities: a critical theory of the informational society', in M. Castells, R. Flecha, P. Freire, H. A. Giroux, D. Macedo and P. Willis (eds) *Critical Education in the New Information Age*, Lanham, MD: Rowman & Littlefield, pp. 37–64.

Harrenz, U. (2006) 'Flows, boundaries and hybrids: keywords in transnational anthropology', retrieved June 2007 from: http://www.transcomm.ox.ac.uk/working%20papers/hannerz.pdf.

Meyer, J.-P. and Brown, M. (1999) 'Scientific diasporas: a new approach to the brain drain', World Conference on Science, UNESCO ICSU, Budapest, June.

17 Have global academic flows created a global labour market?

Simon Marginson

Introduction

Any theorisation of higher education as a worldwide relational set must account for two elements. The first element is the flows across national borders, including flows of people (students, administrators, academic faculty); flows of media and messages, information and knowledge; flows of norms, ideas and policies; flows of technologies, finance capital and economic resources (Marginson and Sawir 2005). The second element is the worldwide patterns of differences that specify, channel and limit global flows: the patterns of horizontal differences in locality, language, pedagogy and scholarship, organisational systems, practices and cultures; and the patterns of vertical difference including those structured by competition, differentiation, hierarchy, inclusion and exclusion, and unequal resources and capabilities.

Higher education with its continuing interplay of global flows and difference/location is shaped in global, national and local dimensions simultaneously (Marginson and Rhoades 2002; Valimaa 2004). It connects to international agencies, governments and national systems, institutions, disciplines, professions, e-learning companies, NGOs and other agencies. While most of the activity within the worldwide higher education environment is nation-bound and the majority remains localised we can identify a distinctive global dimension that appears to be growing in importance. This global dimension or space intersects with each national higher education system and increasingly touches individual institutions, especially research-intensive universities, while also being external to them all. This development has many roots but above all derives from the worldwide roll-out of instantaneous messaging with complex data transfer and the cheapening of air travel. We can observe the emergence of distinctive global systems within worldwide higher education, marked by bounded commonalities, linkages, points of concentration (nodes), rhythms, speeds and modes of movement. Research outputs have become predominantly global in character: there is a single mainstream system of English language publication of research knowledge. There are emerging multilateral approaches to recognition and quality assurance, for example the Washington Accords in Engineering and the UNESCO/OECD protocols on quality assurance. The Bologna

Accord facilitates partial integration and convergence in areas such as degree structures in Europe.

Academic labour, constituted by the work practices of faculty, post-doctoral scholars and researchers and doctoral students, has always combined both a local/national element and a cross-border element. Some scholars and researchers are in open demand in more than one country. Others carry their skills from one country to another using academic work as their migratory bridge. Still more use international visits as a means of securing training or career advancement that can be leveraged back home. Research-related and doctoral activities tend to be more globally universal in character than the more nation-bound and locally idiosyncratic processes of academic appointment, promotion, performance management and remuneration. Historically cross-border movements involved passing from one separated domain, one academic labour market and career system, to another. The questions discussed in this chapter are whether cross-border faculty movements are becoming more frequent and if so whether this is leading to a qualitative change in the worldwide configuration of academic labour. Can we identify a distinctive global domain of academic labour, parallel to the global domain in scientific publications and research collaboration? What are the implications for nationally-based academic labour? Can we detect transformations in the fairly obdurate traditions and rules governing faculty labour and careers? Are some or all nations converging in a global academic career system? What does the evidence tell us?

The chapter draws on data from the Organisation for Economic Cooperation and Development (OECD), recent European literature and US sources (NSB 2006; IIE 2006). The focus is on research universities where the data are strongest and global practices more extensive than elsewhere.[1]

Conceptual notes

Definitions of 'internationalisation' and 'globalisation'

In this chapter the terms 'internationalisation' and 'globalisation' are not understood as mutually exclusive Weberian ideal types or contrasting norms for policy and practice in higher education, so that for example 'internationalisation' is understood as a domain of inter-cultural relations on the basis of equality (Knight 2004) and 'globalisation' as the roll-out of world capitalism (Welch 2002). Rather 'internationalisation' and 'globalisation' are defined in geo-spatial terms and in this chapter treated as otherwise neutral as to educational practices. They are understood as two different dimensions of cross-border human action with differing implications for transformation in higher education, research and academic labour.

'Internationalisation', a long-standing feature of higher education, here means the thickening of relationships between nations ('inter-national' relations). In this national institutions and practices are affected at the margins but essentially remain intact.

'Globalisation' means the enhancement of worldwide or regional (for example pan-European) spheres of action. It has potentially transformative effects within nations and in remaking the common environment in which they relate to each other.

Arguably the dialectic between the two different kinds of cross-border action, global and international, is foundational to the university as an institution. In one respect the university was grounded in European mobility and scholarly Latin; that is, in global relations. It remains so: worldwide disciplinary networks often constitute stronger academic identities than do domestic locations. But from the beginning universities were also locally idiosyncratic and partly open to other powers; and in the nineteenth and twentieth centuries higher education became a primary instrument of nation-building and population management (Scott 1998). Today higher education continues to be partially subject to national culture and government. It is imagined by national policy makers as a primary instrument of the globally focused 'competition state' (Beerkens 2004), which concedes universities a measure of autonomy in order to enhance their effectiveness in cross-border relations. Globalisation does not necessarily imply an end to national regulation. The distinction between internationalisation and globalisation is not a national/global distinction. (Arguably, those who imagine the global higher education environment in terms of a global/national or global/local dialectic, as if there is only one kind of cross-border relationship, have misunderstood that environment.) Internationalisation and globalisation each creates conditions of possibility for the other. They sometimes feed into each other and they sometimes substitute for each other.

Forms of global transformation

Global, international and national practices in higher education are layered on and mixed with each other and this plays out in variable manner in different nations, disciplines, kinds of institution and parts of a single institution. Some cross-border effects are felt directly in institutions on a daily basis through global dealings. Others are mediated by national policy or academic cultures. The patterns of direct/indirect global effect vary by location and over time. In sum, there are three kinds of potential global transformation of the academic profession(s):

(1) Global processes distinct from national ones, that once established are difficult for national agents to block or modify. This might include the formation of a global market in academic labour with the potential to swallow or crowd out national labour markets.

(2) Global systems, relationships and flows that directly engender common changes in different national higher education systems leading to convergence. Examples within higher education include cross-border disciplinary networking, the use of English as the principal language of academic exchange and Internet publishing. An example in academic labour could include convergence in approaches to doctoral training. The question

here is not just the existence and the salience of global flows but whether these flows tend to homogenise national labour markets and career norms.

(3) Parallel reforms by the different autonomous national governments, following globally common ideas and templates, which might lead to some convergence (though rarely to identity) between different national higher education systems. For example, almost everywhere policy and management have been affected by the norms of Anglo-American New Public Management in which national higher education systems are understood as quasi-markets and individual institutions are modelled as quasi-firms.

Transformations made under national auspices, type 3 transformations, may lead to a 'tipping point' facilitating transformations type 1 and 2; particularly in reforms in a national system or single institution reforms focused on opening up higher education across borders.

'Americanisation' in higher education

Contemporary globalisation is associated with 'Americanisation' in higher education and other sectors and more generally, with an Anglo-American linguistic and cultural hegemony in higher education (Valimaa 2004: 29; Marginson, forthcoming). Under any scenario we could expect asymmetries in the global flows between national systems and individual institutions of people, knowledge, ideas and money; but in this era American and to a lesser extent British higher education institutions play a special and dominant role. This affects not just developing nations where capacity is relatively weak (Altbach 2002) but also the more developed national university systems. According to the annual survey of research performance by the Shanghai Jiao Tong University Institute of Higher Education, 71 of the top 100 research universities are in English-speaking nations: 54 in the USA (including 17 of the top 20), 11 in the UK, four in Canada and two in Australia. Another 22 are in Western Europe, six are in Japan and one in each of Israel and Russia. The principal Western European nations are Germany (five), France and Sweden (four each), Switzerland (three) and the Netherlands (two). China and India have none of the leading 100 research universities. China, including Hong Kong and Taiwan, has 19 of the top 500 universities while India has two in the top 500 (SJTUIHE 2006). *The Economist* (2005) refers to a 'global super-league' led by Harvard, Stanford, Yale, Berkeley, MIT, Cambridge and Oxford, universities that draw the best academic personnel from all over the world and enhance career opportunities anywhere. But there are broader advantages conferred by studying and working in the USA that extend beyond the 'super-league'. US doctoral universities in general confirm worldwide career benefits while also opening the way to migration into the United States itself.

The USA is relatively open to foreign academic talent and has the will and means to attract that talent. The foreign doctoral enrolment was 102,084 in 2004–5 (IIE 2006). Foreign-originated personnel have become essential to university and industry research in many fields. Two-thirds of all foreign doctoral students in the USA receive subsidies from their host university and American salaries are relatively attractive. Compared with most other national labour markets the American academic labour market is flexible. The norming of part-time and non-tenure track labour, the weak nexus between remuneration and calendar and major variations in levels of pay and allowances, coupled with the size and differentiation of American higher education, ensures a multiple and varied opportunity structure. There are signs that the flow into the USA is increasing, for example the rising proportion of foreign students within the total doctoral cohort and the growing stay rates of foreign doctoral graduates. Stay rates vary by field of study and nation. Potential migration is especially high for students from China, Israel, Argentina, Peru, Eastern Europe and Iran; and some wealthy countries including the UK, Canada, New Zealand and Germany. Between 1992 and 2001 the stay rate for Chinese graduates in science and engineering jumped from 65 to 96 per cent, and for India from 72 to 86 per cent (Vincent-Lancrin 2004: 32), though stay rates are lower for Korea, Japan, Indonesia and Mexico (Guellec and Cervantes 2002: 92).

One outcome is that net brain drain is a potential problem for all nations other than the USA. In 2003 three-quarters of EU citizens who obtained a US doctorate said they had no plans to return to Europe (Tremblay 2005: 208). As well as Germany losing many doctoral graduates in the USA and the UK, its own capacity to attract foreign faculty and doctoral students has diminished. Berning (2004: 177) remarks that while German research universities are seen as uniformly good there is a lack of highest prestige US-style 'centres of excellence':

> German study courses and degrees have lost part of their former international reputation. This is mainly due to the worldwide expansion and adoption of the Anglo-American HE system, its courses and degrees, but not to a lack of scientific quality in Germany. The consequence is a loss of foreign students from countries close to Germany but now following the Anglo-American mainstream (e.g. East Asia, Turkey). The loss of foreign students may cause a loss of young scientists from abroad too.
>
> (Berning 2004: 177)

'Europeanisation'

The 'Americanisation' of higher education and research is not a political project managed by the US government. It is comprised in the accumulation of the myriad cross-border relations conducted by individuals and institutions. This contrasts with 'Europeanisation' in higher education, which though it is partly constituted bottom-up in the cross-border flows of people and ideas, is also a top-down political project of deliberated convergence. Cross-border educational mobility has been sustained by the Erasmus programme, convergence of degree structures is secured by the Bologna Accord and regional research organisation and cooperation/competition by the European Research Area. If part of the European project consists of negotiating closer collaboration between unchanging sovereign states (internationalisation), another part consists of the creation of pan-European systems and spaces with the potential to modify the role of nation-states (globalisation). Changes of types 2 and 3 are opening European higher education to a larger transformation than explicitly envisaged: 'European countries are creating a process towards an open higher education system and research area which means that a return to a "closed" public higher education system based on the nation-state ... is an illusion' (Enders and de Weert 2004c: 27).

Global mobility and national labour markets

So what then does the evidence tell us? Have the academic profession(s) become subject to internationalisation, or globalisation, or a mix of the two? Enhanced 'internationalisation' would imply that mobility and exchange between faculty across national borders is more intensive and extensive but national faculty labour markets and career dynamics are largely unchanged. 'Globalisation' would imply that at least some core national elements are converging (a transformation of type 2), or dissolving into the global dimension (type 1). In turn this suggests three empirical questions. The first concerns what is happening with faculty and doctoral mobility. Is cross-border movement becoming more extensive and intensive? The second question concerns the global element in academic labour markets. Is this becoming more important, and is it partly displacing national labour markets? The third question concerns what is happening in those national academic labour markets themselves. Are they converging to any extent in their structures (starting points, tenure tracks, securities, criteria and procedure for promotion, differentials, etc.) and in cultures? Is there a tendency to a single cross-national academic labour market or possibly a number of such labour markets?

Global mobility

Here the empirical waters are muddied by the discursive bias in favour of faculty mobility in governmental, university and public zones. Pro-mobility arguments feed into professional norms and are taken for granted in higher education and research policies. Though it varies by nation, Teichler (2004: 11) notes that 'most academics hold cosmopolitan values in high esteem' and internationalising one's knowledge base is a relatively 'safe' method of intellectual growth engaged selectively and at will. Avveduto's (2001) study of faculty and doctoral students in six Italian universities found that 'overseas experience is rated by the vast majority of professors and students as highly desirable and is often cited as a value per se'. Only 26 per cent of the students had studied abroad but 96 per cent of those who had not, wanted to do so (Avveduto 2001: 233). The near universal enthusiasm for mobility is nested in assumptions about the internationalised character of universities, the freewheeling transferability of intellectual capacity and doctoral training, and the contribution of mobility to innovation and competitiveness and as a solution to capacity weaknesses and skill shortages. In turn the assumption that faculty mobility is *desirable* breeds the perception that mobility is *increasing*. This perception is fed also by discussion of globalisation and the ideological assertions about 'borderlessness' in faculty work. It has almost become a given that research is in transition from faculty-driven, curiosity-led and discipline-bound 'mode 1', to multi-disciplinary 'mode 2' shaped by industry applications and government (Gibbons *et al.* 1994; Nowotny *et al.* 2001). In this discourse statements about weakening boundaries between disciplines, and between universities and industry, are loosely joined to talk of internationalisation and the global weakening of boundaries between nations. The argument slides too freely between 'globalisation' and this ambiguous 'borderlessness'. The mode 1/mode 2 thesis is poorly evidenced in empirical terms.

The actual evidence is fragmented and stronger on national labour markets than cross-border phenomena. Luijten-Lub *et al.* (2005: 157) remark that 'there are not many secure data on staff mobility' even in relation to foreign-born academic labour (Mahroum 2001: 220). Data often conflate short-term and permanent mobility. The clearest evidence of increasing mobility is in relation to short-term cross-border movement for academic purposes: research collaborations, conferences and short exchange visits, and recruitment and teaching in the cross-border degree market (OECD 2004a). Research is the primary factor encouraging mobility because of the universal character of dominant knowledges in the sciences. The USA draws the most visiting faculty, with the number of international scholar visitors rising from 59,981 to 89,634 in the ten years after 1994–5 (IIE 2006); though as for foreign student intake it faltered temporarily after 11 September 2001. Within Europe the main receiving countries for researchers are the UK (30 per cent), France (15 per cent), Germany (13 per cent) and the Netherlands (10 per cent) (Luijten-Lub *et al.* 2005: 157). Most European nations report growth in short-term faculty visits. One such case is Norway. 'There has been a substantial increase in all types of journey from 1981 to 2000': about 20 per cent (Smeby and Trondal 2005: 456–7). In the 1990s visits related to cross-border research collaboration increased more rapidly than any other category (ibid.: 457). There is a parallel increase in doctoral student mobility. Many governments subsidise foreign PhD experience. Many universities that once recruited all doctoral candidates locally are now active on the national and the international market (Enders and de Weert 2004a: 146).

To what extent does temporary academic mobility become permanent migration? The Anglophone countries and some others have 'relaxed their immigration laws to attract qualified and highly qualified foreigners, including students, to sectors where there were labour shortages' (Tremblay 2005: 197). The extent to which academic migration is increasing outside the USA is unclear, however. For example there are few data for postdoctoral mobility. According to Enders and de Weert (2004a: 146–7) studies of cross-border mobility in Europe at the postdoctoral stage suggest that mobility is basically stable. This would suggest that while doctoral populations are becoming more cosmopolitan this is not (yet?) associated with greater cross-border mobility at the next stage of faculty employment, except for greater mobility into the USA with its special global role.

For many faculty the trend is not to 'borderlessness' but complexity. Faculty find themselves working with and to a broader range of institutions, communities and stakeholders and in more national and international sites than before. Academic identities are becoming more multiple (Henkel 2005). This points to the possibility of a dual labour market structure in which a global market or markets operate(s) alongside and above national markets.

Global labour market(s)

In its *Science, Technology and Industry Outlook* the OECD (2004c) argues that an intensified global competition for scientific labour, driven by multi-national production, is feeding the evolution of a distinctively global market in R&D that in some research fields is subsuming national labour markets. However, it is less clear that global labour supply is looming larger in R&D located specifically in higher education.

A small number of faculty have an expertise and reputation conferring superior opportunities in many countries, including researchers at the peak of their fields and globally transferable teachers in areas like finance, accounting and, until recently, computing. This small group is strategic for national governments and research universities, augmenting as it does both the national innovation system and position in university rankings, and it has the potential to displace the top end of national labour markets. Nevertheless, it is important not to exaggerate the size of the group. 'One can expect international careers to primarily include a few top academics. Most others, and especially young candidates, still develop national careers' (Musselin 2004a: 72). Moreover a globally mobile pool of high quality researchers does not in itself constitute a single global labour market. The mobile researchers do not necessarily share a single set of conditions, remuneration and career structures.

Rather, what appears to be happening is this. There is an American labour market global in reach – the USA has ten times as many Jiao Tong 'HiCi' researchers as the next nation (Thomson-ISI 2006) – and this sets the upper benchmarks for salaries and research infrastructure support. Other national research systems are being pulled towards American benchmarks by market pressures, so bifurcating between the small upper globally mobile segment and other researchers. The globally mobile elite in each national system is a hybrid, with one foot in the global pool and the other in the national labour market, pulled two and sometimes more ways between career systems, recalling Henkel's point that faculty work is multiple rather than borderless. In 2003–4 the average American doctoral university salary for full professors for 9–10 months was $100,682 and total compensation $125,644, rising to $152,540 in independent private universities; while 6 per cent of full professors earned more than US $200,000 in salary alone (Academe 2006). By comparison Enders and de Weert (2004c: 18) note that the annual income of European professors ranged from €55,000–60,000 in the Netherlands and Germany to €13,000–20,000 in Greece and Eastern Europe.[2] Lee (2002a: 156–8) notes that Singapore's 'recently revised salary scales are internationally competitive and rank among the highest in the region'. Professors earn from US $82,800 to $117,000 per annum, on par with the USA except at the top end. Singapore has set out to create a cosmopolitan and globally competitive higher education system, partly based on expatriate faculty. Some salaries in China are also becoming more globally competitive.

At the same time most students and faculty going abroad continue to use temporary mobility selectively and strategically to advance their careers at home. In some emerging nations such as Malaysia cross-border mobility is integral to advanced training and an ongoing part of the national career system. Temporary mobility early in the career is echoed in later years by study leave trips of shorter duration again used to build scholarly capital realised on return. Musselin (2004a: 66–9) summarises it as follows. 'Most "mobile" academics generally favour careers in their native country and use mobility as a "plus" '; as an add-on to the vitae or an alternative route to national success by queue-jumping, though there can be risks to the prospects at home. In Italy, Avveduto (2001: 236–7) found that most doctoral students see study abroad as a supplement rather than a substitute for their local work, six months being the preferred duration. This kind of foreign experience constitutes a second quasi-global labour pool, again American-centred; but the bifurcation effect in home country labour markets is not as deep. The globally mobile tend to occupy the upper end of national labour markets but without deconstructing traditional remuneration levels.

What is happening to national labour markets?

The power of the 'high-flyers' within a global sellers' market to set the terms of salaries and conditions at the national level, and in the case of large-scale withdrawal to weaken the national research system, creates some potential for partial type 1 transformations in national labour markets. For example, in order to compete effectively for highly sought-after faculty, governments and universities are under pressure to differentiate salaries previously held in a roughly equal position across fields and between individuals at the same level regardless of merit. More generally, within each national system the weight of those with cross-border experience, especially American experience, is probably growing. This again suggests there is potential to relativise national career systems, in the longer run opening them to global influences and parallel nation-by-nation changes, the more so as nations implement increasingly common systems of governance and organisation via neo-liberal reform.

Nevertheless, converging managerial templates and even a common system architecture do not necessarily produce one global higher education system and labour market, even in Europe where conditions for structural and cultural integration are more favourable than elsewhere. Likewise the shaping effects of global experience on academic mentalities, and the competition for elite labour, are not (yet?) undermining career traditions in the larger and more robust nations. Musselin finds no sign of Europeanisation of academic recruitment and careers paralleling the European research framework (Musselin 2004a: 72; 2005: 135). There are continuing significant differences in relation to the legal status of faculty, remuneration and its regulation, language, and procedures for appointment and promotion (Musselin 2004a: 56–62). 'The proportion of staff with and without tenure is highly variable ... each country defines its own career requirements for the profession ... the various stages of a career do not obey the same rules' (Musselin 2003). Diversity between national labour markets inhibits mobility and blocks the formation of large-scale cross-country pools of labour; more so when that diversity is socially and culturally embedded. Likewise there has long been variation in the degree of globalisation by field of study, though there are now convergences in some nations (Enders and de Weert 2004b). Nevertheless Musselin does not close off the possibility of deeper transformation. She notes that foreign recruitment within and into Europe may increase (Musselin 2004a: 74), which would pluralise values and habits in what are still in many ways culturally protected systems. One suspects that Europeanisation and Americanisation both have much further to run.

In just two areas the process of common and parallel reforms unequivocally encourages global mobility and labour market convergence. The first is the adoption of more similar approaches to doctoral training. A number of higher education systems across Europe have shifted paradigms for doctoral training from the Humboldtian model towards the so-called 'professional model' (Enders 2005: 120), contributing to the standardisation of the point of entry of faculty careers and facilitating broader employability. The second area is the negotiation of cross-border recognition of institutions and programmes (OECD 2004b: 24).

Conclusions

In sum, while there is a global element in faculty labour markets it has not subsumed national markets into a single worldwide set of regulations, salaries and conditions. Rather, a small but influential global tier has been imposed on top of the national labour markets where the great majority of faculty continue to be bounded. The global component is comprised by highly mobile researcher/scholars and led from the 'super-league' universities. US higher education provides a large pool of diverse and stratified opportunities. The global element also takes in the rest of the American doctoral sector, some British institutions, and a sprinkling of research universities in Europe and in Asia (Japan, Singapore, Hong Kong) though only a minority of their faculty are potentially mobile on the global scale. The effect of Americanisation is to sustain the US-dominated global pool of high priced high quality researchers, while establishing US higher education for doctoral students and faculty as the primary site of extra-national opportunity. Americanisation does not abolish other national labour markets and career systems. Rather it residualises them on the global scale, in the longer run tending to weaken the reproduction of national traditions, especially in smaller countries.

Except at the top end of academic labour national labour markets are being subordinated and stratified rather than displaced. The most general outcome of globalisation in the academic profession(s) is not the creation of a single global labour market but the shaping of stratification on the world scale between those with global freedoms and those bound to the soil within nations or localities. This leads to (1) the bifurcation of national labour markets and (2) bifurcation on the world scale between nationally employed labour (arranged in a hierarchy between the nations) and predominantly American-aligned globally mobile labour. While most cross-border mobility constitutes 'internationalisation' the growth of the globally employable elite and the increasing stratification effects constitute global transformations. Elite researchers, now in a stronger bargaining position and sustaining globally referenced disciplinary cultures in the research-intensive universities despite more managed settings, are themselves key agents of globalisation in knowledge and culture. It is likely that their full transformative impact in higher education is not yet apparent. They are likely to become increasingly privileged *vis-à-vis* national systems and the majority of faculty whose work is largely teaching centred. This may encourage the fragmentation of the teaching–research nexus and growth in research-only positions; and there are some signs of this, for example in the UK (Enders and de Weert 2004c: 24). A further possibility though is the growth of outsourcing to countries like India where research labour is cheaper, reducing the dependence of the USA on migrants and modifying tendencies to elitification of mobile researchers.

Europeanisation is more likely than Americanisation to create an integrated academic labour market – at least in Europe – because of the commitment to mobile professional labour coupled with the potential for multilateral and bilateral changes to legal, regulatory and financial structures, though little integration of career structures has taken place so far. Given the pulling power of the American labour market, a robust European-wide labour market could develop only if it was bounded by coherent regulatory structures, broadly consistent across the European region in career frames and remuneration levels and eventually viable across Eastern as well as Western Europe. If not, the different European national markets will continue to become more stratified within and because of the global academic setting.

Notes

1 It must be acknowledged that this imparts something of a 'globalist' bias to the argument.

2 These are not Purchasing Power Parity (PPP) comparisons. Accounting for differences in the cost of living narrows the cross-border differentials.

References

Academe (2006) 'Annual report on the economic status of the profession, 2003–2004'. Accessed 10 February 2006 at http://www.aaup.org/surveys/04z/alltabs.pdf.

Altbach, P. (2002) 'Centers and peripheries in the academic profession: the special challenges of developing countries', in Philip Altbach (ed.) *The Decline of the Guru: The Academic Profession in Developing and Middle-Income Countries*, Boston College, Chestnut Hill, pp. 1–22.

Avveduto, S. (2001) 'International mobility of PhDs', in OECD, *Innovative People: Mobility of Skilled Personnel in National Innovation Systems*, Paris: OECD, pp. 243–60.

Beerkens, H. J. J. G. (2004) *Global Opportunities and Institutional Embeddedness: Higher Education Consortia in Europe and Southeast Asia*, Center for Higher Education Policy Studies, University of Twente. Accessed 10 February 2006 at http://www.utwente.nl/cheps/documenten/thesisbeerkens.pdf.

Berning, E. (2004) 'Petrified structures and still little autonomy and flexibility: Country report Germany', in Jurgen Enders and Egbert de Weert (eds) *The International Attractiveness of the Academic Workplace in Europe*, Frankfurt: Gewerkschaft Erziehung und Wissenschaft, pp. 160–82.

Enders, J. (2005) 'Border crossings: research training, knowledge, dissemination and the transformation of academic work', *Higher Education*, 49: 119–33.

Enders, J. and de Weert, E. (2004a) 'Science, training and career: changing modes of knowledge production and labour markets', *Higher Education Policy*, 17, 135–52.

Enders, J. and de Weert, E. (eds) (2004b) *The International Attractiveness of the Academic Workplace in Europe*, Frankfurt: Gewerkschaft Erziehung und Wissenschaft.

Enders, J. and De Weert, E. (eds) (2004c) 'The international attractivness of the academic workplace in Europe – synopsis report', in Jurgen Enders and Egbert de Weert (eds) *The International Attractiveness of the Academic Workplace in Europe*, Frankfurt: Gewerkschaft Erziehung und Wissenschaft, pp. 11–31.

Gibbons, M., Limoges, C., Nowotny, H., Schwartzman, S., Scott, P. and Trow, M. (1994) *The New Production of Knowledge: The Dynamics of Science and Research in Contemporary Societies*, London: Sage.

Guellec, D. and Cervantes, M. (2002) 'International mobility of highly skilled workers: from statistical analysis to policy formulation', in OECD (ed.) *International Mobility of the Highly Skilled*, Paris: OECD, pp. 71–98.

Henkel, M. (2005) 'Academic identity and autonomy in a changing policy environment', *Higher Education*, 49: 155–76.

Institute for International Education (IIE) (2006) Data on US international education. Accessed 1 February 2006 at http://www.iie.org/.

Knight, J. (2004) 'Internationalisation remodeled: definition, approaches, and rationales', *Journal of Studies in Higher Education*, 8(1): 5–31.

Lee, M. (2002a) 'The academic profession in Malaysia and Singapore: between bureaucratic and corporate cultures', in Philip Altbach (ed.) *The Decline of the Guru: The Academic Profession in Developing and Middle-Income Countries*, Boston College, Chestnut Hill, pp. 141–72.

Luijten-Lub, A., van der Wende, M. and Huisman, J. (2005) 'On cooperation and competition: a comparative analysis of national policies for internationalization of higher education in seven Western European countries', *Journal of Studies in Higher Education*, 9(2): 147–63.

Mahroum, S. (2001) 'Foreign scientific researchers in selected OECD EU countries: data sources and analysis', in OECD (ed.) *Innovative People: Mobility of Skilled Personnel in National Innovation Systems*, Paris: OECD, pp. 219–28.

Marginson, S. (forthcoming) 'Global university hegemony', *Critique Internationale*.

Marginson, S. and Rhoades, G. (2002) 'Beyond national states, markets, and systems of higher education: a glonacal agency heuristic', *Higher Education*, 43: 281–309.

Marginson, S. and Sawir, E. (2005) 'Interrogating global flows in higher education', *Globalization, Societies and Education*, 3(3): 281–310.

Musselin, C. (2003) 'Internal versus external labour markets', *Higher Education Management and Policy*, 15(3): 9–23.

Musselin, C. (2004a) 'Towards a European academic labour market? Some lessons drawn from empirical studies on academic mobility', *Higher Education*, 48: 55–78.

Musselin, C. (2004b) 'The academic workplace: up to now it is not as bad … but! Country report France', in Jurgen Enders and Egbert de Weert (eds) *The International Attractiveness of the Academic Workplace in Europe*, Frankfurt: Gewerkschaft Erziehung und Wissenschaft, pp. 141–59.

Musselin, C. (2005) 'European academic labour markets in transition', *Higher Education*, 49: 135–54.

Nowotny, H., Scott, P. and Gibbons, M. (2001) *Rethinking Science: Knowledge and the Public in an Age of Uncertainty*, Cambridge: Polity Press.

NSB (National Science Board) (2006) 'Science and engineering indicators 2004'. Accessed 30 September 2006 at: http://www.nsf.gov/statistics/seind04/

Organization for Economic Cooperation and Development (OECD) (2004a) *Internationalization and Trade in Higher Education: Opportunities and Challenges*, Paris: OECD.

Organization for Economic Cooperation and Development (OECD) (2004b) *Quality and Recognition in Higher Education: The Cross-Border Challenge*, Paris: OECD.

Organization for Economic Cooperation and Development (OECD) (2004c) *OECD Science, Technology and Industry Outlook*, Paris: OECD.

Scott, P. (1998) 'Massification, internationalization and globalization', in Peter Scott (ed.) *The Globalization of Higher Education*, Buckingham: Society for Research into Higher Education/Open University Press, pp. 108–29.

Shanghai Jiao Tong University Institute of Higher Education (SJTUIHE) (2006) *Academic Ranking of World Universities*. Accessed 1 December at http://ed.sjtu.edu.cn/ranking.htm.

Smeby, J.-C. and Trondal, J. (2005) 'Globalization or Europeanization? International contact among university staff', *Higher Education*, 49: 449–66.

Teichler, U. (2004) 'The changing debate on internationalization of higher education', *Higher Education*, 48: 5–26.

The Economist (2005) 'The brains business', 8 September.

Thomson-ISI (2006) Data on highly cited researchers, ISIHighlyCited.com. Accessed 10 April 2007 at: http://isihighlycited.com.

Tremblay, K. (2005) 'Academic mobility and immigration', *Journal of Studies in International Education*, 9(3): 196–228.

Valimaa, J. (2004) 'Nationalisation, localization and globalization in Finnish higher education', *Higher Education*, 48: 27–54.

Vincent-Lancrin, S. (2004) 'Building capacity through cross-border tertiary education', Paper prepared for the UNESCO/OECD Australia Forum on Trade in Educational Services, 11–12 October. Accessed 10 February 2006 at http://www.oecd.org/dataoecd/43/25/33784331.pdf.

Welch, A. (2002) 'Going global? Internationalizing Australian universities in a time of global crisis', *Comparative Education Review*, 46(4): 433–71.

18 Transnational academic mobility in a global knowledge economy

Comparative and historical motifs

Terri Kim

The purpose of this chapter is to analyse the changing relations of academic mobility and knowledge across international borders as part of the geography of higher education, with some reference to the twenty-first century.

The chapter will first look briefly to the past to ask what had been some of the earlier patterns in the international movement of academics and knowledge before we reached the present moment. Thus, the organisation of the chapter is simple. It will provide some comparative examples of academic mobility and universities: first, the early medieval universities in Europe (approximately from 1200 to 1400); second, the late nineteenth and early twentieth century German and Japanese universities; and third, the inter-war period, especially cross-Atlantic academic movements and research knowledge transfer, from Europe and Germany to the USA. Then it looks at the contemporary situation. Specific examples of international academic recruitment policy and practice in Europe and East Asia will be provided before a conclusion is offered.

In this chapter, the term 'transnational' is used to highlight the idea of 'between' or 'above' including institutions that are 'between' or 'above' territorial boundaries. So the emphasis is on individuals and movements which are occurring in 'transnational space'; and not on official inter-action between nations. Therefore, transnational should be differentiated from the conventional understanding of 'international'.

Old patterns

Academic mobility in the sense of crossing territorial borders, and international or transnational academic recruitment are not new phenomena when we look at the history of universities since medieval times. The Bologna University model in the early medieval period (between 1200 and 1400) offers an interesting comparison to the contemporary market-driven, consumer-oriented patterns of university management, and transnational academic mobility and staff recruitment.

However, it was a student-governed university – in particular the power of the foreign students' guilds created a transnational academic political space in Bologna (Cobban 1971: 35–48). A *lingua franca* of medieval Europe assisted in transnational academic mobility. University lecturers were paid directly by student fees and the money relationship between students and lecturers affected the distribution of power in medieval southern Europe (Rashdall 1997; Ridder-Symoens 1992; Cobban 1971: 44). In that sense only, the university was *market-driven*.

However, in the early medieval period, many students went to universities in Southern Europe to qualify for one of the well-paid professions of law, medicine or teaching or in the service of the Church. Cobban (1971) notes: 'As the [early medieval] universities were, *par excellence*, centres for vocational training, gateways to lucrative careers, those who attended did so primarily from a sense of social urgency, from a need to realize professional ambition' (p. 33). It was from the late fourteenth century that members of the aristocracy began to permeate the universities in increasing numbers, and the content of university courses became broader (Ridder-Symoens 1992; Cobban 1971).

Overall, then, teachers in medieval Europe were recruited transnationally. The teaching doctors were hired, elected annually by the students, and dependent upon student fees (*collectae*) for their living (Rashdall 1997). They were teaching labour hired under short-term contracts, who had specialised knowledge but who were denied the exercise of power.

These aspects of academic life in early medieval times are eerily echoed in the present. An increasing number of contemporary academics are moving from one institution to another under short-term contracts. In the UK, the Association of University Teachers Report (AUT 2005) confirms this trend. Of the 334,155 employees in UK higher education in 2003–4, 45 per cent of academics were employed on fixed-term contracts. Two-thirds of academics on teaching-only contracts in 2003–4 were employed on a fixed-term basis, and 91 per cent of those on research-only contracts were fixed-term (AUT 2005).

Thus, the vocational outlook of early medieval university education and academic mobility reverberate – but we now have *policies* that frame transnational academic mobilities. The echoes remind us that it is the forces of change and the patterns of mobility which are of interest – not just the mobilities themselves.

After the fifteenth century, the medieval model waned, and universities evolved as national institutions (Rothblatt 1997) and that affected trans-national mobility quite dramatically. University academics have become positioned within a national frame of institutional development. Accordingly the academic identities are often locked up in national cultural traditions and social structures.

It was after the rise of nationalism and the nationalisation of the university in Europe that Germany developed during the late nineteenth and early twentieth centuries research centres of excellence that were recognised internationally. A large number of researchers, not only from other European countries but also from the United States and Japan travelled to Germany

– later to transfer the German tradition of a research university and its mode of knowledge production to their own national institutions at least up until the outbreak of the First World War (Clark 1983; Tanaka 2005).

The German impact on the United States and Japan was evident in the development of American research universities and Imperial Universities in Japan. In 1905, Berlin University, established within Prussia, had an annual exchange of professors with Columbia and Harvard Universities in the United States (Charle 2004: 403). However, given the emergence of nationalist movements in Europe of the late nineteenth century, this kind of German and US academic exchange was a purposeful, institutionalised academic network – very different from the old *Republique des letters* from the Renaissance onwards. The Second Reich in Germany (1871–1919) gave the Imperial Government the opportunity to utilise the international influence exerted by German research universities in the political arena (Charle 2004: 401). In that period, German academics were invited to Central European and German-speaking countries, the Baltic States, Hungary, and particularly to the United States: the pattern and scale of academic mobility was influenced by Germany's diplomatic alliances (Charle 2004: 416).

During the inter-war period, patterns of transnational academic mobility and new concentration of research knowledge were also affected by the relations between private philanthropy and the university. There were a substantial number of academics crossing the Atlantic in both directions, and many of them were funded by the Rockefeller Foundation established in 1913, and the International Education Board which was also formed by the Rockefeller family in 1923. The specific fields of academic knowledge sponsored by both the Rockefeller Foundation and the International Education Board for scientific research included mathematics, physics, medicine, biology, biochemistry, bacteriology and agricultural studies (Siegmund-Schultze 2001; Kohler 1987).

The Japanese example of nationalist-framed academic mobility is also clear. After the Meiji Restoration (1868) the nationalist mission to acquire and transfer modern scientific knowledge from Western countries, such as the USA, Britain, and especially Germany, was a policy in Japan. Japanese intellectuals first studied applied sciences such as medicine – unlike the classical scientific revolution of the sixteenth and seventeenth centuries in Europe, which began with physics and then spread elsewhere (Bartholomew 1989: 4). Great emphasis on science and technology in the Meiji era was evident in the high percentage of graduates of Tokyo University in scientific disciplines (85 per cent in the 1880s). In this way, the scientific community in Japan had a planned character – planned for the specific purpose of catching up with the Western standard of science as quickly as possible (Nakayama 1974: 209–10).

In the Meiji years, having foreign academics in the universities was vital for the transmission and development of scientific knowledge in Japan since the formation of an indigenous scientific community took time. American and European academics were appointed to professorial posts at major Japanese universities – even at Tokyo Imperial University until the early 1890s. In 1877–8, salaries paid to foreign professors were a third of the budget of Tokyo Imperial University, and during the 1880s, they increased even more (Bartholomew 1989: 64; Umetani 1971). However, the open policy of foreign academic staffing was soon to cease with the strong emphasis on Japanese nationalism at the turn of the century.

Thus, the Japanese mode of academic mobility and university knowledge production was coordinated by strong nationalist agendas and the emphasis was on practical knowledge. In 1870 the principles for the dispatch of students for study abroad emphasised (i) machinery, geology and mining, steel making, architecture, shipbuilding, commerce in Britain; (ii) zoology and botany, astronomy, mathematics, chemistry, law, international relations, promotion of public welfare in France; (iii) physics, medicine, pharmacology, educational system, political science and economics in Germany; and (iv) industrial laws, agriculture, cattle raising, communications, and commercial law in the United States (Nakayama 1974: 218–20). Central intellectual and political figures in Japan's Meiji era modernisation such as Yukichi Fukuzawa, Tenshin Okakura, Ukichi Taguchi, Hirobumi Ito and Arinori Mori had all studied abroad, with the specific mission of the adoption and adaptation of Western knowledge and practice, mainly from Great Britain, the United States, and Germany. Its scale and process were coordinated and controlled by the State (Tanaka 2005: 17–45; Schriewer 2004: 473–87). This was a deliberate and politically organised 'flow' of academic mobility and knowledge.

However, it should be noted that political disasters can also produce 'flows'. The political changes in Germany of 1933 with the rise of the Third Reich led to discrimination, expulsion and emigration of Jewish academics (Medawar and Pyke 2001). The Nazi German period witnessed a specific pattern of academic mobility and knowledge transfer. Many German and Austrian scientists, mostly Jewish, fled to the UK and the USA. Among these and also among Jewish émigrés from Central Europe who moved to the UK and USA, there were distinguished world class professors: for instance, Albert Einstein, Sigmund Freud, Karl Popper, Ludwig Wittgenstein, and Isaiah Berlin. The United States benefited greatly from the peculiar conditions that prevailed in Europe after the rise of Fascism and the outbreak of war. The influx of first-class scholars from Europe to the United States, and their participation in indigenous research teams played a pivotal role in the advancement of knowledge (Nakayama 1974: 228–9). Medawar and Pyke (2001) suggest that the emigration of scientists during the Nazi period was Hitler's loss and Britain's and America's gain. Max Perutz, who received the 1962 Nobel prize together with John Kendrew for their work on haemoglobin, wrote:

> ... the gain was mine. Had I stayed in my native Austria, even if there had been no Hitler, I could never have solved the problem of protein structure. ... We all [the exiled scientists] owe a tremendous debt to Britain. (Medawar and Pyke 2001)

Overall, the Nazi influence in Europe directly and indirectly contributed to the relocation of concentration of advanced research centres from Germany to the USA and the UK, to a very specific form of the transnational mobility of academics and of research knowledge, and to the redefinition of what were international centres of excellence.

In summary, academic mobility in early medieval Europe was 'transnational', laissez-faire and vocation-oriented. According to Cobban (1971), it was a 'severely practical business' (p. 29), conditioned by the socio-economic fields of power and hierarchies of professional knowledge of the time. In late nineteenth and early twentieth century Germany and Japan, the major patterns of academic mobility and knowledge production were 'international', engineered by political nationalism. During the inter-war period, a new form of cross-Atlantic 'transnational' academic mobility and the relocation of concentration of research knowledge and the new mode of applied knowledge production – so-called 'industrialised science' – became visible under the influence of private philanthropy in the United States – such as the Manhattan Project which built the first atomic bomb, and in the rise of Nazi German political nationalism, transnational academic mobility was a forced choice for Jewish scholars.

After World War II, the second half of the twentieth century saw a new wave of migrations in the change of political geography marked by the end of the British Empire and the rise of America within the new Cold War era. The end of the Cold War, the rise of a New Europe based on the enlarged European Union over the last decade, and the global 'war on terror' since the beginning of the twenty-first century have further diversified the traffic of migration.

Contemporary patterns

Since the 1990s the scale and speed of cross-border academic mobility has been increased by new recruitment policy strategies and the liberalisation of trade policies by many national governments (e.g., in the UK, the USA, Australia, Canada, Germany and France, EU and NAFTA), and through WTO/GATS. The immigration policies revised in these countries are specifically favourable towards highly skilled mobile knowledge workers and academics, especially those in science and technology, to meet the demand of advanced knowledge-based economies (Kuptsch and Pang 2006; Tremblay 2005). Simultaneously, the WTO/GATS multilateral negotiations are aiming to liberalise international trade in education and professional services. According to Gibbons (2003), in the so-called global knowledge economy, 'new sites of knowledge production are continually emerging that, in their turn, provide intellectual points of departure for further combinations or configurations of researchers' (p. 112).

To locate and explore this proposition, the chapter will now shift attention to the contemporary geography of transnational flows of academic mobility and new concentrations of knowledge production.

Types of mobile academics and forms of knowledge production

Contemporaneously, it is suggested that differences can be identified between mobile (1) distinguished 'senior' academics, (2) manager-academics, (3) entrepreneurial research-academics, and (4) trained academic researchers and/or teachers. Their patterns and purposes of transnational mobility vary.

For the distinguished 'senior' academics, their locality (i.e., their institutional base) would not affect their transnational mobility. As major thinkers and theoreticians, they are frequently invited to profess their expert knowledge everywhere. Such academics have always been with us. What is now probably more common is that institutionally they are often affiliated to multiple sites. It is not unusual for them to be based in more than two institutions transnationally and simultaneously.

Manager-academics are emerging as a new type of mobile academic leader in the contemporary entrepreneurial universities which is especially visible in the English-speaking, neoliberal market-driven economies such as the UK, the USA, Australia, and New Zealand. For instance, British universities are now recruiting globally not just foreign academics, but also foreign managers. It is becoming their job to change the nature of traditional university governance. British universities are using international head-hunters to recruit manager-academics directly from abroad. To initiate difficult changes inside British universities, the foreign identities of senior managers are seen as an advantage (Kim 2006: 211–17).

In the changing organisational culture inside British universities, ordinary academics are tightly 'managed' as employees under contracts. In professional terms, the role of ordinary academics in the university has been increasingly sub-divided into 'research' and 'teaching'. According to the AUT Report on 'The rise of teaching-only academics' (AUT 2005), barely half of academics in the UK – 55 per cent – are now employed to both teach and conduct research; and two-thirds of those teaching-only contracts are on a fixed-term basis (AUT 2005).

Short-term contracts are more common for foreign mobile academics. For instance, 66.81 per cent of the European academics working in the UK higher education sector are employed on temporary contracts (fixed term or hourly), which is higher than their UK counterpart (39.72 per cent) as of 2001 (European Social Statistics 2002 edition; Re-quoted from William Solesbury and Associates 2005: 85).

Given the nature of academic research, and the strong emphasis on research partnerships and empirical research evidence – especially in the European Research Areas (Martin-Rovet 2003; Morano-Foadi 2005), academic researchers in general have more opportunities to become mobile than those who mainly teach.

The recently published European Research Council's Green Paper 'The European Research Area: new perspectives' (CEC 2007) also stresses the importance of transnational academic mobility for the European Research

Area and highlights the necessity for realising a single labour market for 'researchers' to make new Europe the 'most dynamic competitive knowledge-based economy'.

As a step towards the goal, the European Strategic Forum on Research Infrastructures (ESFRI) established a European 'roadmap' for new and upgraded pan-European research infrastructures, encouraging researchers to create new 'networks of excellence' through the research Framework Programmes and to collaborate effectively with business and other stakeholders, both within and across borders 'in the most cost-effective manner' (CEC 2007: 13–15). Overall, the outcomes of EU research Framework Programmes are positively appraised as having opened up new channels of communication and exchange among different disciplinary specialists to provide a new mode of research and knowledge production that can transcend the national boundaries of academic interests (Benavot *et al.* 2005).

Given the pan-European research policies, for the entrepreneurial research academics, institutional base and academic networking become a very important part of their academic capital. They are mobile, running internationally organised funded-research projects which are often sponsored by national, international or supranational governments, agencies and foundations. Transnational academic competitions for research grants are accordingly becoming increasingly severe. For instance, the ERC Starting Grants call for proposals has received 9,167 research applications submitted by researchers from the European Union member States and associated countries, and yet the budget for the call (approximately €290 m) would result in only around 200–50 substantial grants (ERC Press Release, Brussels, 26 April 2007).

Overall, the transnational mobility of academic researchers has become increasingly common globally. For instance, about 45 per cent of highly cited researchers based in the UK have spent some time working abroad. This is a lower academic mobility rate than that of the cases of other Anglophone countries (such as Canada and Australia), and Germany, the Netherlands, and Switzerland (which has particularly mobile academics); though higher than the US, and considerably higher than that of France and Italy (Bekhradnia and Sastry 2005: 9).

Transnational mobility has also become very popular among junior academic researchers. According to the HEPI Report on 'Migration of academic staff to and from the UK', junior academic researchers account for two-thirds of movement in both directions (Bekhradnia and Sastry 2005: 3), which can be attributed to the increase of short-term contract-based academic employment in general, as well as the emergence of new transnational space for research concentration such as the European Research Area.

Transnational academic mobility can be also attributed to the new organisational management imperatives in many universities (Deem 2006, 2007), which emphasise 'third stream income' to promote applied research agendas and outcomes (McNay 1995; Hatakenaka 2005).

The growth of the 'entrepreneurial research university' as a new model for university organisation has been notable across the globe, in line with new types of knowledge networks and transactions (Kim 2002: 144–5). Universities are now managed as if they are corporations, competing in a global knowledge economy, in which hierarchies of power and wealth are generated by transactions in a new mode of knowledge production which Gibbons *et al.* termed as 'Mode 2'[1] (Gibbons *et al.* 1994).

At the organisational level, Gibbons *et al.* (1994) argue that Mode 2 Knowledge production is based on a complex network of linkages between a number of sub-fields and heterogeneous sites, which leads to further transmutation and reconfiguration of these sub-fields and sites. Accordingly, 'knowledge production, not only in its theories and models but also in its methods and techniques, has spread from the Academy to many different types of institutions. It is in this sense that knowledge production has become a socially distributed process' (Gibbons 2003: 111).

The concept of Mode 2 has become so popular currently as much linked to the contemporary global trends and policy rhetoric of so-called knowledge-based economy. The growing engagement of universities with their regions and localities is an important integrated part of Mode 2 Knowledge production (Harloe and Perry 2004).

However, it should be noted that what is labelled as Mode 2 Knowledge production (Gibbons *et al.* 1994) is not just recent past and contemporary phenomena. For instance, take the case of Japan, especially in the late nineteenth and early twentieth centuries – as illustrated earlier in this chapter.

The Japanese way of modernisation and industrialisation was based on transnational importation and indigenous utilisation of Western scientific knowledge. The whole process of modernisation required academic travels, multiple networks and collaborations inside and outside academic institutions – all of which were carefully selected, coordinated and controlled by the State. The mode of transnational knowledge importation and indigenous application in Japan was a highly hybridised, socially distributed process, involving multiple alliances between academic research, government, industry, and military. Overall, it can be suggested that the major form of knowledge production in Japan was Mode 2 from the beginning.

Equally, it can be argued that mobile academics contribute to the generation and transfer of Mode 2 Knowledge, specifically because of their transnational and dispersed linkages and networks, which are often utilised to increase research coordination and collaboration between institutions, sectors and countries. Regardless of their individual patterns and purposes of transnational movements of the time, however, mobile academics have been part of the global *transfer* of knowledge that is a collaborative and more network-based production. In other words, mobile academics have been engaged more in Mode 2 Knowledge production than Mode 1, in the context of discussions about the 'knowledge economy'.

The term 'knowledge economy' denotes the central role of knowledge in innovation, productivity and sustained economic growth (OECD 1996). It was from the late 1990s that knowledge-based economic growth and concerns about ageing populations in most OECD countries started to accelerate a worldwide competition to attract highly skilled[2] knowledge workers, especially in the science, technology and healthcare sectors (Tremblay 2005; Kuptsch and Pang 2006).

In this trend, the average proportion of foreign academics recruited from abroad in high HDI[3] countries (such as the UK, Australia, and Canada) has been much higher than in medium or low HDI countries in Asia and Africa (Kubler and DeLuca 2006). Thus the significance of so-called 'brain drain' from developing and/or less developed countries to the advanced knowledge-based economies has been discussed as a major international and global issue for sustainable development (Hugo 2006).[4]

Simultaneously, however, the contemporary patterns of academic mobility and knowledge production and transfer are increasingly multilateral and multidirectional in both coordinated and uncoordinated manners in the global expansion of knowledge economy. Transnational networks of mobile academics and virtual collaborations have become viable, and notably increased along with the new ICT-led innovation. International academic migrants are also increasingly maintaining their professional linkages with their home countries (Rizvi 2007; Hugo 2006).

Overall, we are in need of some new analytic framework, scale and paradigm to grasp the contemporary pattern of transnational academic mobility and its spatial relations to knowledge economy. In this era of so-called knowledge economy, knowledge is becoming *industrialised*, along with the mass movement of researchers. The European policies are competitive in this. They are geared to coordinating the global-scale transnational academic mobility in order to create a new transnational 'European space' for innovative research concentrations. For instance, the European Science Foundation's Young Investigator Awards (EURYI) scheme has been designed to attract outstanding young scientists, with between two and ten years' postdoctoral experience, from anywhere in the world to create their own research teams at a European research centre. The European Community Framework Programme's Marie Curie awards have also been providing support for intra-European and international mobility at all career stages, through advice and funding for training, visits, networks, events, fellowships and chairs (William Solesbury and Associates 2005: 98).

Many national governments and agencies[5] have also set out new high skills agendas and revised migration policies subsequently to attract more skilled migrants – for instance, the Leitch Report (2006), 'Prosperity for all in the global economy – world class skills' examines the UK's long-term skills needs and sets out ambitious goals for 2020 to raise UK skill levels.

The findings in these reports confirm the spatial relations of the concentration of knowledge production in the United State and the flows of global transnational academic mobility. According to the National Science

Foundation Survey, in 2002 alone, over 24,500 foreigners earned their doctorates in science and engineering in the USA, and 75 per cent of these foreign-born researchers intended to stay in the USA (Burelli 2004). Similarly, in November 2003, the European Commission reported that 75 per cent of EU citizens who obtained a doctorate in the United States had no plan to return to Europe (Tremblay 2005). Overall, it has been reported that the number of foreign knowledge workers, especially science and engineering experts in the US academia, industry and even the Federal Government has continue to increase to a large extent.

The spatial concentration of research knowledge production is certainly in the United States, which can be verified by the low rate of mobility of US-born academic researchers with doctorates in science and engineering: only 3.1 per cent of them surveyed in the period 1998–2002 had definite plans to move abroad (Burelli 2004).

The concentration of knowledge production in the United States is often identified with the absolute dominance of American universities in the global ranking of universities (in the world university league tables published by e.g. Shanghai Jiao Tong and *The Times Higher*). Such university rankings are frequently cited globally as an authoritative indicator of the world-class university, and often used and abused by many policy makers of the competing nations and regions (such as the EU) to draft new policy agendas (e.g. European Commission (2005) 'Mobilising the brain power of Europe: enabling universities to make their full contribution to the Lisbon strategy'). Such policy documents then have a significant resulting implication on the patterns of global academic movements. For instance, the top seven destinations for those US-born doctorate recipients who did plan to go abroad were Canada, the UK, Germany, France, Japan, Switzerland and Australia (Burelli 2004). Such destinations may have been taken indicatively as alternative sites of global concentration of knowledge production and transaction.

However, looking at local realities is also salutary. There is often a gap between rhetoric and reality. The actual condition of transnational mobility will be reviewed then through the international academic recruitment policy and practice in some of the countries in Europe and Asia.

International academic recruitment policy and practice

The focus of comparison in this section will be on the legal framework of foreign academic staffing in the UK, France, Japan and South Korea.

United Kingdom

The UK government is keen to increase their share of the international higher education market as well as to attract more highly skilled knowledge workers, as clearly indicated in the Prime Minister's Initiative (PMI) running since 1999; a specific target was set for the international higher education market share as 'Vision 2020' (British Council 2004). The High Skilled Migrant Programme (HSMP) and the Science and Engineering Graduate Scheme were launched in 2002 and 2003 respectively. The Migrant Programme permits foreign knowledge workers to come to the UK and settle in, without capital investment, or job offer requirement and the UK government provides a more user-friendly visa service for students to stay in the UK to work on completion of their studies in science and engineering fields.

The Science and Innovation Framework 2004–14 (July 2004) also confirms the UK government's agenda to make Britain 'the most attractive location in the world for science and innovation'. However, no special policy measure has been taken at the national level to improve university academic staff mobility in particular, which is devolved to the institutional level. The UK government expects higher education institutions to operate in an international labour market, and take appropriate measures to ease mobility of academic staff. 'The Bologna Process National Reports 2004–2005' also highlights that 'the large numbers of international staff reflect the UK's openness towards mobility' (Bologna Process National Reports 2004–2005: England, Wales and Northern Ireland: http://www.bologna-bergen2005. no/EN/national_impl/00_Nat-rep-05/National_Reports-England-Wales-N-Ireland_050113.pdf).

In the UK, foreign nationality is not automatically an issue in the academic recruitment process in general. The equal opportunities law requires information about ethnic origin of applicants (instead of nationality), along with age, disability, and gender. In other words, ethnic background is considered a more important criterion than nationality for the surveillance of equal opportunity in academic staffing in UK universities.

France

France also revised the formerly restrictive French immigration policies (so-called *Pasqua* laws) in 1998 to encourage highly skilled immigrants to come to France, by easing the conditions of entry for scientists, scholars and other highly skilled professional workers. However, the legal framework for academic employment in France is quite converse to that in the UK. In France ethnic background is not supposed to be officially documented in job applications. French university staff are civil servants who are *de jure* required to possess French nationality; however, foreign scholars can *de facto* be employed by French universities.[6] However, foreign academics working at universities in France are not given priority as civil servants in the process of issuing *Carte Sejour* (Residence Permit) in France. They are treated equally like any other foreign workers.

Mobility of French teachers and research staff is in general based on mutual agreement of exchange between institutions. Given the established French national system for academic career development structure, international mobility among French academic staff has been relatively constrained. Academic status in the period of international mobility was not easily transferable to the French system. To improve the conditions for international academic mobility from and to France, a new principle of the added value (up to 1 year) of mobility was introduced, which calculates the 'seniority' for teachers–researchers (*'enseignants-chercheurs'*) and 'lecture masters' (*'maîtres de conférences'*) who were mobile to and from a higher education and research institution notably in a member state of the European Community ('Bologna Process National Reports 2004–2005: France': http://www.bologna-bergen2005.no/EN/national_impl/00_Nat-rep-05/National_Reports-France_050125.pdf). However, what is still at stake is to help international mobile careers to develop fast in accordance with the French system of academic career management.

Overall, given the language barriers and a less favourable labour market with the lack of recruitment flexibility and salary incentives, the scale of transnational academic mobility and international academic staffing in France has not been significant when compared with some of the neighbouring competitors in Europe – such as the UK, Germany, Switzerland, and the Netherlands (Tremblay 2005).

Unlike Europe, in North East Asia (represented by China, Japan and Korea), there is no regional integration of higher education areas at the supranational governmental level; nor is there visible change in the national government's immigration policies. However, the national governments and individual universities are very eager to increase international academic exchange links and to recruit foreign academics, as a part of national policy and practice for 'internationalisation'.

Japan

In Japan, the 1982 Special Measures Act for the Appointment of Foreign Staff at National and Public Universities, governing term-limited employment for foreign faculty, was superseded by the *Sentaku Ninkisei* (a system of fixed-term renewable contracts) law so that any educator anywhere in Japan – regardless of nationality or pubic/private job status – could receive term limitation in principle. However, it has been criticised that the policies of term limitation in Japan are in reality far more likely to have the effect of encouraging the retention of local faculty while rendering foreign faculty dispensable (Holden 1999). Overall, it has been said that there is an institutionalised discrimination based on nationality in Japan, in which foreign academics are used as temporary replacements until qualified local candidates can be found. The strong emphasis on Japanese nationalism in university staffing policy has a long tradition that goes back to the late nineteenth century, as reviewed earlier.

South Korea

In South Korea, the government and individual universities are eager to increase international academic exchange links and to recruit foreign academics, as a part of national policy and practice for 'internationalisation'. The Korean government even set a target in 2003 to increase the number of foreign academic staff to 17 per cent in the public sector of higher education, and 30 per cent in all higher education. The so-called 'Brain Pool' scheme has also been implemented as a new incentive to attract foreign academics to South Korea within new fields such as information technology, bio-technology, and the basic sciences (Kim 2005: 95). Major universities in Korea are also in severe competition to increase international competitiveness. Specific measures to assess the level of internationalisation among the Korean universities are typically the number of international publications in the SCI-registered journals, the number of foreign students and scholars recruited, and the number of courses taught in English.

The Korean government's strong desire for drastic change in internationalisation policy was noticeable in the appointment of Professor Robert Laughlin, the American Nobel Prize Laureate in Physics in 1998, to the presidency of the state-run Korea Advanced Institute of Science and Technology (KAIST) in May 2004. KAIST became the first state-funded university in Korea to be headed by a foreigner. The appointment was thought to signal a new form of internationalisation within universities in Korea. However, Laughlin had to step down eventually after staff mutinied against his reform plans. The Korean ambition in pursuit of internationalisation and innovation was triggering cultural clashes, which could lead to more casualties like Robert Laughlin.

After all, unlike in the UK, the USA, Australia, or Canada, foreign academic staff in Korea are *not* employed on the same legal terms as the local staff – they have no legal protection for equality of job opportunities. This is similar to the Japanese case, but perhaps there is more exclusive ethno-nationalism as boundaries of exclusion in Korean academic culture.

In both Japan and Korea, nationality so often affects the overall conditions for employment. Regardless of the official policy agenda of 'internationalisation', foreign academics working in universities in Korea (or Japan) have experienced institutional barriers and xenophobia in faculty life. There is considerable anecdotal evidence of universities' mistreatment of foreign professors in both Japan and Korea. In Korea, foreign academics, especially those in the foreign language departments, are often treated as functionaries rather than professionals. In the existing Korean university system, there is no formal route open for foreign academics to develop their professional careers (Kim 2005: 94–7).

Overall, it is the case in both Japan and Korea that foreign academics can enjoy a higher salary, but are often separated from, and denied equal rights with, the local staff. The cases of Japan and Korea produce an interesting contrast to the British situation, where foreigners are now recruited to senior manager-academic posts (like the foreign Vice-Chancellors in Oxford, Manchester and the London Business School).

Thus, a peculiar form of international transfer of policy rhetoric and local adaptation of the consequence of transfer is occurring in East Asia, which would require more careful research to conceptualise the relations of academic mobility to new concentrations of global knowledge production.

Conclusion

This chapter examined the patterns of transnational academic mobility through a comparative historical gaze to see who moves with what kind of knowledge to where, and what is the influence of structure and agency organising these movements.

International, or even transnational academic mobility has always occurred. What is interesting by taking a long view on these is the ways in which academics and spaces are divided up by politics. For instance, the rise of nationalist universities is characteristic of the collapse of the *pan-European space*, which is the medieval university that academics – whether in Paris, Bologna or Salamanca – inhabited.

Who moves is clearly affected by political circumstances. Political space determines the conditions for all important transnational academic mobility. For example, many young Chinese academics training abroad in the mid-1960s at the time of Cultural Revolution chose to stay abroad for much of their academic career. In Nazi Germany, among those who sought refuge and work overseas were some of Europe's most brilliant intellectuals and scientists.

Academic mobility affects knowledge concentration, which in turn means that we can see the moving, relocating, and creating of centres of excellence. Certainly major efforts are under way to reform the distribution of academic centres of excellence. Aggressive policies are in place to treat other regions as competitors for 'brain gain' and cutting-edge knowledge-economy research.

International and transnational mobility also follows access to the *lingua franca* of the time. It is clearly more difficult for persons (in the twenty-first century) who speak French and German to be transnationally mobile in contrast to their possibilities of mobility in the nineteenth century when German was a critical language for natural and social sciences and French was the language of elegance.

Contemporaneously one of the most striking frames of transnational academic mobility is agencies and policies: the policy rhetoric of globalisation and the global activities of the EU, WTO, World Bank, OECD and major foundations.

For example, the European Union has redefined academic as well as political space and through a series of its Framework Programmes has contributed most energetically to academic mobility flows. Europe is undergoing a simultaneous process of regional integration and international competition. The ongoing process of Europeanisation – i.e., the creation of a 'European higher education area' and a 'European research area' through the Bologna Process and Lisbon Strategies – is a deliberate transnational *industrialisation* of academic mobility and knowledge production. Simultaneously, however, international competition (to increase global higher education market share and to recruit more foreign mobile academics and highly skilled knowledge workers in science and technology) is still visible among the national governments in Europe as reviewed in this chapter.

From an analytical point of view, this is a changing political scaling in the geography of knowledge and the geometries of power, directing the transnational flows of academics, which provides a crucial theoretical call for those working in universities and trying to understand the sociology, anthropology, histories and geographies of these processes comparatively.

These new patterns of transnational academic mobility also require rethinking the concept of brain drain, which has become rather too simple. For instance, the assumption that all academic talents flow into the United States is looking increasingly fragile in the twenty-first century. Apart from anything else, the United States' traditional stance on international academic mobility was contradicted by the 'war on terror', which has made it difficult for foreign students and academics to complete immigration processes in a timely and civilised way.

Similarly, the Korean example in this chapter highlights how it is relatively easy for a government to define and publicise a policy for the internationalisation of national universities, but far more difficult for the government to adjust rapidly the rules of migration (including passports and visas, their finance and taxation structures) and above all it is most difficult for government to alter the national cultures of the universities to make them welcoming to foreign academics.

Regions also vary. In East Asia, for example, there is no sign of regional integration at the supranational level. In East Asia, a most obvious centre for academic research, Mode 2 Knowledge production, and international flows of academic professionals is Japan. But Japan is both in East Asia and – on this academic dimension – extends beyond it to link with the United States, Germany and the UK in terms of applied and pure research. Thus, Japan has not exerted itself to establish an East Asian political space for *transnational* academic flows.

Similarly, China has not – so far – exerted itself to redefine East Asian transnational academic flows. At the moment, China is preparing for the future by encouraging more and more young Chinese to study overseas. Clearly, at some point in the future, China will have developed major world-class universities, it will have very powerful international academic networks, and at that point it may decide to declare itself as a 'political space' for and as the 'obvious' academic centre for all important transnational academic mobilities within East Asia.

Overall, two major processes are occurring:

- very rapid changes in political space, particularly the creation of regional spaces within which transnational academic mobility occurs; and – almost everywhere –
- policies are being written and implemented by international and transnational agencies which include WTO/GATS, OECD, World Bank, NAFTA, and EU.

The world of transnational academic mobilities is getting bigger, and it is seemingly more incoherent. It is indeed difficult to describe, and very difficult to theorise. But it is not incoherent. It is an intentional construction which changes shape at national, regional and international levels probably influenced by ideology and policy. As usual, our social realities and practices are in advance of our theories.

Notes

1 As initially conceptualised by Gibbons *et al.* (1994), Mode 1 refers to a 'traditional' form of 'scientific' knowledge production, legitimation and diffusion generated within a specific disciplinary, cognitive, and primarily academic context. Mode 2, on the other hand, represents a hybridised sense of research knowledge generated outside academic institutions in broader, trans-disciplinary social and economic contexts, blending together the interests of academia, the state, and industry. Gibbons *et al.* (1994) argue that the process of transition from Mode 1 to Mode 2 is well under way, and is in fact 'irreversible' (Gibbons *et al.* 1994: 11). A key change from Mode 1 to Mode 2 is that knowledge production is becoming less and less a self-contained activity.
2 The highly skilled knowledge workers are in general defined as those in possession of higher degrees or extensive specialised/professional work experience (Vertovec 2002).
3 HDI stands for the United Nation's 'Human Development Index'.
4 For instance, in the Philippines, about one-third of college graduates live and work outside the country; and overall 88 per cent of OECD immigrants from LDCs have secondary or higher education (Hugo 2006).
5 E.g. Higher Education Policy Institute's Report on 'Migration of Academic Staff to and from the UK' (Bekhradnia and Sastry 2005), the World Bank Policy Research Working Paper on 'Measuring the international mobility of skilled workers' (Docquier and Marfouk 2004) and the OECD Directorate for Employment, Labour and Social Affairs Report on 'Counting immigrants and expatriates in OECD countries: a new perspective' (Dumont and Lemaître 2004).
6 Similarly, in Germany where professors were public officials of the individual states (Länder), legal restrictions on the employment and advancement of foreign scholars into any teaching or administrative post had been lifted by the 1970s.

References

AUT (2005) 'The rise of teaching-only academics': www.aut.org.uk; http://www.politics.co.uk/microsites/366435/downloads/20_per cent_of_academics_just_teach_as_casualisation_increases_2362005.doc (accessed 23 May 2007).
Bartholomew, J. R. (1989) *The Formation of Science in Japan*, New Haven and London: Yale University Press.
Bekhradnia, B. and Sastry, T. (2005) 'Migration of academic staff to and from the UK', Higher Education Policy Institute (HEPI) Report, October, London: HEPI.
Benavot, A., Erbes-Seguin, S. and Gross, S. (2005) 'Interdisciplinarity in EU-funded social sciences projects', in Kuhn, M. and Remøe, S. O. (eds) *Building the European Research Area: Socio-economic Research in Practice*, New York: Peter Lang: 115–75.

British Council (2004) *Vision 2020: Forecasting International Student Mobility – A UK Perspective*, London: British Council.

Burelli, J. (2004) 'Emigration of US-born S&E doctorate recipients', Washington, DC: National Science Foundation (InfoBrief 04-327), available at: http://www.nsf.gov/sbe/srs/infbrief/nsf04327/nsf04327.pdf (accessed 23 May 2007).

CEC (2005) 'Mobilising the brain power of Europe: enabling universities to make their full contribution to the Lisbon strategy', COM (2005) 152 final, Brussels.

CEC (2007) 'Green Paper: The European Research Area: new perspectives', COM (2007) 161 final, Brussels.

Charle, C. (2004) 'The intellectual networks of two leading universities: Paris and Berlin 1890–1930', in Charle, C., Schriewer, J. and Wagner, P. (eds) *Transnational Intellectual Networks: Forms of Academic Knowledge and the Search for Cultural Identities*, Frankfurt and New York: Campus Verlag: 401–50.

Clark, B. R. (1983) *The Higher Education System: Academic Organization in Cross-National Perspective*, Berkeley: University of California Press.

Cobban, A. B. (1971) 'Medieval student power', in *Past and Present*, 53, November: 28–66.

Coser, L. (1984) *Refugee Scholars in America: Their Impact and Their Experience*, New Haven: Yale University Press.

Deem, R. (2006) 'Changing research perspectives on the management of higher education: can research permeate the activities of manager-academics?', *Higher Education Quarterly*, 60(3): 203–28.

Deem, R. (2007) 'Managing contemporary UK universities – manager-academics and new managerialism', *Academic Leadership: the online journal*, 1(3), Feb. 12. http://www.academicleadership.org/emprical_research/Managing_Contemporary_UK_Universities_Manager-academics_and_New_Managerialism.shtml (accessed 23 May 2007).

Docquier, F. and Marfouk, A. (2004) 'Measuring the international mobility of skilled workers (1990–2000)', Washington, DC: World Bank. Available at: http://econ.worldbank.org/files/38017_wps3381.pdf (accessed 23 May 2007).

Dumont, J.-C. and Lemaître, G. (2004) 'Counting immigrants and expatriates in OECD countries: a new perspective', Paris: OECD. Available at: http://www.oecd.org/dataoecd/27/5/33868740.pdf (accessed 23 May 2007).

European Commission (2002) 'Research networking in Europe – striving for global leadership', Brussels, September. Available at: http://www.dante.net/pubs/Ecbrochure.html (accessed 23 May 2007).

Gibbons, M. (2003) 'Globalization and the future of higher education' in Breton, G. and Lambert, M. (eds) *Universities and Globalization: Private Linkages, Public Trust*, Paris: UNESCO: 107–16.

Gibbons, M., Limoges, C., Nowotny, H., Scott, P., Schwartzman, S. and Trow, M. (1994) *The New Production of Knowledge – the Dynamics of Science and Research in Contemporary Societies*, London: Sage.

Harloe, M. and Perry, B. (2004) 'Universities, localities and regional development: the emergence of the "mode 2" university?', *International Journal of Urban and Regional Research*, 28(1): 212–23.

Hatakenaka, S. (2005) 'Development of third stream activity. Lessons from international experience', *Higher Education Policy Institute Report* (HEPI), November, London: HEPI.

Holden, W. (1999) 'Trends in employment practices at Japanese colleges and universities: longer-term effects of the introduction of the *Sentaku Ninkisei* system', *JALT (Japan Association for Language Teaching) Journal of Professional Issues Professionalism, Administration, and Leadership in Education (PALE)*, 5(2), Autumn: http://www.debito.org/PALE/ (accessed 23 May 2007).

Hugo, G. (2006) 'Research collaboration and mobility: an Australian perspective' Presentation to Forum for European-Australian Science and Technology Co-operation (FEAST) Conference on 'Research Without Borders', Canberra, 29 November.

Kim, T. (2002) 'Globalization, universities and knowledge as control: new possibilities for new forms of colonialism?', in Schuller, T., Istance, D. and Schuetze, H. (eds) *International Perspectives on Lifelong Learning: From Recurrent Education to the Knowledge Society*, Buckingham: Open University Press: 141–53.

Kim, T. (2005) 'Internationalisation of higher education in South Korea: reality, rhetoric, and disparity in academic culture and identities', *The Australian Journal of Education*, 49(1), Special Issue: International Education, C. Joseph, S. Marginson, and R. Yang (eds): 89–103.

Kim, T. (2006) 'Building a business: a comparative note on the changing identities of the British university', in Sprogøe, J. and Winther-Jensen, T. (eds) *Identity, Education, and Citizenship: Multiple Interrelations*, Berlin: Peter Lang: 197–224.

Kohler, R. E. (1987) 'Science, foundations, and American universities in the 1920s', *Osiris*, 2nd Series, 3: 135–64.

Kubler, J. and DeLuca, C. (2006) *Trends in Academic Recruitment and Retention: a Commonwealth Perspective*, London: Association of Commonwealth Universities.

Kuptsch, C. and Pang, E. F. (eds) (2006) *Competing for Global Talent*, Geneva: International Institute for Labour Studies (ILO).

Leitch, S. (2006) 'Prosperity for all in the global economy – world class skills', Final Report, December, London: HMO.

Martin-Rovet, D. (2003) *Opportunities for Outstanding Young Scientists in Europe to Create an Independent Research Team*, Strasbourg: European Science Foundation.

McNay, I (1995) 'From the collegial academy to corporate enterprise: the changing cultures of university?', in Schuller, T. (ed.) *The Changing University?*, Milton Keynes: Open University and SRHE.

Medawar, J. and Pyke, D. (2001) *Hitler's Gift: The True Story of Scientists Expelled by Nazi Regime*, New York: Arcade Publishing.

Morano-Foadi, S. (2005) 'Scientific mobility, career progression, and excellence in the European research area' *International Migration*, 43(5): 133–62.

Nakayama, S. (1974) *Academic and Scientific Traditions in China, Japan and the West* (trans. J. Dusenbury), Tokyo: University of Tokyo Press.

OECD (1996) *Knowledge-based Economy*, OECD/GD(96)102, Paris: OECD.

Rashdall, H. (1997) *The Universities of Europe in the Middle Ages*, 3 vols, reprint of 1936 edition edited by F.M. Powicke and A.B Emden, Oxford: Oxford University Press.

Ridder-Symoens, H. de (ed.) (1992) *A History of the University in Europe, Vol. 1: Universities in the Middle Ages*, Cambridge: Cambridge University Press.

Rizvi, F. (2007) 'Brain drain and the potential of professional diasporic networks' in Farrell, L. and Fenwick, T. (eds) *World Yearbook of Education 2007: Educating the Global Workforce Knowledge, Knowledge Work and Knowledge Workers*, London: Routledge: 227–38.

Rothblatt, S. (1997) *The Modern University and its Discontents: the fact of Newman's Legacies in Britain and America*, New York: Cambridge University Press.

Schriewer, J. (2004) 'Multiple internationalities: the emergence of a world-level ideology and the persistence of idiosyncratic world-views' in *Charle, C., Schriewer, J. and Wagner, P.* (eds) *Transnational Intellectual Networks: Forms of Academic Knowledge and the Search for Cultural Identities*, Frankfurt and New York: Campus Verlag: 473–534.

Siegmund-Schultze, R. (2001) *Rockefeller and the Internationalization of Mathematics Between the Two World Wars: Documents and Studies for the Social History of Mathematics in the 20th Century*, Basel and Boston: Birkhäuser Verlag.

Tanaka, M. (2005) *Cross-cultural Transfer of Educational Concepts and Practices: A Comparative Study*, Oxford; Symposium.

Tremblay, K. (2005) 'Academic mobility and immigration', *Journal of Studies in International Education*, 9(3): 196–228.

Umetani, N. (1971) *The Role of Foreign Employees in the Meiji Era in Japan*, Tokyo: Institute of Developing Economies.

Vertovec, S. (2002) 'Transnational networks and skilled labour migration' Paper presented at the Conference: Ladenburger Diskurs 'Migration' Gottlieb Daimler- und Karl Benz-Stiftung, Adenburg, 14–15 February.

William Solesbury and Associates (2005) 'The impact of international mobility on UK academic research', Higher Education Policy Institute Report, August, London: HEPI.

19 The Chinese knowledge diaspora

Communication networks among overseas Chinese intellectuals

Anthony R. Welch and Zhang Zhen

Introduction: globalisation and knowledge diaspora

Globalisation, as Appadurai has argued, comprises both flows (of capital, labour, information and imagery), and also disjunctures, including between the local and the global. Media images from abroad may conjure up aspirations for lifestyles, or forms of modernity, that cannot be satisfied locally (Appadurai 2001: 6), or at least only for a small elite.

There are further disjunctures within discourses of globalisation, of course, notably by proponents of economic globalisation. National political leaders, for instance, particularly from the wealthiest nations, often tout the advantages of cross-border capital flows, while actively seeking to restrict cross-national labour flows. In recent years, the UK, Australia and the USA have all, for example, erected legal, and in some cases physical barriers to those fleeing oppression, or seeking a better life in another country, who are demonised as illegals, or queue jumpers. In the Australian case, the national government went as far as excising certain offshore islands, so that even those who reached their apparent safety, could still be denied the legal rights bestowed on anyone who landed on Australian soil.

At the same time, however, many of these same wealthy nations have established or refined specific programmes that target the highly educated, who gain preferential treatment for migration purposes. It is precisely this group, of course, whose migration represents one of the most significant losses to the home country. The stratified nature of the global knowledge network (Altbach 1994, 2002) underlines the fact that flows of intellectuals are still very largely from the South to the North. As Solimano (2002) argues, the global inequality of knowledge creation and application is exacerbated, since developed countries compete to attract research talent from developing countries, who then consolidate the already strong knowledge base in the former (Hugo 2002), at the cost of the latter.

In research terms, a by-product of this trans-national talent flow has been the creation of substantial knowledge diasporas, particularly in OECD countries, and a renewed focus on the differential effects of global migration, including by the highly-skilled. National Science Foundation data showing that only half of international doctoral or post-doctoral candidates in the USA return to their country of origin within two years, is likely to be replicated in Australia. Indeed, for those from China and India who study in the USA, the figures are as low as 10–12 per cent. In the decade to the late 1990s, approximately half of the doctoral recipients from China sought and received opportunities for further study and employment in the United States (Johnson and Regets 1998). The impact on innovation, in the form of research productivity, and patent applications is also substantial (Özden and Schiff 2005).

Data from Saxenian show that, of Silicon Valley's Asian population in the late 1990s, 77 per cent of Indian residents held at least a masters degree, while for Chinese residents the figure was 86 per cent, and Taiwanese 85 per cent (Saxenian 2006; Kapur and McHale 2005: 113). Australian and Canadian data show similar figures (Li 2005; Welch 2007b). In Australia, for example, which shows the highest nett brain gain of all OECD countries (Docquier and Abdeslam 2006: 180), the proportion of skilled migrants rose from 39.8 per cent of the total in 1990–1, to 46.8 per cent by 2003–4, (Parliamentary Library 2004; Welch 2007b) while for certain groups, for example China-born migrants, it was more than half. Indeed, of long-term Chinese immigrants to Australia, over 80 per cent currently have degrees, and fall within the three highest occupational categories, while significant numbers have moved into academic posts, usually after taking their PhD at an Australian university (Hugo 2005; Welch and Zhang 2005).

That the emphasis on the highly educated has become all the more important in recent times, is a further reflection of the change towards more knowledge-based economies (and, arguably, the further commodification of education). The global circulation of epistemic currents, including among diasporic communities, is also part of this new orientation, which challenges our notion of space and place (Tsolidis 2001).

Of late, however, the hierarchical structure in knowledge distribution and dissemination has become less fixed, as the loci of power and growth are becoming multiple, and more dispersed (Meyer *et al.* 2001). This more multi-polar quality of the global knowledge network means that the diaspora option can be instrumental in narrowing the North–South scientific gap (Brown 2000; Meyer and Brown 1999; Meyer *et al.* 2001; Zweig and Fung 2004). Knowledge transfer (via, for example, the United Nation's Transfer of Knowledge through Expatriate Nationals [TOKTEN] programme), while by no means wholly effective, is nonetheless integral to diaspora policy, which seeks to strengthen bonds between knowledge-intensive places and less intensive ones. For example, Choi (1995) observed that many Asian-background academics in American higher education keep in close contact with their countries of origin, maintaining scientific and academic relationships with colleagues and institutions at home. From this perspective, the huge Chinese diaspora, estimated to be around 35 million worldwide, of whom many are highly skilled, can be seen as a potential resource, rather than an instance of brain drain. For China, deploying the diaspora option is now a priority (Zweig and Fung 2002; Welch and Zhang 2005), representing a more nuanced response to issues of brain drain. Programmes such as the '985 Project' (that from 1999 was planned to pour approximately Rmb. 30 billion [approximately US$4 billion], differentially, into China's top ten universities, with the explicit goal of making them 'world class', and to recruit top (Chinese) scholars from throughout the world, to work in them), and the newer '111' programme, that is designed to recruit Chinese intellectuals from abroad to mainland universities, even on a periodic basis, represent further strategies to deal with brain drain. Such knowledge bridges, built with overseas Chinese intellectuals, many of whom are keen to contribute to the homeland, from abroad, are in part responsible for China's rapidly rising scientific stature – from 38th position on international rankings of academic output, in 1979 to fifth in 2003 (Li 2005), notwithstanding some remaining structural impediments (Cao 2004; Shen 2000; Welch 2008).

These knowledge networks are part of the wider phenomenon of increased global mobility, especially by diasporic intellectuals, and the trans-national networks they establish, undergirded by the greater density and diffusion of information technology, are each tilting the balance towards countries such as Taiwan (Luo and Wang 2002), Israel, China and India, whose highly-skilled scientists and technologists, often with experience in Silicon Valley, are busily '... creating far more complex and decentralised, two-way flows of knowledge, capital and technology' (Saxenian 2006: 6). (To foster such networks, the Taiwanese intellectual diaspora in Silicon Valley, for example, created the Monte Jade Science and Technology Association, the Chinese its equivalent (Yuan Hua Science and Technology Association), and Israelis the SIVAN group.)

The Chinese intellectual diaspora in Australia

But does this finding hold true for knowledge diasporas in other parts of the world? How do intellectual diasporas maintain connections to the motherland, and to other parts of the diaspora? The following study focused on the growing, and diverse Chinese knowledge diaspora in Australia, which although part of the North, with well-developed infrastructure and a relatively strong research presence internationally, occupies an *entrepôt* status, both attracting significant numbers of intellectuals, scholars and students, but also suffering its own form of brain drain, largely to the USA, and to a lesser extent to the UK and Europe (from which it also draws). In this sense it can be compared with Canada, for example, although the latter's proximity to the US system arguably makes it particularly vulnerable.

The study was conducted at a large research university in one of the capital cities in Australia. The university, among the elite 'Group of Eight', is one of the older institutions in Australia, having been founded during the mid-nineteenth century. For well over a century, the university has played a leading role in teaching and research in Australia. International cooperation and exchanges have been emphasised as an important strategy for institutional development. One of the largest universities with a wide range of disciplines, the university also has a long history of China relations (Holenbergh 2005) and currently hosts over 8,000 international students, of which the largest component are mainland Chinese students. A rising numbers of its academic staff are also from the People's Republic of China (PRC).

A tentative list of mainland Chinese academic staff was compiled using university and faculty websites (Table 19.1), and the Mandarin spelling (*hanyu pinyin*) system adopted in China. Ethnic Chinese born in places other than the mainland use a different system to spell their names (Tsang 2001). Details of universities from which they obtained their first degrees further confirmed their mainland Chinese identities. A range of variables (specialty, professional rank, gender and age group) was deliberately included in the sample, in the interests of range, and semi-structured in-depth interviews were employed.

Forms of contact

On the whole, interviewees were interested in maintaining contact with Chinese scholars in general, and mainland scholars in particular. As Table 19.2 shows, all the interviewees established scientific communication with their mainland counterparts. Zhuang perceived this type of communication and collaboration as conducive to building up the reputation of Chinese and fostering China's national competitiveness.

> Of course, I hope Chinese can communicate and collaborate with one another at global level. For one thing, this can enhance the reputation of Chinese (scholars) in the international community. For another, it can strengthen China's competitiveness in the global economy. I would like to cooperate with Chinese scholars at home and abroad. To me, this kind of cooperation will be more beneficial. (Zhuang, cross-discipline)

The forms that communication took included reciprocal visits, publication in mainland journals, and teaching, and was generally considered important by the interviewees.

Table 19.1 Interviewee details

Name	Gender	Age group	Speciality	Highest degree and origin	Rank	Length of stay
Chen	M	40–5	Cross-discipline	PhD Australia	Lecturer	11 years
Ding	F	40–5	Social Science	PhD Australia	Senior Lecturer	12 years
Li	M	40–5	Engineering	PhD China	Professor	13 years
Shi	F	40–5	Health Science	PhD Australia	Senior Lecturer	9 years
Wang	M	40–5	Health Science	PhD Australia	Senior Lecturer	16 years
Zhuang	M	40–5	Cross-discipline	PhD Australia	Lecturer	16 years

Table 19.2 Summary of interviewees' communication channels with mainland scholars and overseas Chinese intellectual diasporas

		Personal contact		Conferences and conventions		Publication		Staff/student exchange	
		MLS	OCS	MLS	OCS	MLS	OCS	MLS	OCS
Chen	Cross-discipline	+/–	–	+/–	–	–	–	+/–	–
Ding	Social Science	++	++	++	++	++	+	+	+/–
Li	Engineering	++	+	+	+	+	+	++	+
Shi	Health Science	+	++	++	++	+	+	+/–	–
Wang	Health Science	++	–	+	–	+	+	+	–
Zhuang	Cross-discipline	+/–	–	–	–	–	–	+/–	–

Legend: ++ = very important; + = important; +/– = somewhat important ; – = not important
MLS = mainland scholar; OCS = overseas Chinese scholar.
Note: A communication channel was designated as 'very important' when it involved collaboration; 'important' when there were successive communications; 'somewhat important' when there was evidence of sporadic communication; 'not important' when no communication was evident.

Worth of collaboration

All respondents confirmed the value of trans-national collaborations. Li, for example, viewed mobility as conducive to expanding the scientific/professional network and an important medium for transmitting knowledge and expertise.

> We receive at least 15 visiting scholars from China each year. Nearly every big research institute in China has sent their staff here to get trained. When they came back, they may bring back some of our academic findings … In the past ten years, about 30 students got their PhD degree here. They come from different parts of China. The impact has been spread. As our graduates settled around the world, so was the network. (Li, engineering)

Wang was highly appreciative of his collaboration with mainland counterparts.

> I enjoy the collaboration with Chinese counterparts. That is why I went back seven times last year … In terms of contribution, uh … I don't think it is more or less because I am Chinese after all. (Wang, health science)

Ding viewed the relationship between her and her alma mater as like that of a child and parent, hence her commitment to lecturing in her alma mater. Noticing that the mainstream specialist English-language journals had limited readership in China, she saw publishing in Chinese journals as an important means to disseminate academic findings to her mainland peers.

In 2001, I went back and there were more or less differences in the way they treated me. My feeling was, for example, when the child had been away from home for a long time, the parents welcomed their child as a guest. It is a long period of time that we have not been together ... My Alma Mater wants me to go back and conduct workshops or seminars for the students. If time permits, I am very happy to and I think I am committed to doing so. (Ding, social science)

Previously, I did not pay much attention to publishing papers in Chinese journals. Gradually, I found out that many Chinese scholars did not read articles in foreign journals. If I wanted the findings to have greater impact, I should publish in both English and Chinese journals. Now, I pay much attention to translating the article into Chinese and publishing in Chinese journals. (Ding, social science)

A culture shared

The qualities of Chinese scholarship, industrious study habits, and courtesy were appreciated by the interviewees, as also the relative ease and familiarity of dealing with other Chinese.

About half of the class are Chinese students. During the lecture, they account for more than half. This is because local students pay less attention to discipline. (Ding, social science)

When I talk with my former colleagues, we still communicate as old friends and colleagues. However, when I came back and talked to the junior staff or junior scientists, they paid very high respect to me. Obviously, this is because of the philosophy, the thousands of years of Confucianism. (Wang, health science)

Clearly, sharing the same cultural and linguistic backgrounds contributed to a greater closeness in scholarly communications. These expressions of commitment and willingness to cooperate with the home country support other recent studies in the area (Meyer *et al.* 2001). In the current study, there was an important two-way dimension to the relationship between expatriate Chinese intellectuals and the mainland. On the one hand, individuals benefited from new research techniques, the rich array of English language literature, major conferences, and cutting-edge research communities. On the other hand, a universal commitment was evident among this group, to utilise the resources of the knowledge centres, including new communications technologies, in the interests of the gigantic periphery of China. In this way, it was felt, the gap between centres and peripheries could be partly alleviated as the strength of the former contributes to the development of the latter.

Notably different from previous studies of Asian intellectual diaspora (Choi 1995), none of the interviewees kept in contact, or collaborated, with regions such as Taiwan, Hong Kong or Singapore. One possible reason seems to be the dramatic growth rate in China's economy, which has grown at an annual rate little short of 10 per cent since 1990, and the priority attached to the development of higher education since that earlier study, with special reference to science and technology. While commitment was strong however, outcomes were often weak. Although all interviewees kept in contact with the home country, four of them (Ding, Shi, Chen and Zhuang) indicated that they did not have any concrete collaboration, or collaborative outcomes, from the professional contact with their mainland peers. Interviewees described multiple channels of communication which contributed to a complex and uneven picture of scholarly relations.

Factors affecting variations in communication

As noted above, efforts were made to embrace a range of dimensions within the sample, and factors such as status, gender, shared research interests, and forms of leadership contributed to the quality of collaboration found.

Gender and academic rank

Commensurate with research on the gendered nature of the academic profession (Stiver Lie and O'Leary 1990; Welch 2005), female interviewees noted the importance of building up their career before they formed any collaborative relationships. This led to a certain paradox for these two scholars: the opportunity for, and scope of cooperation was determined by professional rank, while their promotion opportunities were based on their individual research abilities. Although each expressed it slightly differently, they both felt that the time and energy needed to build their career had impinged on their capacity to collaborate with mainland colleagues.

> In the past five years, I have paid much attention to conducting individual research. This is for the consideration of professional development. I believe there will be more collaboration in the future, as I assume a senior position. (Ding, social science)

> During the past nine years, I have been working hard to build up my reputation. I did not have enough time and energy to collaborate with mainland scholars. (Shi, health science)

Interestingly, Chen stated that mainlanders tended to collaborate with Chinese expatriate scholars of higher rank, again perhaps a confirmation of the longstanding hierarchical quality in Chinese society, associated with its Confucian heritage.

Perhaps, they have different ideas of with whom and how to conduct cooperation. They would prefer collaborating with Professors. (Chen, cross-discipline)

Research interest

Three interviewees viewed the lack of development of their field in China as a constraint upon building up cooperation with China. Both Chen and Shi identified this as the very reason for their lack of communication and collaboration with overseas Chinese scholars.

> In the journals I read, I can see more and more Chinese names ... I do not have any contact with them because of the difference in research interests. As for scholars, the communication is spontaneous if they share the common interest. It does not mean that I may contact you because you are Chinese. (Chen, cross-discipline)

> In my specific field, China is lagging behind the developed countries. This is mainly because China is a developing country and problem concerned is to ensure its people adequate food and clothing. (Shi, health science)

Zhuang viewed the complex demands of his specific research arena as a major constraint to developing professional relationships with Chinese scholars at home and abroad.

> Because my field crosses two disciplines, I can hardly find anyone who is good at both. I am expert at one field but not the same in the other. So I hope to find someone who is at least quite competent at the second. It's not easy. (Zhuang, cross-discipline)

Leadership

The importance of this concept is underlined by the fact that it was experienced as both a positive and a negative. That is, it can both facilitate but also constrain effective scholarly contacts between Chinese expatriate scholars and the home country. Specifically, Shi related both successful and frustrating experiences with mainland counterparts at the administrative level.

> I discussed with some colleagues my intention to cooperate with their institution. They told me there was no job vacancy and just suggested I talk to another person. It was like ball rolling (buck passing). What I wanted was to see whether I would cooperate with them. I did not want to apply for a position there. So I felt disappointed ... However, the president of C2 University was more straightforward, 'We have almost everything. What we are short of is high calibre personnel like you.'

I responded, 'Although your university is not my Alma Mater, your university is my first priority.' (Shi, health science)

In all, three interviewees (Shi, Zhuang and Chen) recalled similar experiences when meeting mainland delegations, notably that there were no follow-up activities after the visit. As a result, the interviewees still were unclear how to establish collaboration with Chinese institutions.

I have met one high-level delegation from China. The delegation head assured me that China needed quality personnel like me. But where can I find out the bridge for building the linkage? There is no answer. (Shi, health science)

Interviewees' perceptions of their communication with Chinese scholars in general and the mainland scholars in particular are best represented on a continuum of positive and negative responses, on which they move back and forth. Despite their interest in collaborating with Chinese scholars, academic status and research interests are two limiting factors. While communication between scholars with common interest is spontaneous, leadership support and recognition by the mainland counterpart are critical to ongoing success.

Our findings as to the impact of academic status, and research interest and relevance, on scientific communication and collaboration bear out those of Choi (1995), who observed that the higher status of more senior academics ensures easier access to, and utilisation of, resources, and hence affords more opportunities for professional collaboration. She further argued that the lower levels of infrastructure associated with less developed countries, which make it difficult to support highly specialised work in the field, can act as a brake on international collaboration. In this regard, it has been argued that the comprehensiveness of a developed indigenous scientific community is a prerequisite to the mobilisation and utilisation of the expatriates' expertise (Meyer and Brown 1999). According to some, the lack of specialisation and differentiation in Chinese scientific community is a token of the marginalisation of Chinese scholarship. While the significant injection of resources into key universities via national projects such as 211 and 985 over the past decade or more, and the impressive priority accorded the development of higher education, have begun to reshape Chinese higher education, and notably lift research performance, marginalisation is still evident, as is further illustrated below.

The quality of Chinese leadership is a notable aspect of interviewees' experience of complication in establishing relationships with the mainland. What seems crucial is for leaders of Chinese HEIs to have a better understanding of the cutting-edge of the discipline. Without such knowledge, it is difficult for them to target and attract high calibre talent. Without improvements in leadership, the aim of developing world-class universities is unrealistic, notwithstanding major financial investment. Emphasis on highly-skilled personnel should not just be rhetoric: a meaningless slogan. Respect and recognition of leadership play a significant role in facilitating and fostering the mobilisation and utilisation of Chinese expatriate scholars. Further, support and recognition should not be verbal. For most Chinese delegations, the main objective, at least on the agenda, is to promote mutual understanding, and build up linkages for future collaboration. The problem here is that, in practice, the mission of the delegation often ends when their visit ends.

Marginalisation

As indicated above, the global knowledge network is still weighted towards the wealthier countries, principally restricted to OECD membership, and English-language environments (Altbach 1994, 2002; Crystal 1997). Neither places China within 'core' knowledge environments, at least not yet. The concept of marginalisation highlights an awareness of China's lack of access to the fruits of, and limited contribution to, the international knowledge network, in particular the often still limited involvement by mainland scholars in scientific communication and collaboration with external peers. It also reflects a perception of the lower quality of the Chinese scholars' work in a larger sense connected to less access to resources, and the academic atmosphere and heritage within the mainland Chinese scientific community.

Notwithstanding some differences, significant overall similarities in interviewees' perceptions of China's limited participation in international knowledge network emerged. Interviewees indicated that the most influential journals in the fields were from the North, in general, and the Unites States, in particular.

> The most influential journals are from North America, mainly, with several from the European countries. (Chen, cross-discipline)

Equally, interviewees pointed out that the mainland scholars remained much less prominent in the internationally recognised journals in their fields.

> Even with a growing number of Chinese contributors, the mainland scholars are quite limited as the contributors are overseas Chinese in the western academes. (Shi, health science)

The inadequate quality of many (but not all) mainland scholars' work was seen by interviewees as the primary reason that they were not able to get their papers published.

> The Chinese academics, largely, find out what others did, copy the model and develop it into a model that suits the Chinese. (Shi, health science)

> Papers in the Chinese journal seem to be quite simple. The discussion section has lack of depth and comprehensiveness in comparing and

> contrasting one's findings with those of the others. (Zhuang, cross-discipline)

Two interviewees (Ding and Zhuang) cited lack of access to the latest information in the fields as an important factor contributing to the quality issue of the mainlanders' research.

> It is more convenient here to access information and it is easier to maintain the frontier status. Through the library website, almost all the latest issues of the most influential journals in the field can be read on the computer. Most of the Chinese universities may not be able to subscribe to these journals because the lack of financial input. (Zhuang, cross-discipline)

In addition, Chen and Zhuang viewed language as a constraint for mainland scholars in getting their papers published.

> As for mainland scholars who have been educated domestically, I think it is quite difficult for them to get their papers published. To publish in those journals, it requires at least some years' accumulation both in language and in specialized knowledge. (Chen, cross-discipline)

> Here, we have a research team and the members can help you polish the language in the article. I don't think they have this type of support and there is no one to help with the language. (Zhuang, cross-discipline)

As expected, most interviewees (Chen, Li, Wang and Shi) stated that the current academic atmosphere within China's scientific community constrained Chinese scholars' involvement in science and research.

Quantity and quality

Two interviewees (Shi and Wang) raised the relationship between quantity and quality as problematic. They stated that mainland scholars tended to publish more articles, rather than better ones.

> Most Chinese academics, they publish their articles because they want promotion. Writing papers is part of their task. My former colleagues told me it was not necessary to publish in internationally recognized journals and the second-class domestic journal was ok. (Shi, health science)

Li, Chen and Shi all voiced a concern that Chinese academics tended to emphasise practical achievements, with less effort given to basic research. However, this may be understandable in today's China, where chances to make one's fortune and one's career have been increasing due to its stellar economic resurgence (China's annual per capita GDP growth rate of almost 10 per cent since around 1990 has been world leading).

> In my specific field, the mainland scholars I met placed great emphasis on joint-degree programs, or inviting foreign academics to teach students in China. They were not interested in pure academic cooperation. (Chen, cross-discipline)

> In terms of research, I think my Alma Mater is lagging far behind as compared to Australia. Although there were new buildings and facilities, they were busy with daily treatment (i.e. clinics). They did not emphasize the research or have the funding to support research. They did not put research on their agenda. (Shi, health science)

In addition, two interviewees (Li and Wang) noted that scientific research was influenced greatly by academic heritage and that teachers had great influence on students. This was the reason why the mainlanders' work was put in a simple or unsophisticated way.

> Because most Chinese academics were educated there, they inherited the old way to conduct research. (Wang, health science)

However, all the interviewees stated that the Chinese way of conducting research could be changed as more and more overseas Chinese returned.

> I think Chinese academics do quite well in academic research. The key point here is that they have a different way of writing papers. I believe the Chinese way of conducting research can be changed as more and more overseas Chinese return. (Li, engineering)

> Without attracting and utilizing more overseas Chinese academics, China can hardly keep up with international development. The group of personnel is the huge potential for China's development in science and technology. (Shi, health science)

As mentioned, interviewees related the marginalisation of Chinese scholarship to the fact they work in Australia, one of the centres of scientific activity. Lack of language proficiency and resources, as well as the traditional academic atmosphere and heritage, contributed to less active participation by mainland scholars' in the international scientific community. All interviewees believed, however, that experienced returnees with overseas degrees would provide a solution to the problem.

Stratification

The findings regarding the influence of the lack of resources on the invisibility of the mainland scholars substantiate previous studies in the field. Research on the impact of the world economy on the international knowledge network reveals a direct, causal relationship between the two (Altbach, 1987, 1995, 2002; Choi, 1995; Tefera and Altbach 2003; Meyer *et al.* 2001; Welch 2007a, 2008).

This is no less true in China. Notwithstanding the rapid growth that the Chinese economy has enjoyed over the last decade and a half, the fruits of this growth have been very unequally distributed, thus segments of the economy remain bogged in backwardness, with low literacy rates and considerable poverty. The fruits of growth and investment in higher education too, are very unequally distributed across China. Therefore, while a rising number of mainland scholars will take a much more active role in the international knowledge network, these will stem almost exclusively from China's most eminent institutions – for the foreseeable future, most Chinese scholarship will retain its marginalised status.

Interviewees reflected considerable awareness of the extent of stratification within Chinese higher education, and expressed considerable consensus regarding its effects. Both Wang and Shi were highly appreciative of the work conducted by academics of the Chinese university.

> I visited the web site of C1 University one day. Amazingly, there were so many higher-level papers published in *Science* and *Nature*. In China, top level is top, internationally top. But the medium level is quite low. (Wang, health science)

> To my knowledge, only C1 has conducted relevant research. During my contact with Professor X, I find out that his ideas and research are cutting edge. However, when I went back my alma mater, I noticed that they advanced with moderate progress. (Shi, health science)

Further, two interviewees specifically noted the impact of the unbalanced development of different disciplines in Chinese higher education.

> As you may notice, China has been quite expert at certain skills in hard science. However, it lags far behind in many fields in soft science. (Chen, cross-discipline)

Indeed, Zhuang perceived it as a constraint to setting up a professional relationship with the mainland peers in his field (although not with others).

> Collaboration in science and engineering is easier and more productive. This is because China is strong in these fields, with so many good undergraduates. (Zhuang, cross-discipline)

The stratified structure of the Chinese higher education system has been intensified in recent years with the national government using selective schemes such as the well-known 211 and 985 Projects, to pour much-needed resources into key universities (with the aim of fostering an elite category of world-class universities), at the cost of lesser institutions. As part of the project, having internationally trained professors is an important indicator. This is the reason that there are several research-oriented HEIs, with excellent facilities and overseas educated academic staff, operating at the highest international level despite the fact that the Chinese higher education system as a whole is still lagging behind.

This phenomenon is highly illustrative of the existence of centre and periphery at global and national level, and reflects both economic factors, and China's national developmental priorities. While some research points to a number of universities in newly industrialised states such as China approaching the status of world-class research institutions, it remains the fact that the leading research-oriented universities in the North still occupy the top tier. The underlying truth is that higher education structure is becoming multi-polar, in the context of ever more intense competition. Even within the centre, there are centres and peripheries, for example, the so-called Ivy League in the United States, the Russell Group in the UK, and the Group of Eight in Australia.

Conclusion

The findings above regarding the impact of problems of language proficiency, the bias of citation indices, and differences between Chinese and Western ways of conducting research, and on the mainland scholars' differential status in the international scientific community support previous studies on academics in the third world (Altbach 2002, 2004; Welch 2005). These reveal that, as publication in the prestigious scientific journals, mostly edited in the North, remains the *sine qua non* of academic validity, academics from the South are still placed at a significant disadvantage, because of a common lack of language proficiency and unfamiliarity with the Western research system (Altbach, in Altbach and Umakoshi 2004: 7–11).

The findings as to the significance of the scientific knowledge and expertise of Chinese intellectual diasporas to China's development again support the mainstream research on the diaspora option which conceptualises the exodus of the highly skilled as a substantial, if at times temporary, loss and at the same time a potential resource to be mobilised by the country of origin (Brown 2000; Lowell 2001; Meyer *et al.* 1997; Meyer and Brown 1999; Meyer *et al.* 2001; Tefera 2004; Wickramasekara 2002; Zweig and Fung 2004). This is all the more so in light of the deepening interconnectedness of the world, especially the research world, in an era of thickening, and denser, global information and communications technologies.

The notion of the diaspora, embodying the key notion of interstices and in-betweenness, presents a further challenge to the taken-for-granted status of the nation state in education. The development of global knowledge diasporas, further challenge us to reconsider this assumption. For researchers in education, they hold out the promise of new lines of research, based on alternative premises. At the same time, they also herald, in concert with rises in new and denser forms of information technology, novel ways of conducting research in both the natural and social sciences, and ways of contributing to the development of research and development in the homeland, and forming knowledge bridges that can be of benefit to both sides of the relationship.

Bibliography

Altbach, P. G. (1987). *The Knowledge context: Comparative perspectives on the distribution of knowledge*, Albany, NY: State University of New York Press.

Altbach, P. G. (1994) 'International knowledge network', in T. Husen and T. N. Postlethwaite (eds) *International Encyclopedia of Education* Oxford: Pergamon Press, pp. 2993–8.

Altbach, P. G. (1995) Foreword: 'International knowledge networks and the "invisible college" of scientist and scholars', in H. Choi (ed.) *An International Scientific Community: Asian Scholar in the United States*, Westport, CT: Praeger, pp. ix–xi.

Altbach, P. G. (2002) 'Centers and peripheries in the academic profession: the special challenges of developing countries', in *The Decline of the Guru: The Academic Profession in Developing and Middle-Income Countries*, New York: Palgrave, pp. 1–21.

Altbach, P. G. (2004) 'Globalization and the university: myths and realities in an unequal world', *Tertiary Education and Management*, 10(1): 3–25.

Altbach, P. and Umakoshi, T. (eds) (2004) *Asian Universities: Historical Perspectives and Contemporary Challenges*, Baltimore: Johns Hopkins University Press.

Appadurai, A. (2001) 'Grassroots globalisation and the research imagination', *Globalization*. Durham, NC: Duke University Press, pp. 1–21.

Brown, M. (2000) 'Using the intellectual diaspora to reverse the brain drain: some useful examples'. Retrieved 26 March 2005, from http://www.uneca.org/eca_resouces/Conference_Reports_and_Other_Documents.

Cao, Cong (2004) 'Chinese science and the "Nobel Prize" complex', *Minerva*, 42: 151–72.

Choi, H. (1995) *An International Scientific Community: Asian Scholars in the United States*, New York: Praeger.

Crystal, D. (1997) *English as a Global Language*, Cambridge: Cambridge University Press.

Docquier, F. and Abdeslam, M. (2006) 'International migration by educational attainment 1990–2000', in Özden, Ç. and Schiff, M. (eds) *International Migration, Remittances and the Brain Drain*, Washington, DC: World Bank, pp. 151–200.

Hall, S. (1996) 'The formation of a diasporic intellectual', in Morley, D. and Chen, K.-H. (eds) *Stuart Hall: Critical Dialogues in Cultural Studies*, London: Routledge, pp. 484–503.

Holenbergh, R. (2005) 'Relations in higher education, Australia and the People's Republic of China: a study of educational linkages, with special reference to the University of Sydney'. Unpublished PhD thesis, University of Sydney.

Hugo, G. (2002) 'Migration policies designed to facilitate the recruitment of skilled workers in Australia', *International Mobility of the Highly Skilled*, Paris: OECD, pp. 291–320.

Hugo, G. (2005) 'Australian migration transformed', *Australian Mosaic*, 9: 1.

Johnson, J. M. and Regets, M. C. (1998) 'International mobility of scientists and engineers to the United States: Brain drain or brain circulation?' Retrieved 25 March 2005, from http://www.nsf.gov/sbe/srs/stats.htm.

Kapur, D. and McHale, J. (2005) *Give us Your Best and Brightest: The Global Hunt for Talent and its Impact on the Developing World*, Washington, DC: Centre for Global Development.

Li, P. (2005) 'Immigration from China to Canada in the age of globalisation. issues of brain gain and brain loss', *People on the Move: The Transnational Flow of Chinese Human Capital*, Hong Kong University of Science and Technology, October 2005

Lowell, B. L. (2001) *Policy Response to the International Mobility of Skilled Labor*, International migration papers 45. Geneva: International Labor Office.

Luo, Y.-L. and Wang, W.-J. (2002) 'High-skill migration and Chinese Taipei's industrial development', *International Mobility of the Highly Skilled*, Paris: OECD, pp. 253–69.

Meyer, J.-P., and Brown, M. (1999) *Scientific Diasporas: A New Approach to the Brain Drain*, World Conference on Science, UNESCO ICSU Budapest, June.

Meyer, J.-B., Kaplan, D. and Caran, J. (2001) *Scientific Nomadism and the New Geopolitics of Knowledge*, Oxford: UNESCO.

Meyer, J.-B., Charum, J., Bernal, D., Gaillard, J., Granes, J., Leon, J., Montenegro, A., Morales, A., Murica, C., Narvaez-Berthelemot, N., Parrado, L. S. and Schlemmer, B. (1997) 'Turning brain drain into brain gain: the Colombian experience of the diaspora option', *Science Technology and Society*, 2(2): 285–315.

Özden, C. and Schiff, M. (eds) (2005) *International Migration, Remittances and the Brain Drain*, Washington, DC: World Bank, especially Chelleraj, G., Maskus, K. and Mattoo, A., 'Skilled migrants, higher education and US innovation', pp. 245–59.

Parliamentary Library (2004) *Australia's Migration Programme*, Research Note 48, 2004–5. http://www.aph.gov.au/library/pubs/rn/2004-05rn48.pdf.

Saxenian, A. (2006) *The New Argonauts. Regional Advantage in a Global Economy*, Cambridge, MA: Harvard University Press.

Shen, H. (2000) 'Academic freedom and academic duty in Chinese universities', in OECD, *Current Issues in Chinese Higher Education*, Paris: OECD, pp. 21–35.

Solimano, A. (2002) *Globalizing Talent and Human Capital: Implications for Developing Countries*, Santiago: UN.

Stiver Lie, S. and O'Leary, V. (eds) (1990) *Storming the Tower: Women in the Academic World*, London: Kogan Page.

Tefera, D. (2004) *Brain Circulation: Unparalleled Opportunities, Underlying Challenges, and Outmoded Presumption*. Paper prepared for the Symposium on International Labour and Academic Mobility: Emerging Trends and Implications for Public Policy. Retrieved April 5, 2005, from http://www.wes.org/ewenr/symp/DamtewTeferraPaper.pdf.

Tefera, D. and Altbach, P. (eds) (2003) *African Higher Education*, Bloomington: Indiana University Press.

Tsang, E. W. K. (2001) 'Adjustment of mainland Chinese academics and students to Singapore', *International Journal of Intercultural Relations*, 25: 347–372.

Tsolidis, G. (2001) *Schooling, Diaspora and Gender*, Buckingham: Open University Press.

Welch, A. (2005) *From Peregrinatio Academica to the Global Academic*, The Internationalisation of the Academic Profession, The Professoriate, Profile of a Profession, Dordrecht, Springer.

Welch, A. (2007a) 'Blurred vision: public and private higher education in Indonesia', *Higher Education* (in press).

Welch, A. (2007b) 'Cultural difference and identity', in Connell, R. *et al.* (eds) *Education, Change and Society*, Oxford: Oxford University Press, pp. 155–87.

Welch, A. (2008) 'Higher education between the Dragon and the Tiger Cubs: China–ASEAN relations in higher education in the GATS era', in D. Jarvis and A. Welch (eds) *The Dragon and the Tiger Cubs: China, ASEAN and Regional Integration*, London: Palgrave (in press).

Welch, A. and Zhang, Z. (2005) 'Zhongguo de zhishi liusan – haiwai zhongguo zhishi fenzijian de jiaoliu wangluo' (Communication networks of the Chinese intellectual diaspora) *Comparative Education Review* [Beijing], 26(12): 31–7 (in Chinese).

Wickramasekara, P. (2002) *Policy responses to skilled migration: Retention, Return and Circulation*, Geneva: International Labor Organization.

Zhang, G. and Li, W. (2002) 'International mobility of China's resources in science and technology and its impact', *International Mobility of the Highly Skilled*, Paris: OECD, pp. 189–200.

Zweig, D. and Fung, C. S. (2004) 'Redefining the brain drain: China's diaspora option', Center on China's Transnational Relations, Working Paper No. 1. Retrieved 19 April 2005, from http://www.cctr.ust.hk/articles/pdf/redefining.pdf.

20 Internationalisation and the cosmopolitical university

Rodrigo Britez and Michael A. Peters

Introduction

In his book *Globalization*, Zygmunt Bauman (1998) points out that mobility has become a byword of contemporary reality, 'nowadays we are all on the move' (p. 77). Precisely, the current context of global connectedness and interaction generates a reality of increased mobilities and desires to be mobile by individuals and corporations. In this context, student populations at research universities around the world have become both more numerous and internationally diverse. This phenomenon is not merely related to the growing global demand for higher education, but also is a direct result of the increasing dependency of states and higher institutions' influence and wealth on their capacity to participate and strategically position themselves in global markets. In those instances internationalisation of higher education as part of a set of strategies to position higher education systems and institutions in a global context seems to be informed by the demands of neoliberal capitalist economies and by a neoliberal cosmopolitical concept of university.

Basically, the neoliberal position emphasises the view of international students primarily as a strategic economic resource or a source of revenue for university institutions. Simply put, neoliberalism sees the export of institutional education services abroad as an economic export. This position is adopted by states in neoliberal capitalist economies and subsequently enforced and encouraged by national education systems to pursue an economic agenda even at the expense of the achievement of any political purposes on internationalism. We argue that in such instances cosmopolitanism and the lure for cosmopolitan experiences and cosmopolitan practices become part of marketing apparatus no different from those observed in the international recruiting of workers for transnational corporations. More importantly, we argue that these neoliberal practices seem to ignore alternative ways of thinking transnational spaces rather than viewing them as economic spaces of exchange or cultural spaces subordinated to the economy.

In this chapter, we discuss some of the issues that surround inter-nationalisation of higher education as a way to open a discussion about the construction of an alternative cosmopolitical vision of the university which is necessary if the university is to fulfill any of its historic tasks concerning the creation of globally aware citizens. We begin with a historical overview of the notion of internationalisation and indicate the way in which currently it has been used in higher education to refer to specific strategies to answer to globalisation trends. We also indicate the way it has become subordinated to a neoliberal metanarrative of development that contains a particular understanding of globalisation and cosmopolitanism.

In the second, third and four sections we indicate that economic and technological globalisation has resulted not only in the growth of international education but also in the increasing significance of transnational spaces where accelerated patterns of interaction and worldwide connectedness can be best characterised in terms of global flows and networks. In this networked environment internationalisation of higher education refers to strategies to attract students and also to specific patterns of movement. We maintain that the neoliberal metanarrative informing strategies of internationalisation not only ignores the complexity of those patterns of interaction, connectedness and movement, but also implies modes of insertion of higher education into transnational spaces, as receptors or senders of certain flows. The way in which students' movements are managed by university institutions and systems leads us to reflect about the cosmopolitical project of university implicit in those strategies.

In the last section we present different concepts of cosmopolitanism linked to projects of political integration in transnational spaces influencing university institutions. We argue that cosmopolitical neoliberalism looks at the cultivation of students as consumers ignoring the potential social and cultural disjunctures in current globalisation projects. Moreover, we maintain that this neoliberal project essentially ignores the potential contributions of university institutions to the creation of public transnational spaces. Finally, against this we reflect on a vision of a cosmopolitical project of university as alternative to the one implicit in neoliberal internationalisation strategies.

Reconfiguring the concept of internationalisation

Internationalisation is a set of processes in search of a concept and theory of internationalism that has yet to be articulated. Most often the use of the term internationalisation figures as a *strategy* with an emphasis on 'how to' questions rather than a reflective discourse examining political ends or purposes. Increasingly the term has become a significant part of strategic plans of universities, especially in the western world but often the concept is not thought through or developed in line with the purposes of the university but rather seen as a simple synonym for 'study abroad' or the recruitment of overseas students, especially by universities in neoliberal economies that focus on 'export education'.

Today, 'internationalisation' in higher education has become a common phrase used by the decision makers in higher learning institutions to refer to specific strategies implemented as an answer or solution to globalisation trends. Internationalisation is understood in most cases in narrow and instrumental terms. As Nelly P. Stromquist (2007) notes, it most often characterises the search for markets for students, 'rather than positioning the university's knowledge at the service of others' (p. 81). In this case, internationalisation as a strategy becomes subordinated to a particular understanding of globalisation closely linked with a dominant political discourse as a term 'widely used only in one-dimensional economic sense' (Beck 2004: 135).

In the current context, internationalisation in most cases has to be understood very differently from 'internationalism'. The latter term is closer to the cultivation of a cosmopolitan perspective while the former refers in practice 'to greater international presence by the dominant economic and political powers, usually guided by principles of marketing and competition' (Stromquist 2007: 82).

Yet the close connection between the root concept of internationalisation is thrown into some relief in its connection to internationalism understood as a theory of international relations and opens up the discourse of internationalisation to the consideration of cosmopolitanism and to the prospect of a form of internationalisation tied to political purposes inherent in notions of cosmopolitanism and the cosmopolitical university. One of the benefits of this conceptual move is that it enables us to understand that there are different projects of cosmopolitanisation: for instance, one attached to a dominant discourse of economic globalisation, others linked to the development of cosmopolitan perspectives and practices. In this case, a neoliberal economic metanarrative of cosmopolitanism becomes the dominant view. Narratives of the cosmopolitan operate as 'bylines of globalisation' which is to say that historically it is linked with the movements of people across borders, 'an outlook of those who look and journey beyond borders – whichever borders apply; of itinerant sages and scholars, warriors and aristocracies, merchants and moneylenders, journeying craftsmen, monks and pilgrims. The headings change with the times' (Pieterse 2006: 1248).

But contrary to the notion of the mere movement of people, goods and ideas, the notion of cosmopolitanism essentially refers to the ethos of travelling: institutionalised expectations, ethics, and overall the actual practice and experience of movement across borders and territories. Nowadays, everyone travels; however, the ethos of our travel is quite diverse according to the circumstances. Analogously, it is important to question what kind of cosmopolitanisation we are referring to. In other words, if cosmopolitanism refers to being a world citizen, then what are the experiences or practices of world citizenship and how are they fostered and enhanced by curricula, academic and administrative practices?

In this chapter, we argue that presently the narrative of cosmopolitanism that dominates the discourse of internationalisation of higher education institutions operates as a marketing strategy of corporate universities informed by neoliberalism rather than a critical position encompassing the political, social and cultural dimensions relevant to the practice and experience of being a world citizen. Thus, it becomes part of normative project of cosmopolitanism, disassociated from practice – a neoliberal cosmopolitical project of university most often associated with the doctrine of 'free trade'.

The implementation of this cosmopolitical project certainly diminishes the value of study in university institutions. What makes the university different from a corporation? In part, it is the offering of something different than a banal form of cosmopolitanisation, from travel as a kind of surface tourism. Only universities that attempt to differentiate themselves from the corporate form and response to globalisation can be genuinely called cosmopolitical in the true sense of the term. By this we mean those institutions that offer opportunities for the development of intellectual, social and life skills in their graduates, of the practice and experience of being a cosmopolitan citizen and that offer something more than mere accreditation or perfunctory training for the entrance into transnational labour markets and into a form of 'world citizenship'.

In short, such institutions offer a space to consider cosmopolitanism as an experience and forms of *political action*: to recognise its many faces rather than merely as an abstract, empty, ethical or normative position. We might say that those higher learning institutions recognise 'cosmopolitanism from below' the actual experience of world citizenship dominated by multiethnic diasporas, migrant experiences and grassroots, as well as transnational enterprises.

Why is this important? Because of the increasing relevance of two fundamental aspects in the contemporary historical period of globalisation for the provision of quality education: networks and multiculturalism (Castells and Ince 2003: 107). In other words, we can argue for the necessity of an alternative cosmopolitical project of university where 'multiethnicity and multiculturalism can be viewed as applied cosmopolitanism' (Pieterse 2006: 1255).

Beck (2004) indicates that cosmopolitanisation refers to a multi-dimensional process, involving the formation of multiple identities and multiple loyalties, as well as the emergence and spread of multiple transnational lifestyles (p. 34). Life in an age of globalisation becomes a cosmopolitan reality, but globalisation itself speaks of a multidimensional process that cannot be reduced solely to an economic discourse or a one-dimensional economic perspective.

Globalisation speaks of the 'intensification of worldwide social relations which link localities in such a way that local happenings are shaped by events occurring many miles away and vice versa' (Giddens 1990: 181). In those terms, Beck's (2004) position that 'cosmopolitanisation' is not merely 'economic globalisation' seems correct. These processes of interaction are not new, and globalisation processes in the past have shown the interdependence of communities across the planet. However, what is new is the emergence of a cosmopolitan perspective of reality, a self-consciousness that indicates the emergence of a social imaginary of reality that emphasises multiple levels of interdependence, the tearing down and collapsing of some of the categories of political, cultural and social organisation articulated in the first period of modernity.

In this context, higher education experiences a number of pressures not merely related to the primacy of economic demands and discourses. However, pressures related to the primacy of an 'internationalisation project are manifest in the dominant discourse of economic globalisation', as well as observed in subtle responses affecting academic programmes, faculty, and students, and in the creation of administrative structures and new hierarchies of privilege (Stromquist 2007: 81). For instance, mechanisms to expand the project of global education harmonise with a dominant metanarrative of globalisation and can be observed in the GATS agreements on higher education as well as in the links and growing partnerships between business firms and educational institutions. In the United States the growing dependence of universities on external resources creates common patterns of development which influence the strategies adopted to answer those pressures, thus emphasising processes of integration of colleges and universities into the 'new economy' (Slaughter and Rhoades 2004) as predominantly commercial enterprises.

However, universities are not corporations but more complex institutions that have accumulated a number of contradictory roles scarcely related solely to economic development. Universities are 'imagined communities' (in Benedict Anderson's sense) that have accumulated with time the changing aspirations and expectations of society at a time that encapsulated a number of contradictions. Those contradictory dynamics are characteristic of the particular tradition within an overall university system, the primacy of specific functions, and the position of the institutions in national systems of education. For instance, the basic functions of the university were not merely related to the production and application of knowledge or training of a skilled labour force but also operate as a mechanism of selection and formation of dominant elites, as well as the generation and transmission of ideology (Castells 2001: 210).

The central question that we want to pose is that of universities considered in relation to internationalism rather than internationalisation? It is a significant question because internationalisation is commonly seen as an all-encompassing concept that integrates many different activities such as forms of academic mobility, research collaboration on international development projects in higher education, curricular aspects in terms of the scope of programmes and courses ('area studies') offered or changes in curriculum of specific disciplines. It is also increasingly use as rhetorical device to describe international exchanges in higher education, exchanges across nation states, related to trends of a particular ethos of movement , and in the case of students, related to the aspirations for an international experience in education that have often little to do with cosmopolitan perspectives. What might a theory of internationalism in relation to the university look like, what normative orientations would it imply and how might it guide the university in its practical strategies of internationalisation? These questions also require a better understanding of the way in which internationalisation differs from globalisation.

Student mobility and internationalisation of higher education

The latest edition of the *Global Education Digest: Comparing education statistics across the world*, published by the UNESCO Institute for statistics (UNESCO 2006) clearly shows an aspect of this global context of increasing mobility and the growth of international education. The increase of students mobility, of 'international mobile students' has been marginal in relation to the total enrolment of students pursuing tertiary education. The flow of students moving abroad in pursuit of tertiary education has jumped by 41 per cent between 1999 and 2004 from 1.75 million to 2.5 million outside their home countries at a time that enrolment in higher education has increased dramatically from 92 to 132 million.

This marginal growth in international mobile students has a contradictory correlation with the steady rise of economic globalisation. Mobility has generated a complex picture on the provision of cross-border education as well as the way in which students' mobility affects destination and sender countries and education systems. Today, the United States, Japan, Australia, the United Kingdom, Germany, France and Australia account for 68 per cent of student mobility. It is also noticeable that the greatest percentage and the most growth until recently are in Anglo-American neoliberal capitalist economies of the United States, Australia, the United Kingdom, New Zealand and Canada.

While the United States continues to be the favoured place of destination for graduate education, since 2001 there has been a diminishing share of enrolment of the total of international students, at a time when the UK and Australia emerged as competing places of destination to large shares of undergraduate students. An article in the *New York Times*, 'U.S. slips in attracting the world's best students' (Dillon 2004) indicates how the confluence of increased visa restrictions after September 2001 and the aggressive competition over the recruiting of international students by other international providers, countries like the UK and Australia, are affecting the enrolment of international students at United States universities. In the same article, Tim O'Brien, at that time international development director at Nottingham Trent University in England, explained the diminishing share of enrolment of international students in United States university institutions in the following terms.

> International education is big business for all of the Anglophone countries, and the U.S. traditionally has dominated the market without having to try very hard ... Now Australia, the U.K., Ireland, New Zealand and Canada are competing for that dollar, and our lives have been made

easier because of the difficulties that students are having getting into the U.S.

(Dillon 2004: 7)

The pattern of concentration of the destinations of student mobility continued in the case of the 15 major countries of destination, as shown in the rise in their share of the total of international students from 76 per cent to 82 per cent between 1994 and 2004 (UNESCO 2006: 47), but caveats on the type of mobilities observed account for a more complex picture.

In the case of graduate education, the US seems to retain a large share of the mobility of highly skilled students in sciences and technology. This is in part explained by the role taken by higher education institutions in partnership with transnational corporations, as well as a long history of state research funding strategies. The partnership with corporations is not only limited to research activities, but is also linked to the recruitment of highly skilled workers for those corporations. Research universities in the US attract flows of graduate international students not only to sustain the research activities in those institutions, but also to serve as centres of recruitment of highly skilled workers. The fact is that research centres at universities in the US are heavily dependent on the constant flow of international graduate students to sustain the activities of their research parks. Corporations also rely on attracting flows of highly skilled workers from foreign students graduating from US institutions. The current clamour by corporations in the US over restrictions on visas for foreign workers is directly associated with international students that graduate from higher education institutions in the US. An article in *The Washington Post*, 'Gates cites hiring woes, criticizes visa restrictions' (Vise 2005) mentions some of the comments made by Bill Gates, president of the Microsoft corporation, in a 2005 technology panel at the Library of Congress illustrating this matter in unambiguous terms,

'We are very concerned that the U.S. will lose its competitive position. For Microsoft, it means we are having a tougher time hiring,' Gates said. 'The jobs are there, and they are good-paying jobs, but we don't have the same pipeline.' Microsoft conducts 85 percent of its research in this country. 'We are very tied to the United States' when it comes to doing research and development on the company's Windows and Microsoft Office products, he said ... Gates said the combination of tighter visa restrictions and increasing opportunity in rapidly growing economies in China and India means that more foreign students who study at U.S. universities are returning home to work, rather than seeking jobs in the United States.

(Vise 2005: 13)

The visa restrictions in the United States and the imperative to recruit international students for transnational corporations are not lost by those who pursue international education regardless of the motivations that they may have to study abroad. As Rizvi (2005) indicates, 'the motivations of students wanting to invest in international education vary ... [but] the desire to eventually immigrate has now been identified as one of the most important factors' (Rizvi 2005: 179).

Recruiting strategies (AEI 2005) are informed by the idea that international students are, to a great extent, strategic economic assets or new sources of revenue for university institutions and states (Middlehurst and Woodfield 2004). This is associated in part with the international trend towards seeing education primarily as a trade commodity.

Currently, the international market of education is a great source of profits, comprising approximately 3 per cent of the market of global services and already generating more than US $30 billion in revenues by 1998. For instance, in 2003–4 'export education' was Australia's fourth largest export generating $5.9 billion to the Australian economy.

Finally, all countries are developing strategies to tap into the flows of international labour through higher education systems. We see a complex picture where countries like the US attempt to accommodate, in contradictory ways, strategies to tap into flows of graduate students in order to recruit potential highly skilled workers. We see strategies by countries like the UK (Johnes 2004), Australia, and others, to trade educational services at an international level, while other countries, like the Philippines, are concentrated on strategies to trade skilled labour. The Philippines is one of the largest labour-exporting countries in the world (OECD 2003), and their national system of higher education accommodates the training of highly skilled workers in certain fields (e.g. nurses, teachers) to the requirements of foreign markets that demand their services.

These individual country strategies indicate a complex picture that is outside the scope of this chapter. However, this points to a context in which countries and universities are trying to position themselves in transnational spaces.

Networks and power

One of the most important characteristics of globalisation processes is the intensification of the flows of capital, goods and services, ideas, cultural symbols, and people. As Castells (1999) argues, technology has enabled the emergence of a new space of organisation for dominant activities of the world: from 'a space of places' to a 'space of flows'. Informational technologies allow the digitalising of 'different types of text (pictures, sounds, words)' (Schirato and Webb 2003: 59), thus the convergence of different media, facilitating the processing and transferring of information. As Schirato and Webb (2003) point out, those technologies facilitate the storage of ever-increasing amounts of information as well as the medium for its distribution in 'real time' (p. 59).

Hence, these technologies rather than being solely technologies of material mobility, provide the means for virtual mobilities. Henceforth, the term 'space of flows' refers to a space of interaction where the mobility of the information contained in a book, a letter or a newspaper is no longer material because the information itself acquires a virtual form; it is immaterial in itself. Thus, information or any kind of code, including money, can be converted into any asset for instant transportation.

Those technologies are the ones closely related with current forms of global integration, providing 'affordances' for reshaping the main spheres of human activity, not only the economy. What we see is that the speed and mass of information flows provide the basis for the development of dissimilar processes of integration. For instance, while financial flows become increasingly global and interdependent, the material movement of labour and people become increasingly dependent on states' policies and network strategies. This is to say that, while capital becomes unbounded by operating through virtual mobilities, the free circulation of labour across state borders becomes increasingly problematic.

To understand this contradiction is precisely to understand that processes of global integration have been dominated since the 1980s by the meta-narrative of a 'distinctive strand of neoliberalism' which emerges 'as the dominant paradigm of public policy in the West and continues to exert influence' (Peters and Besley 2006: 31).

This dominant narrative has encapsulated globalisation under a universal logic, as the basis for the global reconstruction of all aspects of society. In a sense, it is projects that have captured the policy agendas of most western countries, under the basic tenet of assuming human beings primarily as individual subjects of an economic rationale driven by self-interest. At the centre of this ideology, mobility is seen as a key to integration and wealth production. But, as we indicated above, it is also producing new forms of disadvantage and difference.

One of the fundamental problems with this neoliberal narrative is precisely the lack of reflexive engagement with the potential consequences and complex dynamics of increasing transnational mobilities. The way in which people mobilise is based on complex dynamics that include the creation of meaning and cultural values, which are not necessarily subject to a dominant individualist economic rationale. Thus, it is within an understanding of these patterns of communication and movement that we can begin to understand their effects on higher education.

In those instances, internationalisation of higher education as a set of strategies informed by the metanarrative of neoliberalism offers a poor understanding of these processes and their significance. The organising principles of movement are neither markets nor exclusively commercial concerns, but issues such as information, resources, trust and cultural values. Thus, movement is defined in terms of relations and flows.

For instance, Meyer (2001) indicates the way that international intellectual mobility of knowledge networks at universities operates through networks linking diaspora members with their countries of origin. The relationships that enable this form of travel are quite different from the ones that characterise the linking to transnational corporations operating through 'head hunter' companies recruiting skilled workers to be shipped to transnational markets of labour. Different instances of international mobility of people are carried under a different ethos, expectations, purposes and strategies.

The question 'what flows are universities tapping into?' is not merely a question about strategy but also about purposes and political ends. If the consideration is merely to attract new sources of revenue, in the form of student recruitment, internationalisation of education begins to acquire forms of an advertising campaign selling the fantasy of a cosmopolitan experience, not dissimilar from those used by transnational 'body-shopping' firms.

Those marketing campaigns can acquire bizarre formats, as seen in a recent article in the *Guardian* entitled 'Reality TV hunt for students' (Hemmens 2007). The article describes a planned reality show in which students from India will compete to obtain five scholarships at five UK universities (Leeds, Warwick, Cardiff, Middlesex and Sheffield):

> The show then goes live in July, with tests selecting winners subject by subject. It runs until November, following the winners to university. BSkyB will air the show in Britain. Fees for overseas business undergraduates at Leeds for 2007–8 are nearly £9,000. The vice-chancellor of Leeds, Michael Arthur, said the business school had about 70 Indian students, mostly graduates. 'This will help Leeds raise its profile further in India and show potential students how much the university has to offer.'
>
> (Hemmens 2007: 3–4)

We argue that by adopting certain strategies university institutions choose modes of integration with transnational spaces that define positions within networks as receptors or senders of certain flows. The sources of wealth and influence of nation states and university institutions, as well as the source of exclusion across transnational spaces, becomes linked to the capacity to sway those mobilities. For instance, in an increasingly globalised economy, we see an increasing dependence on a global workforce. As well as the reliance of the more productive segments of the economy, a 'new economy' becomes linked to a constant flow of skilled workers and highly skilled knowledge producers, as well as cultural producers.

The purpose and content of movements that influence the position of university institutions in distribution networks (e.g. as places of generation of ideas, accreditation, or access to transnational labour markets) becomes more than a question about advertising. Instead, the content of flows requires a serious reflection about the way in which differences are managed within higher education institutions. In short, it is to discuss the cosmopolitical project of university implicit in strategies of internationalisation.

Three concepts of the cosmopolitical university

To talk of the cosmopolitical university is immediately to invoke a globally-oriented institution that aims at the cultivation of globally minded citizens. In short, it is oriented to the cultivation of cosmopolitan citizens rather than national citizens.

As Derek Heater (2004: 218) indicates, the idea of 'citizen of the world' though vague has been characterised by 'the conviction that the world citizenship ideal has a practical validity and moral worth', which has been a persistent feature of western political thinking. Indeed, the root stock of the word first used in 1614 to mean 'citizen of the world' derives from the Greek *kosmopolites* (*kosmos* meaning 'world', *polites*, meaning 'citizen', and *polis* meaning 'city'). 'Cosmopolitanism', with first recorded use in 1828, registers the idea that there is a *single moral community* based on the idea of freedom and thus in the early twenty-first century is also seen as a major theoretical buttress to the concept of universal human rights that transcends all national, cultural and state boundaries.

The notion of 'citizen of the world' or 'global citizens', in its oldest incarnation is associated with ideas of cosmopolitanism. But, the capacity of cosmopolitans to proclaim the idea of a moral community and to travel has always been dependent on the capacity of states to guarantee safety and movement. At this point, Bowden (2003) points out an obvious dilemma confronting the idea of cosmopolitan global citizenship:

> For cosmopolitan advocates of global citizenship there is an inescapable dilemma that is still to be addressed with any degree of satisfaction. If cosmopolites embrace and advocate only Western liberal-democratic values at the expense of non-Western values, then they are not truly multicultural pluralist cosmopolitans at all. Rather, they are (at best) cultural imperialists, perpetuating the Western Enlightenment's long history of universalism-cum-imperialism. On the other hand, if repelled by this prospect, cosmopolitans instead embrace cultural pluralism, that is, if they embrace all (or a broad range of) values, then it may very well be the case that they lack any, as Pagden suggests. And as Arendt rightly points out, as nothing more than human beings in general they lose all significance. (p. 360)

In this chapter, we do not directly address this dilemma although it is clear that the formulation avoids the fact that ideas that spring from one locality can take on universal significance as in science, the adoption of universal number systems and also the ideology of human rights. However, we will indicate that cosmopolitan values that transcend all national, cultural and state boundaries are generally considered an essential component of cultivating cosmopolitan perspectives of globally minded citizens. At this point a number of questions become obvious: what kind of cosmopolitan values? what kind of globally minded citizen?

Besides moral and political (or legal) cosmopolitanism there is also a form of economic cosmopolitanism associated with the work of Adam Smith who sought to diminish the role of politics in the economic realm. Said to originate from Quesnay, the notion of economic cosmopolitanism has been promoted strongly in the twentieth century by Friedrich Hayek and Milton Friedman, and taken up in a particular form of neoliberalism that now characterises the World Trade Organisation.

In a liberal framework the three most prominent forms of contemporary cosmopolitanism are: Kantian moral cosmopolitanism represented by the discourse of human rights and, perhaps, institutionally by the United Nations; Kantian political cosmopolitanism represented by the likes of Habermas, Rawls, Beitz, Pogge and cosmopolitan democracy, argued by Held; and finally, economic cosmopolitanism currently best exemplified by a form of neoliberal 'free-trade'.

Furthermore, each of these concepts of cosmopolitanism informs competing projects of political integration in transnational spaces influencing university institutions. More precisely, within those projects are the ideas influencing the type of globally minded citizens to be cultivated by universities.

For instance, cosmopolitan neoliberalism assumes citizens as consumers. This perspective assumes that cosmopolitanism is only a type of global commodity subordinated to the demands of capital. Students are considered consumers in transnational spaces, while university institutions provide narratives and expectations of world citizenship where cosmopolitan experiences and consumption become one and the same.

Neoliberalism assumes a world unbounded in which nation states operate exclusively under the logic of the economic activity of supranational spaces. In these circumstances, international students are considered not only a mere reflection of the erosion of boundaries and frontiers but also part of an ambivalent reality dominated by economic rationalities and perspectives.

The cosmopolitan values that dominate this concept are clear: the values of the consumer of transnational spaces. Cosmopolitan refers to a specific type of traveller: one who is able to choose where to be and to live without subjecting his or her own cultural values to the exchange and test of their host culture. In other words, universal values like freedom of movement are part of an image of the cosmopolitan citizen but they are restricted to those able to purchase and afford movement.

Habermas (2003) points out some of the problems of the assumptions made by the advocates of this project, especially given the consideration of the potentially unintended consequences of a project articulated primordially in economic terms that creates forms of social integration of segments of the global population while encouraging forms of exclusion and marginalisation for vast segments of the world population.

Furthermore, the attempt to cultivate globally minded citizens subordinated to this kind of cosmopolitanism is characterised by empty forms of political practices. Subtle feelings and growing sensibilities toward unfamiliar spaces become void. In other words, this is the cultivation of a type of cosmopolitan citizenship that does not demand any kind of responsibility or awareness towards others, toward their cultures, languages and traditions. Consequently, it cultivates perspectives that ignore the fact that for most of the people on this planet exclusion is still operating through the government of spaces and territories, and over a large array of cosmopolitan experiences and differences.

Moreover, we argue through the chapter that strategies of internationalisation of higher education subordinated to the primacy of this form of cosmopolitical vision of university not only ignore the social and political roles that universities have played through time but also are unable to enhance educational experiences through the cultivation of cosmopolitan perspectives about the diversity and the preservation of the diversity of knowledges, languages and cultures.

Again, Appadurai (1996) noted that 'diversity is a particular organization of difference. The question is what kind of organization?' (p. 24). It is possible to argue that, if we are going to speak of a cosmopolitical project of university, we also must refer to the way in which the 'economy of diversity' is managed in the academy.

We could assume that difference is managed in the academy according to the type of policies applied, and to the point of interest in this chapter, by the type of cosmopolitical project that generates those political practices. In those terms, it may be that the official discourse of the university on internationalisation is one of an essentially empty nature driven by strategy and little awareness of broader philosophical goals or purposes. For instance, to state the goal of promoting globally minded citizens when it is used as a marketing tool, or to enunciate diversity by simply asserting the recruitment of students of colour, international students, or scholars as if diversity 'is mechanical good' (Appadurai 1996: 24).

In this chapter we maintain that alternative ideas of the cosmopolitical university are possible. For instance, Kantian moral and legal cosmopolitanism are two projects that still have potential as alternative projects of social integration. Both projects refer to the construction of democratic universes based on the construction of supranational political formations that point to the silent aspect of a project based on the idea of a cosmopolitan citizen as a consumer of markets: 'markets, unlike political entities cannot be democratised' (Habermas 2003: 95). Alternatives are necessary if we take into consideration the inability of cosmopolitical concepts of university informed by neoliberalism to address two critical aspects for the future development of higher education institutions.

First, the management of diversity: what makes different colleges and universities of specialised research centres or professional credential spaces today? Appadurai's answer is the 'university is also about thought and reflection, cultivation and conscience, disinterest and abreaction, literacy and cosmopolitanism' (Appadurai 1996: 27). Because liberal arts remain quintessentially cosmopolitan they provide a space for the cultivation of specific cosmopolitan habitus of research and inquiry.

However, this is only possible today, with humanities that are able to escape traditional frameworks of reference. Thus the humanities must be able to escape their local origins and trajectories and broaden their accounts to take in the radical pluralism existing as part of a new globalism recognising the claims of local autonomy made by first peoples, indigenous peoples, sub-state cultural minorities, international religious movements, youth cultures, gender groups, and all sorts of political associations (Peters 2007: 8).

The idea is that the creation of habitus of research cultivates a cosmopolitan perspective rather than being merely vocational and offering professional training of graduate students. The care and cultivation of habits of research and inquiry is based in the cultivation of a specific type of 'cosmopolitan self', thus is the object of post-humanistic pedagogies that focus on projects of organisation of difference that cultivate a perspective that seriously engages with the values of diversity.

First, the quality of the academic experience is not based in quantity but the acquisition of habitus of quality control. In Appadurai's (1996) words, 'the true scarcity is not of great books – an odd idea – but opportunities to impress upon students the right norms of quality control' (p. 25). In other words, quality in the academy is tied to the creation of ecologies for organising diversity: a culture of diversity, rather than cultural diversity. It is dependent on political administrative practices, a management of diversity that allows the creation of an institutional climate 'that is actually hospitable to diversity: one which puts diversity at the centre of the curriculum and the demographics of the university, rather than at its statistical or conceptual margin' (Appadurai 1996: 26). Without a 'conscious commitment to the mutual value of intellectual and cultural university', it is not possible to create a 'habitus where diversity is at the heart of the apparatus itself' (Appadurai 1996: 26).

Today, quality education in research institutions requires the cultivation of a 'cosmopolitan perspective', as the habitus of research and inquiry. For university systems, university institutions, and university sectors becoming globalised in complex institutional settings the questions remain: What types of education will modern universities provide, to whom, and in which spaces? How will the cosmopolitan political practices of universities be established? The potentials of modern universities or their eventual irrelevance as educative and research spaces will probably be defined in those terms, as well as the potential venues of stratification within higher education systems.

The second critical aspect about the future development of higher education institutions is the social role of universities: what will be the social role of universities in transnational spaces? This is not only an ethical question about the type of university, but also the political project that we would like to see developed.

In conclusion, if we ask the question: 'what kind of "cosmopolitan selves" is a project of university cultivating?' we are also asking questions about ethics and politics (Peters 2007: 8), and according to the project of cosmopolitical university, these questions will be answered in different ways.

We assume that the potential of the modern university as a part of a democratic project will examine cosmopolitan political practices, looking for a humanistic view of cosmopolitanism, as the one explicitly adopted by Derrida (2001): recuperating ancient concepts of friendship, the ethics of hospitality, forgiveness, and the gift and the invitation that outlines his account of responsibility to the other (Peters 2007: 8). Only in those instances will projects of internationalisation of higher education also include places of critical resistance and dissidence against cosmopolitanisation processes, and cosmopolitan political practices made under the claim of universal humanism or one culture – a claim of universal superiority characteristic of fundamentalist movements.

References

AEI (2005) *Australia's Competitors in International Education*, Canberra: AEI, Australian education international News. Retrieved 10 March 2007, from http://aei.dest.gov.au/AEI/PublicationsAndResearch/Publications/CompAnalysis July05_pdf.

Appadurai, A. (1996) 'Diversity and disciplinarity as cultural artifacts', in C. Nelson and D. P. Gaonkar (eds) *Disciplinarity and Dissent in Cultural Studies*, New York: Routledge.

Bauman, Z. (1998) *Globalization*, New York: Columbia University Press.

Beck, U. (2004) 'Cosmopolitan realism: on the distinction between cosmopolitanism in philosophy and the social sciences', *Global Networks*, 4(2): 131–56.

Bowden, B. (2003) 'The perils of global citizenship', *Citizenship Studies*, 4(3): 349–62.

Castells, M. (1999) 'Flows, networks, and identities: a critical theory of the informational society', in M. Castells, R. Flecha, P. Freire, H. A. Giroux, D. Macedo and P. Willis (eds) *Critical Education in the New Information Age*, Lanham, MD: Rowman & Littlefield Publishers.

Castells, M. (2001) 'Universities as dynamic systems of contradictory functions', in M. Castells, J. Muller, N. Cloete, and S. Badat (2001) *Challenges of Globalisation*, Pinelands: Maskew Miller Longman.

Castells, M. and Ince, M. (2003) *Conversations with Manuel Castells*, Cambridge: Polity Press.

Derrida, J. (2001) *On Cosmopolitanism and Forgiveness*, New York: Routledge.

Dillon, S. (2004) 'US slips in attracting the world's best students', *New York Times*, December 21. Retrieved 30 March 2007, from http://www.nytimes.com/2004/12/21/national/21global.html?th.

Giddens, A. (1990) *The Consequences of Modernity*, Cambridge: Polity Press.

Habermas, J. (2003) 'Toward a cosmopolitan Europe', *Journal of Democracy*, 14(4): 86–100.

Heater, D. (2004) *A History of Education for Citizenship*, New York: Routledge Falmer.

Hemmens, W. (2007) 'Reality TV hunts for students', *The Guardian*, 7 April. Retrieved 10 April 2007, from The Guardian Unlimited website.

Johnes, G. (2004) 'The global value of education and training exports to the UK economy', British Council. Retrieved 10 March 2007, from http://www.

britishcouncil.org/global-value-of-education-and-training-exports-to-the-uk-economy.pdf.

Meyer, J. P. (2001) 'Network approach, versus brain drain', *International Migration*, 39(5): 91–110.

Middlehurst, R. and Woodfield, S. (2004) *The Role of Transnational, Private and For-Profit Provision in Meeting Global Demand for Tertiary Education*, Commonwealth of Learning, UNESCO. Retrieved 25 April 2007, from http://www.col.org/colweb/webdav/site/myjahiasite/shared/docs/03Transnational_Report.pdf.

OECD (2003) *Trends in International Migration: SOPEMI, 2002 Edition*, Paris: OECD. Retrieved 10 June 2006, from http://www1.oecd.org/publications/e-book/8103061E.PDF.

Peters, M. A. (2007) 'The humanities in deconstruction: raising the question of the post-colonial university', *Access: Critical Perspectives on Communication, Cultural & Policy Studies*, 26(1).

Peters, M. A. and Besley, A. C. (2006) *Building Knowledge Cultures: Education and Development in the Age of Knowledge Capitalism*, Lanham: Rowman & Littlefield.

Pieterse, J. N. (2006) 'Emancipatory cosmopolitanism', *Development and Change*, 37(6): 1247–57.

Rizvi, F. (2005) 'Rethinking brain drain in the era of globalization', *Asian-Pacific Journal of Education*, 25(2): 175–93.

Schirato, T. and Webb, J. (2003) *Understanding Globalization*, Thousand Oaks: Sage Publications.

Slaughter, S. and Rhoades, G. (2004) *Academic Capitalism and the New Economy*, Baltimore: Johns Hopkins University Press.

Stromquist, N. P. (2007) 'Internationalization as a response to globalization', *Higher Education*, 53(1): 81–105.

UNESCO (2006) *Global Education Digest 2006*, Montreal: UNESCO Institute for Statistics. Retrieved 18 April 2007, from http://www.uis.unesco.org/TEMPLATE/pdf/ged/2006/GED2006.pdf.

Vise, D.A. (2005) 'Gates cites hiring woes, criticizes visa restrictions', *The Washington Post*, 28 April. Retrieved 25 April 2007, from http://www.washingtonpost.com/wp-dyn/content/article/2005/04/27/AR2005042702241.html.

21 The social web

Changing knowledge systems in higher education

Bill Cope and Mary Kalantzis

To a greater extent than is often acknowledged, the modern university is a creature of the society of the printing press. Until the turn of the twenty-first century, print was the medium of scholarly communication. It was the source of book learning. Now, quite suddenly, digital text is beginning to displace print as the primary means of access to the knowledge of academicians and as the dominant medium for the delivery of instructional content. This chapter explores some of the consequences of this change. To what extent do digital technologies of representation and communication reproduce the knowledge and pedagogical systems of the half-millennium long history of the modern university or how far do they disrupt and transform them?

To answer this question, this chapter will first explore key aspects of contemporary transformations, not just in the textual forms of digital representation, but the emerging social forms that digitisation reflects, affords and supports. This we call the 'social web', a term we use to describe the kinds of relationships to knowledge and culture that are emerging in the era of pervasively interconnected computing. What, then, are the impacts and potentials of these changes on two of the fundamental missions of the university: knowledge formation and teaching?

Today, universities face significant challenges to their traditional position in society – contemporary knowledge systems are becoming more distributed and learning ubiquitous. Where does this leave the university – as a historically specialised and privileged place for certain kinds of knowledge and learning, as an institutionally bounded space? What do these changes mean for the mission and structures of a renewed university in the era of digital communications? These are large questions, which we can only begin to answer in a schematic way in the space of this chapter.

The social web

The first printed book, Gutenberg's 1452 Bible, had no title page, no contents page, no page numbering. Extant copies show the signs of ecclesiastical, manuscript culture – the beautifully illuminated marginalia which, until the era of print, gave the written word an aura of authority that raised it above the spoken word of everyday experience. It took another fifty years for the textual architecture of the printed word to take its modern form, and with it, new forms of textual authority.

By 1500, the end of the period of 'incunabula', eight million books had been printed. It was not until then that printed text came to be marked by the structures of graduated type and spatial page design, and the information hierarchies of chapter headings, section breaks and subheadings. Navigational devices were added in the form of tables of contents and running heads. Alphabetically ordered indexes were added. And the text was divided into uniform and easily discoverable units by means of the most under-rated and revolutionary of all modern information technologies – the page number (Febvre and Martin 1976; Eisenstein 1979).

These textual forms became the ground for representations of knowledge and patterns of teaching in its characteristically modern form. Petrus Ramus, a professor at the University of Paris in the mid-sixteenth century, could be regarded as the inventor of the modern textbook, laboriously laying out in print the content of what students were to learn by way of a sectionalised knowledge taxonomy. Eleven hundred editions of Petrus Ramus's texts were published between 1550 and 1650. Walter Ong credits Ramus with no intellectual originality in the content of the texts, but with an ingenious sense for the emerging epistemic order in which knowledge was analytically laid out and spatially ordered, replacing the authority and pedagogy of rhetoric and dialogue with the atomistically compartmentalised and formally schematised knowledge of modern academe and pedagogy (Ong 1958).

Also characteristic of the textual forms of the emerging print culture was the premium it placed on accuracy, from the standardisation of spelling in vernacular languages, to the processes of editing, proofing and correction. Even after printing, errata were used to correct the text, and text was further corrected from edition to edition – a logic intrinsic to the fastidiousness for detail and empirical verity which marked the emerging lifeworlds of the thinkers and teachers of the early modern academy.

Not merely textual, printed texts came to be located in an intertextual universe of cross-referencing. The announcement of author and title did not just mark the beginning of a work. It situated that work and its author in a universe of other texts and authors, and marked this with the emerging conventions of librarianship, citation and bibliography. Moving away from the rhetorical tradition, authors used footnotes and referencing, not only as a sign of the erudition upon which authoritative text was necessarily grounded, but also to distinguish the author's distinctive and ostensibly original voice from those of the textual authorities or research data upon which they were relying (Grafton 1997).

No longer simply a matter of identification of authorial voice, the new social conventions of authorship became the boundary markers of private intellectual property, the copyright of authors as originators of ideas being embodied in specific forms of words. Knowledge as intellectual property expressed in written text, owned by the individual author and alienable as commodity, was to be found in incipient forms as early as in fifteenth-century Venice (Rose 1993).

This regime of textual knowledge became a key foundation of the modern university, a point of clear break from its monastic origins. It was both a symptom and an enabler in the development of characteristically modern ways of attributing human origins to ideas, of ascribing authority to these ideas, and of developing modern pedagogy that melded the voice of the teacher with the voice of the writer of the authoritative text.

The purpose of this quick sketch is to consider what is new and not new about the emerging regime of digitised text. Widespread digitisation of parts of the text production process began in the 1970s with phototypesetters that were driven by rudimentary word processing programs (Cope and Kalantzis 2001a). During the 1980s and 1990s, word processing and desktop publishing became near-universal tools of authorship. Academics who had previously handwritten their articles, books and teaching notes, and passed them on to typists, started to spend a good part of their working days keyboarding digital text. The logic of their work, however, remained to a large degree within the Gutenberg orbit, marking up the information architectures of their text in the typographic mode, designed to be printed or pseudo-printing in the form of PDF (portable document format) digital replicas of the printed page.

Three decades into the digitisation process, we may well still be in an era of what Jean-Claude Guédon calls 'digital incunabula', in which the full potentialities of digital text have barely been explored, let alone exploited (Guédon 2001). Information is locked up in PDFs which are designed for printing out rather than the functionalities of search, access and copying offered by more advanced digitisation technologies. Such texts-for-print are not marked up by structure and semantics, so even the best search mechanisms offer little more than what can be achieved through word collocation algorithms, far less adequate in some crucial respects than the traditions of indexing and cataloguing from the era of print.

Moreover, some things that are purported to be new about digital text, are not so new at all. For all its apparent novelty, 'hypertext' is nothing other than a version of the process of referencing to be found in the tradition of page numbering and catalogue listing established over the past five centuries. What is the link other than a way of making the same old distinction of individual authorship, delineating the boundaries between one piece of intellectual property and the next, and a sign of deference to the authorities on which a text is based?

As for the much-vaunted novelty of the 'virtual', what more is the digital than a reincarnation of the modes of representation of distant people, places and objects that made books so alluring from the moment they became cheaply and widely accessible? Also, books and their distribution systems, no less than today's networked communities, allowed the creation of dispersed communities of expertise, mediated by local interlocutors in the form of pedagogues who gave specialised classes (Cope and Kalantzis 2004).

Some things about the world of digital communications, however, may turn out to be very different from the world of printed text. Just how different remains to be seen, and the full impact upon universities may take decades to become clearer. Or it may happen sooner.

Several features of the new communications environment stand out. One is a change to the economies of cultural and epistemic scale. Whilst something like a thousand copies need to be sold to make a print run viable, there is no difference in the cost of one person or a thousand reading a web page, or a print-on-demand book. The immediate consequence is that the amount of published and accessible content is rapidly growing and the average number of copies accessed of each academic work is declining (Waters 2004). These are ideal conditions for the development of ever more finely grained areas of knowledge, cultural perspectives and localised applications of knowledge. So significant is this change that knowledge itself may change. What is the enduring validity of universal and universalising perspectives? How do they accommodate the particular? How does the local connect with the global? Furthermore, with the development of Unicode and machine translation, scholarly communication beyond the local may not for much longer have to be expressed in the language of global English, and if it is, it is in the specialised discourses of academic technicality less dependent for their aura of reliability on the 'good style' of native English speakers.

Another key feature is the intrinsic multimodality of the new media. The elementary modular unit of text manufacture in the Gutenberg (and then ASCII) era was the character. Digital texts make written words and images of the same stuff, pixels, and sound of the same stuff as pixels – the zeros and ones of semiconductor circuitry. In everyday life, we have experienced this radical conflation of modes throughout the media, from illustrated books and journals (previously, in lithographic processes as a simple matter of technical convenience images were mostly placed on pages of their own), to video, to the Internet. Academe, however, has stayed steadfastly wedded to text, with the increasing incursion, however, of diagrams and images into the text (Kress 2003). Will the new media destabilise the traditional textual forms of book, article or essay, paper and thesis? In what other ways might knowledge be represented today, and particularly in the areas of the sciences, the arts (Martin and Booth 2007) and design?

Perhaps most significant, however, is what we call a shift in the balance of textual agency between the author and the reader (Kalantzis 2006a; Kalantzis and Cope 2006). Here are some examples and symptoms of this change. Whereas print encyclopedias provided us with definitive knowledge constructed by experts, Wikipedia is constructed, reviewed and editable by readers and includes parallel argumentation by reader–editors about the 'objectivity' of each entry. Whereas a book was resistant to annotation (the size of the margins and a respect for its next reader), new reading devices and formats encourage annotation in which the reading text is also a (re)writing text. Whereas the diary was a space for time-sequenced private reflection, the blog is a place for personal voice that invites public dialogue on personal feelings. Whereas a handwritten or typed page of text could only practically be the work of a single creator, 'changes tracking', version control and web document creation such as Google Docs make multi-author writing easy and collaborative authorship roles clear. Whereas novels and TV soaps had us engaging vicariously with characters in the narratives they presented to us, video games make us central characters in the story where we can influence its outcomes. Whereas broadcast TV had us all watching a handful of television channels, digital TV has us choosing one channel from amongst thousands, or interactive TV in which we select our own angles on a sports broadcast, or making our own video and posting it to YouTube or the web. Whereas broadcast radio gave listeners a programmed playlist, every iPod user creates their own playlist (Kalantzis 2006b). We call this rebalancing of agency, this blurring of the boundaries between authors (and their authority) and readers (and their reverence), 'the social web'. If print limited the scope for dialogue, the electronic communications web opens up that scope.

Each of these new media is reminiscent of the old. In fact, we have eased ourselves into the digital world by using old media metaphors – creating documents or files and putting them away in folders on our desktops. We want to feel as though the new media are like the old. In some respects they are, but in other respects they are proving to be quite different.

The earlier modern regime of communications used metaphors of transmission – for television and radio literally, but also in a figurative sense for books, curricula, public information, workplace memos and all manner of information and culture. This was an era when bosses bossed, political leaders heroically led (to the extent even of creating fascisms, communisms and welfare states for the good of the people), and personal and family life (and 'deviance') could be judged against the canons of normality. Not only have things changed in today's everyday life – the most advanced of contemporary workplaces devolve responsibility to teams and ask workers to buy into the corporate culture. Neoliberal politics tells people to give up their reliance on the state and to take responsibility into their own hands. Diversity rules in everyday life, and with it the injunction to feel free to be true to your own identity.

Things have also changed in a homologous fashion in the social relations of representation. Audiences have become users. Readers, listeners and viewers are invited to talk back to the extent that they have become media co-designers themselves. The division of labour between the creators of culture or knowledge and their consumers has been blurred. The direction of knowledge flows is changing. In fact, the flows are now multifarious and in many directions. Consumers are also creators, and creators are consumers. Knowledge and authority are more contingent, provisional, and conditional-based relationships of 'could' rather than 'should'. They are more open to contestation and to critical reading on the basis of personal experience and voice. Knowledge and culture, as a consequence, become more fluid.

This is what we mean by a shift in the balance of agency, from a society of command and compliance to a society of reflexive co-construction. It might be that the workers creating bigger profits for the bosses, that neoliberalism 'naturally' exacerbates disparities in social power, and that proclamations of diversity are a way of putting a positive gloss on inequality. The social outcomes, indeed, may at times be disappointingly unchanged or the relativities even deteriorating. What has changed is the way these outcomes are achieved. Control by others has become self-control; compliance has become self-imposed. New media are one part of this broader equation. The move may be primarily a social one, but the technology has provided new affordances and social aspiration has helped us image uses for available technologies even beyond the imaginings of their inventors.

Where does this leave the university as a source of epistemic authority? What is the status of Wikipedia, written by tens of thousands of unnamed persons who may or may not have passed the credentialing hurdles of higher education, the authority of individual expert voice or institutional credentials? What is the status of an academic's blog? How do we reference mini-lectures on YouTube, and measure the validity of one YouTube video against the next or a refereed article? How do we assess practice-based and multimodal theses, publications and exhibitions?

The means of production of meaning in the social web are also deceptively the same, and different, to what has preceded. Eschewing the Gutenberg look-alikes of word processing, desktop publishing and postscript files is a new tradition of semantic and structural markup (as opposed to visual markup, for one rendering). This tradition originated in the IBM labs of the 1960s as Standard Generalised Markup Language, but rose to widespread prominence with Berners-Lee's HTML in the early 1990s, and subsequent refinement as XML and more recently the Resource Definition Framework of the 'Semantic Web' (Cope and Kalantzis 2004). This second generation Internet was dubbed Web 2.0 in 2003, and is manifest in widespread application web-based social networking technologies including wikis, weblogs, podcasts and syndication feeds. In the words of the unnamed author or authors of the Wikipedia Web 2.0 entry, it is also a 'social phenomenon embracing an approach to generating and distributing Web content itself, characterized by open communication, decentralization of authority, [and] freedom to share and re-use'.

Distributed knowledge systems

Universities today face significant challenges to their historical role as producers of socially privileged knowledge. More knowledge is being produced by corporations than was the case in the past. More knowledge is being produced in the traditional broadcast media. More knowledge is being produced in the networked interstices of the social web, where knowing amateurs mix with academic professionals, in many places without distinction of rank. In these places, the logics and logistics of knowledge production are disruptive of the traditional values of the university – the for-profit, protected knowledge of the corporation; the multimodal knowledge of audiovisual media; and the 'wisdom of the crowd' which ranks knowledge and makes it discoverable through the Internet according to its popularity.

The new, digital media raise fundamental questions for the university. How can it connect with the shifting sites and modes of knowledge production? How can it stay relevant? Are its traditional knowledge-making systems in need of renovation? What makes academic knowledge valid and reliable, and how can its epistemic virtues be strengthened to meet the challenges of our times? How can the university meet the challenges of the new media in order to renovate the disclosure and dissemination systems of scholarly publishing? How can the university connect with the emerging and dynamic sources of new knowledge formation outside its traditional boundaries?

To a greater extent than is frequently acknowledged, the rituals and forms of print publishing were integral to the modern republic of human and scientific knowledge. Publication was contingent upon peer review, it represented a point of disclosure in which other scientists could replicate findings or other humanists could verify sources. Until publication, academic knowledge remains without status, unassimilable into the body of knowledge that is the discipline and without teachable value. Publication is an integral part of the academic knowledge system.

Pre-publication, peer review as a method of scientific knowledge validation began to evolve from the seventeenth century, with Oldberg's editorship of the Philosophical Transactions of the Royal Society (Guédon 2001; Biagioli 2002; Willinsky 2006; Peters 2007). Post-publication, bibliometrics or citation analysis emerged as measure of ranking of the value of a published piece. The more people who cited an author and their text, the more influential that person and their work must have been on the discipline. This thinking was refined in the work of Eugene Garfield and his Institute for Scientific Information.

The system of academic publishing, however, reached a now well-documented crisis point at the beginning of the twenty-first century. The bulk of academic journal and book publishing was still dominated by commercial publishers producing to the economies and production logics of print – even their electronic versions were by and large in print-reproduction PDF form. The commercial publishers came under increasing fire for the slowness of their publication processes contrasted with the immediacy of the web, the relative closure of their networks of editorial control contrasted with the more democratic open-ness of the web, but most importantly for the rapidly increasing cost of journal subscriptions and books in contrast to the free content on the web (Bergman 2006; Willinsky 2006; Peters 2007; Stanley 2007). The background to this growing critique was one of the most remarkable phenomena of the evolving world of the Internet, that is freely accessible intellectual property in the form of software code (Raymond 2001; Stallman 2002; Williams 2002), content tagged with Creative Commons licenses (Lessig 1999, 2001, 2004; Benkler 2006) and, more specific to the case of academic knowledge, the rise of open access journals (Bergman 2006; Willinsky 2006; Peters 2007).

These developments in an economic domain that Benkler calls 'social production', are not, however, without their own difficulties. John Willinsky speaks lyrically of a return to the days when authors worked beside printers to produce their books (Willinsky 2006). However, academics do not have all the skills or resources of publishers. Nor is playing amateur publisher necessarily the best use of their time. The new economy of social production, moreover, is removing the economic basis for publishing as a form of employment and as a way of helping fund professional associations and research centres which have historically gained revenue from the sale of periodicals and books. Tens of thousands of people used to work for encyclopedia publishers, even if some of the jobs, such as that of the proverbial door-to-door salesperson, were less than ideal. Those who write for Wikipedia have to have another source of income to sustain themselves. What would happen to the significantly sized global scholarly publishing industry if academics assumed collective and universal responsibility for self-publishing?

Open-access, moreover, does not necessarily reduce the points of closure in academic publishing: its English language and developed world bias; the self-replicating logic which gives visibility to established journals and the insider networks that support them; its bias to the natural sciences at the expense of the social sciences and humanities; its valuing of journal articles over books; the intrinsic lack of rigour of most refereeing, without reference to explicit criteria for valid knowledge; and its logic of ranking in which academic popularity ranks ahead of academic quality, and self- and negative citation carries the same weight as positive external citation (Peters 2007).

The Internet in its initial forms, in fact, perpetuates many of precisely these deficiencies. Google is the brainchild of the son of a professor who translated Garfield's citation logic into the page rank algorithm which weights a page according to its 'backward links', or the people who have 'cited' that page by linking to it. When is such a process unhelpful populism, mob rule even, in the newly democratised republic of knowledge? And what do we make of a knowledge system in which even the wisdom of the crowd can be trumped by the wisdom of the sponsored link?

In 1965, J. C. R. Linklider wrote of the deficiencies of the book as a source of knowledge, and imagined a future of 'procognitive systems' in the year 2000 (Linklider 1965). He was anticipating a completely new knowledge system. That system is not with us yet. We are still in the era of digital incunabula.

In semantic publishing technologies, however, we see possibilities not yet realised, in which all the world's knowledge is marked up within developing disciplinary discourses and meaningfully accessible. In the social web, we can gain an inkling of dialogical processes in which academics, professionals and amateurs may advance knowledge more rapidly, take greater intellectual risks, and create more creatively divergent and globally distributed bodies of knowledge and theoretical paradigms than was possible in the slower and more centralised knowledge production systems of print publishing.

If it is the role of the university to produce deeper, broader and more reliable knowledge than is possible in everyday, casual experience, what do we need to do to deepen this tradition rather than to surrender to populism? What needs to be done about the knowledge validation systems of peer review and the dissemination systems of academic publishing? These are fundamental questions at this transitionary moment. Their answers will not just involve new publishing processes. They will entail the creation of new systems of knowledge production, validation and distribution.

Ubiquitous learning

At the height of the dot.com boom, online education was forecast to be one of the key industries of the new 'knowledge economy' (Drucker 2000). Universities began to forge relationships with media conglomerates and operators of Internet portals with names like NextEd, UNext, Pensare and the Global Universities Alliance. They were attracted by opportunities to extend their reach beyond the geographically delimited market of their past (determined by who lives nearby or is prepared to live nearby, a kind of location-based monopoly) to the possibility of competing with universities everywhere. Their business models were built upon what appeared to be the low costs of online teaching – with overheads apparently reduced to computer servers on the Internet and tutors in chat-rooms instead of the expensive real estate and labour-intensive processes of traditional teaching and learning. They were also attracted by the proposition that the value in their 'product' could be transferred from location and fixed infrastructure to an internationally bankable 'brand'.

Since the dot.com crash of 2000, many of the most-hyped endeavours have disappeared into obscurity or bankruptcy (Carr 2001; Mangan 2001). What survived into the second half of the decade of the 2000s was surprisingly modest – a few private, for-profit online universities offering graduate professional programmes in business, teaching and nursing, of which the University of Phoenix and Jones International University are perhaps most notable. As for online learning platforms, the two largest, Blackboard and WebCT, merged in 2005. Much to the chagrin of the champions of Open Source, Blackboard was granted a patent on its e-learning technology in 2006, then proceeded to take action against its near commercial competitors (see www. boycottblackboard.org). Even in 2007, and despite its aspirant monopoly position, Blackboard only had a $180 million turnover, was spending a third of that on marketing and in one reading of its accounts, was trading at a loss (see Blackboard's 2007 Annual Report).

Apart from the questionable extent of the impact of online teaching in higher education, the impact on teaching and learning has been questionable, too. Online learning in higher education often involves little more than the reproduction through digital media of traditional higher education pedagogies – a week-by-week sequence of lecture presentations (written scripts or recorded video), virtual classroom discussions, assignments to upload and tests to take. The didactic relation of teacher to student remains essentially unchanged. The sources of epistemic authority remain unchanged, too, as textbook and readings are copied into digital formats to be downloaded by students. Indeed, the translation into a digital environment often makes the curriculum seem more didactic than one more nuanced by person-to-person contact.

The full potentials of the digital may take some time to be realised. One such potential is pedagogical. Here, the key question emerging from a world increasingly influenced by the epistemic norms of the social web may be, how do we teach in a world where people are more inclined and able to build their own knowledge and understandings from a mix of sources than to receive the pre-packaged wisdoms of authorities? James Paul Gee speaks of the increasingly anachronistic lack of engagement in traditional, transmission pedagogies as contrasted with the identity-engaging pedagogies of video gaming (Gee 2004, 2007). What pedagogical or assessable status might a teacher afford to YouTube video? How might equally generative learning spaces be created for students inured to the communicative practices of MySpace or FaceBook? How might server-based collaborations be managed so that students get involved in more joint work? How might lateral peer-to-peer learning relationships be nurtured, along with peer assessment on social networking principles? How might we develop non-linear pedagogies which allow alternative navigation paths according to the prior knowledge and preferred ways of knowing of diverse learners (Cope and Kalantzis 2001b)? These key pedagogical questions arise not only from the changing dispositions of new generations of students, but from a reading of the kinds of knowledge and epistemic sensibilities that may be more relevant to the 'knowledge economy' (Peters 2007), adaptive communities and cosmopolitan citizenship.

Another potential is to shift the sites of higher education or to blur the boundaries between higher education institutions and the sites of application of learning. More of today's learning happens close to the specifics of everyday life – on the job, for instance, or at the software interface. More of the minutiae of what we need to know to be fully functioning workers, citizens and persons we learn in the pedagogic spaces of training programmes, help menus and by immersion in communities of practice which provide support scaffolds for new entrants (Wenger 1998). How do universities, sites of formal education par excellence, respond? What does it mean for the level of generality of their curricula – should they be geared up or down? To what extent should universities join the markets for learning anywhere and anytime, just in time and just enough? How can universities work with the disruptive potentials of e-learning, or should they resist in order to maintain their brand credibility?

One thing seems clear: that universities will find themselves enmeshed in new geographies, in which the local meets the global, and the public-institutional meets the private-domestic and the pragmatics of workplaces. To be anywhere and everywhere, they will have to adjust their pedagogies so the general and theoretical is able to engage with the local and the practical, and in extremely divergent sites. The distinction between on-campus and off-campus may also be blurred and programme delivery mechanisms blended. Students may move between one mode and another, or join a class based on multiple and readily available alternative modes. Increasingly, regular face-to-face courses are using online content management systems, such as the open source Moodle, for delivery. From this point, it is a small step to offer the course online. The future of online higher education, in other words, may not be as a separate alternative to on-campus delivery. These alternative modes may in fact be integrated in a seamless relation to each other.

Yet another potential of online and blended delivery is to shift the demographics of the student body. Universities are under increasing pressure to push the frontiers of equity as they respond to the demands of the knowledge society. How could twice the percentage (or more) of the population go to university? What would happen to the knowledge and learning of elite institutions, if they stooped to the logic of mass delivery? What if they had to develop a new economics of online provision in order to open opportunities for entry to historically excluded groups located around the corner and around the world? There are many demographically identifiable groups for whom residential or full time higher education is not an option, usually because of overriding commitments to work, family, military service, or other factors. Many people cannot afford the fees, and if they have to live nearby, the board and lodging.

The challenges raised by this demographic shift are, as much as anything, pedagogical. Online higher education will increasingly be situated within lifeworld settings which were formerly 'outside' of the university – in workplaces, in homes, in other countries, in communities which have not traditionally enjoyed access to higher education. This raises enormous issues about diversity in its every sense – how university teaching engages effectively with widely different people located in widely varied learning settings; how, in other words, the teaching/learning relationship is redefined.

The idea of a less expensive, more accessible university education could certainly open the horizons of access for historically under-represented groups. However, this can only be achieved by identifying efficiencies that are peculiar to online learning ecologies.

Efficiencies were created in traditional teaching contexts by having professors lecture large numbers of students in lecture halls and graduate assistants hold tutorials. Online learning is rarely efficient in these ways. It takes the professor far longer to translate the oral discourse of the classroom into a publishable written discourse; and without their direct participation in online discussions and other forums, the learner has no more engagement with the professor than they would by reading a textbook. By and large, the alternatives are either an unsatisfactory learning experience for the student or a huge amount of work for the professor.

Efficiencies and effective learning can, however, be achieved by creating energetic horizontal communities of knowledge construction and peer review amongst learners. Graduate students, emeritus professors and programme alumni can act as tutors who are close to the intellectual agenda of the programme. And professors could be accessible through online conferences and conversations. The key challenge is to create efficiencies through mass customisation, not massification. This means finding fundamentally new ways of creating efficiency. The online analogue to the large lecture hall is the hundreds of students consuming the professor's generic content which has now been published online. This is the massification model of efficiency.

The key question for online learning needs to be, how can a multitude of programmes be customised so that each has a feel of its own as a learning community? For instance, the energies and distinctiveness of each learning community needs to be constructed as much by the learners as the content transmitted by the professors. If the learning is engaged, practical and rooted in learner needs and experiences, each class in each course will develop a distinctive feel of its own which fits the sensibilities of the group of learners, and reflects the learning dynamic that emerges within the group. This requires new and more open pedagogical approaches, a new place for content, and new facilitation roles on the part of instructors. The efficiencies here are created by a layered approach – peer-to-peer learning, teaching assistant led teaching, instructional and technology specialist support, with faculty contributing in a 'light touch' overall content development and pedagogical design role.

Emerging technologies and social relationships of the 'new media' have the potential to change the contexts and forms of teaching and learning in higher education. The word 'ubiquitous' captures key aspects of this potential. The implications for our heritage institutions of higher learning are enormous. Whilst technology does not in and of itself change the social world (many so-called 'learning management systems' achieve little but to replicate traditional classroom relations), its affordances may open possibilities that could not previously have been realised.

One potential is to blur the traditional institutional, spatial and temporal boundaries of 'education'. Another is to transform pedagogical relationships, changing the balance of agency between teacher/text and learner, in which learners become collaborative co-designers of knowledge and even learning itself. Still another is to change the modalities of learning, in which forms of representation are increasingly multimodal and written text sits alongside and sometimes within multimedia communications.

The changes we are witnessing today could be deeply disruptive of the discursive, epistemological and interpersonal forms of heritage higher education systems. The challenge for technologists and educators is to work together to explore relationships of learning that are more apt to today's social conditions, more dynamic, and which engage learners more effectively.

References

Benkler, Y. (2006) *The Wealth of Networks: How Social Production Transforms Markets and Freedom*, New Haven, CT: Yale University Press.

Bergman, S. S. (2006) 'The scholarly communication movement: highlights and recent developments', *Collection Building*, 25(4): 108–28.

Biagioli, M. (2002) 'From book censorship to academic peer review', *Emergences: Journal for the Study of Media & Composite Cultures*, 12(1): 11–45.

Carr, S. (2001) 'Rich in cash and prestige, Next struggles in its search for sales', *The Chronicle of Higher Education*, 47(34): A33–5.

Cope, B. and D. Kalantzis (eds) (2001a) *Print and Electronic Text Convergence. Technology Drivers Across the Book Production Supply Chain, From the Creator to the Consumer*, Melbourne: Common Ground.

Cope, B. and M. Kalantzis (2001b) 'e-Learning in higher education', in M. Kalantzis and A. Pandian (eds)*Literacy Matters: Issues for New Times*, Penang: Universiti Sains Malaysia, pp. 193–217.

Cope, B. and M. Kalantzis (2004) 'Text-made text', *E-Learning*, 1(2): 198–282.

Drucker, P. (2000) 'Putting more now into knowledge', *Forbes*, pp. 91–7.

Eisenstein, E. L. (1979) *The Printing Press as an Agent of Change: Communications and Cultural Transformation in Early-Modern Europe*, Cambridge: Cambridge University Press.

Febvre, L. and H.-J. Martin (1976) *The Coming of the Book*, London: Verso.

Gee, J. P. (2004) *Situated Language and Learning: A Critique of Traditional Schooling*, London: Routledge.

Gee, J. P. (2007) *Good Video Games + Good Learning: Collected Essays on Video Games, Learning and Literacy*, New York: Peter Lang.

Grafton, A. (1997) *The Footnote: A Curious History*, London: Faber and Faber.

Guédon, J.-C. (2001) 'In Oldenburg's long shadow: librarians, research scientists, publishers, and the control of scientific publishing', from http://www.arl.org/resources/pubs/mmproceedings/138guedon.shtml.

Kalantzis, M. (2006a) 'Changing subjectivities, new learning', *Pedagogies: An International Journal*, 1(1): 7–12.

Kalantzis, M. (2006b) 'Elements of a science of education', *Australian Educational Researcher*, 33(2): 15–42.

Kalantzis, M. and B. Cope (2006) *New Learning: Elements of a Science of Education*, Cambridge: Cambridge University Press.

Kress, G. (2003) *Literacy in the New Media Age*, London: Routledge.

Lessig, L. (1999) *Code and Other Laws of Cyberspace*, New York: Basic Books.

Lessig, L. (2001) *The Future of Ideas: The Fate of the Commons in a Connected World*, New York: Random House.

Lessig, L. (2004) *Free Culture*, New York: Penguin Press.

Linklider, J. C. R. (1965) *Libraries of the Future*, Cambridge, MA: MIT Press.

Mangan, K. S. (2001) 'Expectations evaporate for online MBA programs', *The Chronicle of Higher Education*, 48(6): A31–2.

Martin, E. and J. Booth (2007) *Art-Based Research: A Proper Thesis?*, Melbourne: Common Ground.

Ong, W. J. (1958) *Ramus, Method and the Decay of Dialogue*, Cambridge, MA: Harvard University Press.

Peters, M. A. (2007) *Knowledge Economy, Development and the Future of Higher Education*, Rotterdam: Sense Publishers.

Raymond, E. (2001) *The Cathedral and the Bazaar: Musings on Linux and Open Source by an Accidental Revolutionary*, Sebastapol, CA: O'Reilly.

Rose, M. (1993) *Authors and Owners: The Invention of Copyright*, Cambridge, MA: Harvard University Press.

Stallman, R. (2002) *Free Software, Free Society*, Boston, MA: GNU Press.

Stanley, C. A. (2007) 'When counter narratives meet master narratives in the journal editorial-review process', *Educational Researcher*, 36(1): 14–24.

Waters, L. (2004) *Enemies of Promise: Publishing, Perishing and the Eclipse of Scholarship*, Chicago: Prickly Paradigm Press.

Wenger, E. (1998) *Communities of Practice: Learning, Meaning and Identity*, Cambridge: Cambridge University Press.

Williams, S. (2002) *Free as in Freedom: Richard Stallman's Crusade for Free Software*, Sebastapol, CA: O'Reilly.

Willinsky, J. (2006) *The Access Principle: The Case for Open Research and Scholarship*, Cambridge, MA: MIT Press.

Index